HISTORIC PHOTOS OF
NEBRASKA

TEXT AND CAPTIONS BY TAD STRYKER

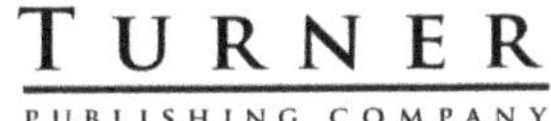

Houses, fenced lots, and commercial buildings abound in this 1868 photograph of Omaha, facing east toward the Missouri River. Arundel C. Hull, who is responsible for this and several other images in this book, was a protégé of well-known William H. Jackson, who followed the construction of the Union Pacific Railroad through Nebraska, Wyoming, and Utah. Hull married and raised a family in Fremont.

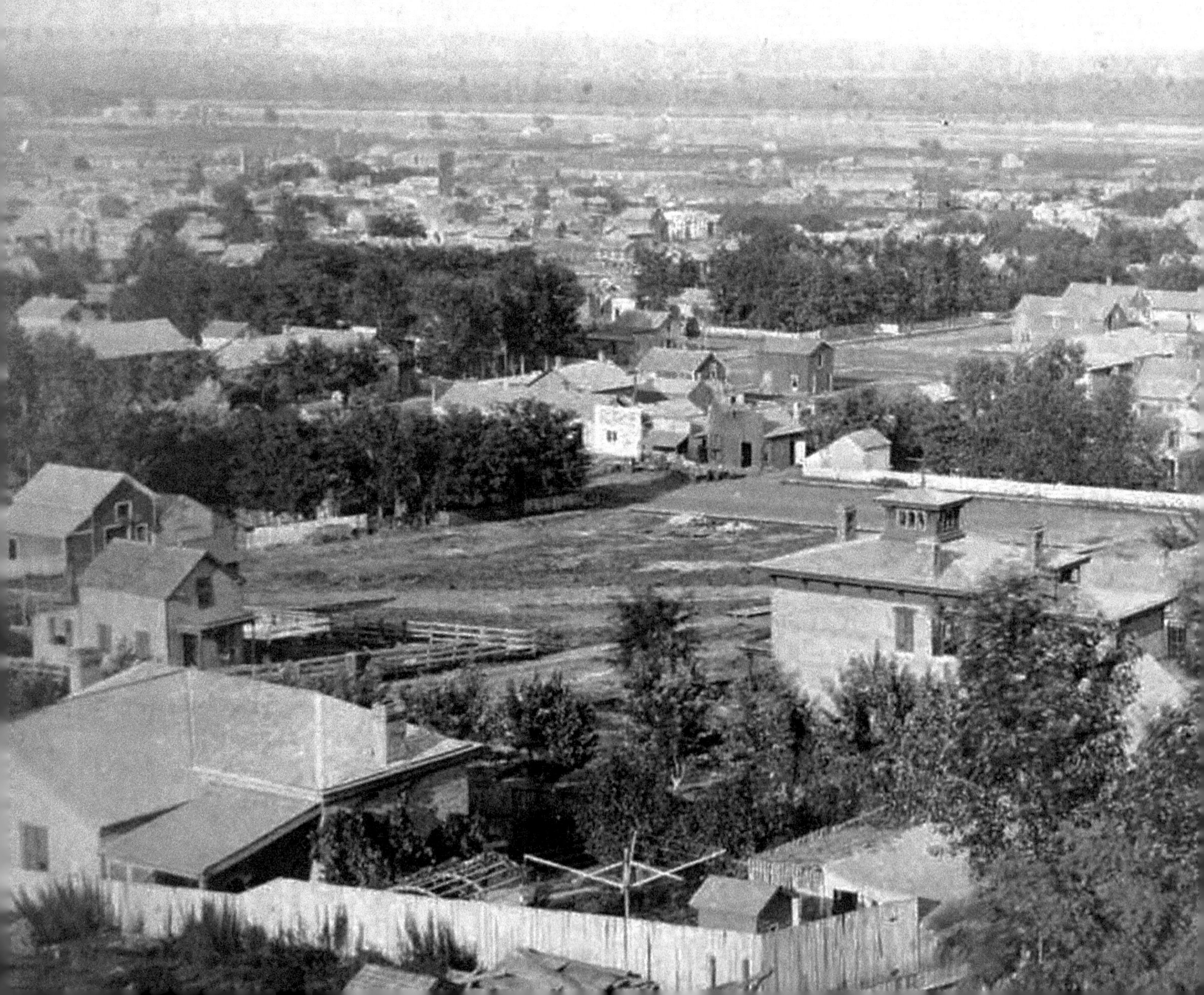

HISTORIC PHOTOS OF
NEBRASKA

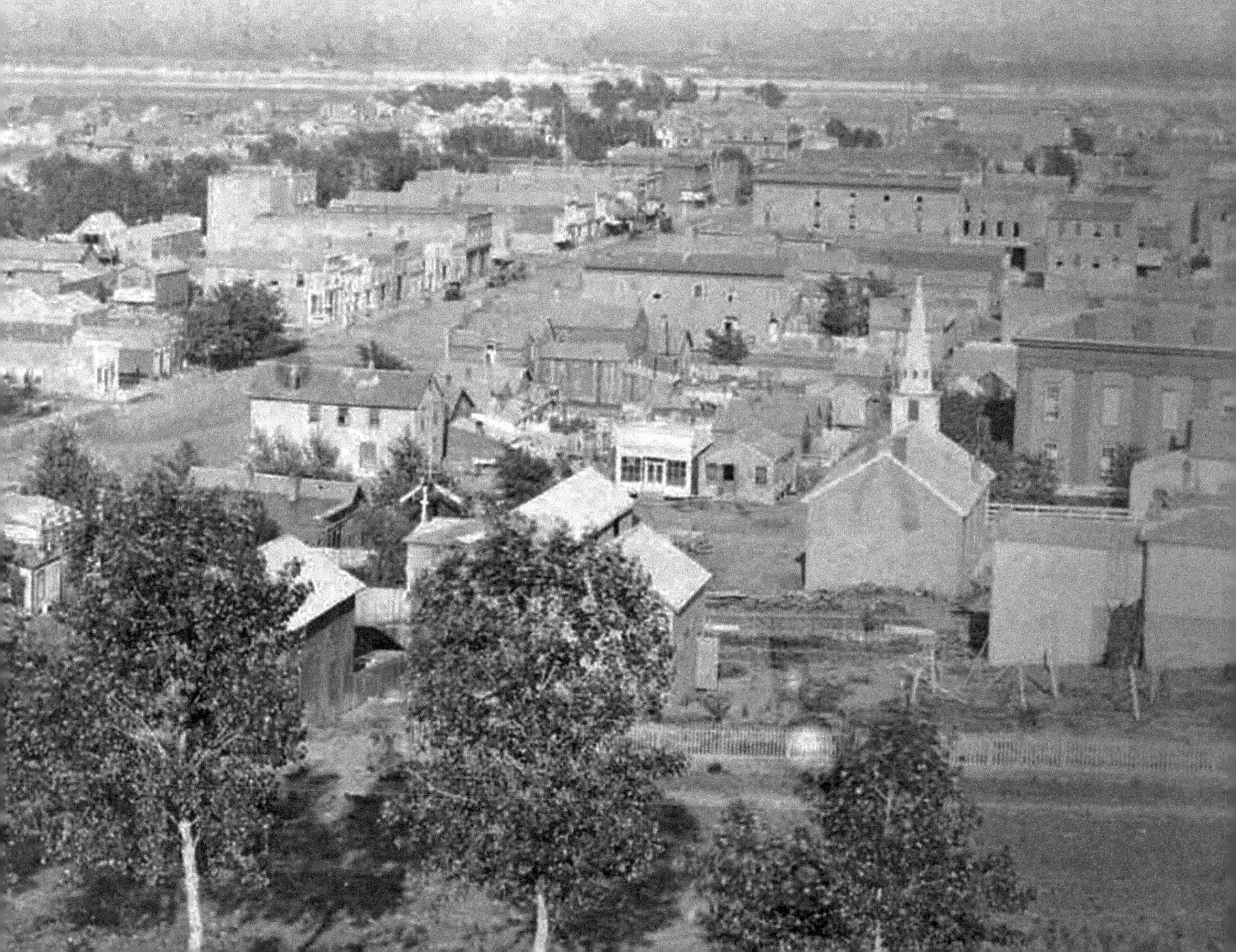

Turner Publishing Company
4507 Charlotte Avenue • Suite 100
Nashville, Tennessee 37209
(615) 255-2665

www.turnerpublishing.com

Historic Photos of Nebraska

Library of Congress Control Number: 2009939391

ISBN: 978-1-59652-570-2

ISBN: 978-1-68442-111-4 (hc)

Printed in the United States of America

10 11 12 13 14 15 16 17—0 9 8 7 6 5 4 3 2 1

Contents

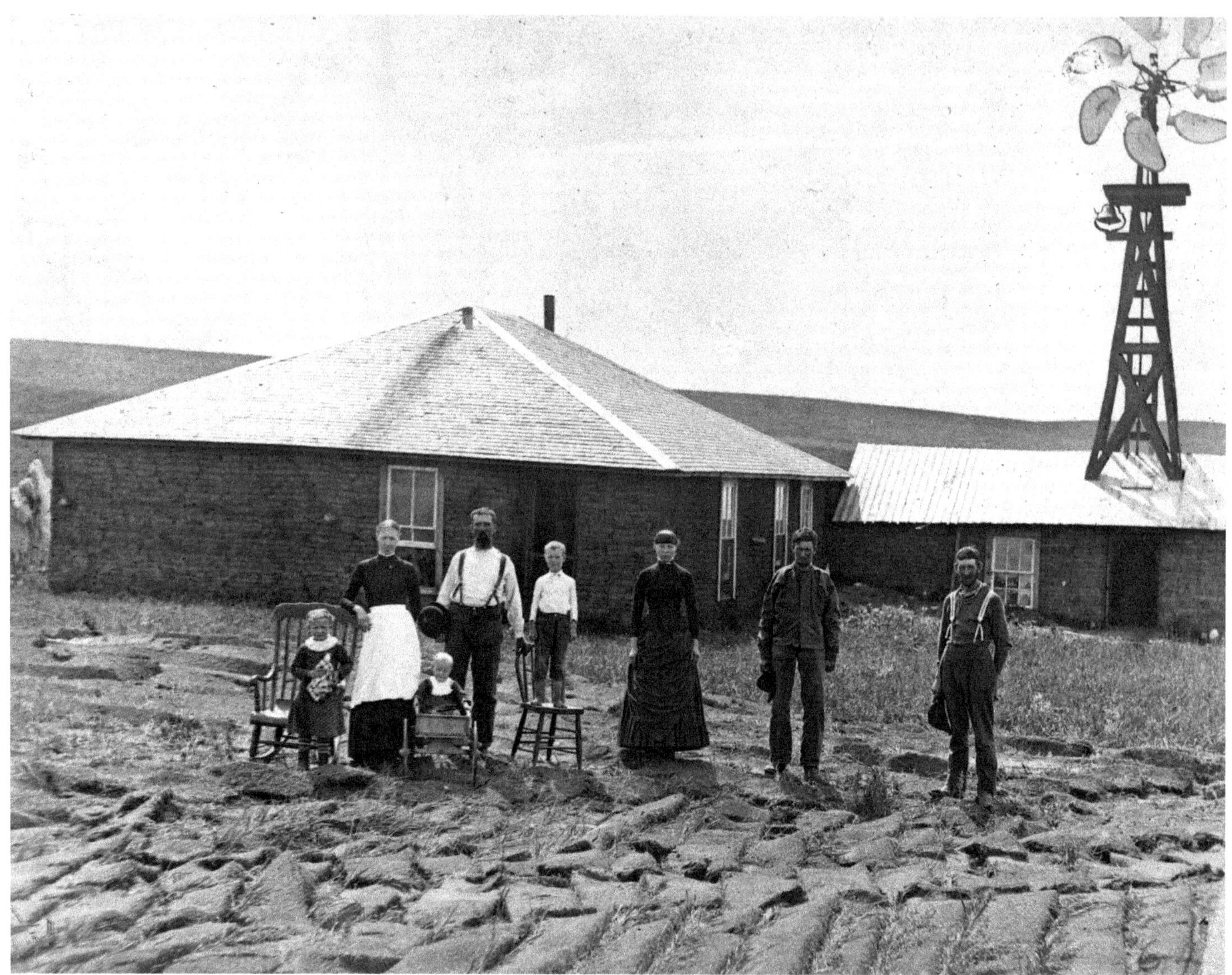

Solomon D. Butcher, the best-known nineteenth-century photographer of Nebraska, took numerous photographs of his Custer County neighbors who were living their version of the American dream, eking an existence out of the stark landscape. This image was recorded around 1885 and features a peaked roof worthy of note, rows of freshly turned sod, and an unusual windmill. The family is unidentified.

Acknowledgments

This volume, *Historic Photos of Nebraska,* is the result of the cooperation and efforts of many individuals and organizations. It is with great thanks that we acknowledge the valuable contribution of the following for their generous support:

Boys Town Hall of History, Boys Town, Hall of History and Father Flanagan House Museum
Denver Public Library
Library of Congress
Nebraska State Historical Society

This book would not have been possible without the assistance of the staff of the Nebraska State Historical Society, especially Karen Keehr, curator of visual and audio collections, and assistant curator Linda Hein.

The writer also wishes to thank Mary Landkamer, curator of the Custer County Historical Society, and Mardi Anderson, local historian and archives volunteer at the Buffalo County Historical Society, who helped identify photos from the Solomon D. Butcher collection and clarify their historical significance.

Thanks are also due the Boys Town Hall of History and its associate curator, Mark Daniels; to Tom Buecker, curator of Fort Robinson Museum; and to the staff who oversee the newspaper microfilm archives at the Bennett-Martin Library in Lincoln.

The writer referred to Solomon D. Butcher's 1905 *Pioneer History of Custer County,* and Samuel Clay Bassett's 1916 *Buffalo County, Nebraska, and Its People: A Record of Settlement,* vol. 2, and made extensive use of the Internet in researching this book. Buffalo County Historical Society sites at www.rootsweb.ancestry.com were especially helpful, as were NOAA weather sites, the www.genealogytrails.com site, and the official Web sites of various cities and counties throughout Nebraska.

With the exception of touching up imperfections that have accrued with the passage of time and cropping where necessary, no changes have been made. The focus and clarity of many images is limited by the technology and the ability of the photographer at the time they were taken.

Preface

Hidden where the tall grass prairie meets the High Plains, possibly somewhere near the spot where the 100th Meridian crosses the first transcontinental railroad, are the paradoxes of Nebraska.

When you think of diversity and significance, Nebraska doesn't immediately come to mind. Stability is more the ticket. Yet all three components apply. Nebraska has subtle beauty, depth, and staying power. The photographs in this book are just a small window into its soul. You'll see citizens battling the elements and weathering economic storms. You'll see the indigenous peoples who met conflict with white settlers. You'll see the founders of grassroots political movements and the inventors of widely used products.

Too bad it is such a flat and boring state, right? Well, that's one of the great myths of Nebraska—right up there with cow-tipping outings and jackalope hunts—as anyone who lives in the Sandhills or Pine Ridge could tell you. Nebraska is a place where six distinct ecosystems meet in the Niobrara River valley near Valentine. It's a tilted, irregular landscape which at Panorama Point, just southwest of Kimball in the corner of the Panhandle, is loftier than mile-high Denver. Then it falls off at the rate of seven feet per mile moving east along the Platte River. By the time the landscape winds its way through the rolling hills of eastern Nebraska to the Missouri River and heads downstream to Rulo, where all the water that drains from the Platte and Missouri valleys flows by, the elevation has dropped more than 4,500 feet.

The people are just as varied. We're traditional, yet community-minded. Tight-fisted, but warmhearted. Practical, although forward-thinking. Nebraskans are stingy when it comes to paying property taxes, but notoriously loose with our purse strings when it comes to traveling to Lincoln—and across the nation—to watch the Cornhuskers play football. We are people who can appreciate both the talkative tippler Bob Devaney and the taciturn teetotaler Tom Osborne, because both coaches got the job done on the field and helped build an institution that has forged a gut-level sense of pride and unity among Nebraskans of all stripes.

Since the days of the Mormon and Oregon trails, most Americans have thought of Nebraska as a place to pass through, or in this day of commercial air travel, to fly over. This book features the pioneers who decided to stay, and their descendants.

Nebraska is a state that has stood up for the "little guy"—at least, for those who seem to be living a decent, disciplined life. Notable populist agitators used to call Nebraska home, and there is still an underlying distrust of big Eastern corporations. Yet some of the world's most successful businesses—Berkshire Hathaway, Mutual of Omaha, ConAgra Foods, T. D. Ameritrade, Cabela's, and the Union Pacific Railroad—are headquartered here. Even so, the state's economy is still anchored in its grain fields and cow pastures.

These are some of the paradoxes of Nebraska.

Politically, the state tends to be conservative, but the seeds of reform continue to sprout in both of its major parties. It's reliably Republican in presidential elections and in the House of Representatives, but appears unwilling to trust anyone with too much power. Nebraskans really like to mix things up in the U.S. Senate and the governor's mansion—since the start of World War II, citizens have put the GOP in office only slightly more often than the Democrats.

Nebraska is a state tested by extreme weather. It is prone to drought, floods, and blizzards, constantly whipped by changeable winds, and terrorized by the most capricious storm of all, the tornado. It logically follows that the state has one of the nation's sparsest populations. So Nebraskans don't take much of anything for granted, especially when it comes to economics. It can take a doggoned long time to get a road paved here.

A lot of us still do old, ordinary things like saving for the future. Even the state legislature understands frugality—a rainy-day fund helped keep the state's budget in the black during a severe economic downturn during the first decade of the twenty-first century. Nebraska isn't a trendy state. If you're looking for the latest fashions, don't look here first.

There's a certain durability to Nebraska, which tends to avoid financial peaks and valleys—although the Cornhusker State has not been immune to severe economic downturns, including the Panic of 1893, the Great Depression of the 1930s, and the farm crisis of the late 1970s and early 1980s. And businesses with a lengthy pedigree, like the locally owned Vise-Grip factory in DeWitt, have been sold and their jobs outsourced. That said, economic hardship is not the first battle that Nebraskans have faced, and it won't be the last. Our durable spirit is on display here, as are the paradoxes that forged it.

—*Tad Stryker*

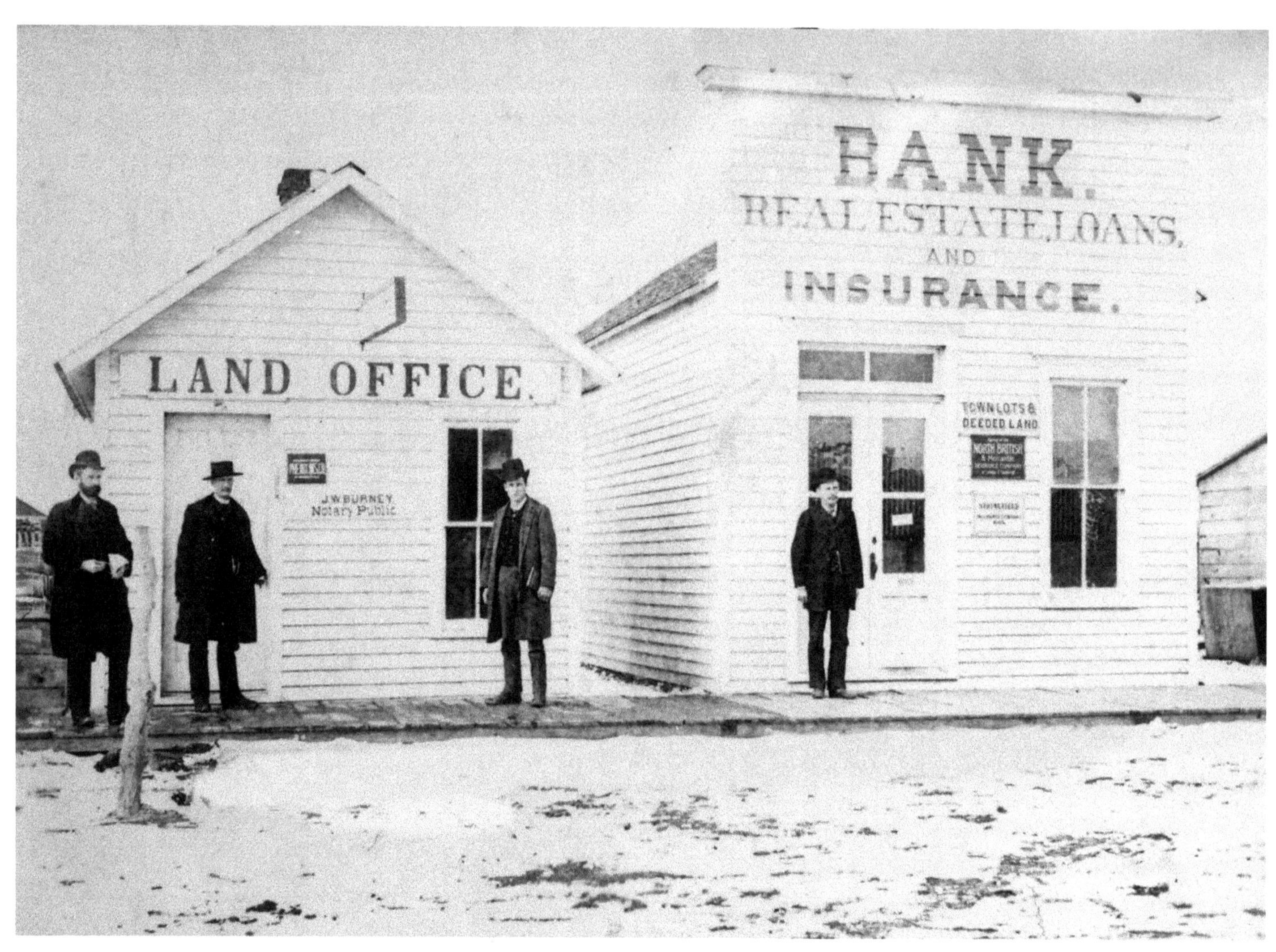

In another up-and-coming settlement just west of Trenton, this late 1880s photograph shows the Stratton real estate office at left with its agent, John W. Burney (second from left) and the first bank in town, which was run by Charles Shurtleff (at far-right).

Frontier Nebraska

(Before 1892)

From the outset, there was struggle in Nebraska. Long before the 1803 Louisiana Purchase defined it as a possession of the United States, its inhabitants had endured the extremities of the Northern Great Plains climate. And although the American Indians are generally touted as living in harmony with the land, they tended to have as much trouble getting along with each other as other races would in succeeding generations.

The Spanish believed they were the first European power to lay claim to the region. In 1720, Pedro de Villasur left Santa Fe with a small war party looking for trespassing French fur trappers. The Spaniards reached the confluence of the Loup and Platte rivers, only to be massacred by Pawnee. By that time, a French explorer named Bourgmont had already named the wide, sandbar-infested Platte the "Nebraskier," a variation of an Otoe word for "flat water." Nebraska has been greatly affected by the Platte ever since.

The French and Spanish started an intense competition for trade rights, which meant making agreements with the Pawnee, Lakota, Ponca, Cheyenne, Arapaho, Omaha, Otoe, and others who had prior claim. The British and Americans arrived later, joining the series of treaties that the newcomers would break.

In 1823, a U.S. Army engineer named Stephen Long labeled much of the region a "Great Desert." Soon afterward, the discovery of gold in California and fertile land in Oregon launched the era of the Oregon and Mormon trails, with more than half a million people migrating through the area that would soon be mapped and politicized by the Kansas-Nebraska Act of 1854. Military outposts like Fort Kearny and Fort McPherson were set up to keep peace along the trail, and Fort Robinson soon followed to help monitor the conflict that culminated with the Lakota wars of the 1870s.

Photography came to Nebraska too late to capture the most dynamic moments of American expansion westward, but photographs of these three forts give us an idea what life was like for the soldiers who watched the overland trails decline and the transcontinental railroad come in. Solomon D. Butcher's in-depth and sustained photography of central Nebraska settlers has been a godsend to historians. It is featured liberally here to illustrate the transition from territorial status to statehood and those who were early on the scene, struggling to tame the land.

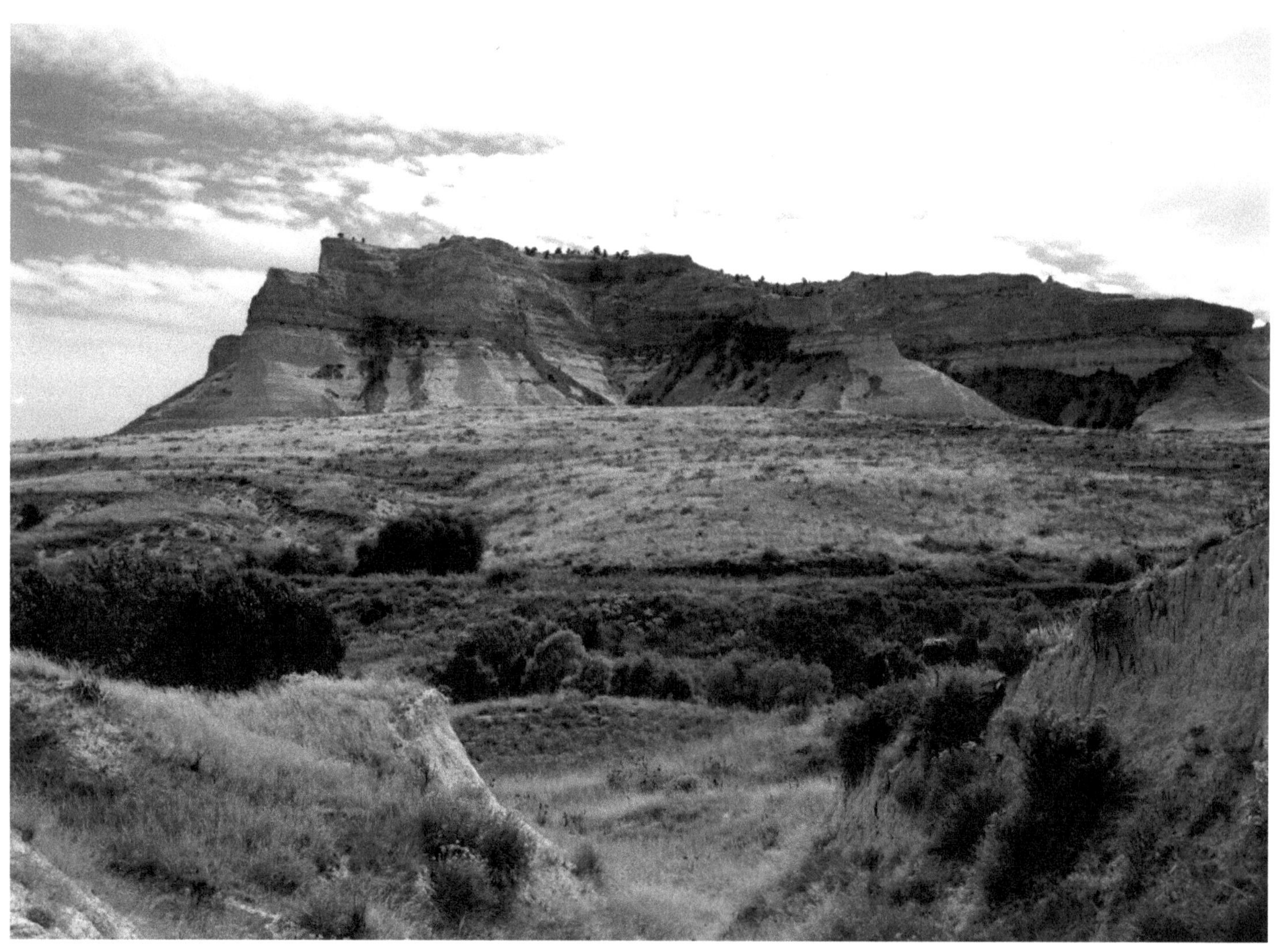

A majestic landmark along the Oregon Trail, Scott's Bluff was already well known to many of the travelers who passed through adjoining Mitchell Pass in their Conestoga wagons. The site is named for Hiram Scott, the unfortunate 24-year-old fur trader whose bones were discovered nearby in the spring of 1830.

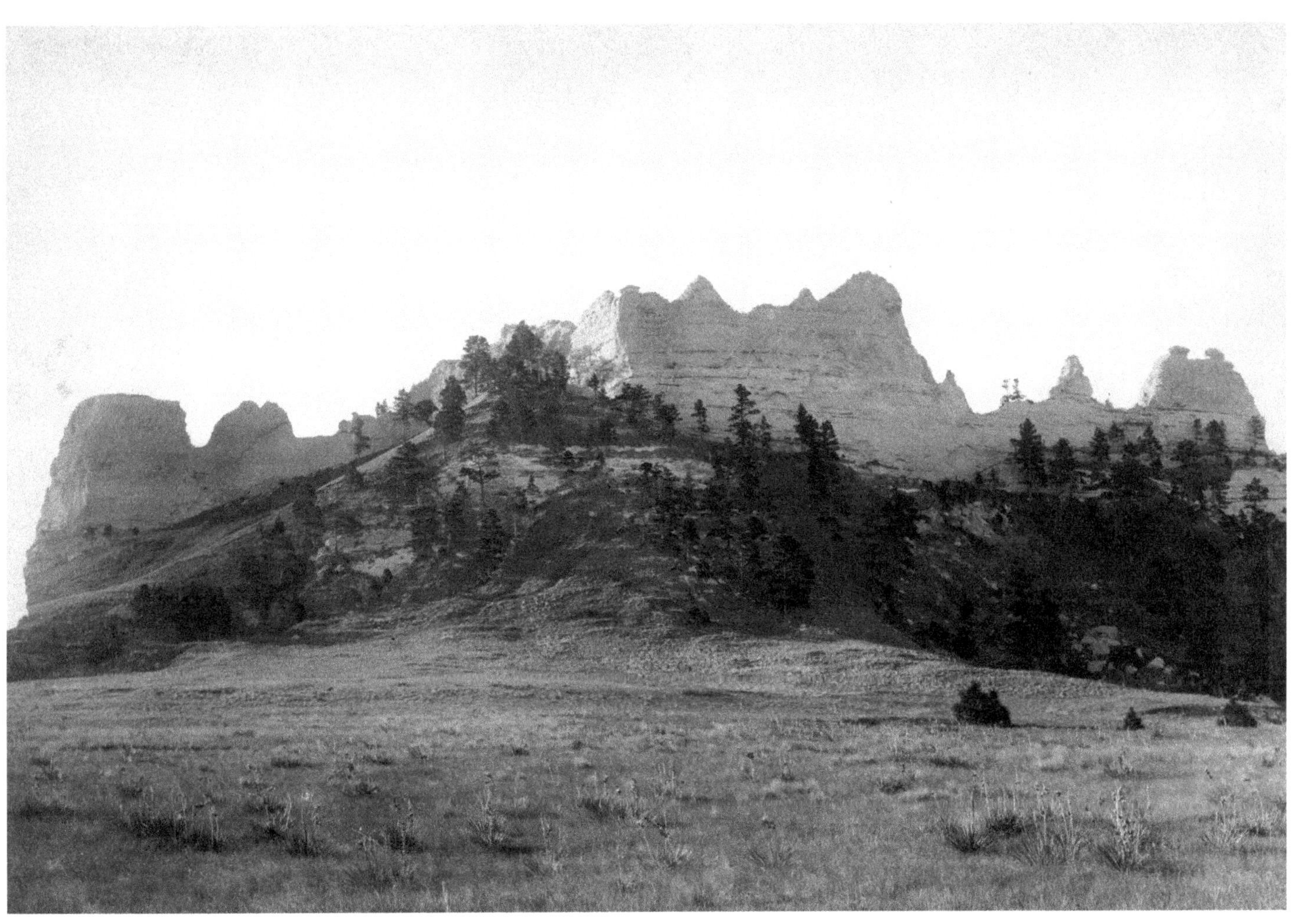

Located near Crawford, Crow Butte was the site of an October 1849 standoff between Crow families and Sioux warriors. Legend has it that after fleeing to the top, the entire Crow contingent escaped the third night by killing a pony and using its hide to make ropes to lower themselves down an unguarded portion of the butte. The oldest man stayed, keeping campfires burning to deceive the Sioux, who gave him liberty for his bravery.

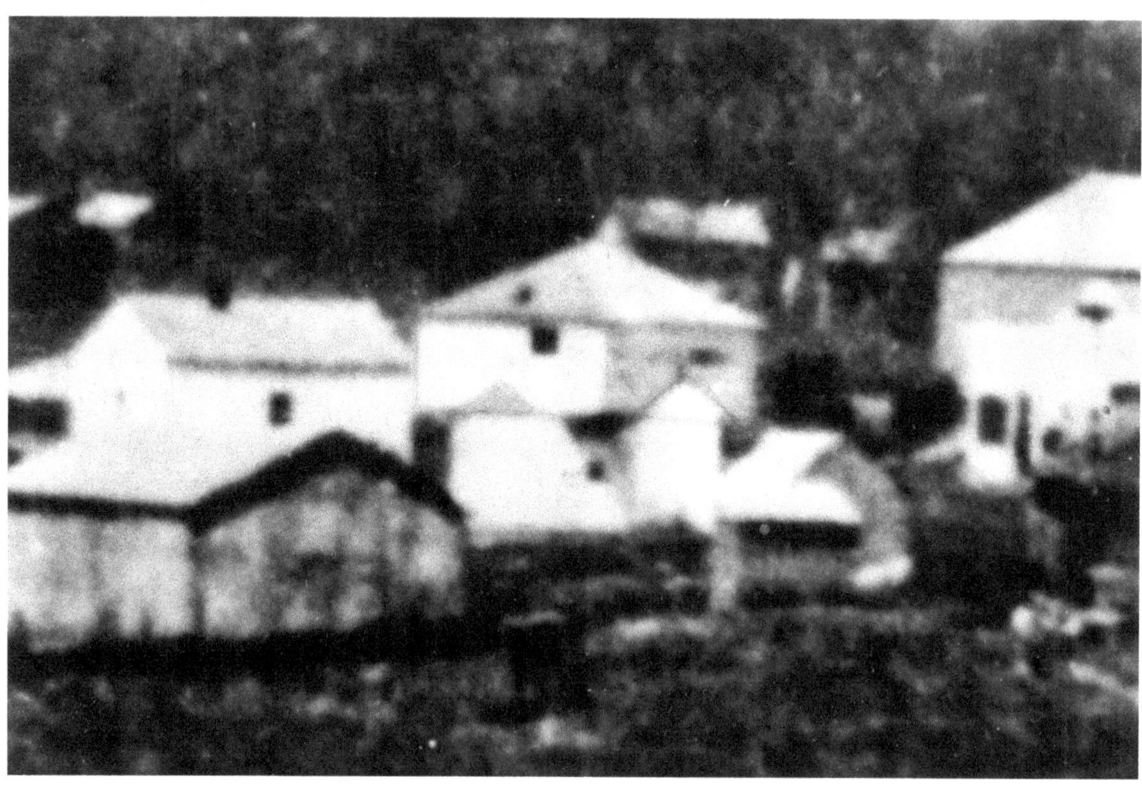

This 1858 photograph by Samuel C. Mills shows the parade grounds and officers' quarters at Fort Kearny, near present-day Kearney. A U.S. Army base established in 1848, it was one of the main stopping points along the Oregon Trail, serving as a way station, supply depot, and message center for westward travelers along the Great Platte River Road. Fort Kearny would become a freighting station and a home station for the Pony Express before its abandonment and dismantling in 1871.

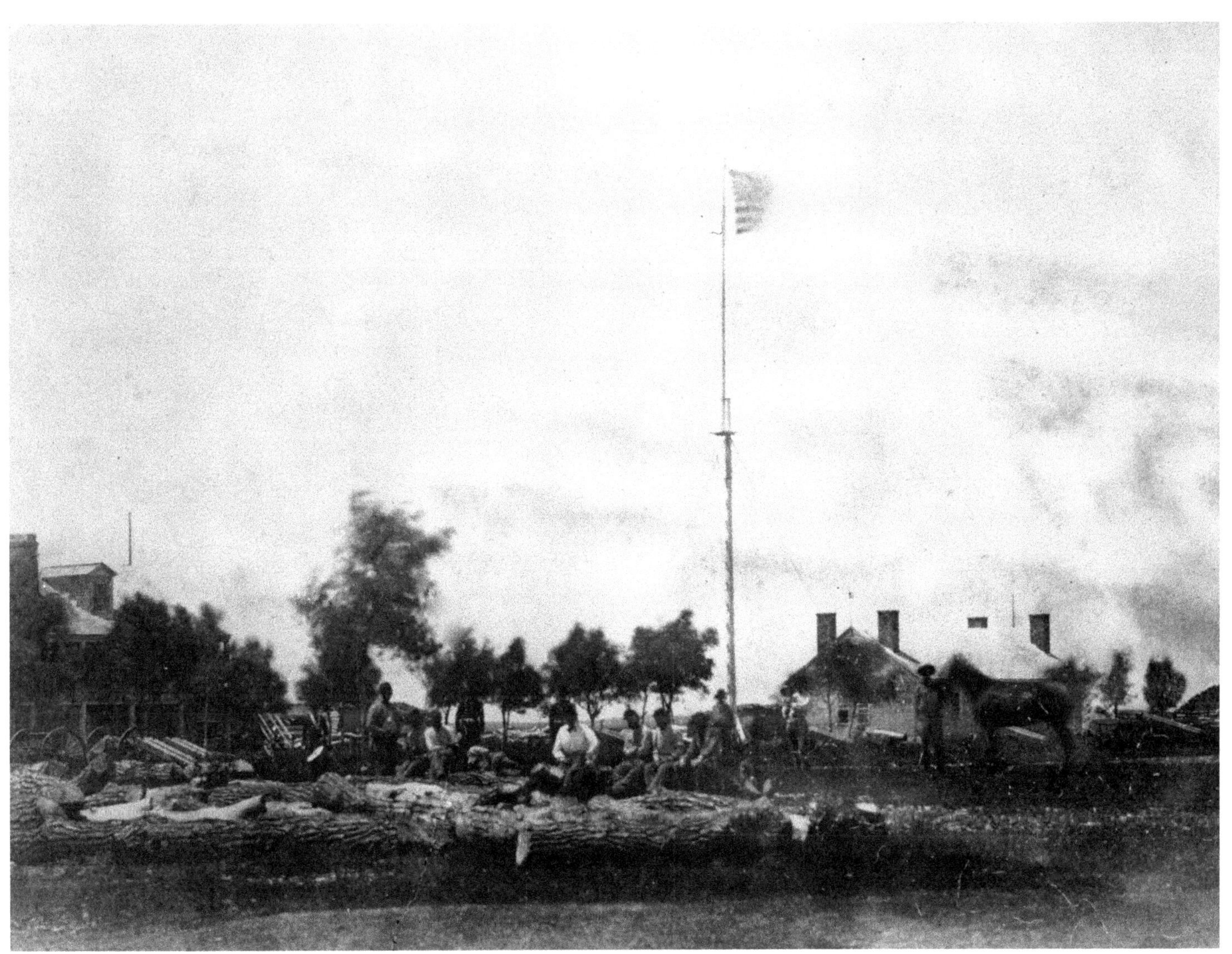

Shown here around the 1860s, Fort Kearny must have been a welcome sight to the thousands of pioneers who had already traveled more than 300 miles from Independence, Missouri, on their way west during the mid nineteenth century. From June 1848 to June 1849 alone, at least 4,000 wagons passed the fort, according to the journals of Lieutenant Daniel P. Woodbury, who had built the fort with the help of 175 soldiers.

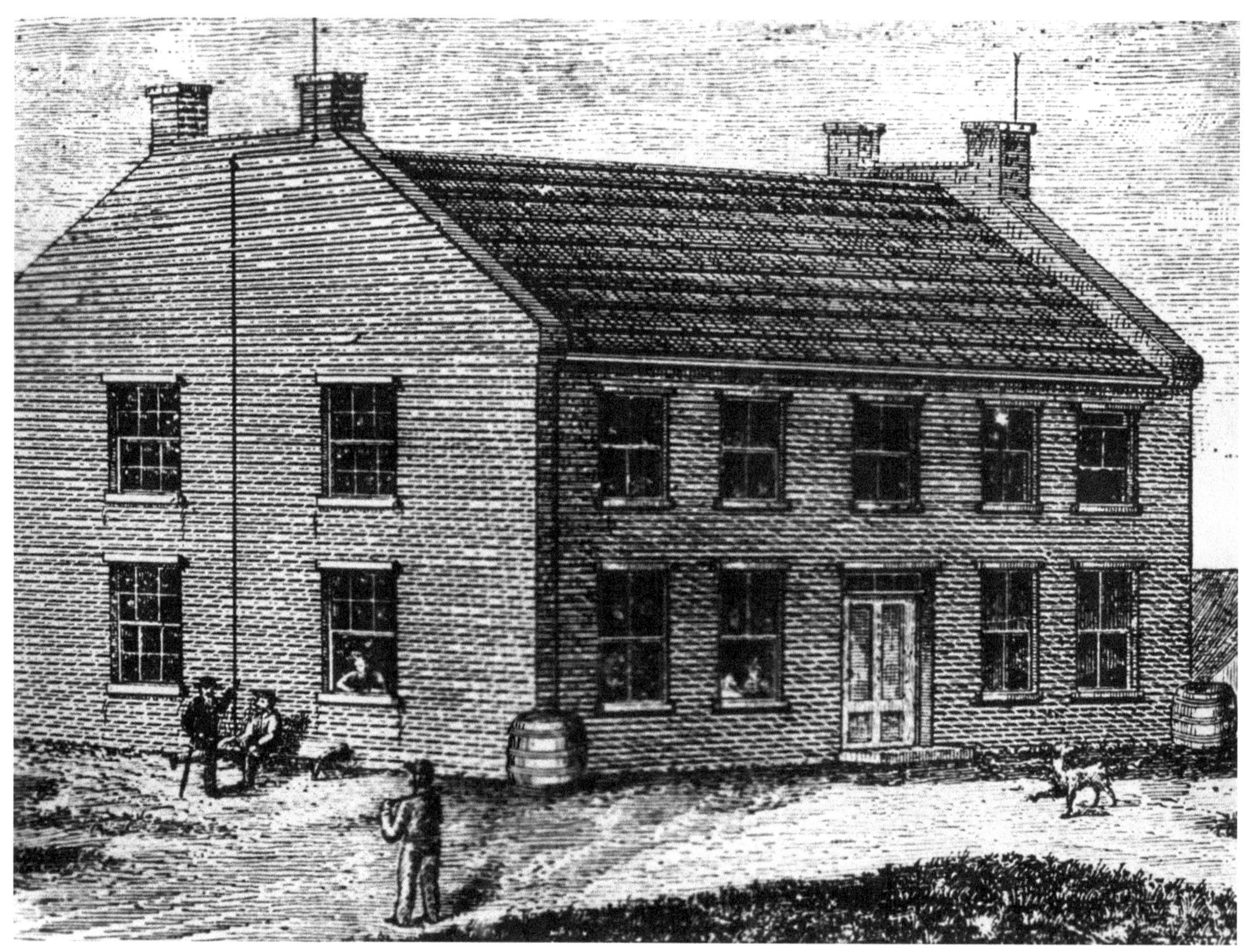

Built and donated by the Council Bluffs and Nebraska Ferry Company, Nebraska's first territorial capitol housed the first two sessions of the legislature, in 1855 and 1857, then was used as general offices by the Union Pacific Railroad.

James Butler "Wild Bill" Hickok had a murky reputation based on his experiences as a Union spy, wagonmaster, gambler, gunfighter, and U.S. marshal. In July 1861, Hickok worked at Rock Creek Station, a freighting and Pony Express outpost near Fairbury, and became incensed at former owner David McCanles, who named him "Duck Bill" because of his long nose. Hickok killed McCanles and a companion as they tried to collect a payment from the new owners.

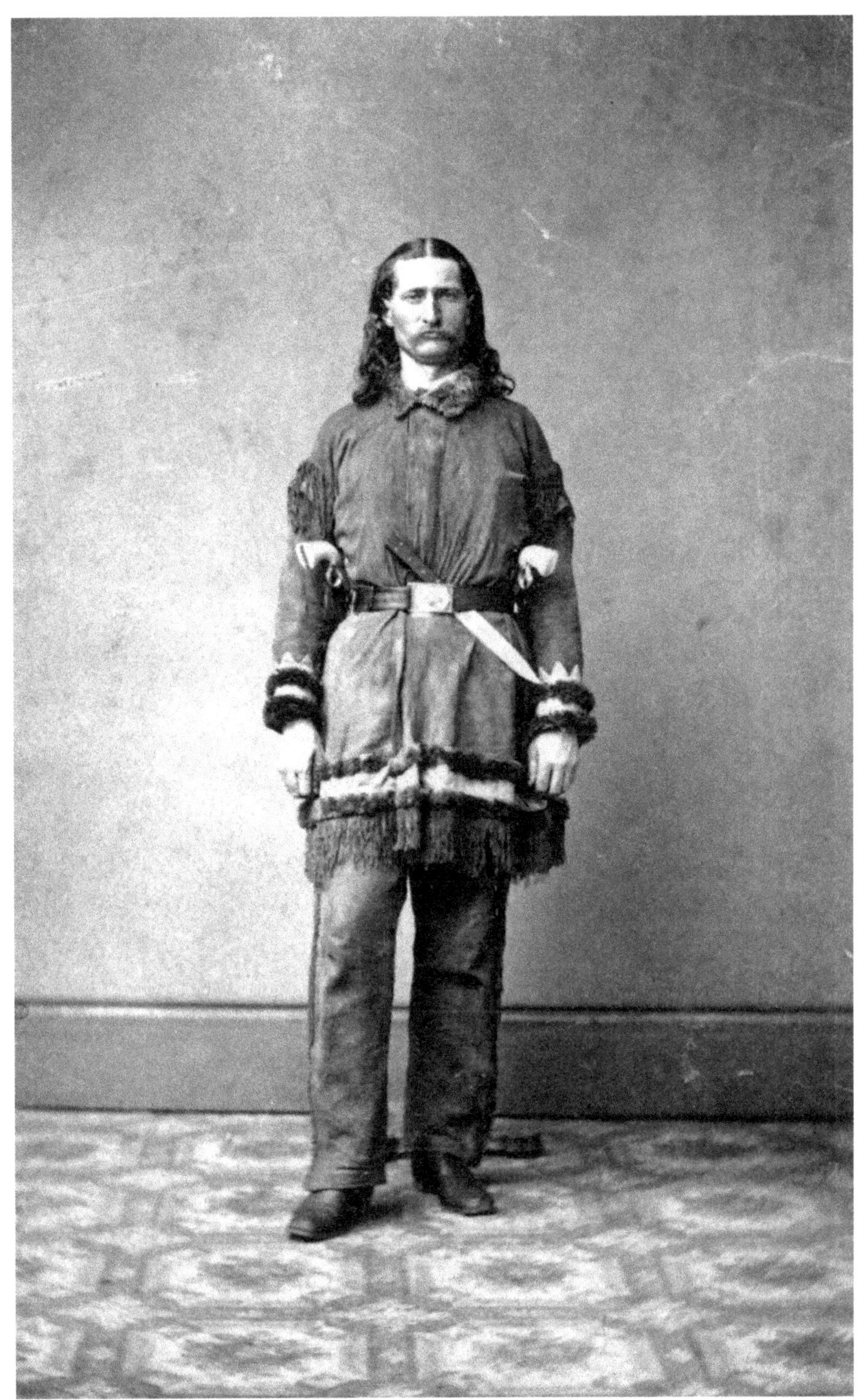

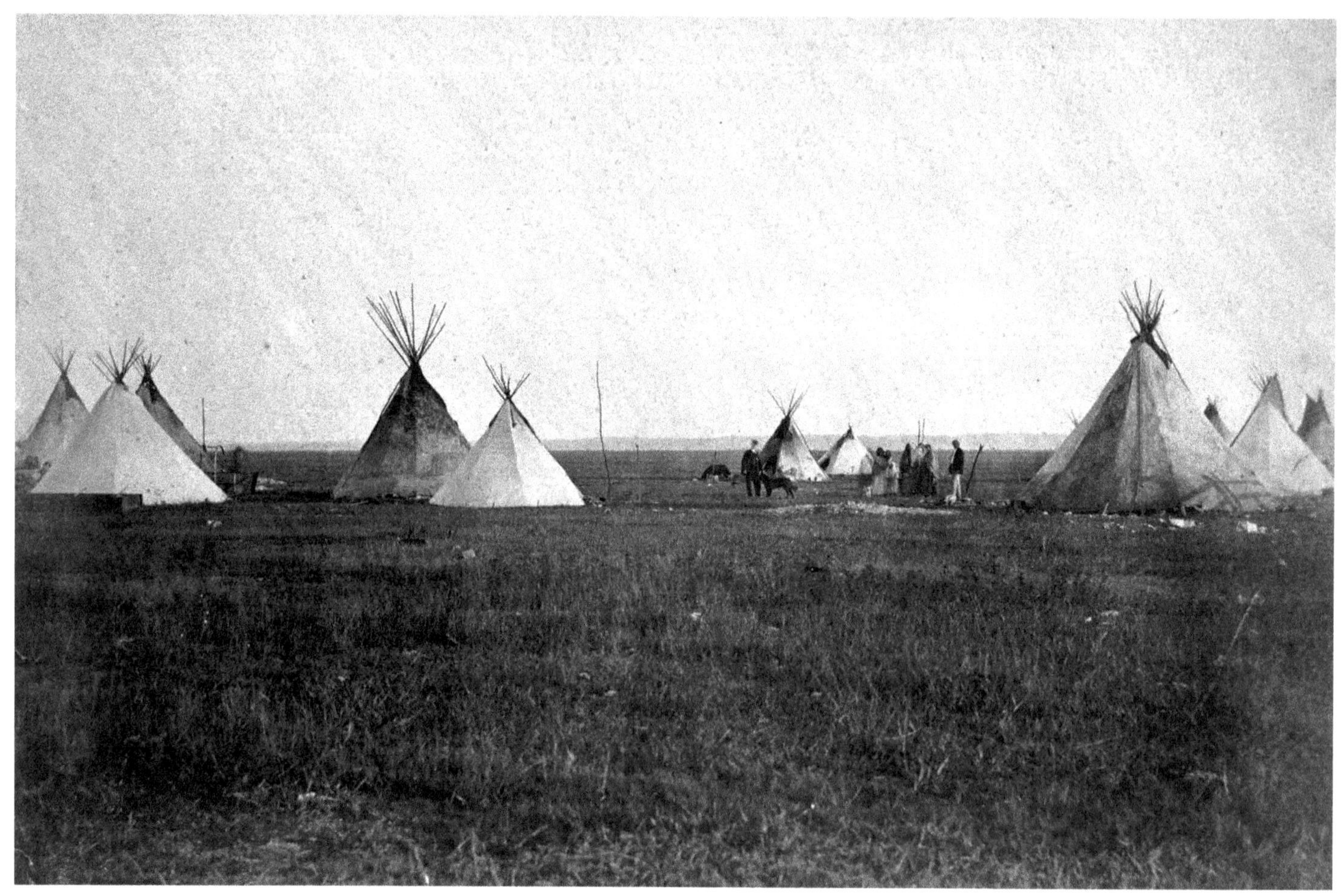

This 1867 photograph by Arundel Hull shows Sioux men and women and U.S. Cavalry soldiers near North Platte. Tepees were a common sight at the confluence of the North Platte and South Platte rivers, which from ancient times forward had been a meeting place for various tribes. As the main source of law enforcement on the frontier during the 1860s, the U.S. Army had a difficult job protecting settlers and natives from each other.

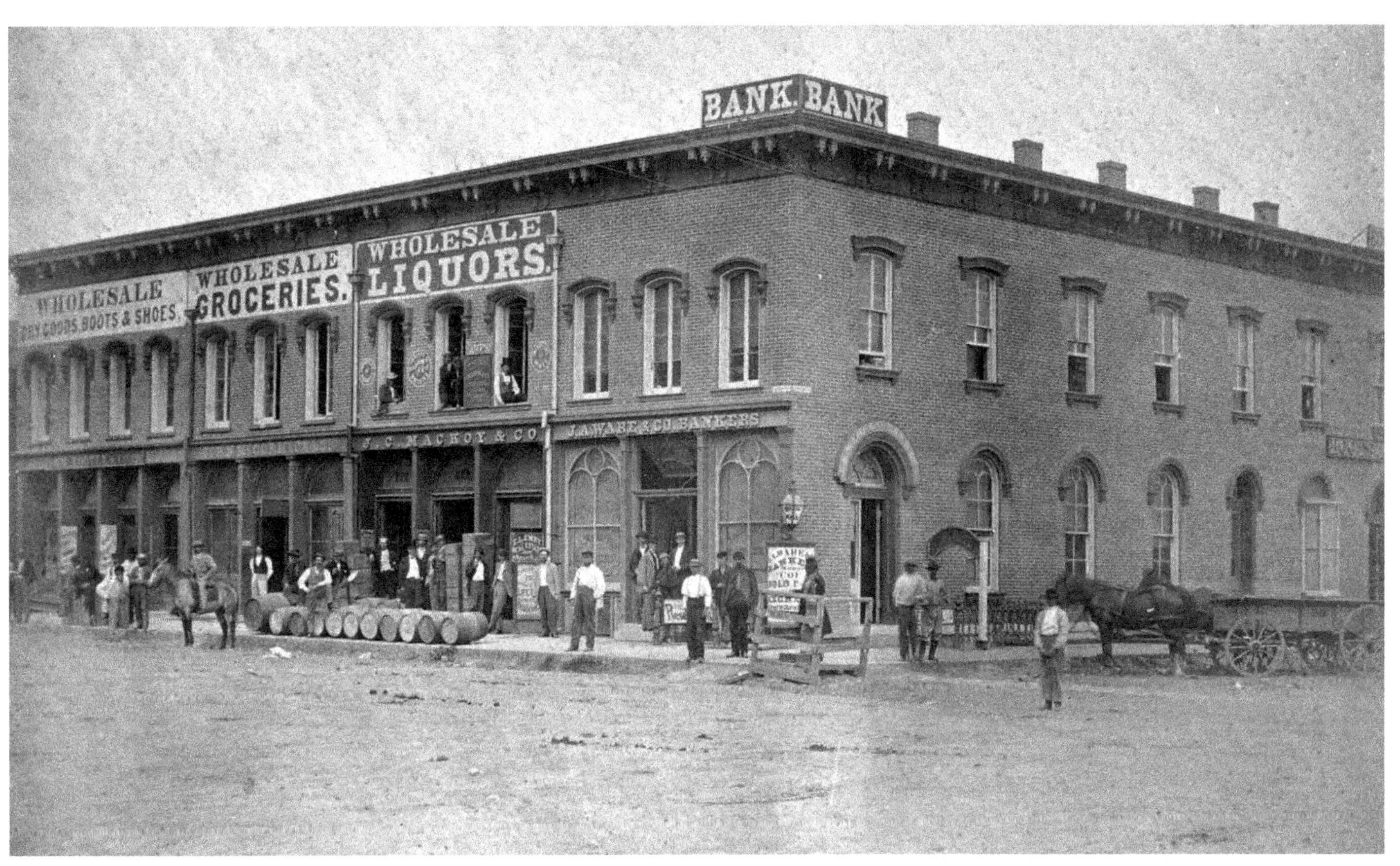

William A. Paxton, a well-known Omaha financier, built the Ware Block, named for his wife, Mary Jane Ware. This 1868 image shows Ware Block workers, who helped facilitate the sale of everything from boots, shoes, and dry goods to real estate, groceries, and liquor. J. A. Ware, a banker from Nebraska City, opened a branch of his bank in this block, later selling it to a group of investors who included former territorial governor Alvin Saunders.

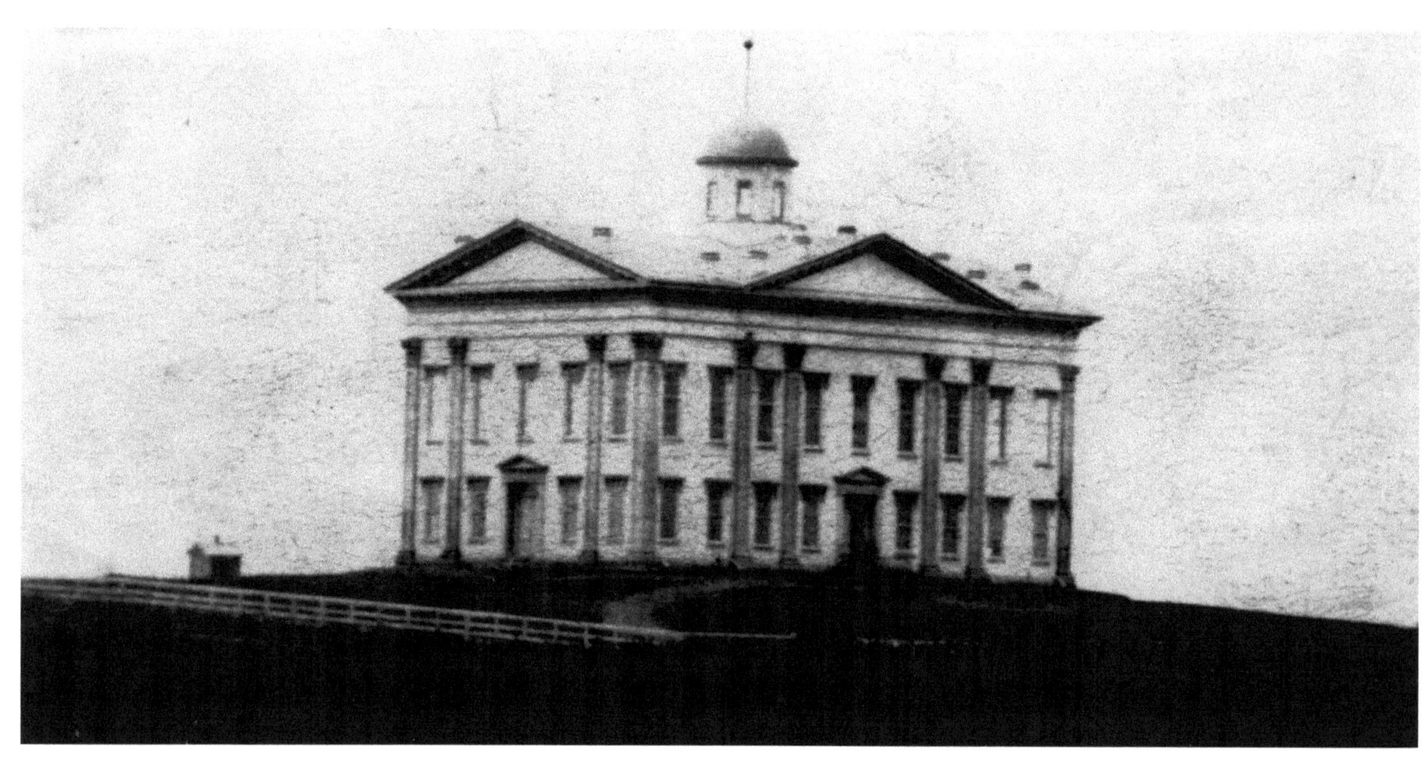

The second Nebraska territorial capitol was constructed in 1857 on Capitol Hill, at 20th and Dodge streets in Omaha. It served in its official capacity up to the time of the state's admission to the Union on March 1, 1867, then briefly served as the state government headquarters until August, when the capital moved to Lincoln. The second capitol was torn down in 1872 to make way for Omaha High School (today's Omaha Central High).

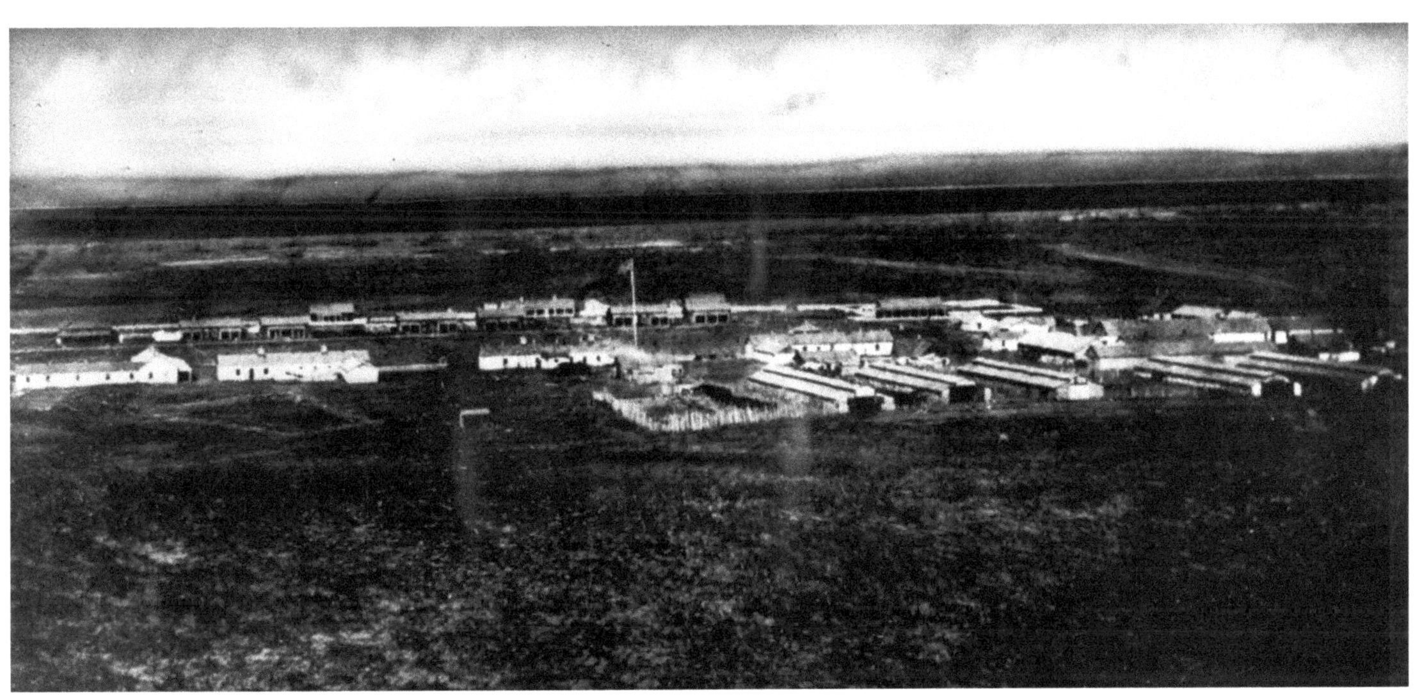

The U.S. Army wanted to add an outpost between Fort Kearny and Fort Laramie to protect westward travelers, so Fort McPherson was built in 1863 near present-day Maxwell. This panorama was recorded around 1870, about the time a young civilian scout named William F. "Buffalo Bill" Cody was discovered by dime novelist Ned Buntline, who had come to Fort McPherson in search of material. The fort was abandoned in 1880 and a national cemetery is located there today.

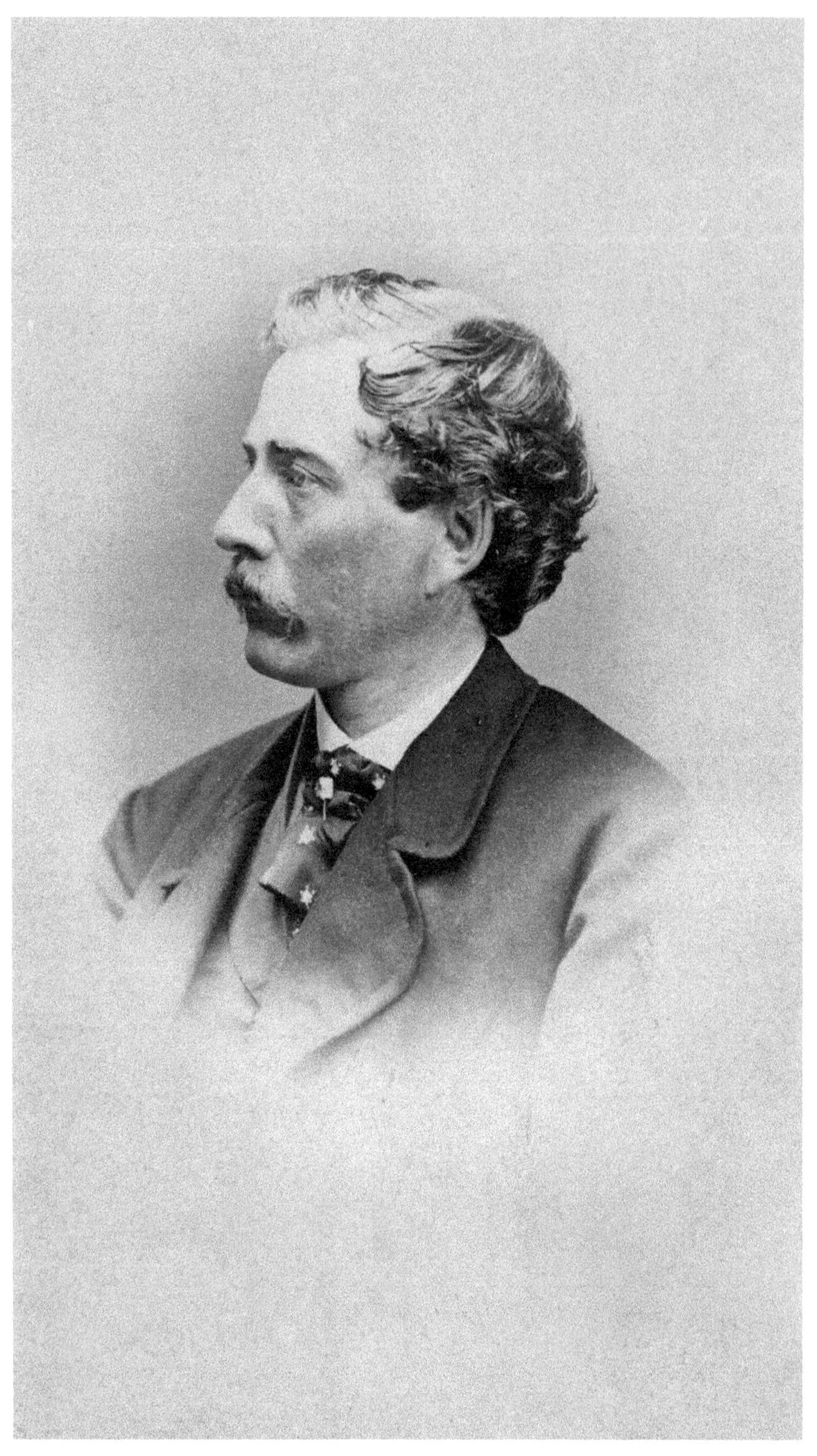

Known as the father of Arbor Day, J. Sterling Morton was a newspaper publisher in Nebraska City. He later served as Nebraska's acting territorial governor and later as Secretary of Agriculture. He had a background in agriculture, and advocated tree planting in the nearly treeless state. Arbor Day soon became a state holiday, celebrated on Morton's birthday, April 22, and thereafter was adopted as a holiday across the nation. "The Tree Planters' State" was Nebraska's official nickname from 1895 to 1945.

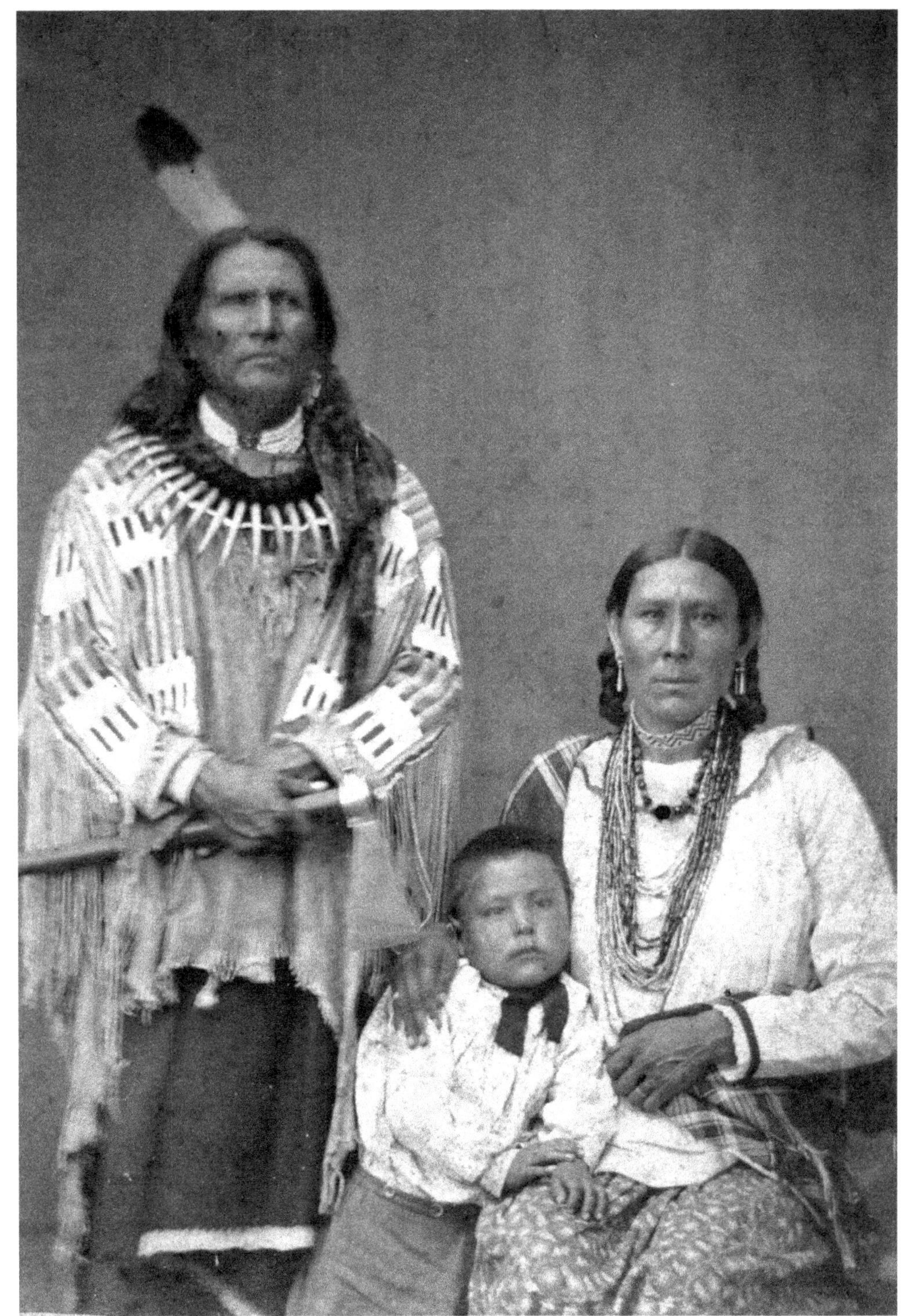

Standing Bear, shown here with his wife and a child, was a Ponca chief in northeast Nebraska whose 1879 trial in Omaha called into question the way the United States had been treating Indians for decades. The decision recognized Indians' rights as citizens, including habeas corpus. It couldn't bring back his son and daughter who had died as a result of the Poncas' relocation to present-day Oklahoma, but it started changing minds about Indian policy.

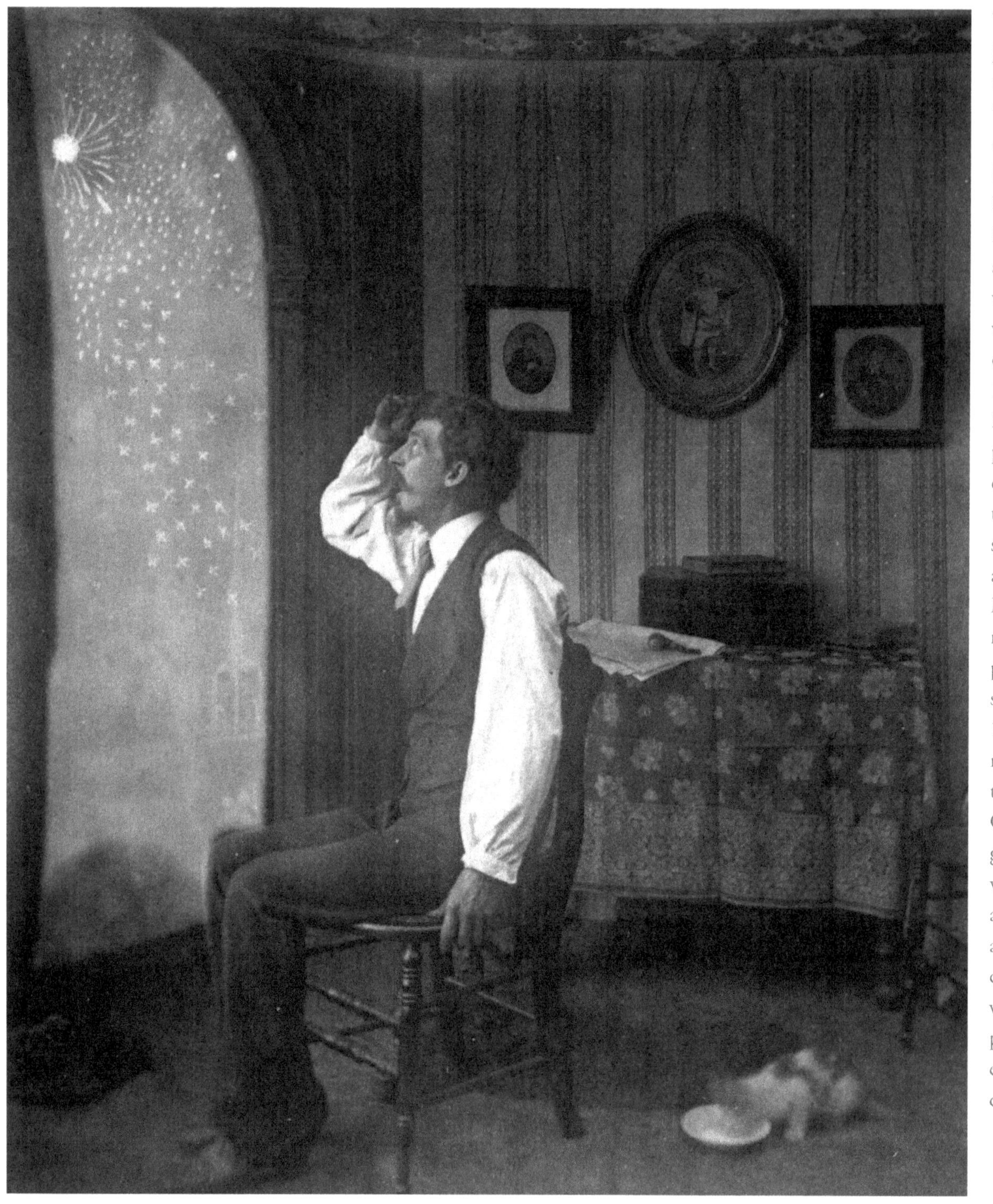

This drop-jawed, wide-eyed man gazing at "grasshoppers" outside his door was intended as humor, but the voracious intruders did not amuse Nebraskans who suffered widespread crop devastation in the 1870s. The Rocky Mountain Locust plague of 1874-75 cut a wide swath through eastern and southeast Nebraska and other states. Measurements revealed that at its peak, the greatest swarm encompassed 198,000 square miles—greater than the area of California. The grasshoppers vanished as rapidly as they had come and today are considered extinct, with various theories put forward to explain their strange demise.

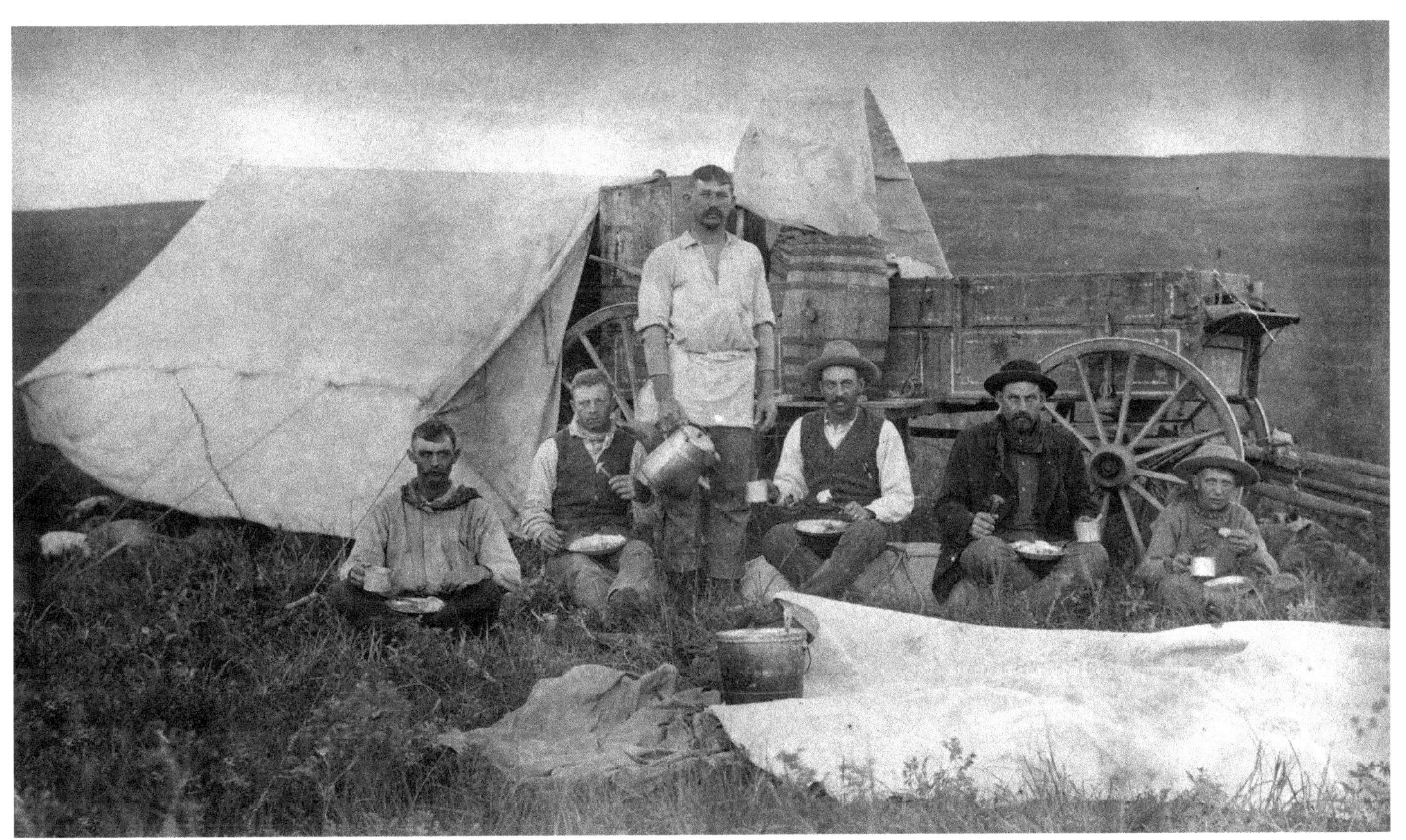

Taking a welcome break to enjoy a meal at the Birdwood Ranch near Sutherland, these cowboys may have been part of a larger group on a cattle drive from Texas, or they may have been stationed in western Nebraska. Either way, the tent and chuck wagon indicate a mission requiring at least several days to complete.

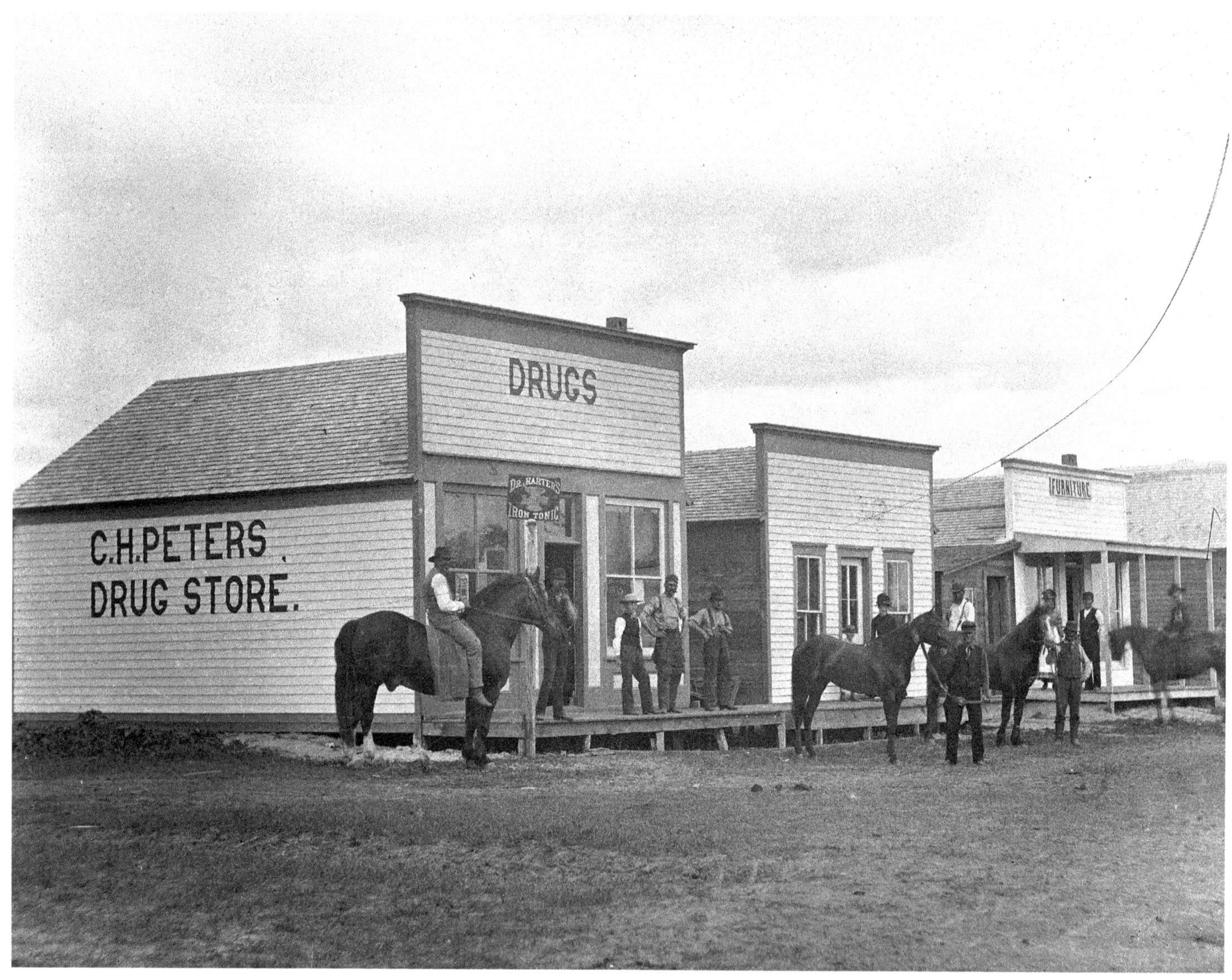

C. H. Peters traveled with a group of settlers from Brush Creek, Iowa, to the northern edge of Custer County and helped form the tiny settlement of West Union, where he built the drug store featured in this Solomon D. Butcher image. The settlement, whose population reached 100 in 1900, was just west of present-day Sargent, but the businesses eventually moved or closed. The town is long gone, with only farm and ranchland remaining where buildings once stood.

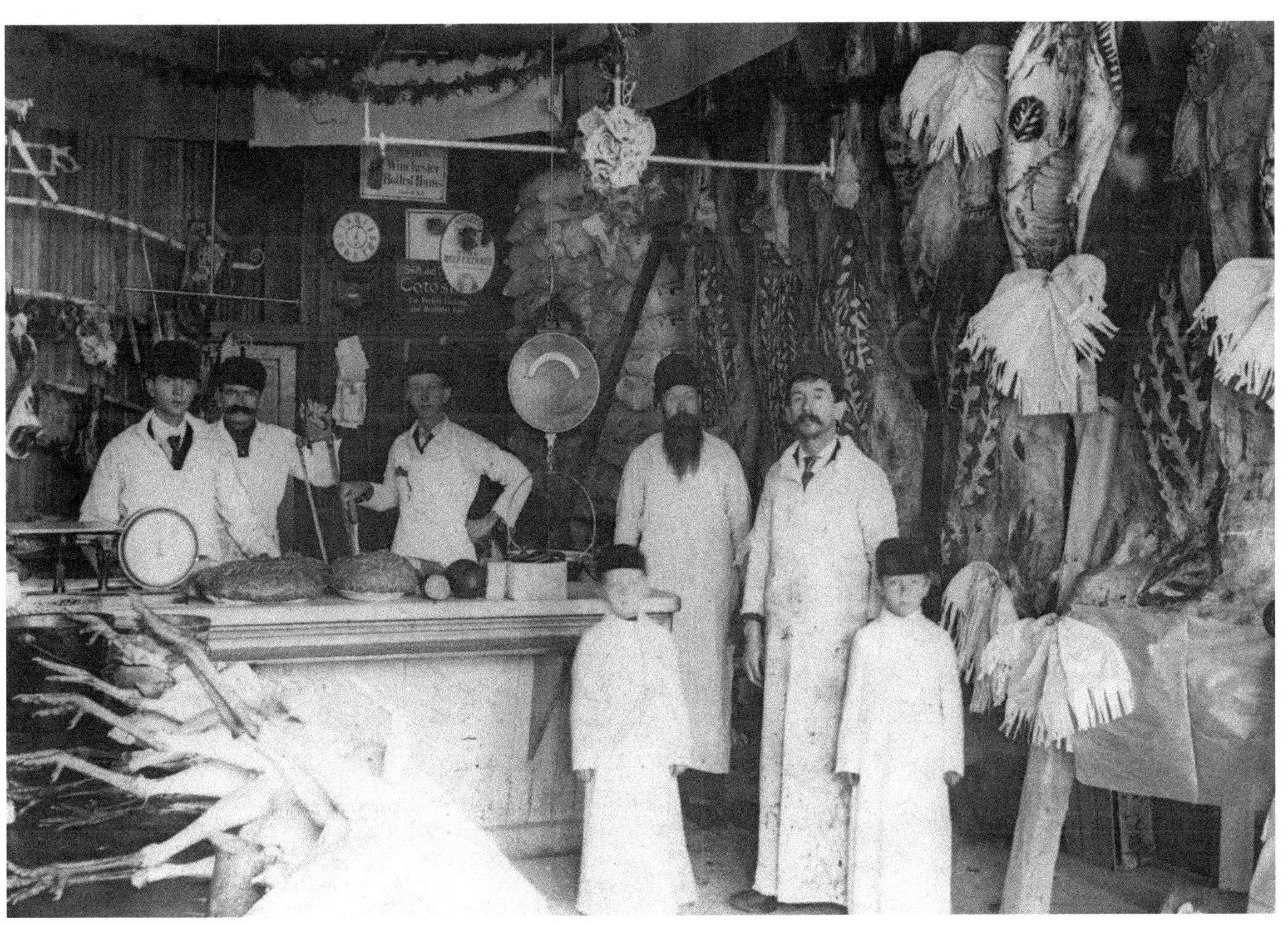

Weilers Butcher Shop, a family business located at 214 N. 10th St. in Lincoln, opened between 1884 and 1888. At right, next to the unidentified rabbi, is Valentine Weiler, the shop's owner. His sons, Francis Weiler (left) and Valentine Weiler, Jr., stand beside him. The younger Val Weiler went on to start one of Nebraska's most successful enterprises, Valentino's Pizza, opening at 35th and Holdrege streets in 1957. Francis eventually started another Lincoln restaurant.

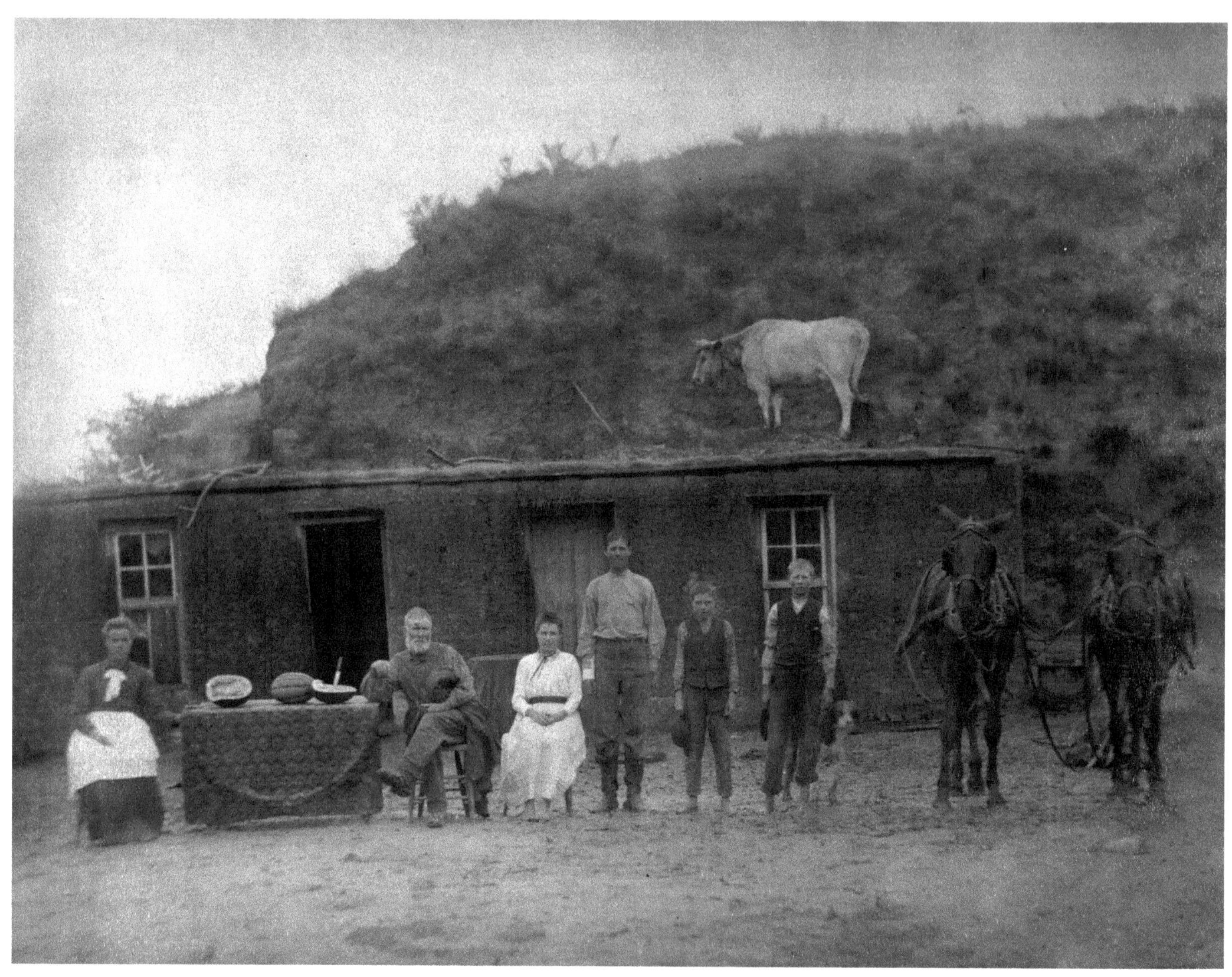

Possibly the most famous Solomon Butcher image shows the Sylvester Rawding family north of Sargent in the summer of 1886. Rawding claimed that the lump visible above his eye was a war wound. He also claimed that his stepson (the tallest of the three boys) later evicted him and forced him to move to an old soldiers' home in Kansas. The truth seems to have been that the lump was a cyst and Rawding moved by his own choice after a disagreement.

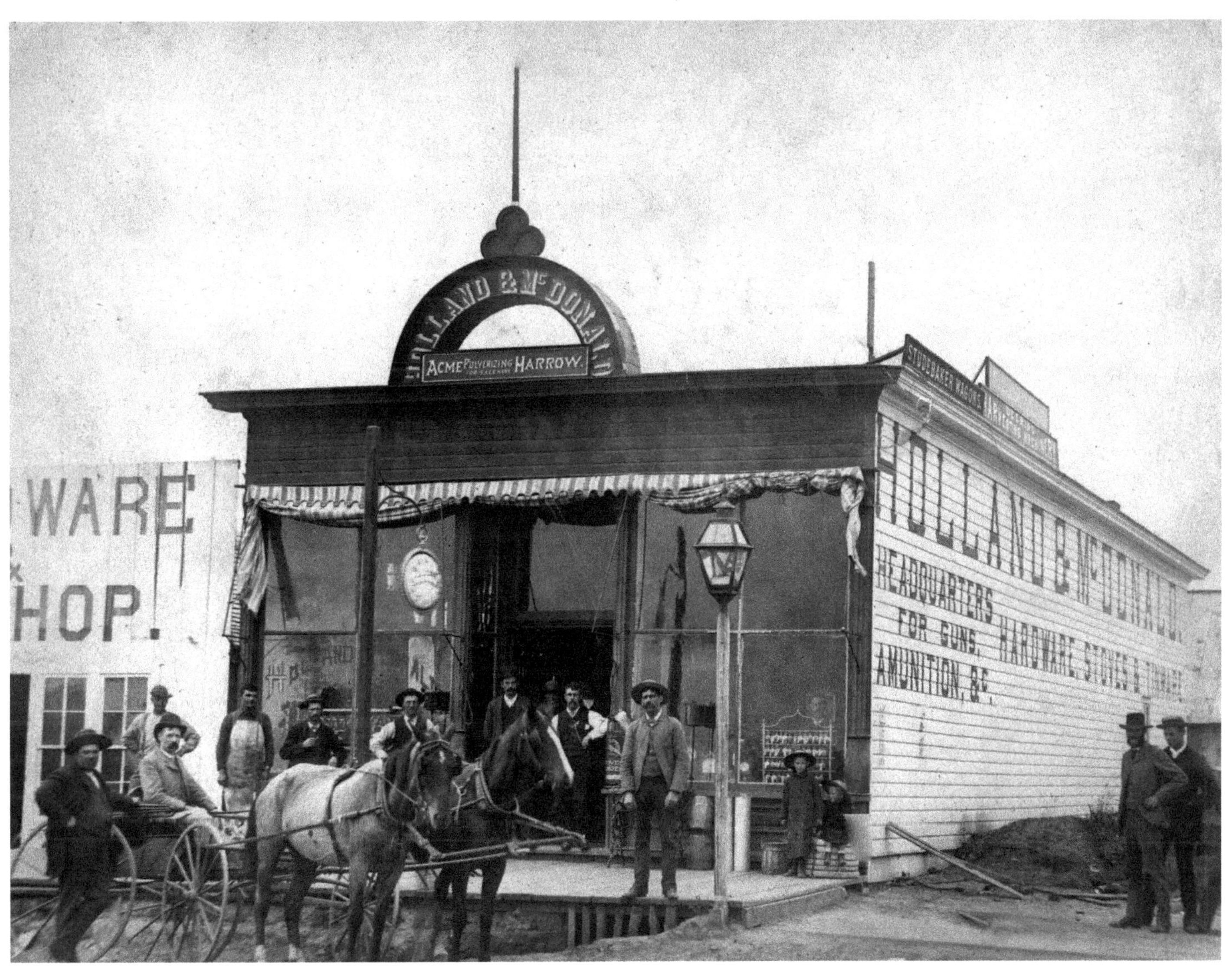

The Custer County seat enjoyed its new hardware store, complete with wooden platform sidewalk, built in 1884. The city was named for a discarded Indian bow discovered in 1880 by Wilson Hewitt, a homesteader who petitioned for a post office on his land. After several suggested names were rejected by the government because they were already taken, Hewitt hit the jackpot with "Broken Bow."

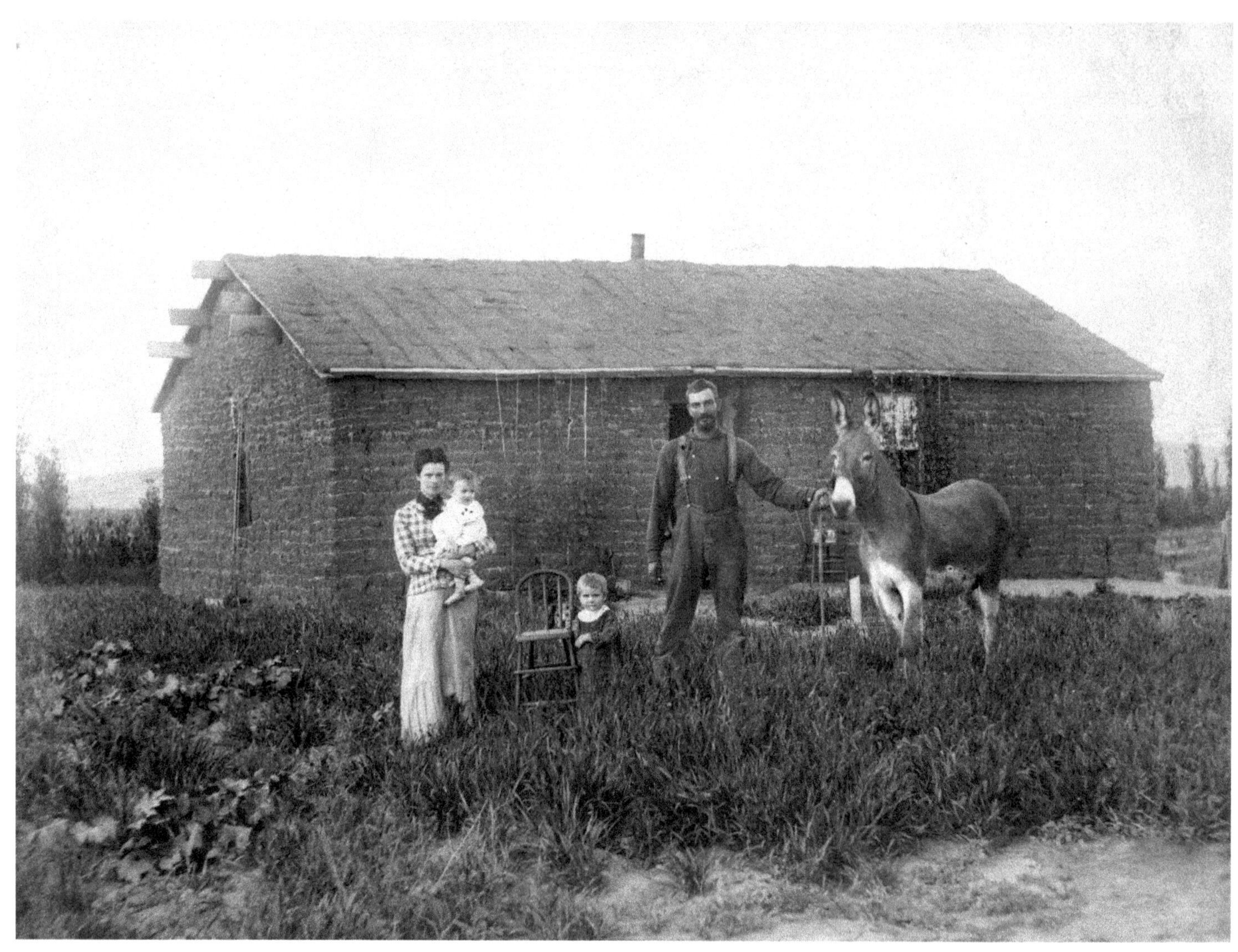

This is J. D. Semler with his donkey in hand, his wife, Lillie (holding their daughter, Daisy), and their son, George, with the shy family dog hiding behind George's chair. The family is shown in 1886 at the Semler sod house near Woods Park, east of present-day Sargent.

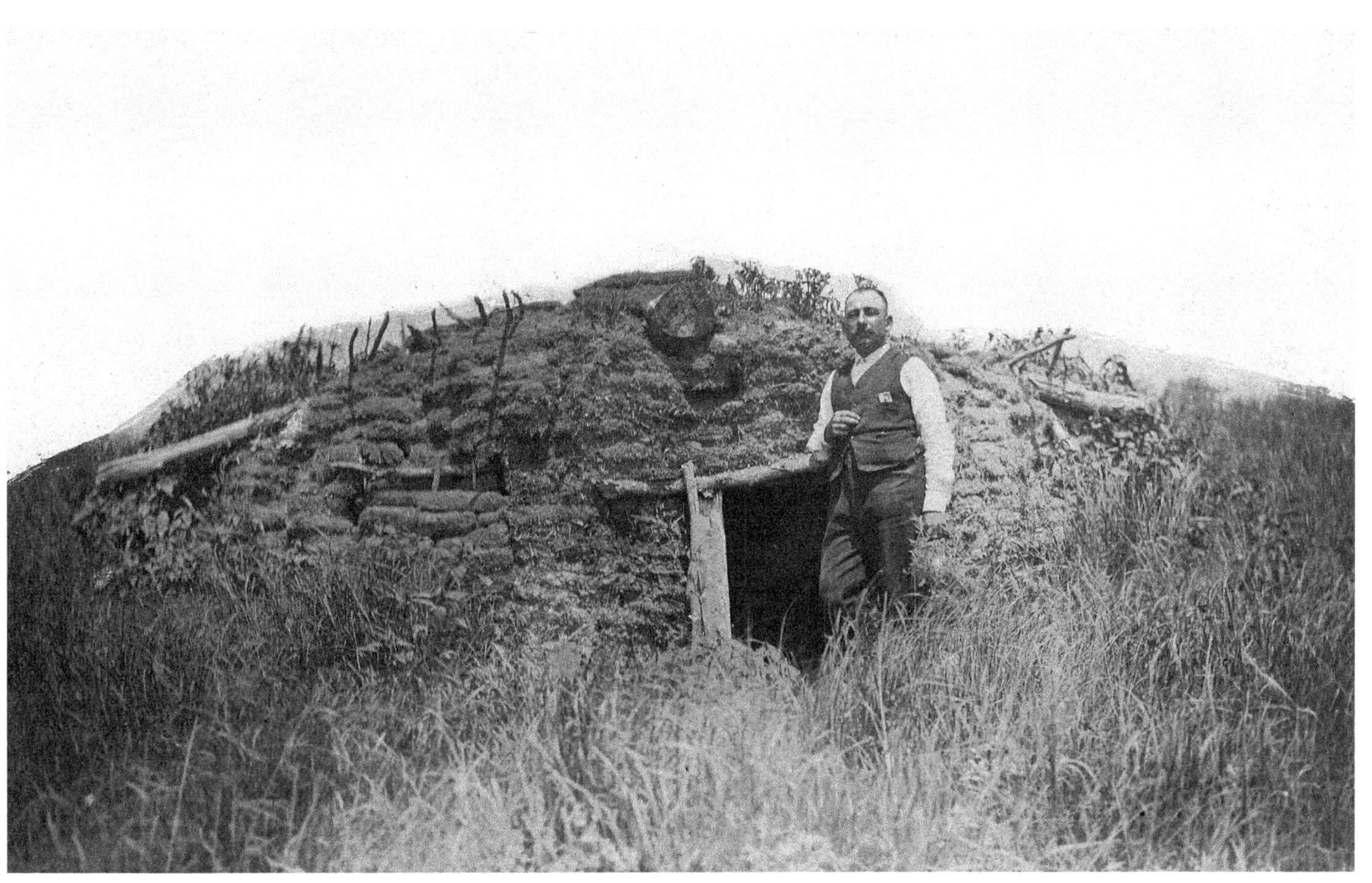

Solomon Butcher, shown in this 1886 self-portrait in front of his first Custer County dugout home, moved to Nebraska from Ohio in 1880 with his parents in a pair of covered wagons. He tried his hand at homesteading but found he wasn't built for farm life. In addition to his photographic endeavors, he also taught school and became a salesman, but always respected those who could make a go of it on the farm.

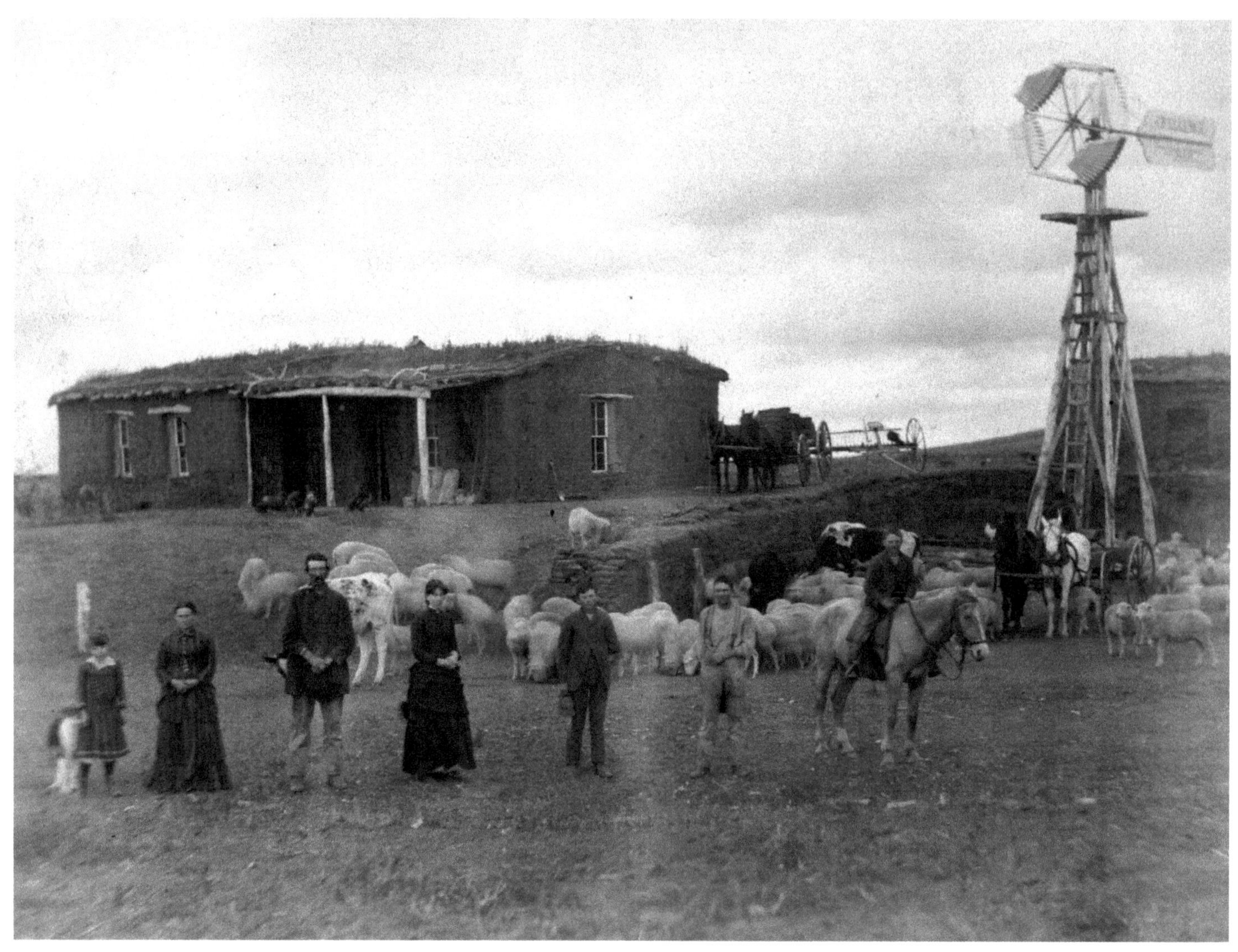

William Moore and his family display all their worldly wealth—including cattle, sheep, pigs, teams of horses, a windmill, and farm implements—in this 1886 Solomon Butcher photograph taken at the Moore sod house near Sargent. The photographer traveled by horse and wagon to his many photo shoots.

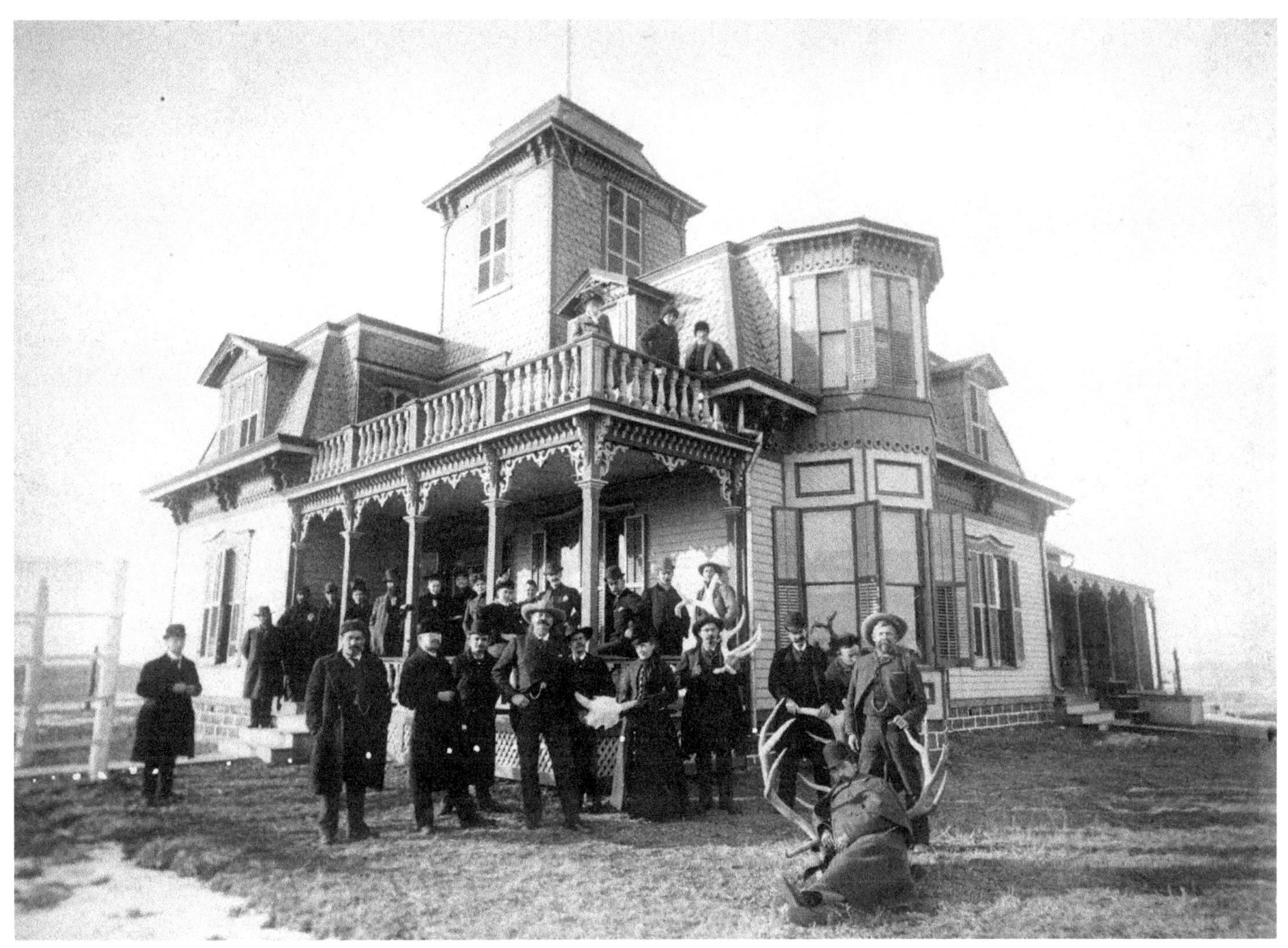

Despite their stormy marriage, Colonel William F. "Buffalo Bill" Cody and his wife, Louisa, often entertained guests at Scouts Rest, their home near North Platte built in 1886. Cody, who was on the road with his Wild West tour every summer starting in 1883, often lamented that he never saw the place when the fields were green. He stands at center with Louisa, who is helping him hold a cow skull.

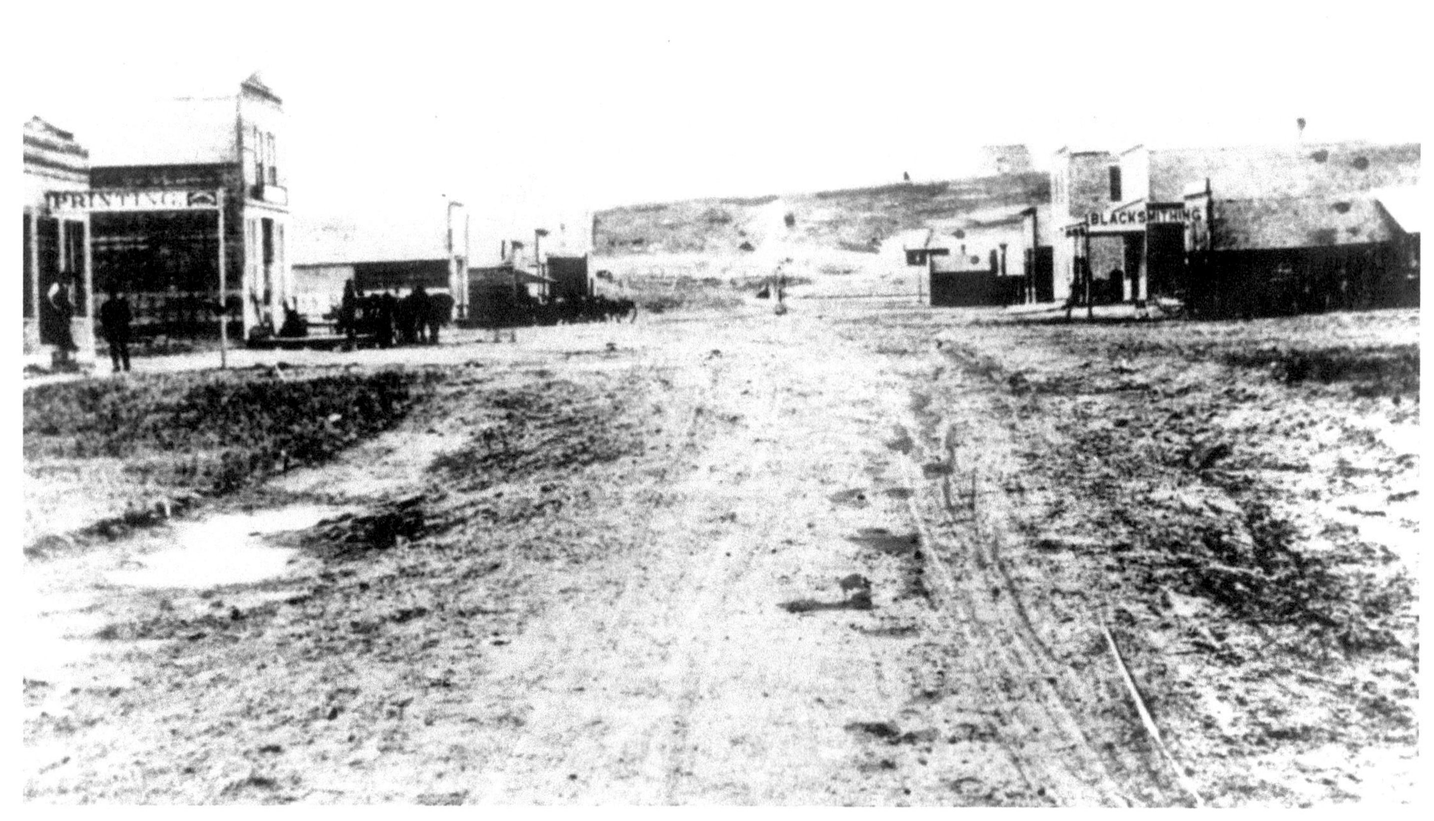

Sloughs flank this muddy street in the Hitchcock County town of Trenton, on the High Plains in southwestern Nebraska, around the mid-1880s. Shown here, a printer and a blacksmith are among the businesses serving settlers in this early view of the town.

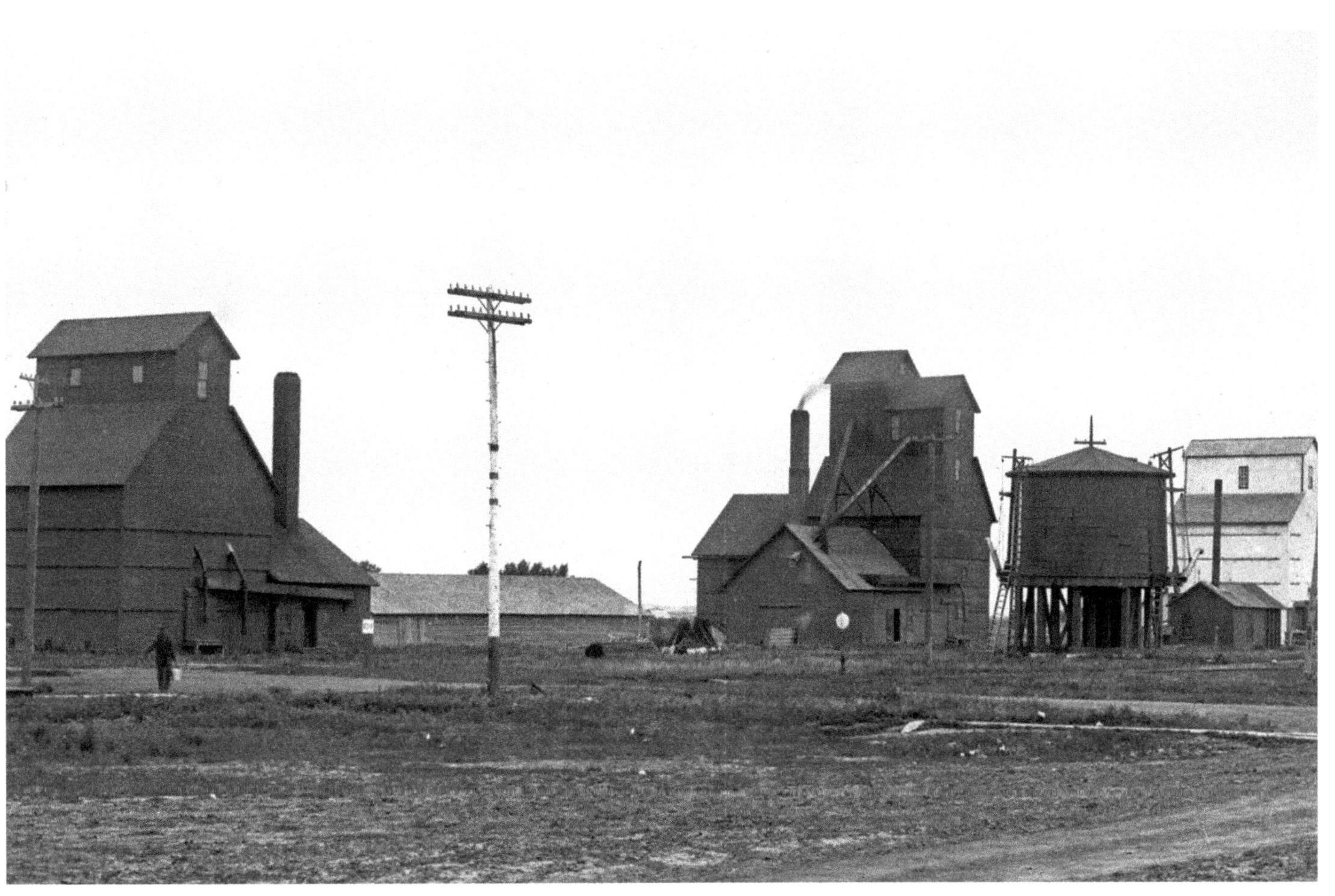

Grain elevators and a railroad water tank dominate this nineteenth-century image of Blue Hill. Located between the Republican and Little Blue rivers, Blue Hill was platted in 1878 and within four years boasted a population of 1,000. The town survived a devastating downtown fire in 1890 and its population has remained relatively stable into today.

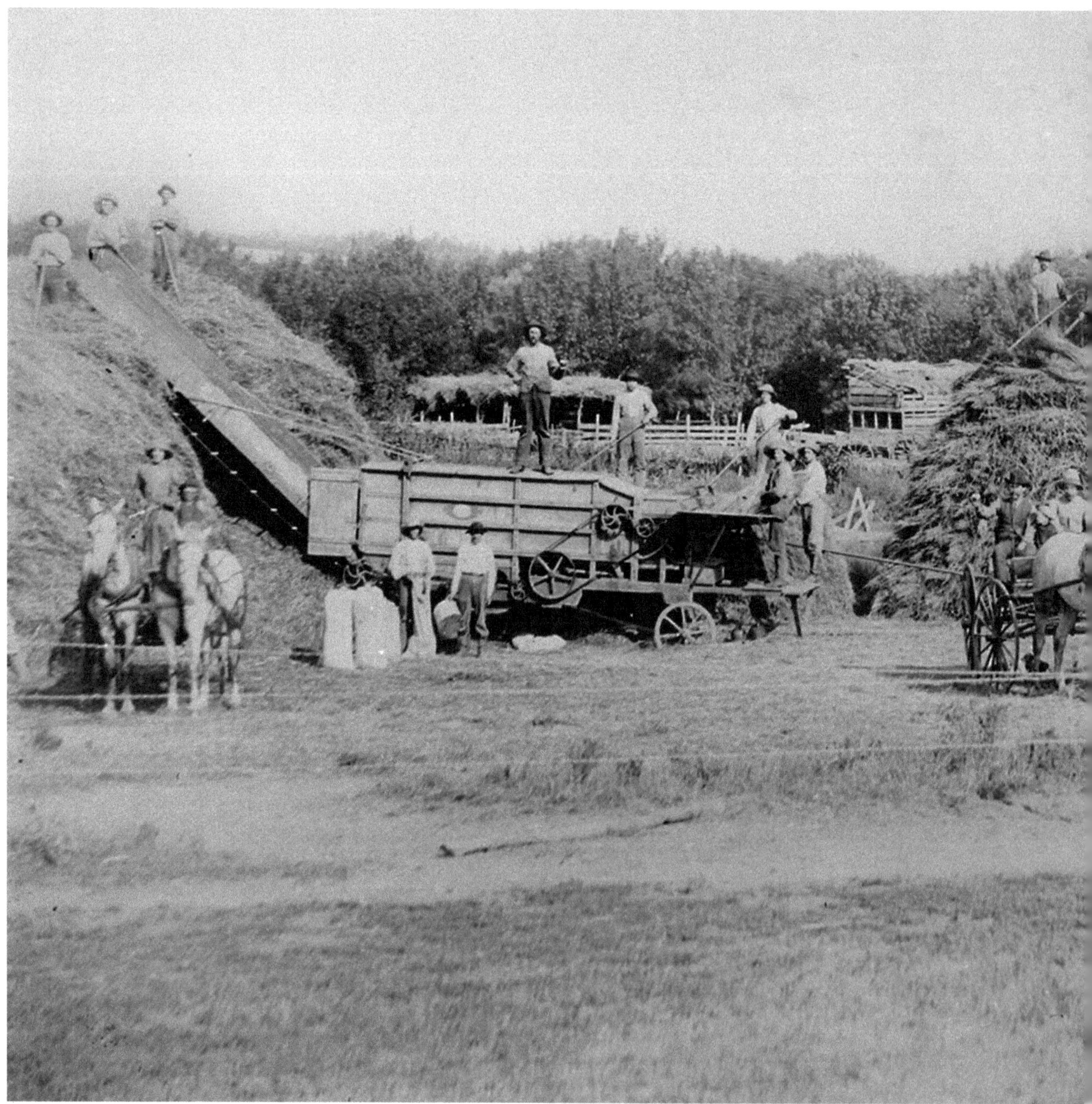

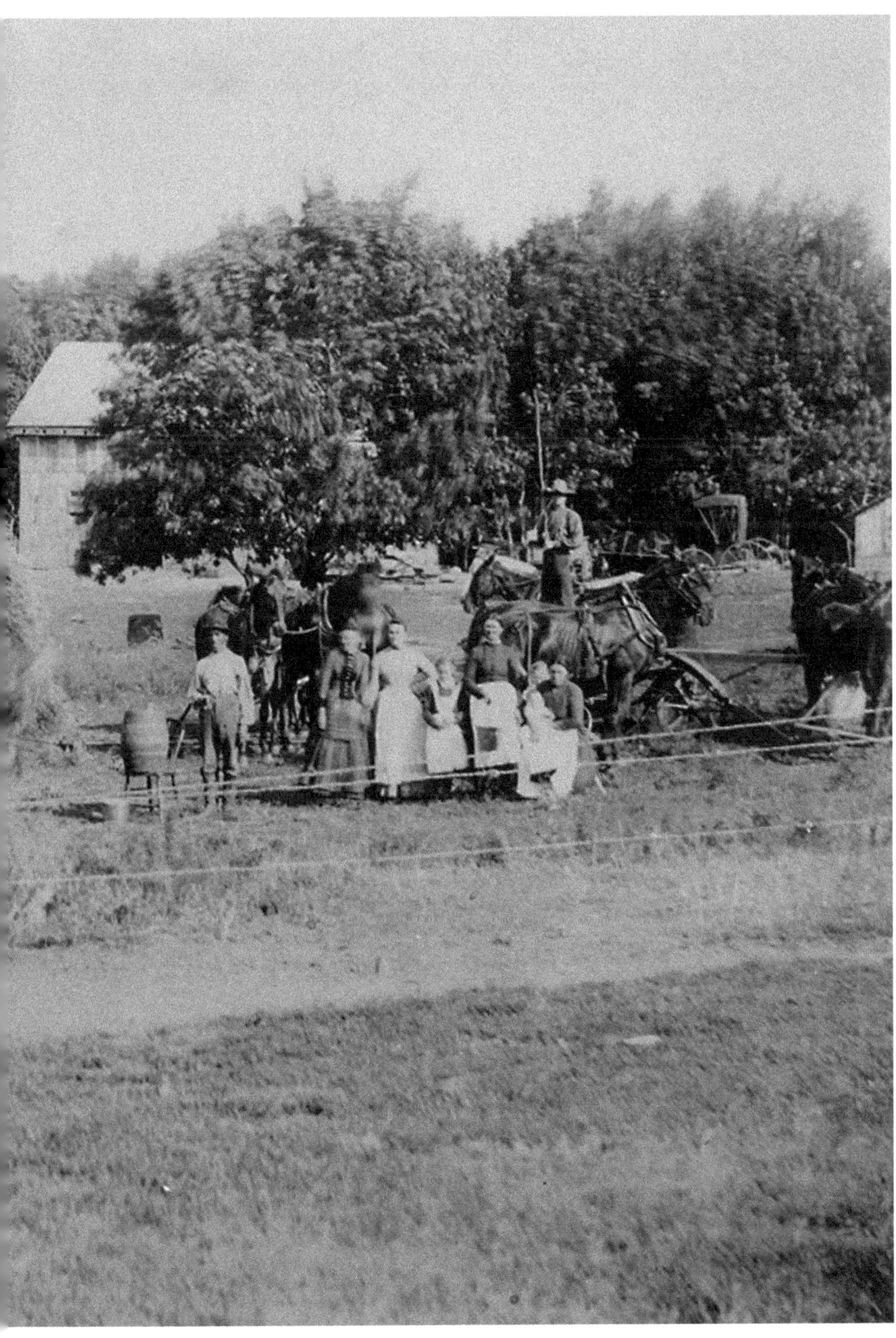

The arrival of a threshing crew was big news on the farm as friends and neighbors pitched in to help get the work done. Lined up for a group shot in 1888 in a farmyard near Wilber are horse-drawn wagons, the chain-driven threshing machine, men with pitchforks atop stacks of the harvest, teams of horses (in a circle at right to power the thresher), and women of the family, in charge of feeding all the helping hands.

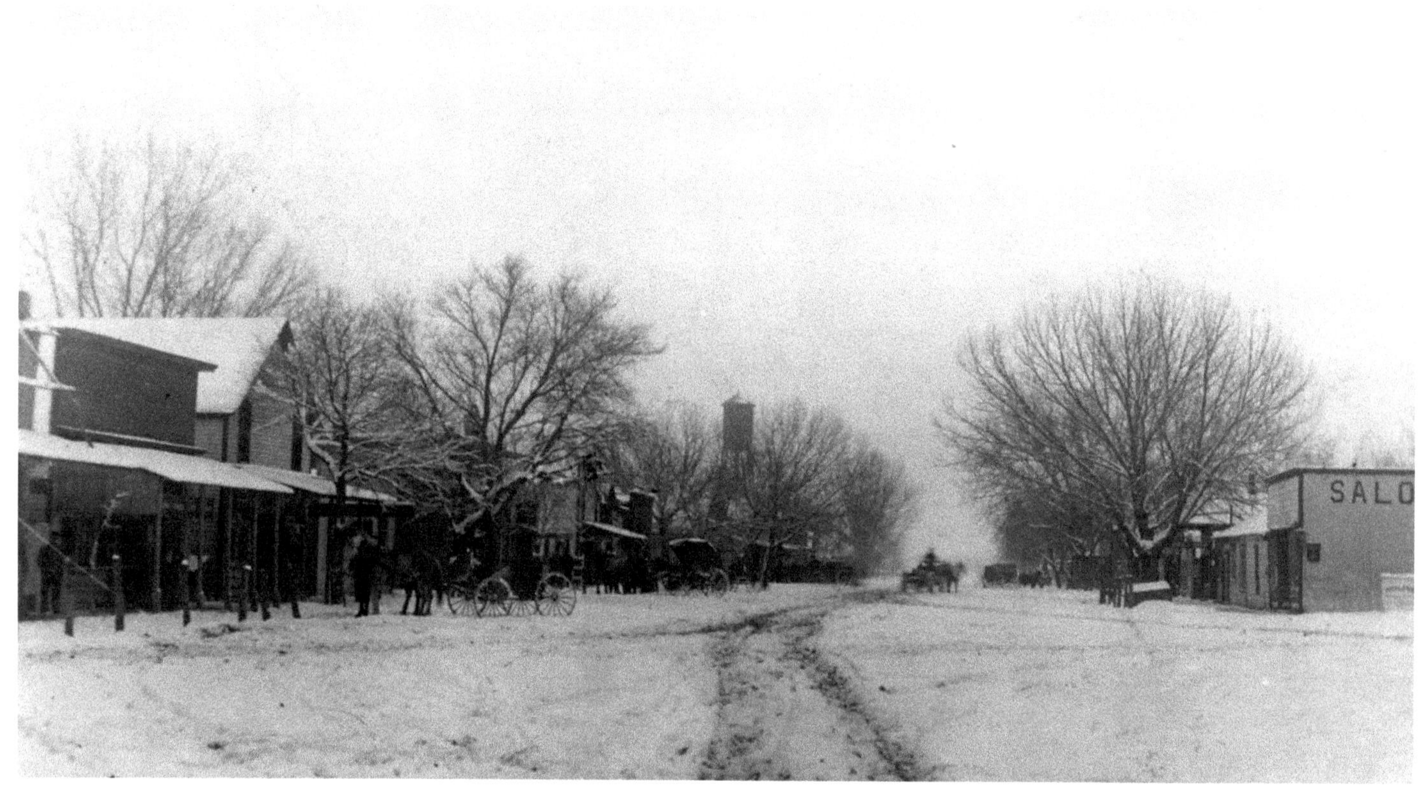

Several unattended carriages are tied up along this wintry street in early Ewing, in northeastern Nebraska, as a lone wagoneer heads off into the distance. A large water tower is visible through the treeline at center. Nebraska is no stranger to snowy winters, and worse. On January 12, 1888, a fast-moving blizzard tore through the state without warning, sending mild temperatures plummeting and claiming the lives of children on their way home from school.

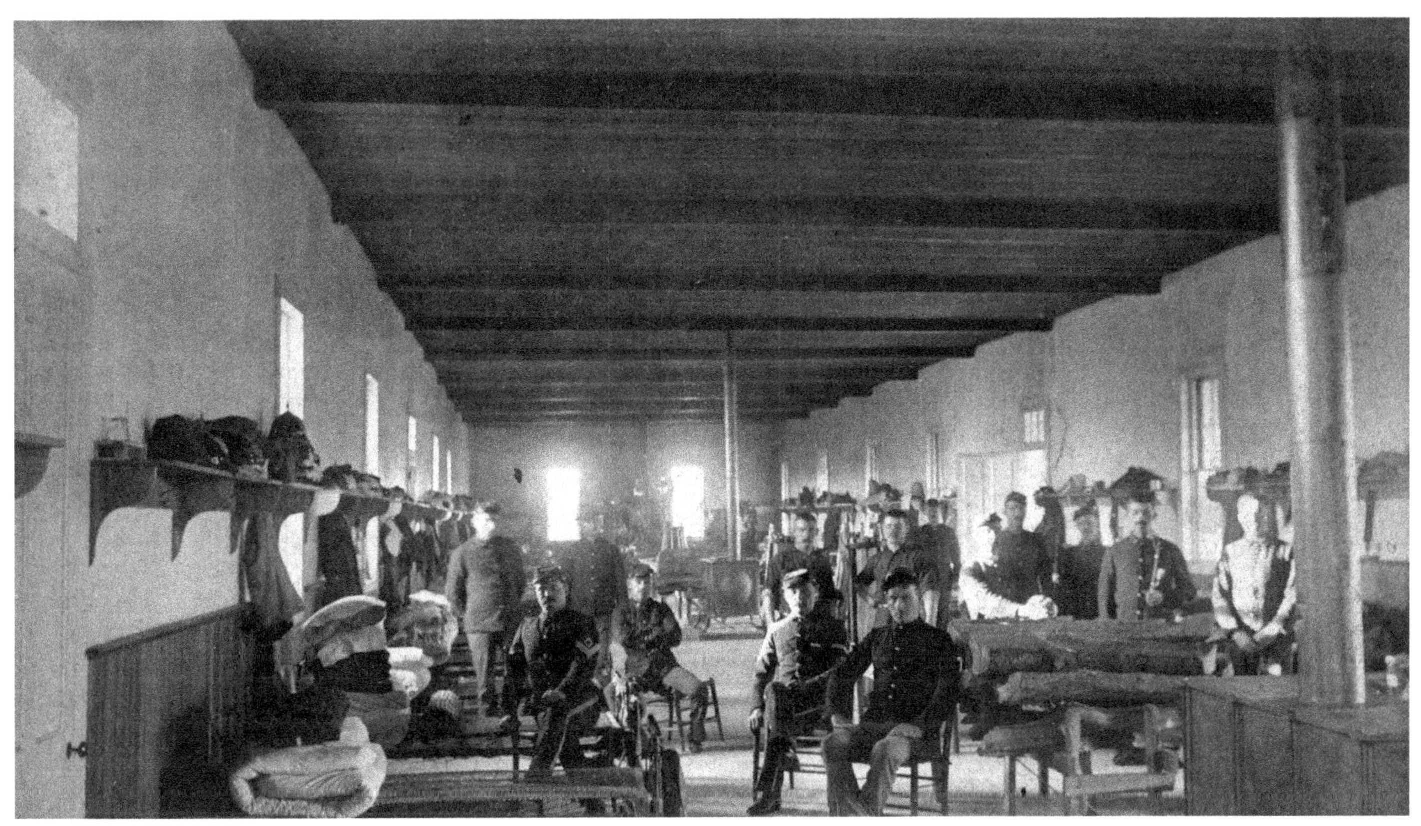

Fairly roomy but rather Spartan, the interior of the barracks of the Eighth Infantry, Fort Robinson, was warmed by potbellied stoves. The fort was established near present-day Crawford in 1874 and played an important role in the Sioux wars from 1876 to 1890. In 1877, the Oglala Lakota (Sioux) war leader Crazy Horse was killed at Fort Robinson as he struggled with military guards to avoid imprisonment.

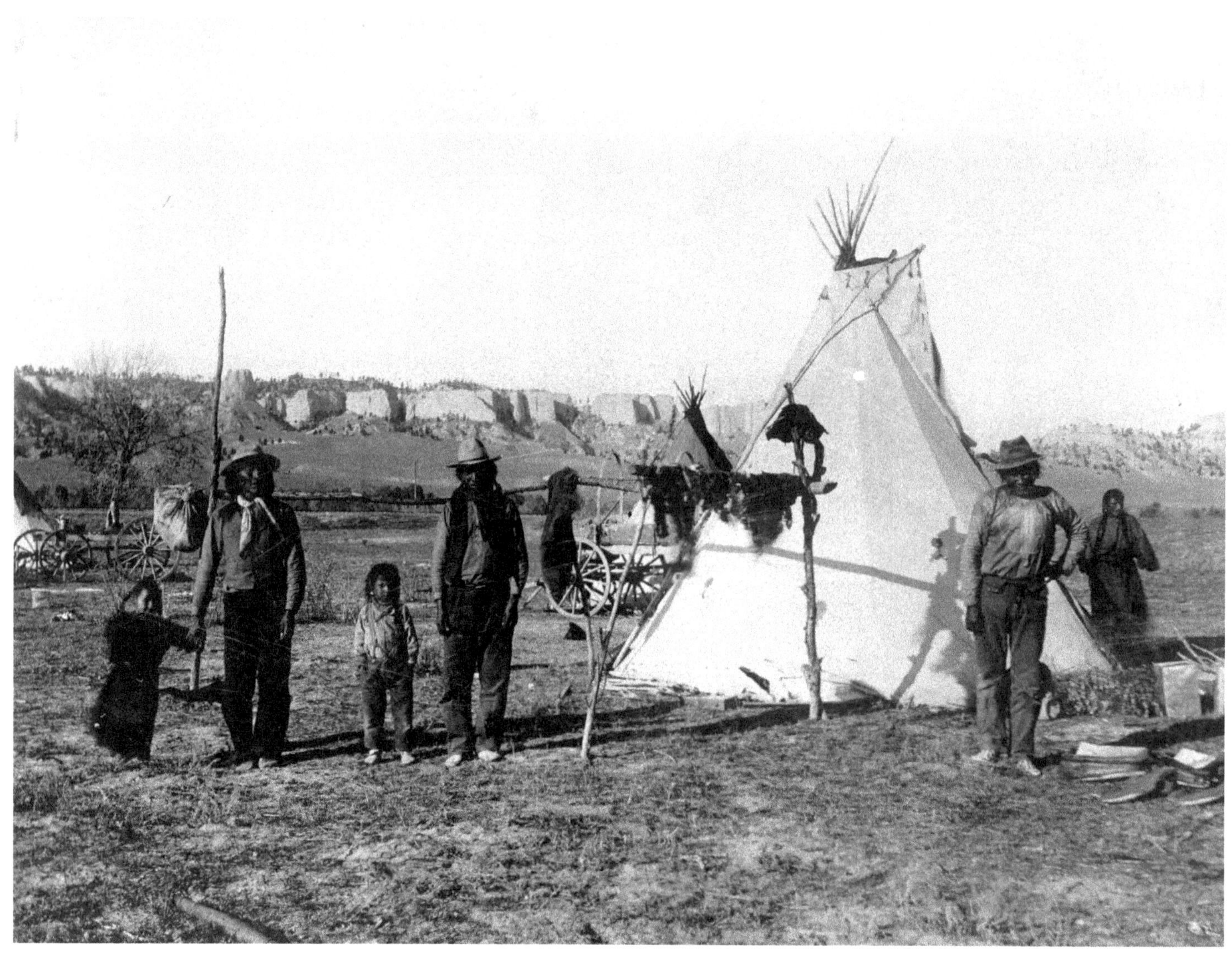

The nomadic Lakota were the dominant force in northwest Nebraska through most of the 1800s, but were largely displaced and confined to reservations by the turn of the century. These Lakota have adopted the clothing and means of transport introduced by settlers. Behind them runs a railroad track.

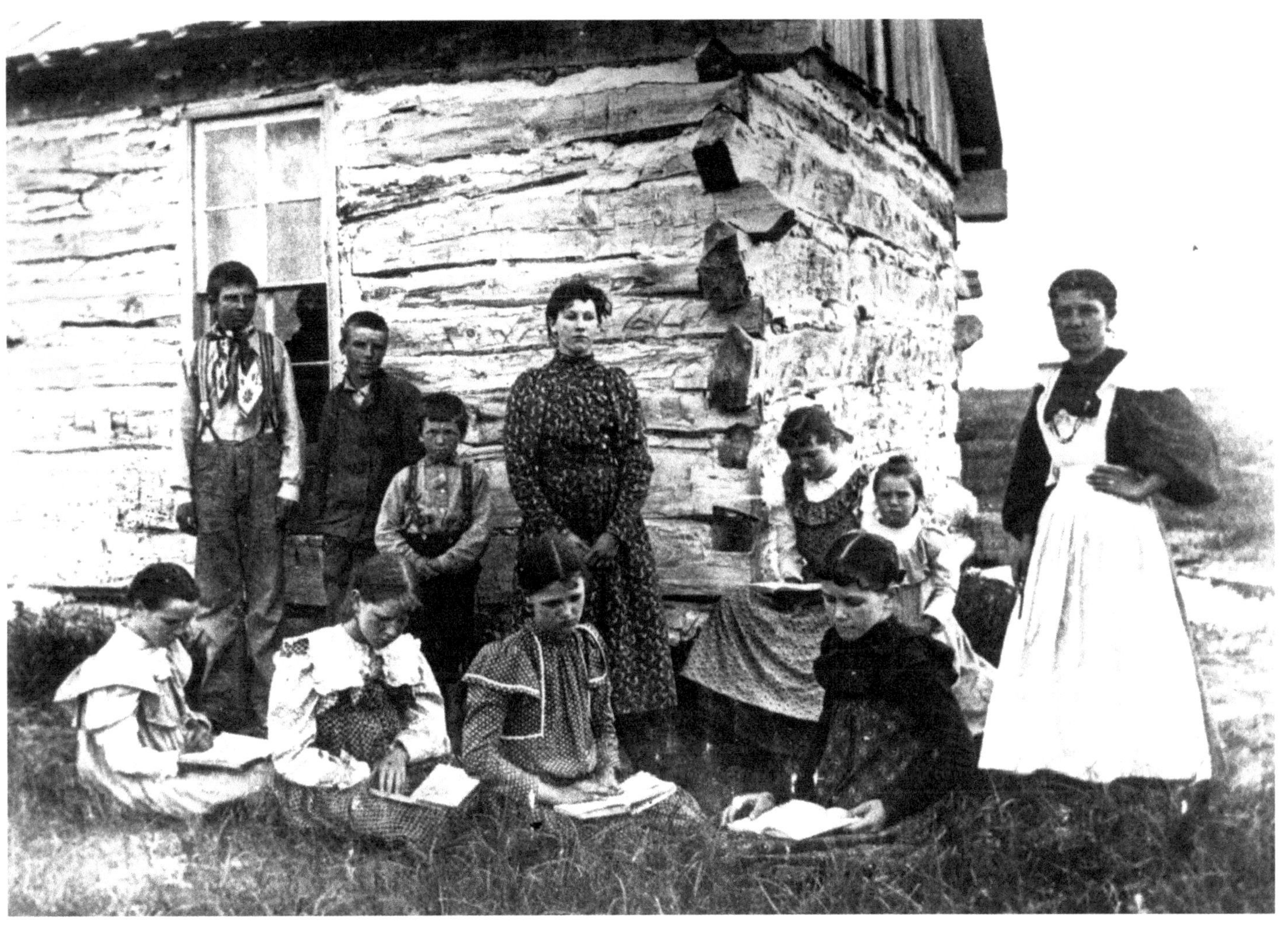

These schoolchildren don't look too eager to continue their studies outdoors, even under their teachers' watchful eyes. The schoolhouse, on Pine Creek in Holt County, was made of hand-hewn square logs.

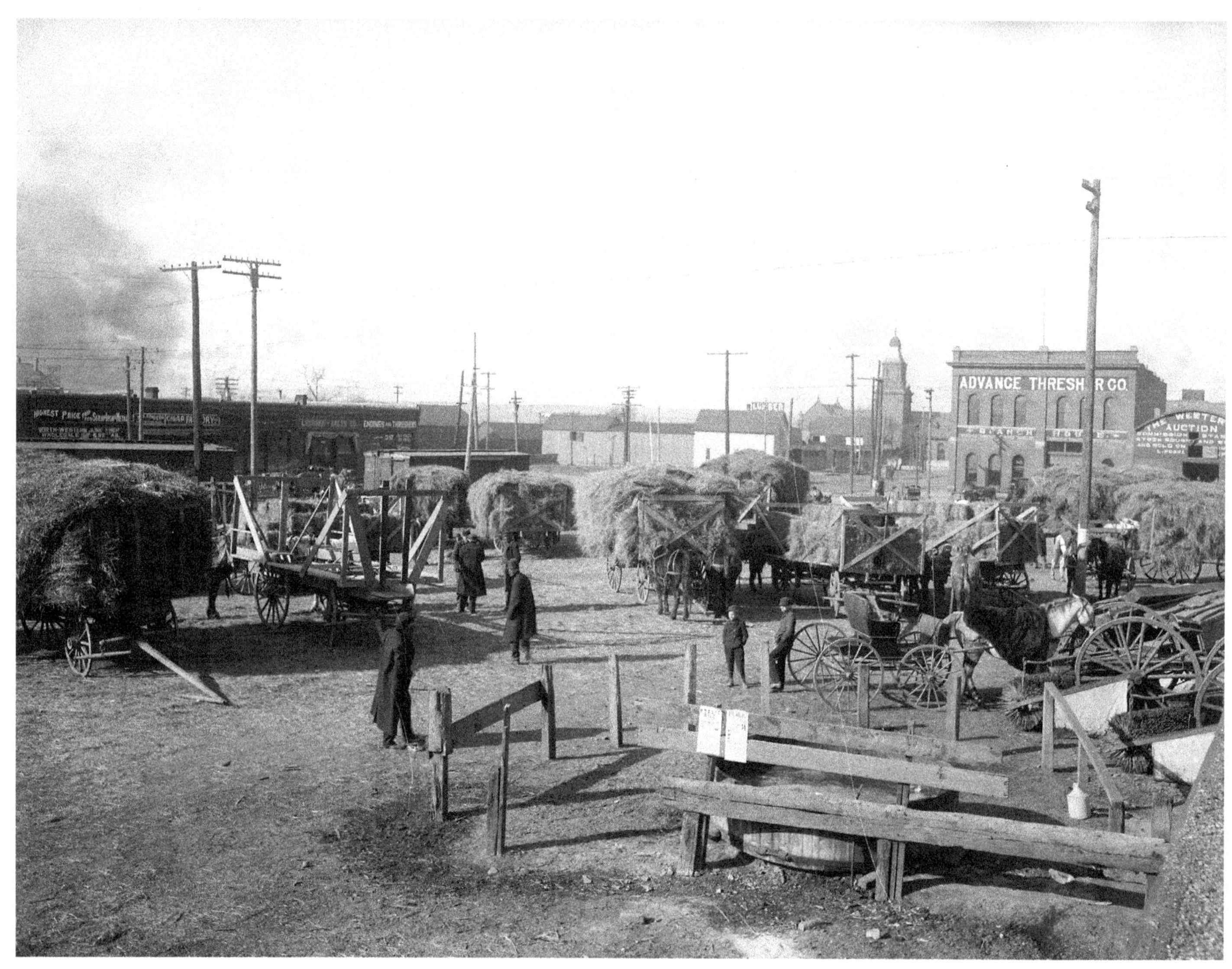

Flatbeds loaded with hay from nearby farms were a typical sight in the late nineteenth century in Lincoln's Haymarket District, which was known for its railroad stations, bars, brothels, and more than a few seedy characters.

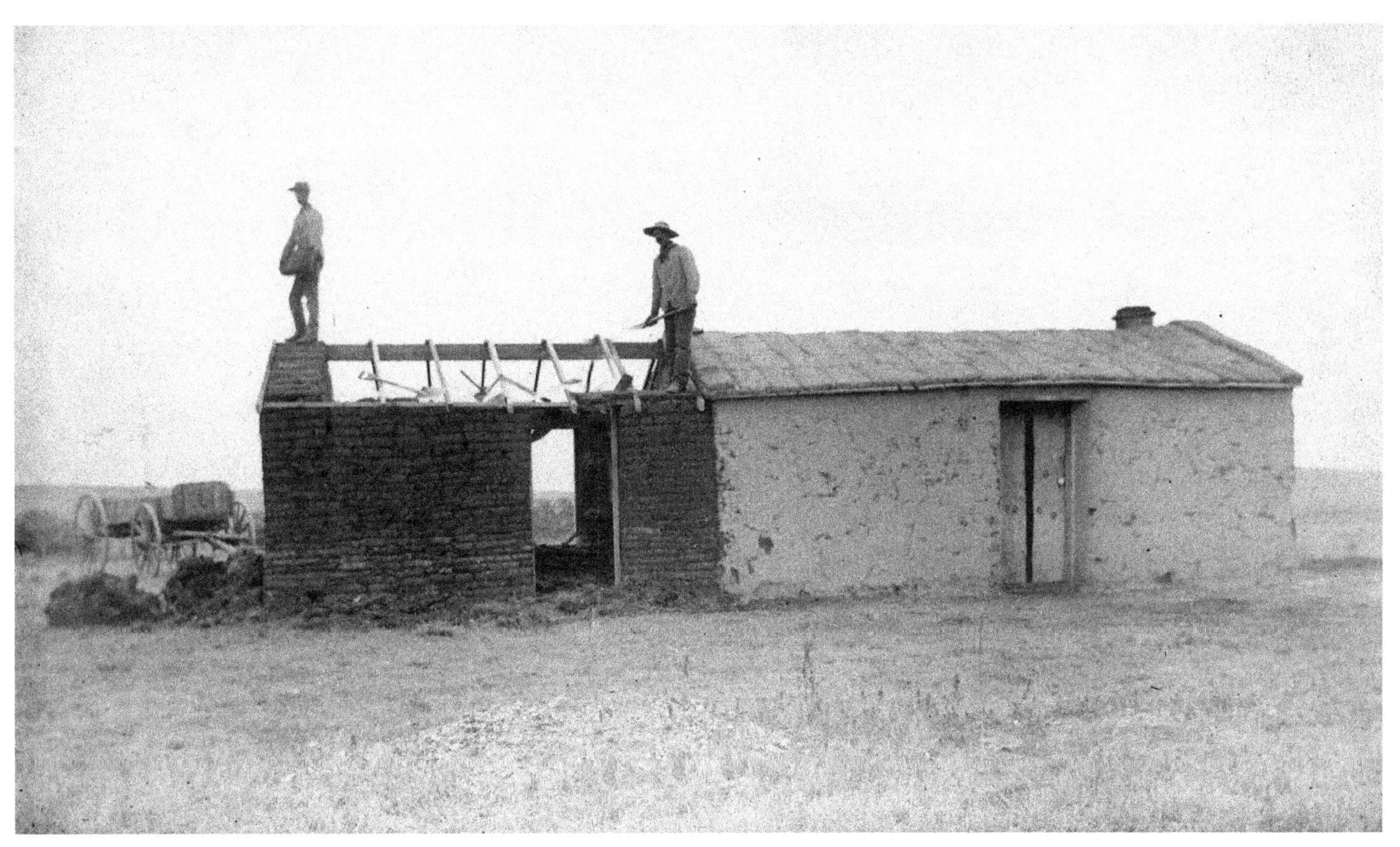

The Frank Roach sod house in Keith County was getting an addition in 1890. Encouraged by the Union Pacific Railroad, which had land to sell, settlers began to arrive in Ogallala and surrounding regions in significant numbers from 1882 to 1884. A decade later, an *Omaha World-Herald* story said that "two-thirds of the 2,500 population are in destitute circumstances" owing to famine caused by drought and hard economic times.

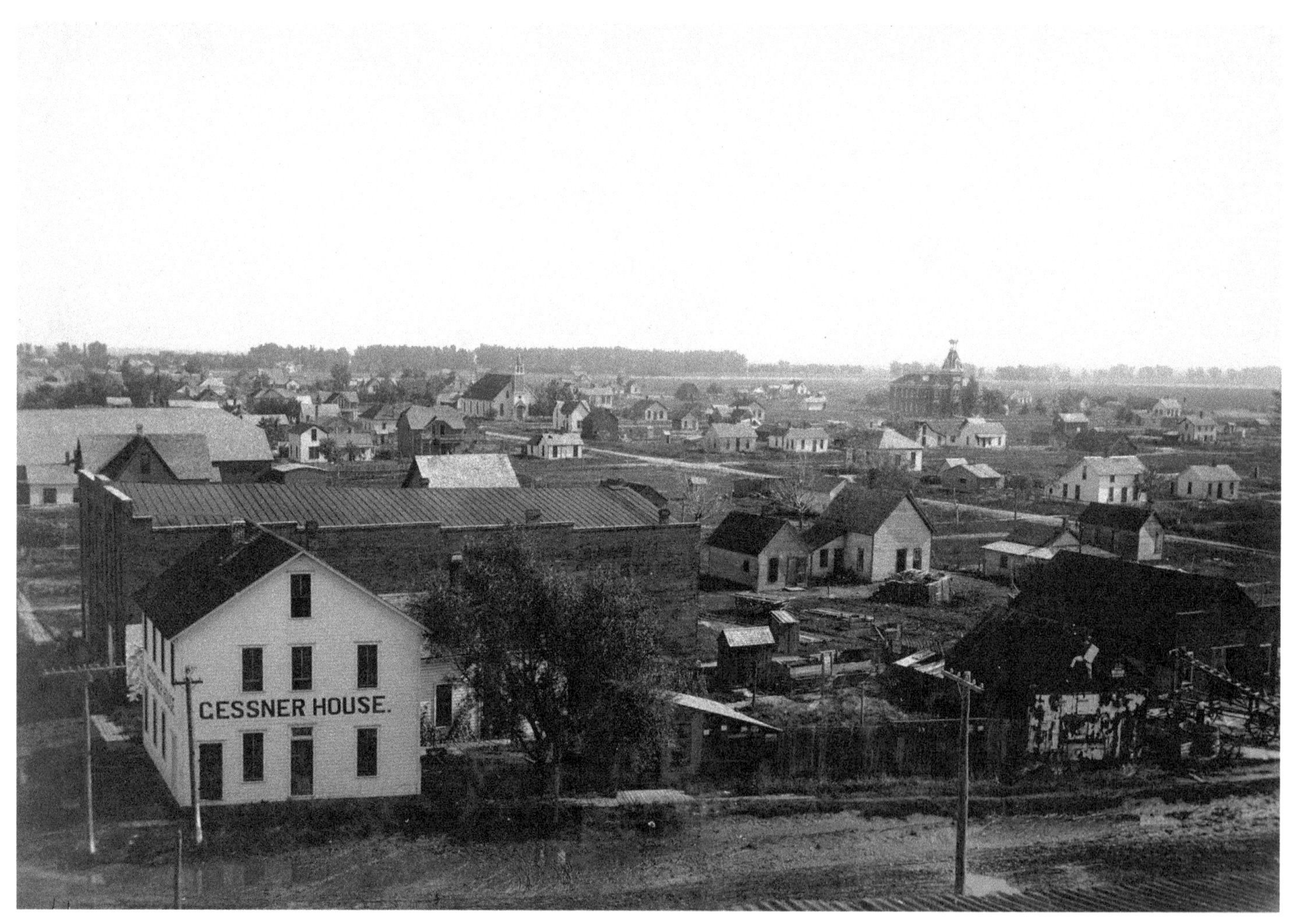

Plum Creek was founded in 1860 and a trading post established there. An attack by Cheyenne warriors in August 1864 killed 13 settlers, destroyed the post, and forced residents to flee to Fort Kearny for safety. In 1874, a town was incorporated, and in 1889, to commemorate a famous Revolutionary War battle, the town's name was changed to Lexington. Solomon Butcher captured this image not long afterward.

Progressive Nebraska

(1892–1911)

Such a toll in human effort and emotion was required to settle the isolated, treeless expanses of Nebraska that people were stretched to the breaking point. Many had been goaded by journalists and legislators to "go west," drawn along by their own dreams of a free life on their own land and lured by railroad promotional men to claim the exact spot they now found themselves living on. Was it tougher than they thought it would be? Perhaps. Some returned to their roots in the East, but most stayed, battling it out on a daily basis. Their dugouts and "soddies" gave way to modern frame houses, and they built cities and towns.

Many of the farmers and ranchers struggling on the prairie began to organize into cooperatives, and eventually the People's Party—better known by the term "Populist"—was born. Some of its most ardent promoters were Nebraskans. The nation's biggest political figures soon came calling as the state found itself at the center of the Progressive Era, with its women's organizations and Chautauqua speakers pitching a moralistic message centering on the prohibition of alcohol, a progressive income tax, and voting rights for women. Two of the nation's most prominent statesmen—William Jennings Bryan and George Norris—were Nebraskans. As the economy weathered booms and busts, the state rose to its high-water mark politically with six seats in the House of Representatives from 1893 to 1933, and despite his three losses in presidential races, Bryan established a reputation as one of the best orators in American history.

Having gained the territorial capital from Bellevue through political maneuvers, Omaha lost the state capital to Lincoln in roughly the same way. Omaha started a sustained period of growth as the state's center of commerce through manufacturing, transportation, and food processing while Lincoln became the center of government and home to Nebraska's land-grant university. Meanwhile, improvements in technology helped both farmers and city dwellers become more productive. Colleges were founded and public schools spread widely.

Out west, the romantic days of cattle drives ending at raucous railheads like Ogallala had pretty much vanished, but William F. Cody was still at home on his ranch at North Platte, where he had invented the sport of rodeo and become one of the world's most famous men as founder of "Buffalo Bill's Wild West." Nebraska was officially on the map.

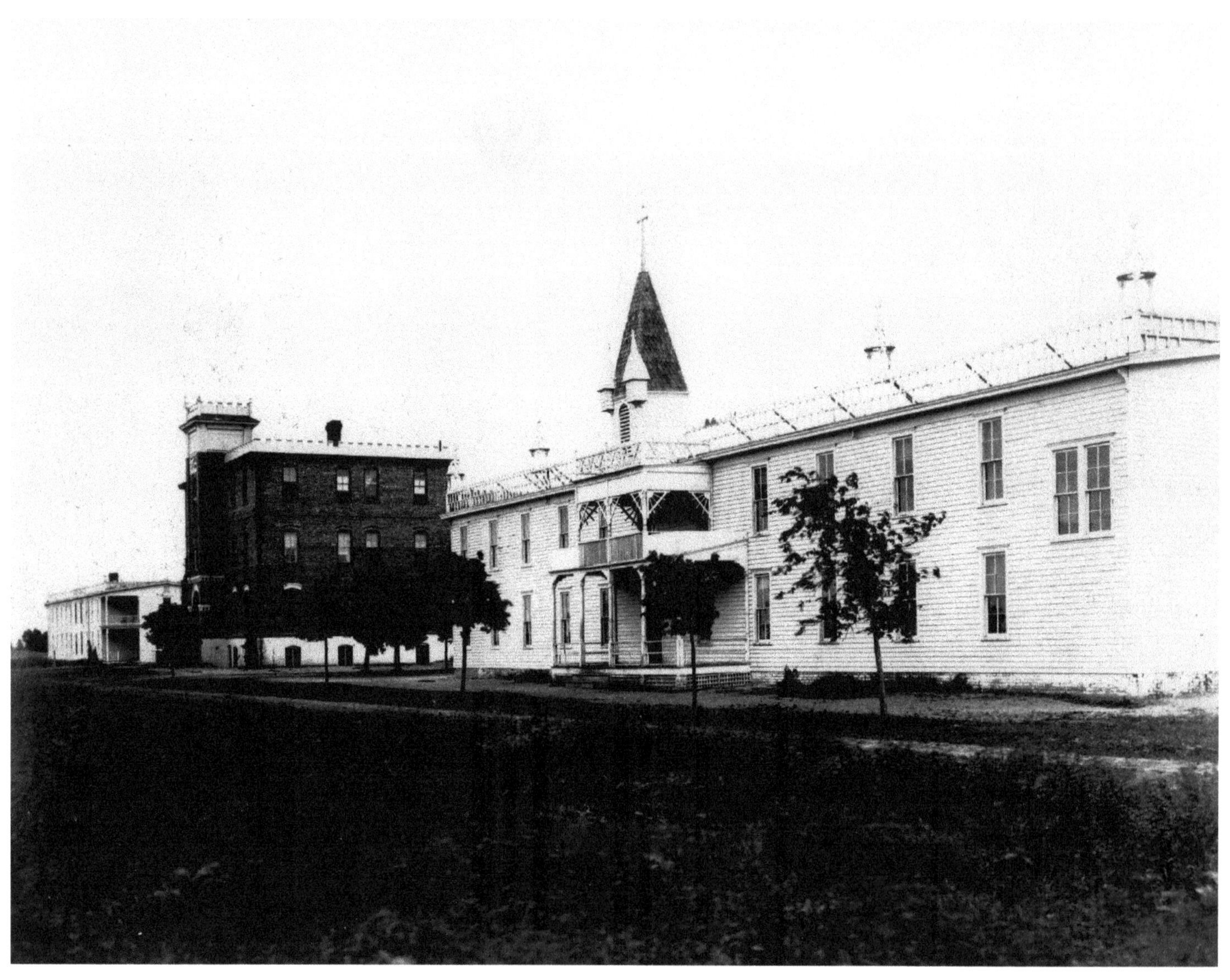

The Platte Valley Institute opened on the east edge of Kearney as a coeducational school in September 1892, about the time this image was recorded. Six years later, it became a military academy for boys and several new buildings were constructed. Then five cadets died in the influenza epidemic of 1918. Funding declined, and Nebraska's last surviving military academy closed its doors in 1923. In the 1950s the facility would serve as a retirement home.

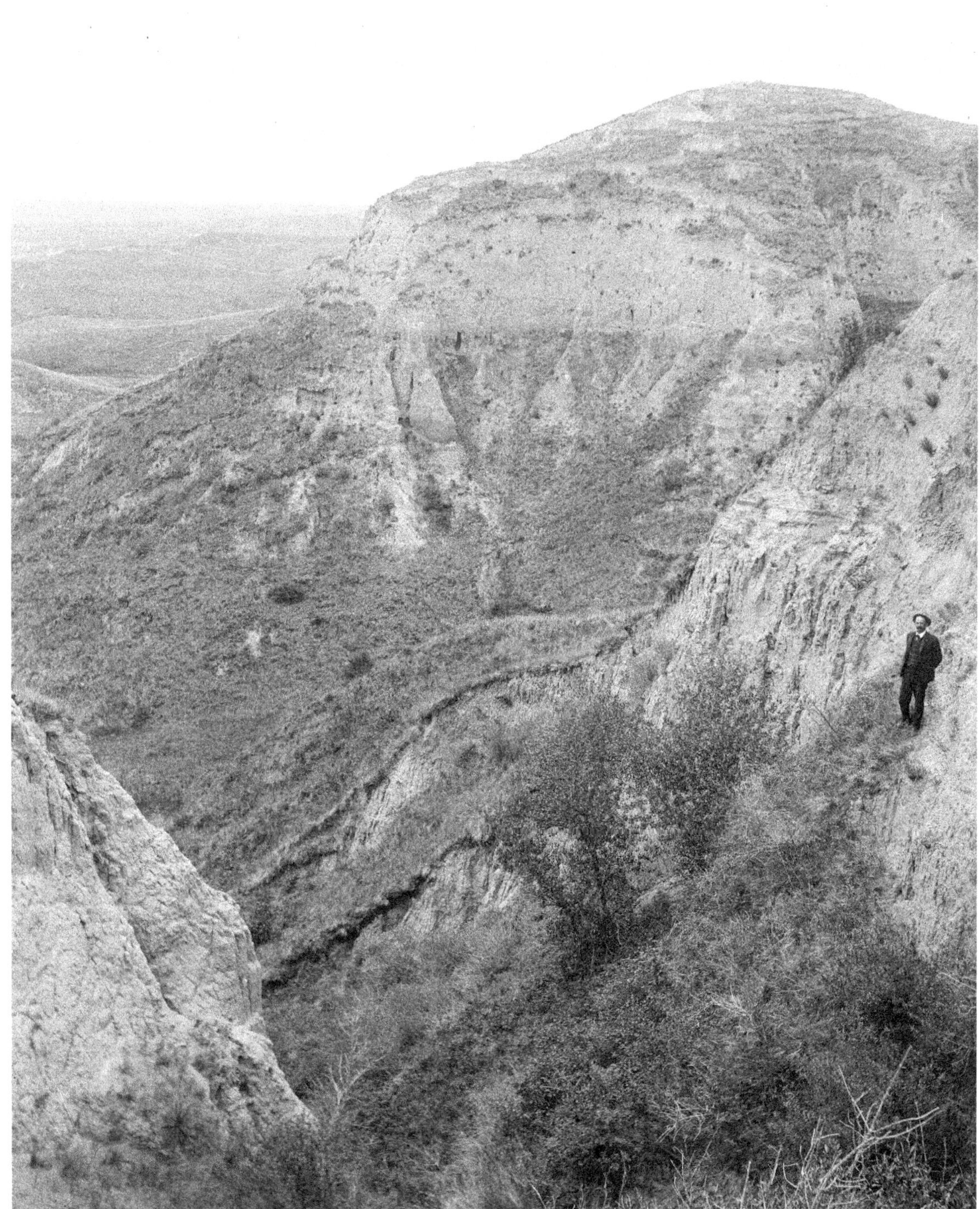

Cattlemen who depended upon the open range to sustain their herds were natural rivals of settlers who raised crops. This is Devil's Gap near Oconto, the site where in 1878, farmers Luther Mitchell and Ami Ketchum were lynched and their bodies burned by a gang led by cattleman I. P. "Print" Olive, who had tried to force Mitchell and Ketchum into abandoning their homesteads. A miscarriage of justice led to Olive's release from prison, despite his conviction for the murders. Landowner John Bridges, shown here in 1892, was not involved.

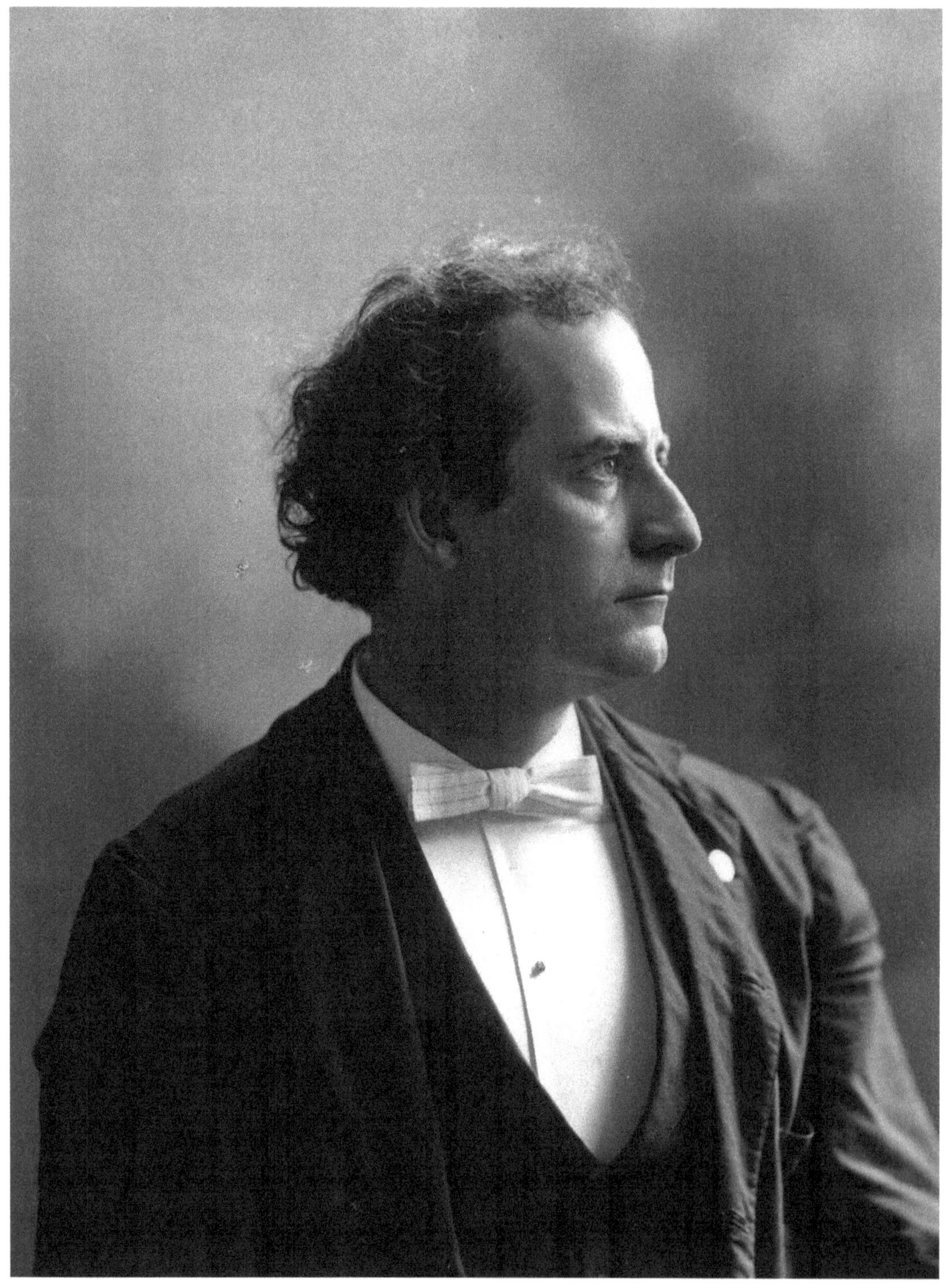

Lincoln attorney William Jennings Bryan burst upon the national political scene as a presidential candidate in 1896, about the time this photograph was taken. A highly moralistic man, with a "glance as penetrating as a searchlight" as described by fellow Nebraskan Willa Cather, Bryan championed economic relief for farmers and blue-collar "toilers" throughout the nation. He was largely responsible for dismantling the Democratic Party's historic Jeffersonian distrust of a strong central government.

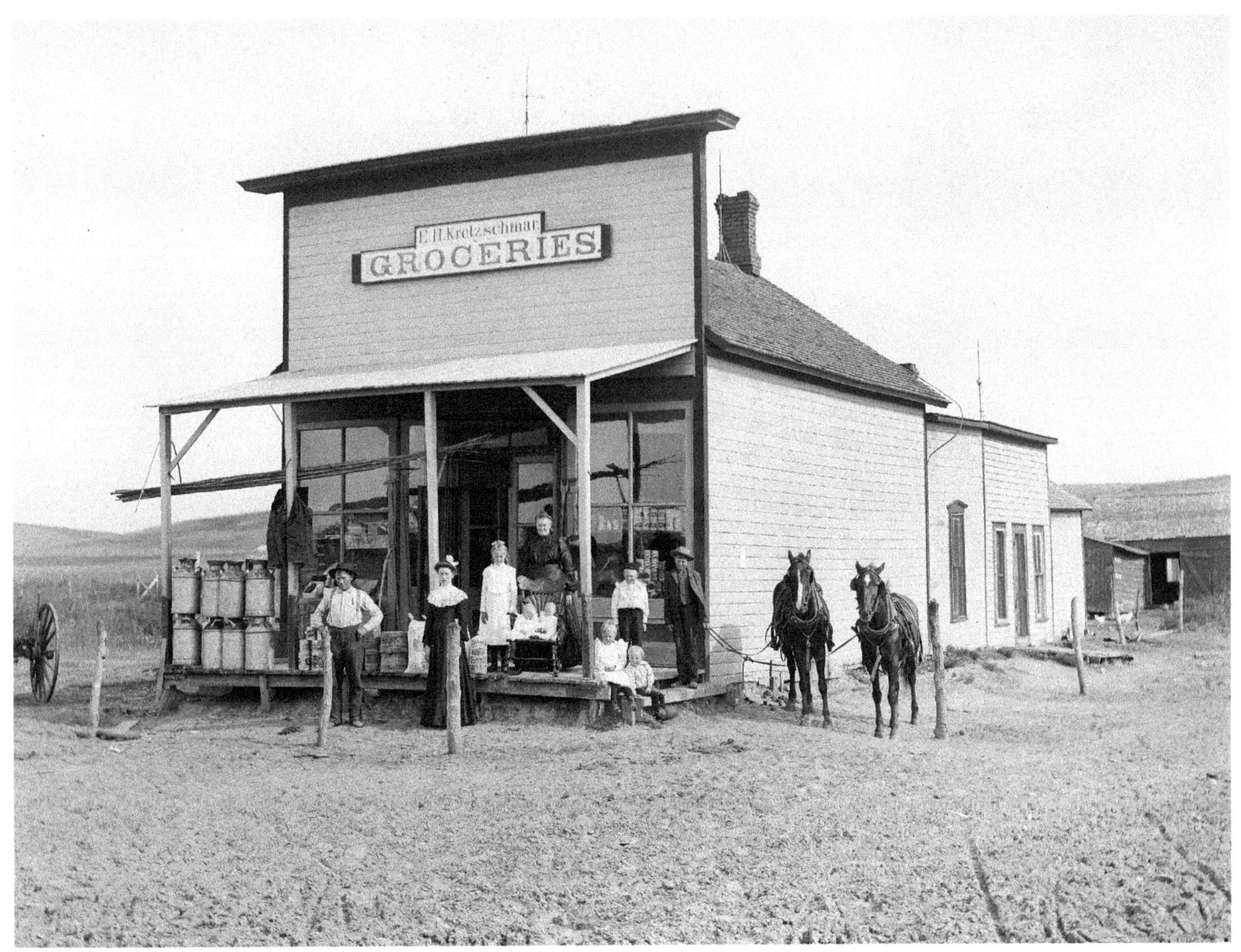

E. H. Kretzschmar ran a grocery store in Sartoria, a tiny Buffalo County settlement along the South Loup River just west of Pleasanton. The grocery store appears to have been a family affair, from Kretzschmar on down to a pair of newborn twins. Sartoria existed from the 1880s to the 1920s with a population as high as 40. Though few in number, the townspeople enjoyed Fourth of July celebrations, ice cream socials, box suppers, revival meetings, and school activities.

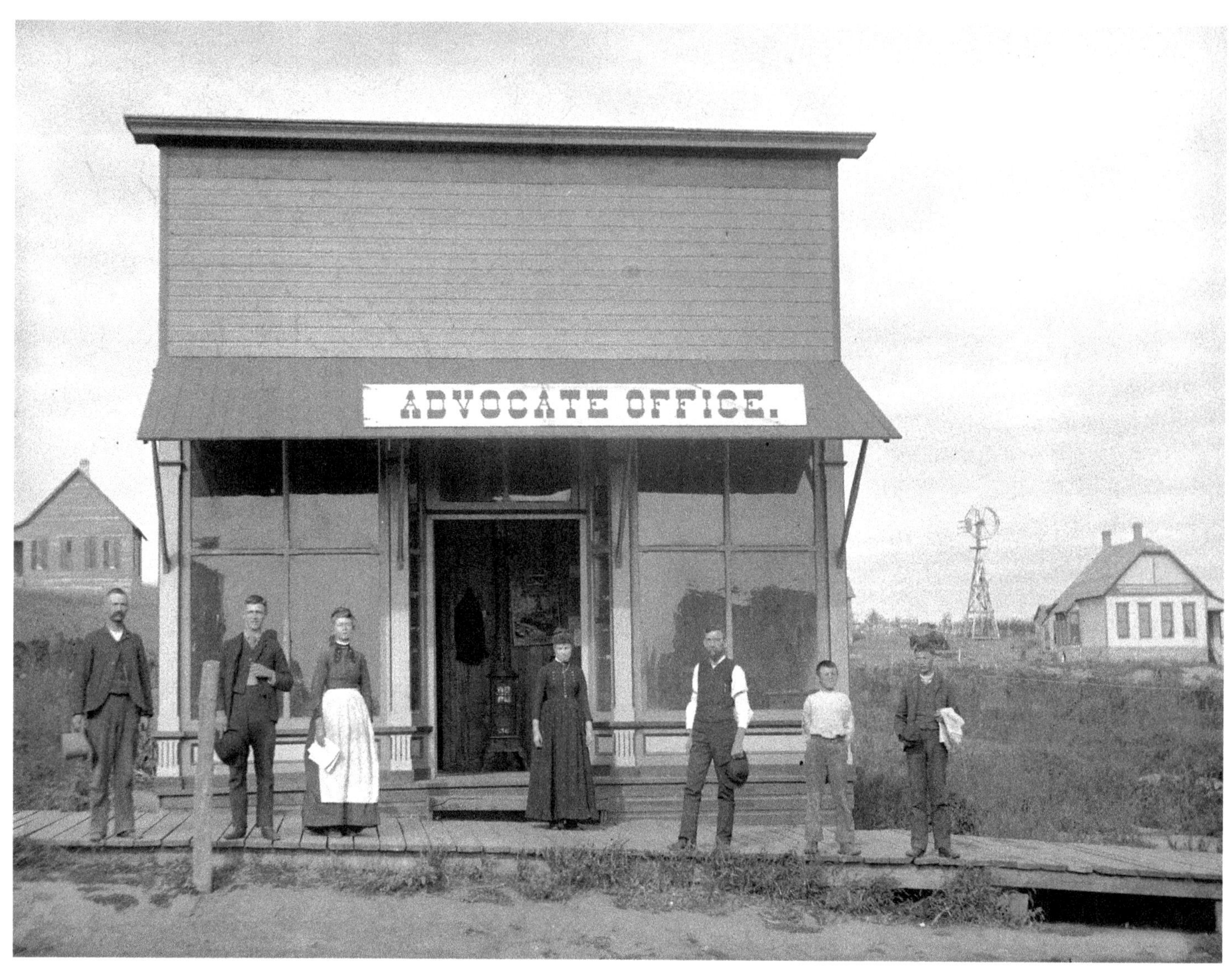

The *Advocate* was an early newspaper in Ansley, located south of Sargent in Custer County. Butcher's 1901 book, *Pioneer History of Custer County,* says the Advocate started operations in Ansley in 1896 and went out of business within five years. The *Advocate* staff, along with family members, are shown standing on the wooden sidewalk in front of the office.

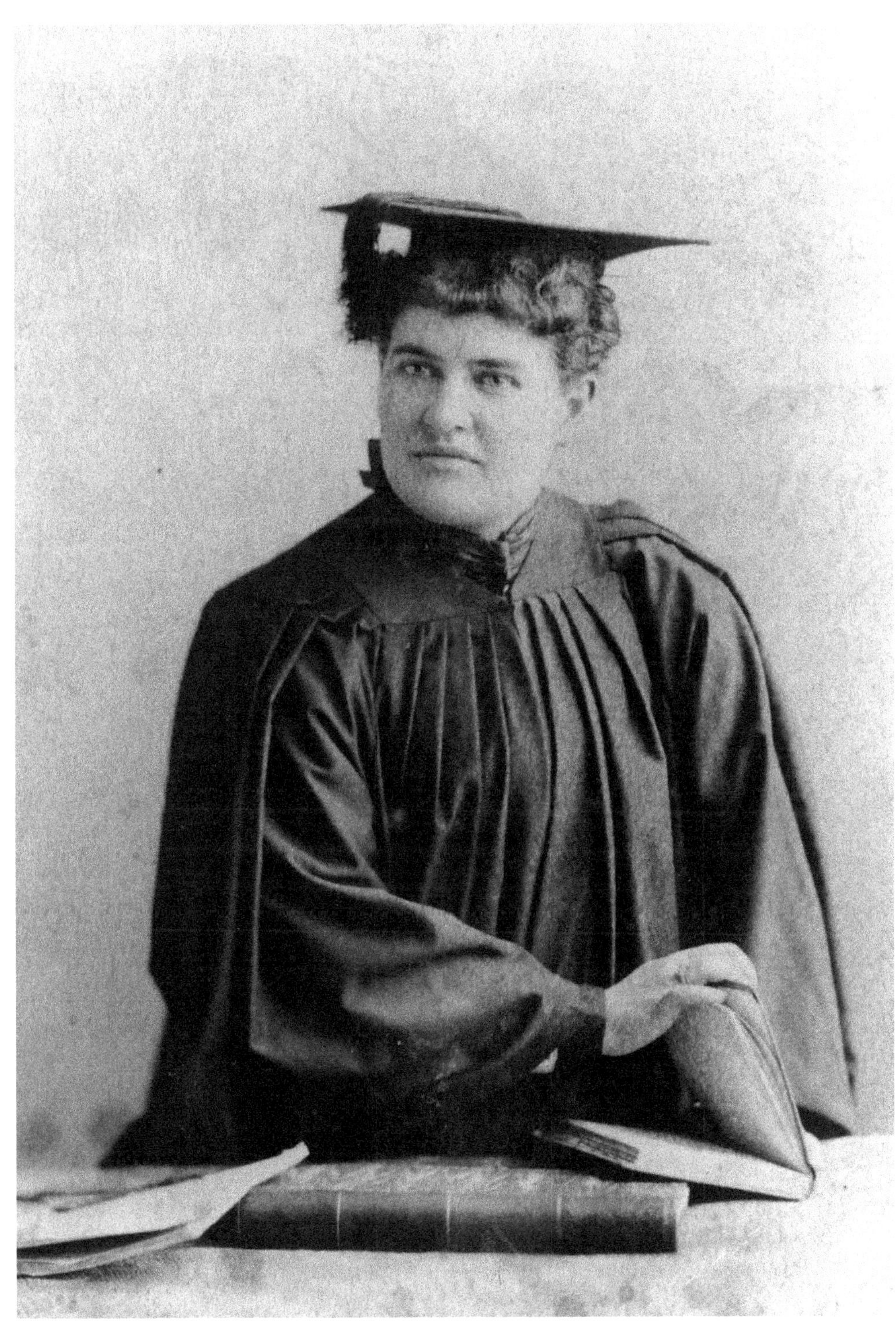

Willa Cather graduated from the University of Nebraska in 1895 and launched a writing career. She won the 1923 Pulitzer Prize for *One of Ours,* about the World War I letters of her cousin G. P. Cather, the first Nebraska officer to die in the war. Most of her books drew upon her extensive knowledge of life on the Plains, including *My Antonia, Death Comes for the Archbishop,* and *O Pioneers!*

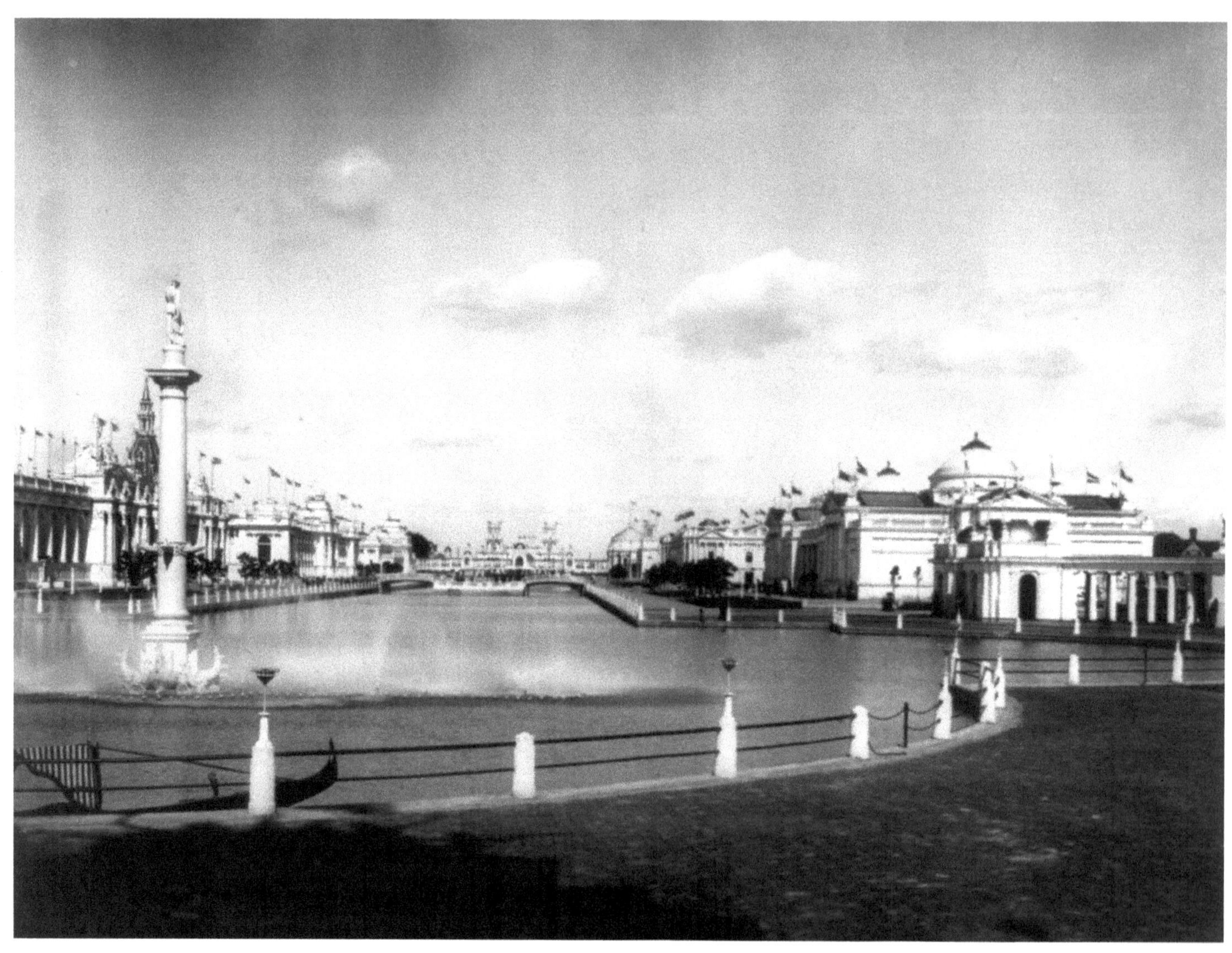

Possibly the most widely publicized event ever staged in Nebraska was the Trans-Mississippi and International Exposition and Indian Congress, held in Omaha June 1–October 31, 1898. The event was intended to showcase the economies of the western United States and stimulate a recovery after the financial panic of 1893. This is a view of the Grand Court, looking east past the Agricultural Building. The man-made lagoon was 8 blocks long and more than 300 feet wide.

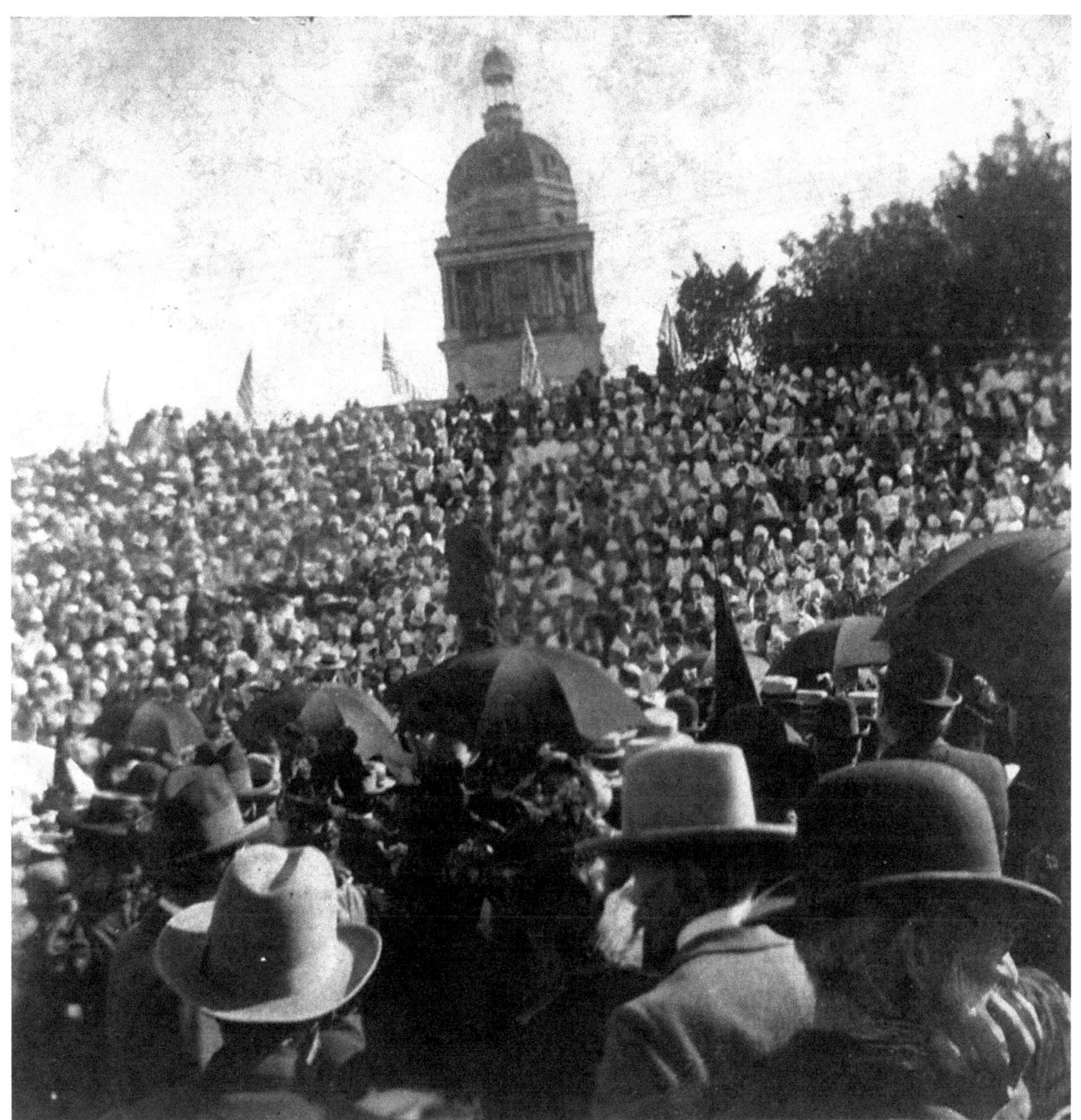

With the second Nebraska state capitol as a backdrop, a Spanish-American War rally was held in Lincoln in 1898. Among the speakers that day were Governor Silas Holcomb, and two former Republican governors of Nebraska who both had served as Civil War officers—John M. Thayer and Robert W. Furnas.

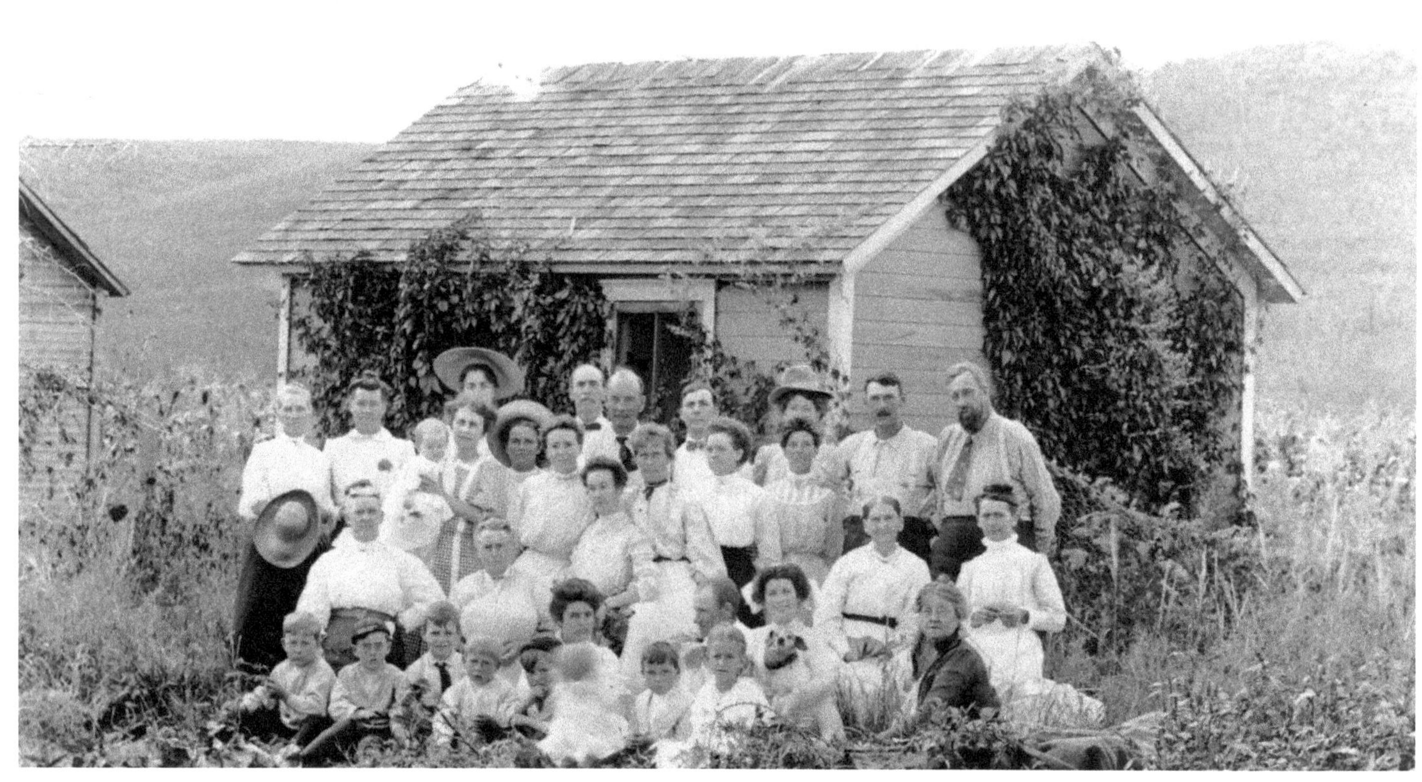

A group of women's auxiliary members in Mullen (likely a church group) and their families pose for a group portrait. Ladies' groups like this one feared that alcoholic beverages would be the downfall of the nation. They were the grassroots supporters of the prohibitionist and women's suffrage movements during the late nineteenth and early twentieth centuries, and they eventually gained the active support of Nebraska politicians William Jennings Bryan and George Norris.

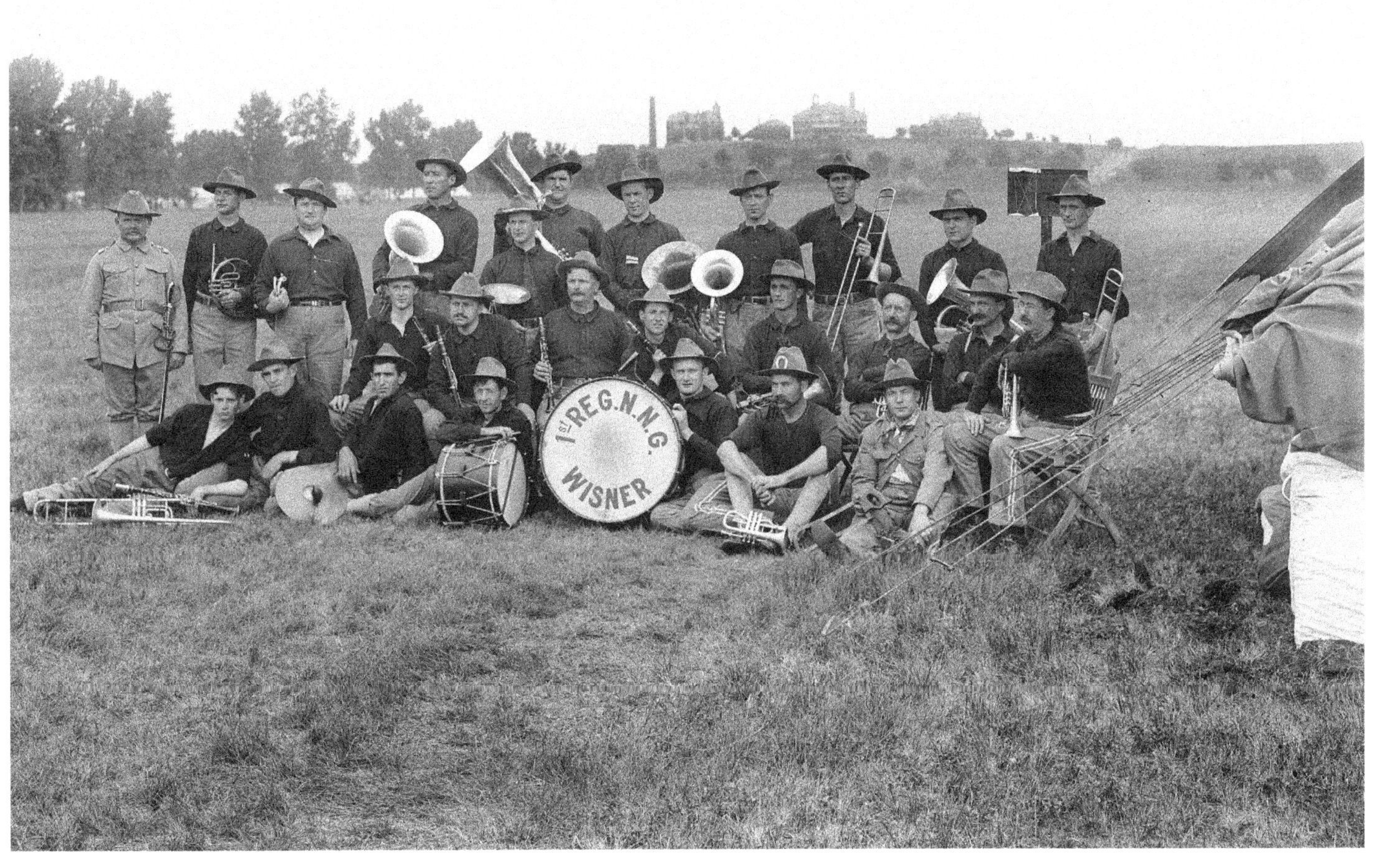

In 1900, Solomon Butcher photographed this well-outfitted First Regiment band in camp with the Nebraska National Guard at the west edge of Kearney. Whether the hacksaw (far right, front row) was used as a musical instrument remains a mystery.

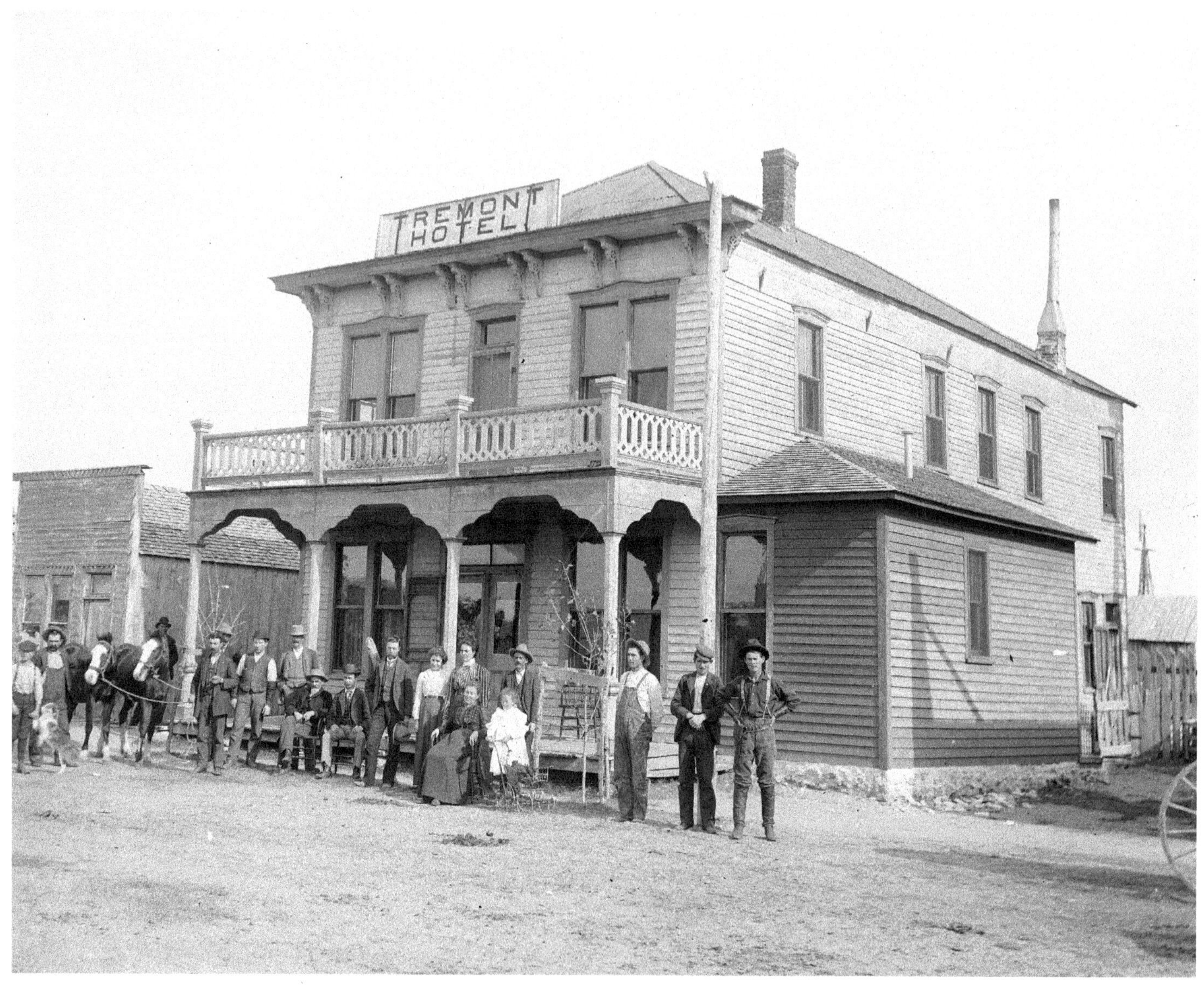

Springview was organized shortly after a November 1884 election determined that the portion of Brown County north of the Niobrara River would become Keya Paha County. Springview would go on to defeat the nearby town of Burton in a hotly contested fight to become the county seat. The Tremont Hotel, shown here in 1900, was one of four hotels operating in town in the early twentieth century.

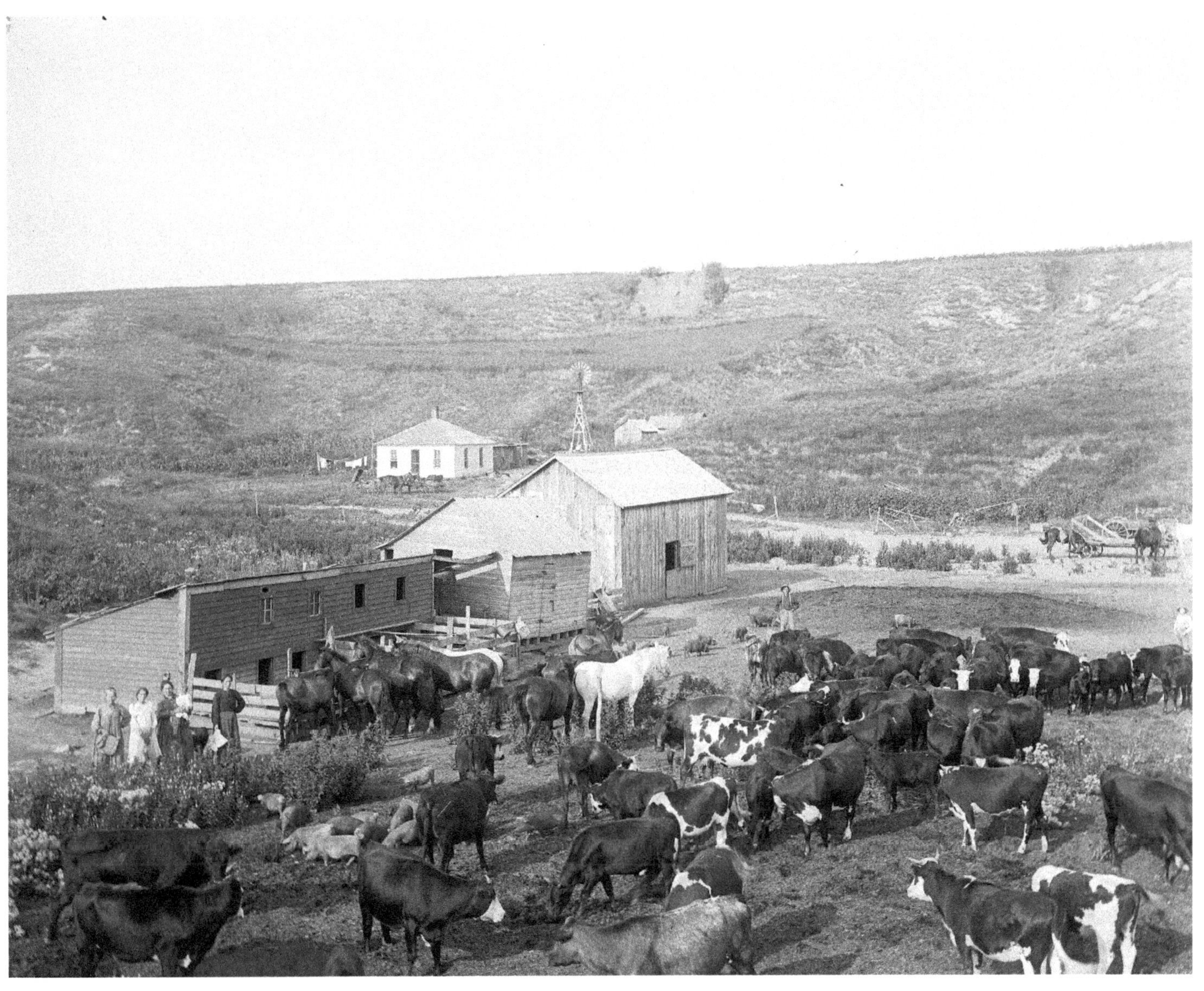

Horses, cattle, hogs, and cropland all look to be in good shape at the Elam Bean ranch north of Amherst here in 1901. Four women, one of them pregnant, and two boys are watching over the well-run farmyard.

President Theodore Roosevelt made a much-publicized tour of the western United States in 1903 to see Yellowstone National Park and the Grand Canyon, among other sights. His train passed through Nebraska and is shown here as it stopped in Fairmont.

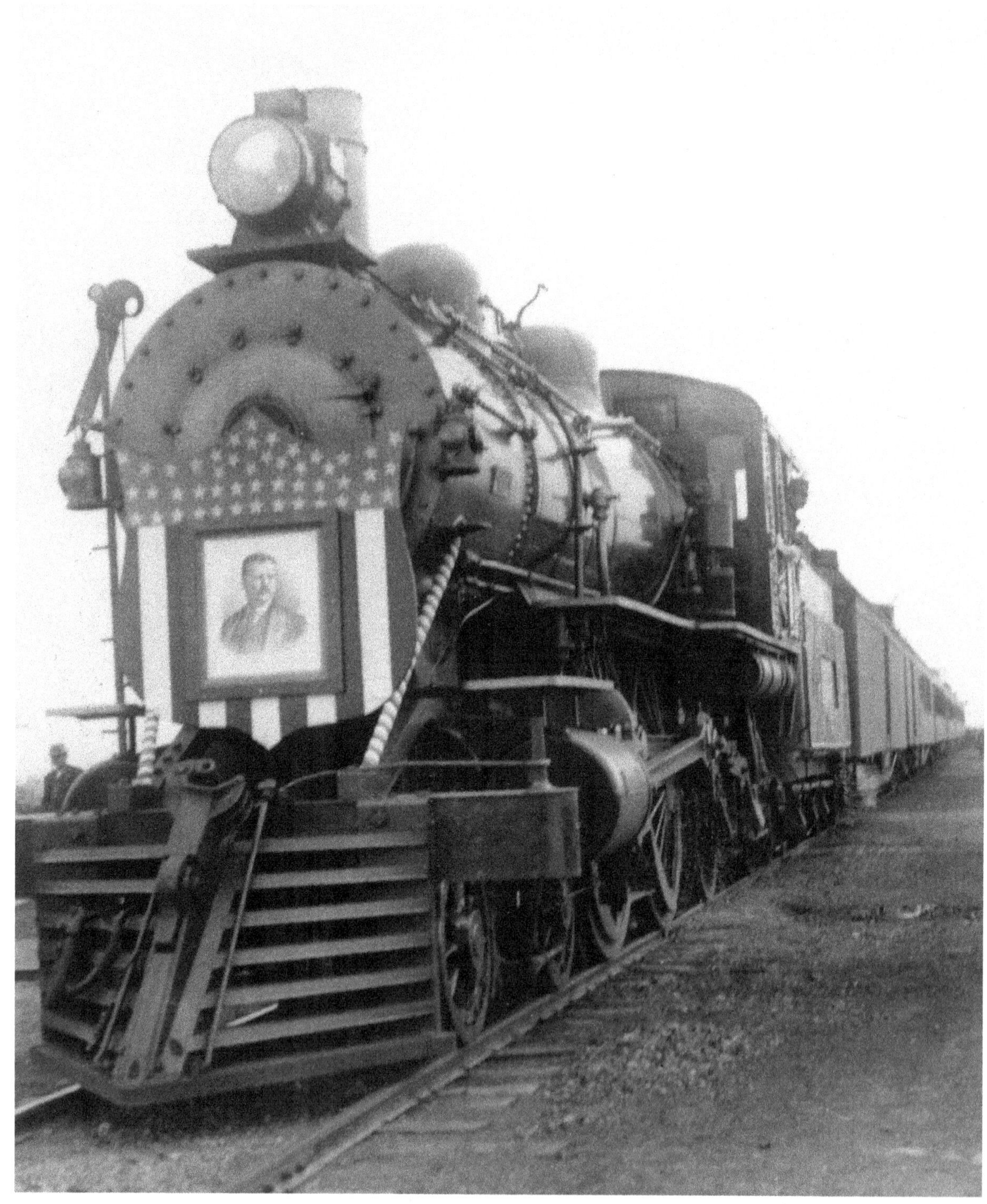

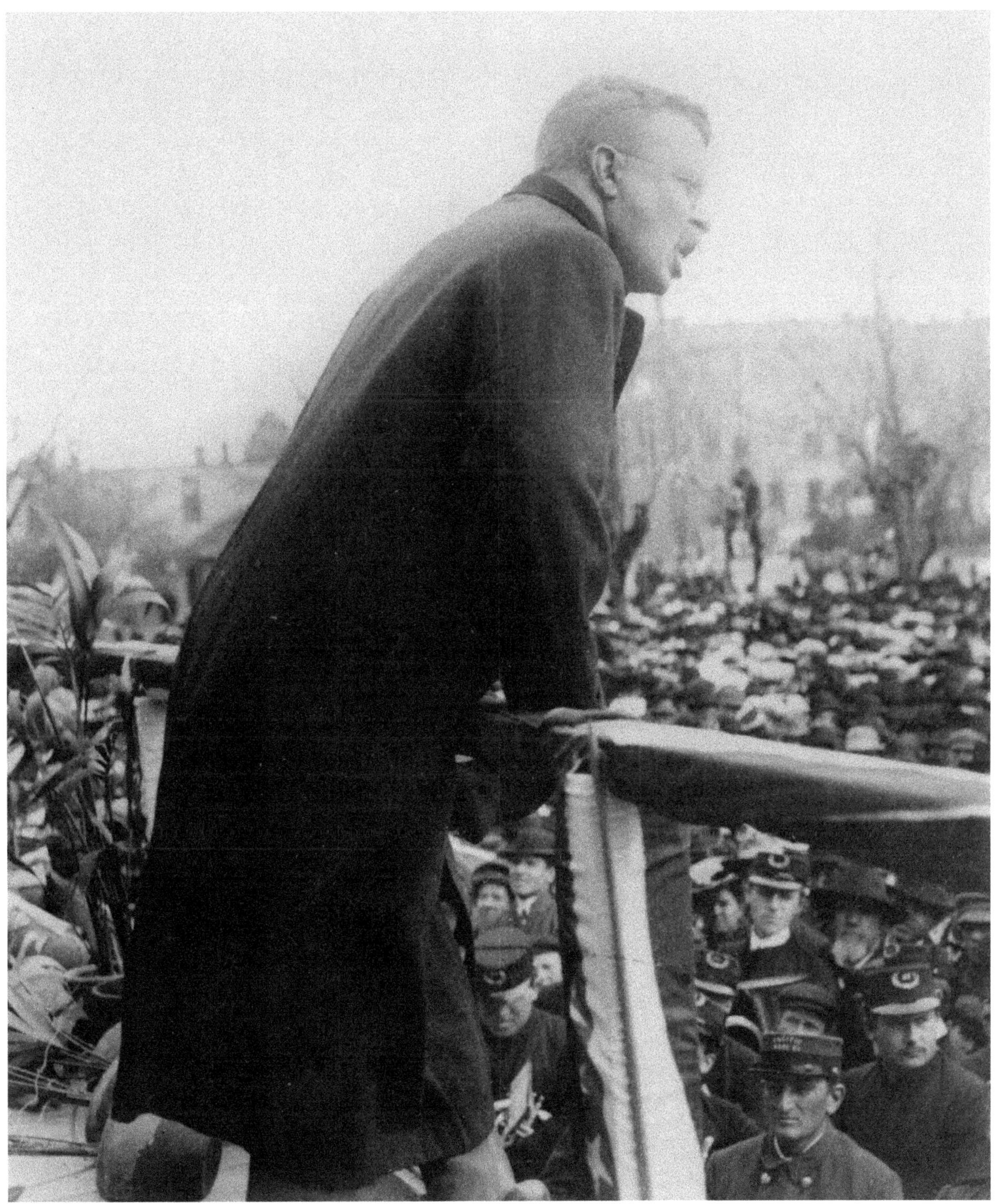

On his tour of the western United States in 1903, President Roosevelt passed through several Nebraska communities, and here is shown speaking from the rear of his train to a crowd gathered to see him in Grand Island.

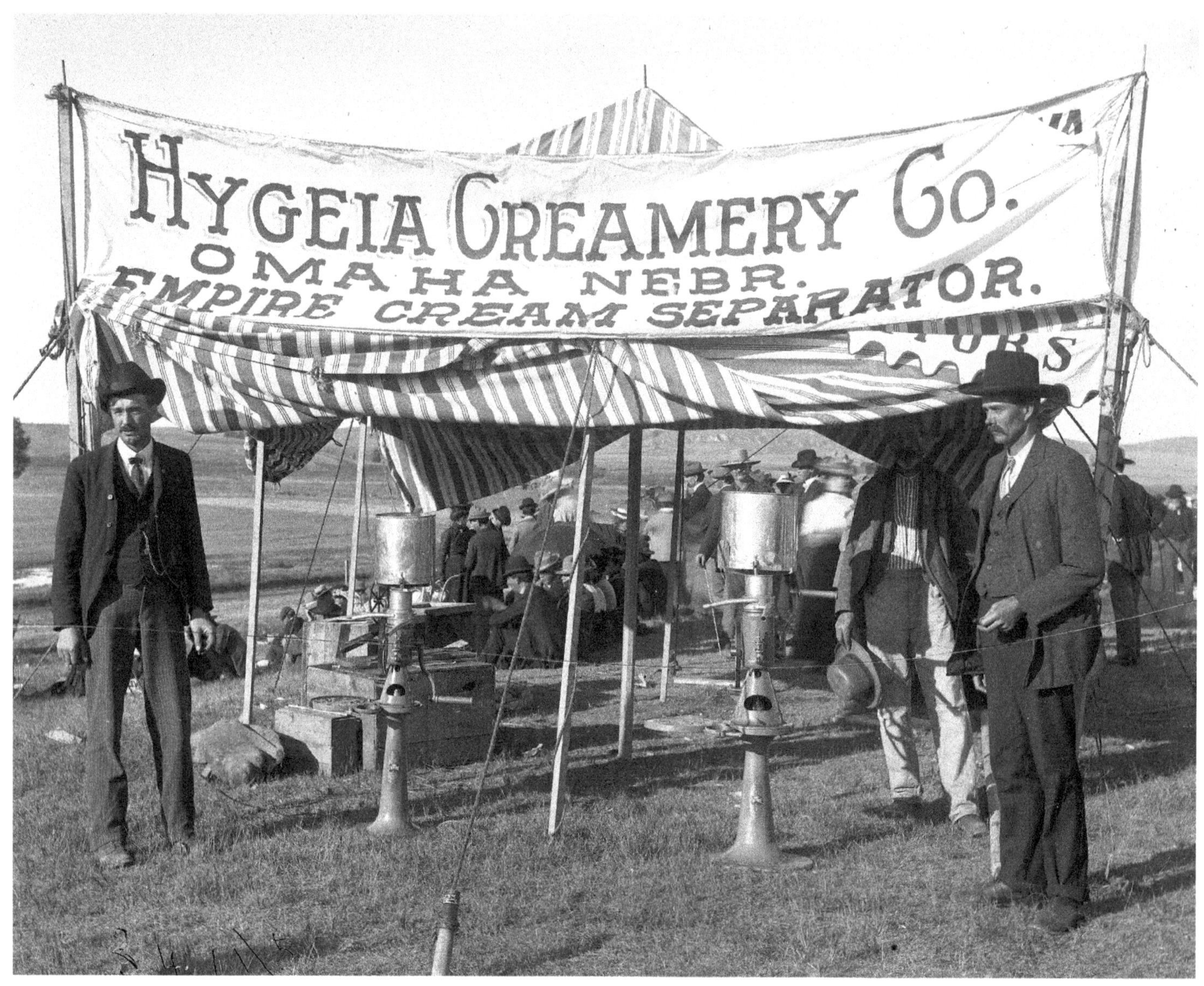

These two salesmen traveled west from Omaha in search of willing buyers for their new cream separators at the 1903 Custer County Fair in Broken Bow, an annual attraction that photographer and homesteader Solomon Butcher probably enjoyed many times.

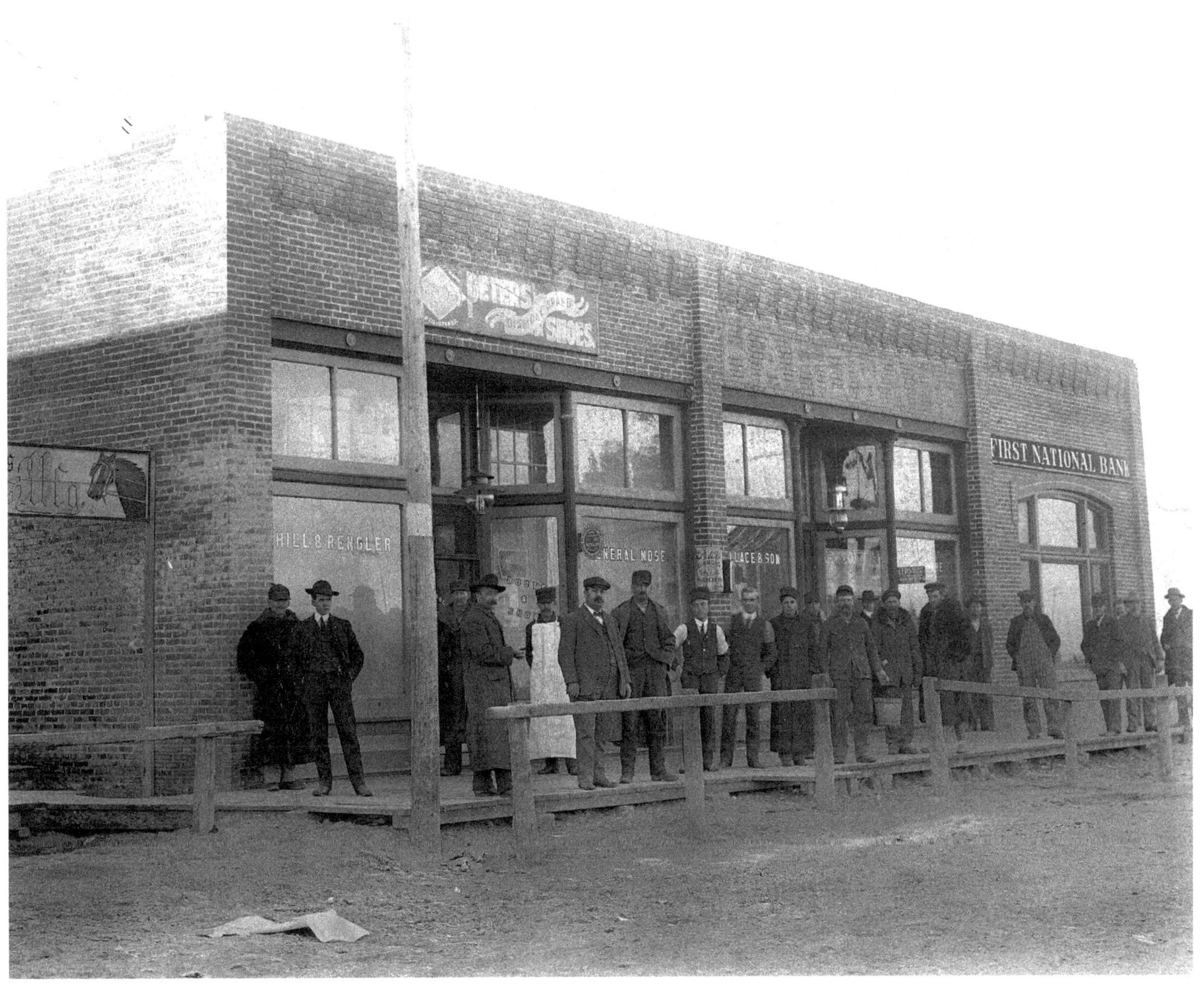

On a frosty winter day in 1904, employees and passersby line up for a photograph on the wooden sidewalk in front of the First National Bank Building in Overton. At far-left is a sign advertising C. Berger Harness Manufacturing. Other businesses in the block include Hill & Rengler Boots and Shoes, and Lace & Son General Merchandise and Hardware.

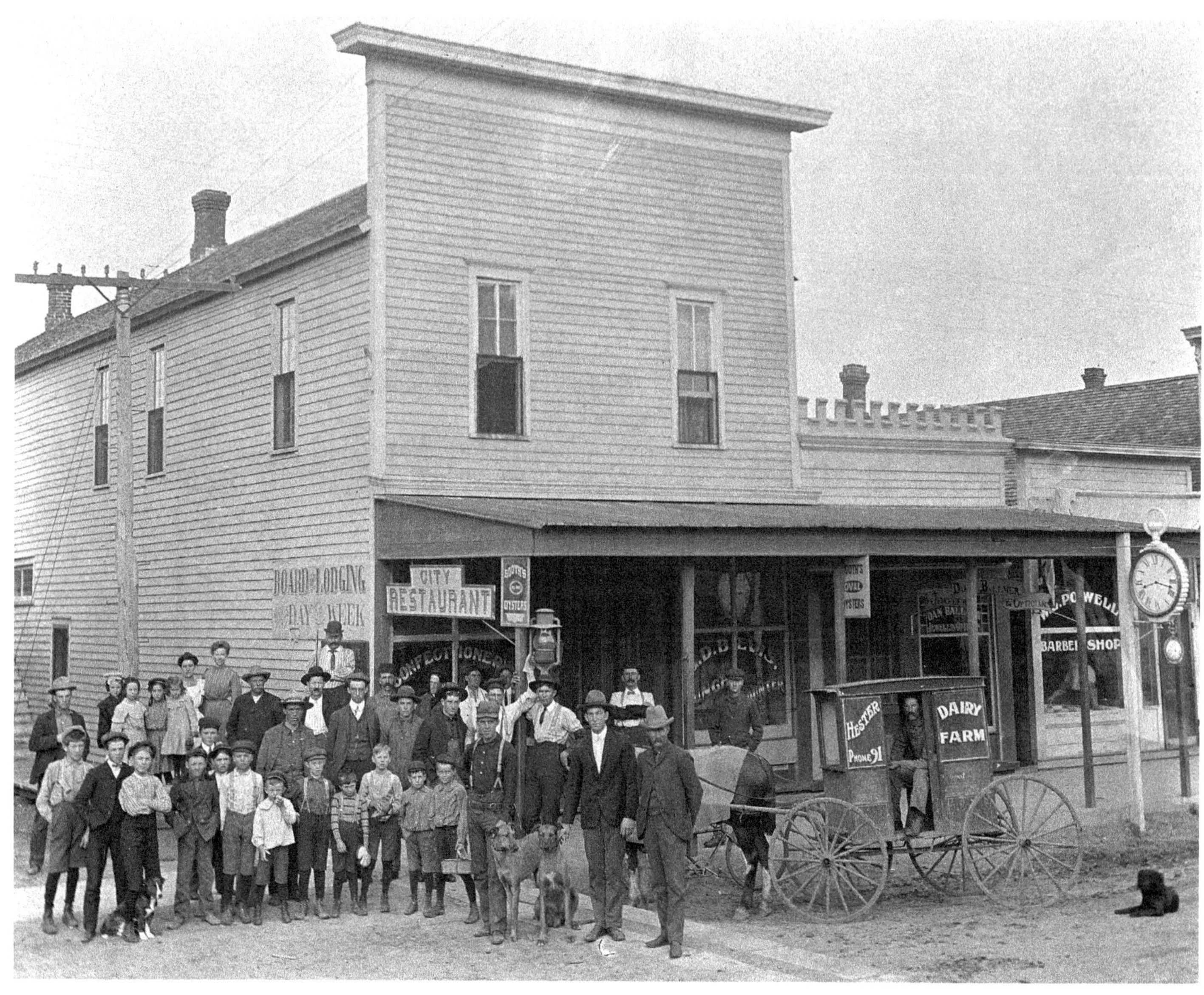

Solomon Butcher captured this small crowd in 1904—including a deliveryman from a local dairy—on one of his innumerable glass plate negatives at the City Restaurant, noted as the oldest store building in Cozad. Nearby are the Ballmer Jeweler & Optician Shop and the Powell Barber Shop. Cozad was built on the 100th Meridian—"where the humid East meets the arid West"—and was the childhood home of acclaimed Ashcan artist Robert Henri. (Born Robert Henry Cozad, Henri's family founded the town.)

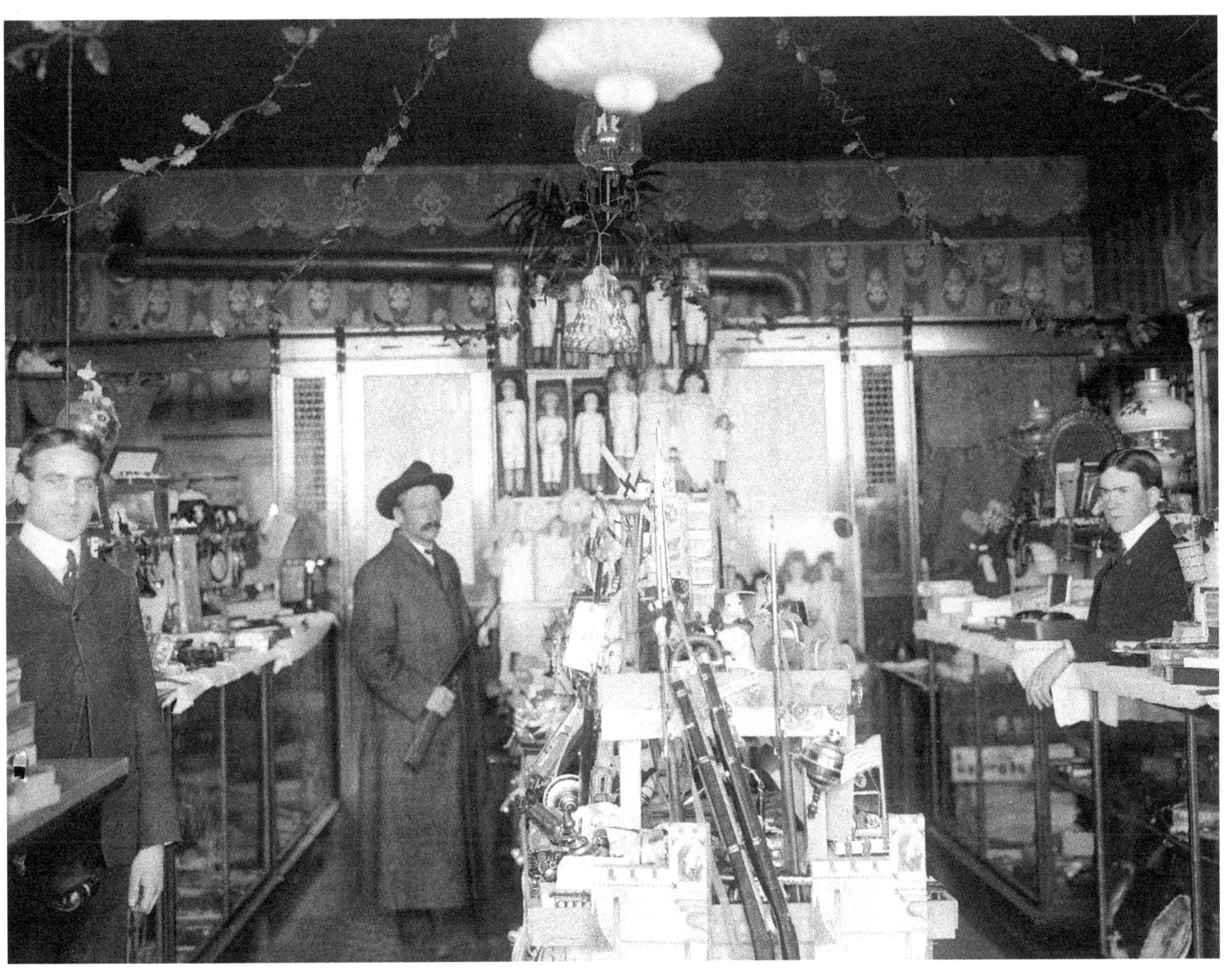

Despite its festive Christmas wares, the drugstore in Overton appears to have been a very serious place to work—and guard—in 1904, judging by the looks on these men's faces.

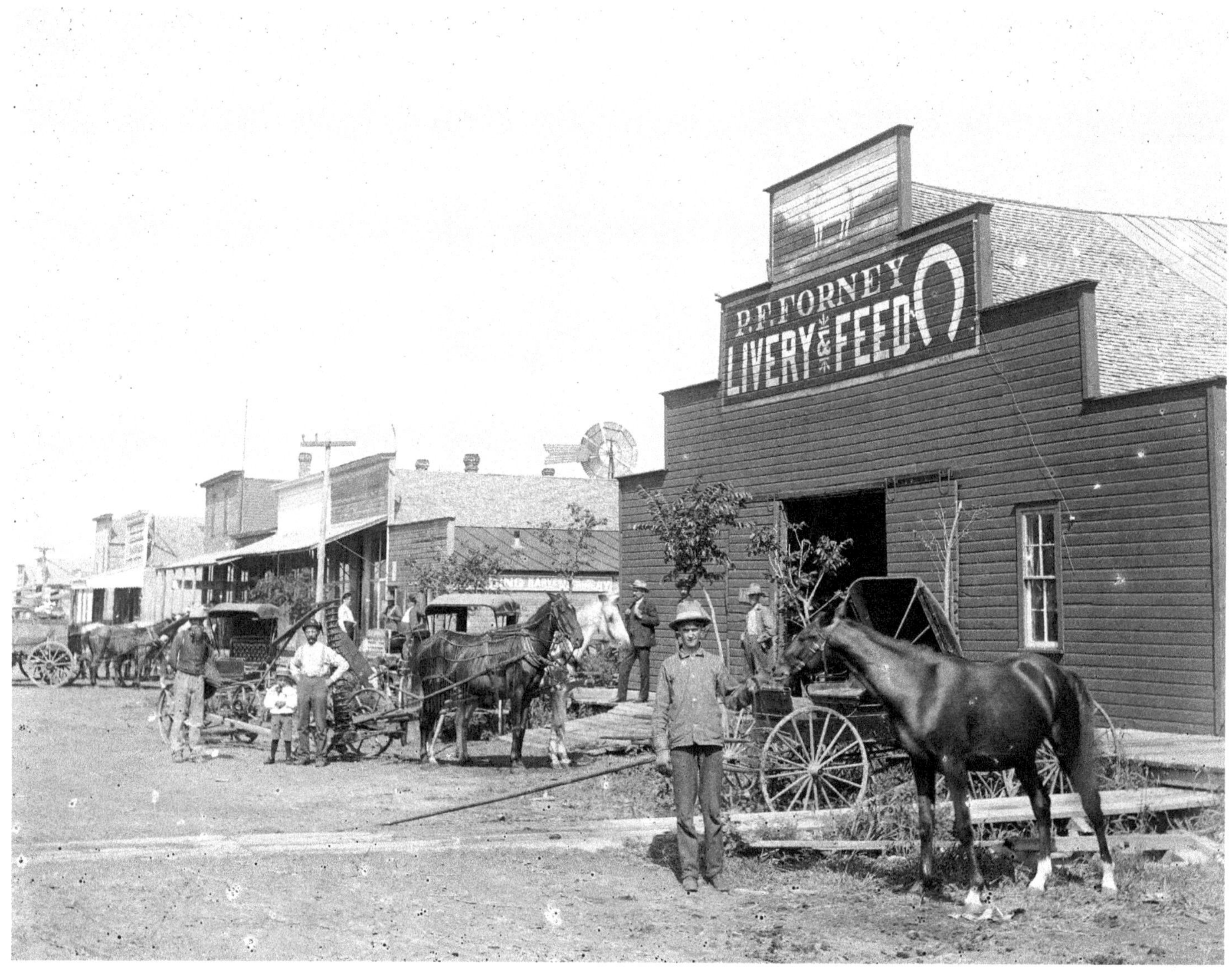

Horse-drawn farm implements and carriages still dominated the streets of Merna in 1904, where newly planted trees show promise outside the P. F. Forney Livery & Feed store. Built on the Burlington Railroad and named for the youngest daughter of the first postmaster, Merna is located in central Nebraska, where the Sand Hills trail into the rolling canyon country north of the Platte Valley.

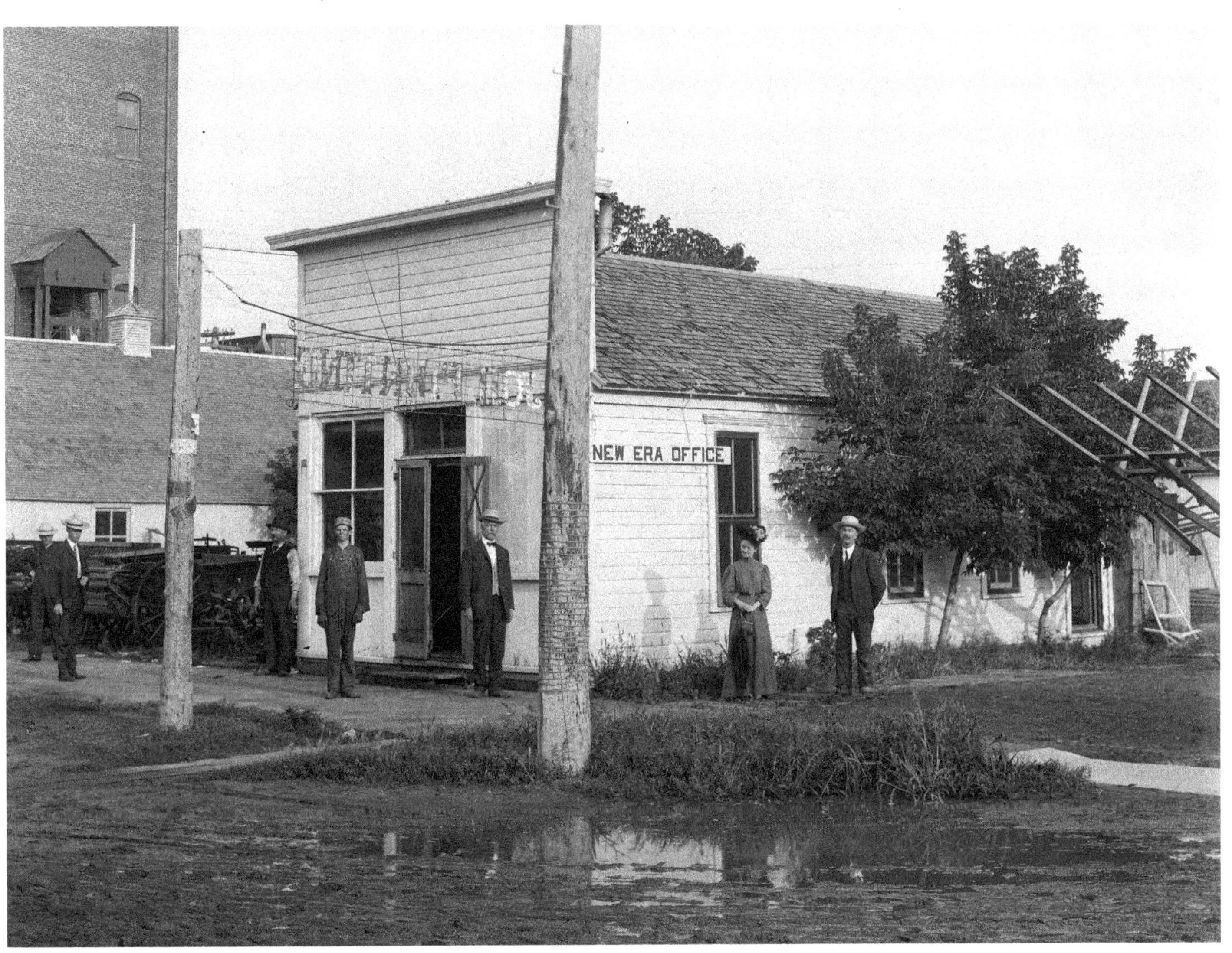

The *New Era* newspaper was started in 1883 in Kearney but didn't stay solvent much beyond 1904. The town was originally named Kearney Junction because of its location at the junction between the Union Pacific and Burlington & Missouri railroads and its proximity to Fort Kearny, the U.S. Army fort established nearby in 1848 to guard travelers on the Oregon Trail. The different spellings stem from a misspelling in the original post office paperwork.

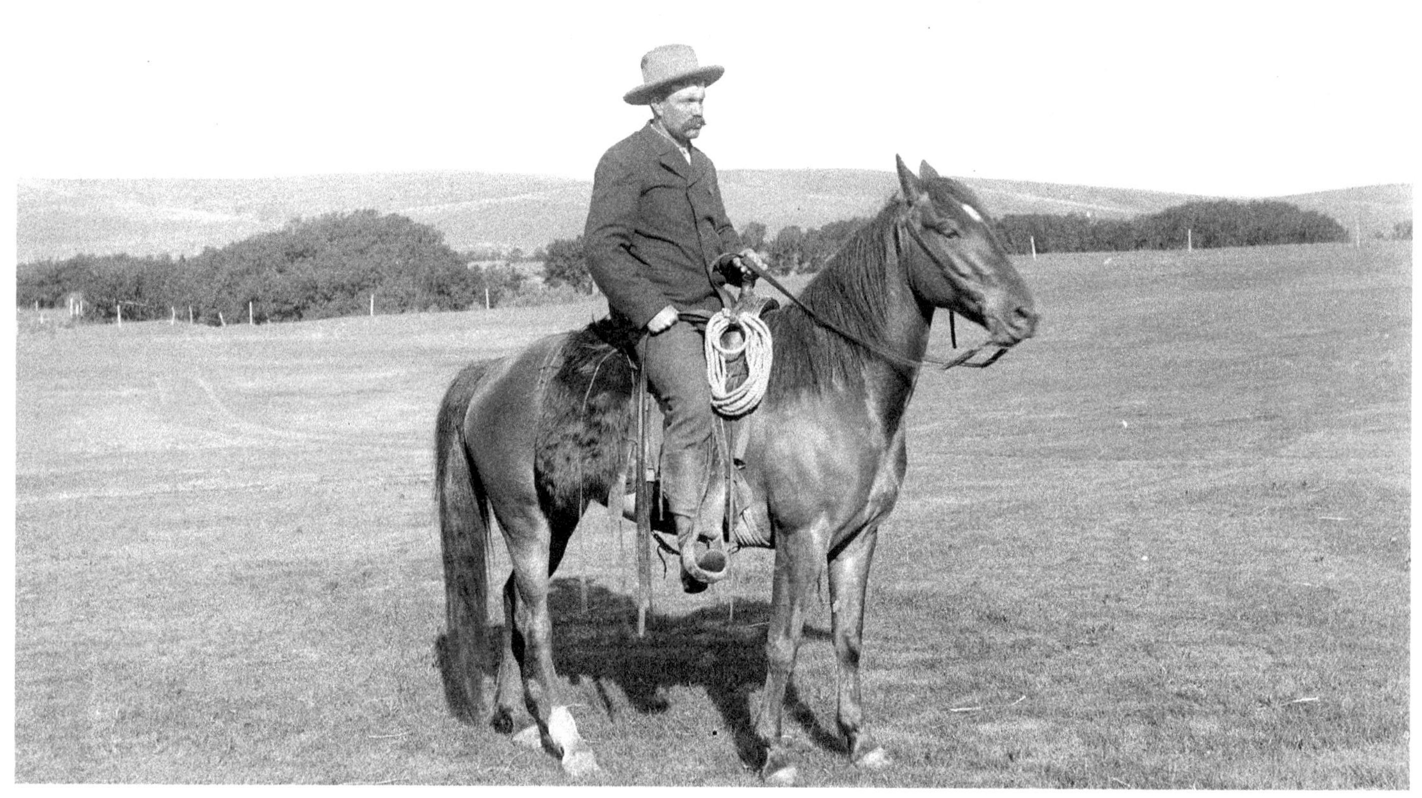

James Farley was a veteran cowboy from Missouri who came to Nebraska by way of Dodge City, Kansas, in 1878 and eventually made his headquarters in Custer County, where he befriended infamous cattle king Isom Prentice "Print" Olive. He also knew Frank North, who partnered with William F. Cody to buy a ranch on the Dismal River. Farley is 54 years old here in 1904.

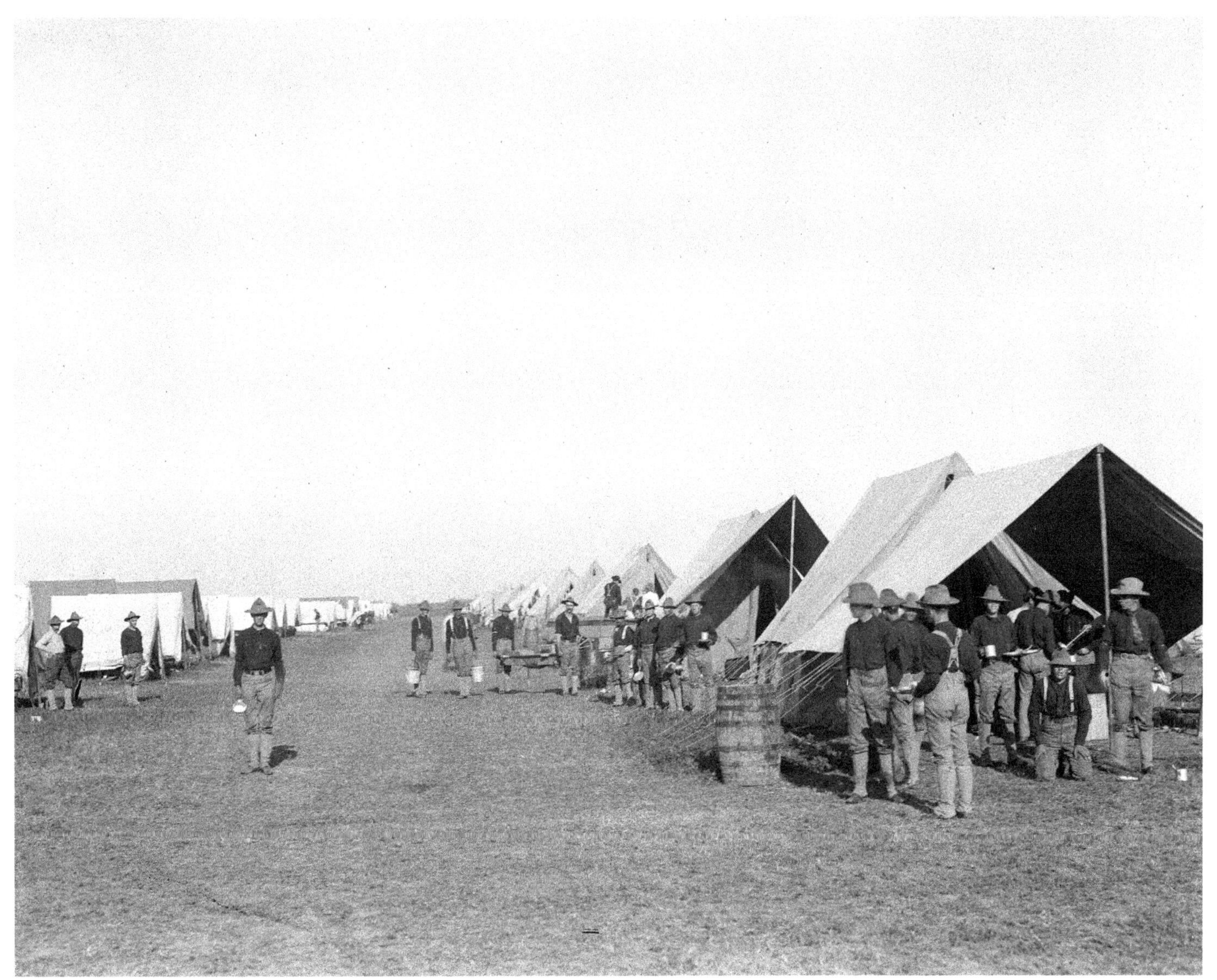

Nebraska National Guardsmen, shown in camp at the west edge of Kearney in 1905, wield tin cups and saucers as chow time approaches.

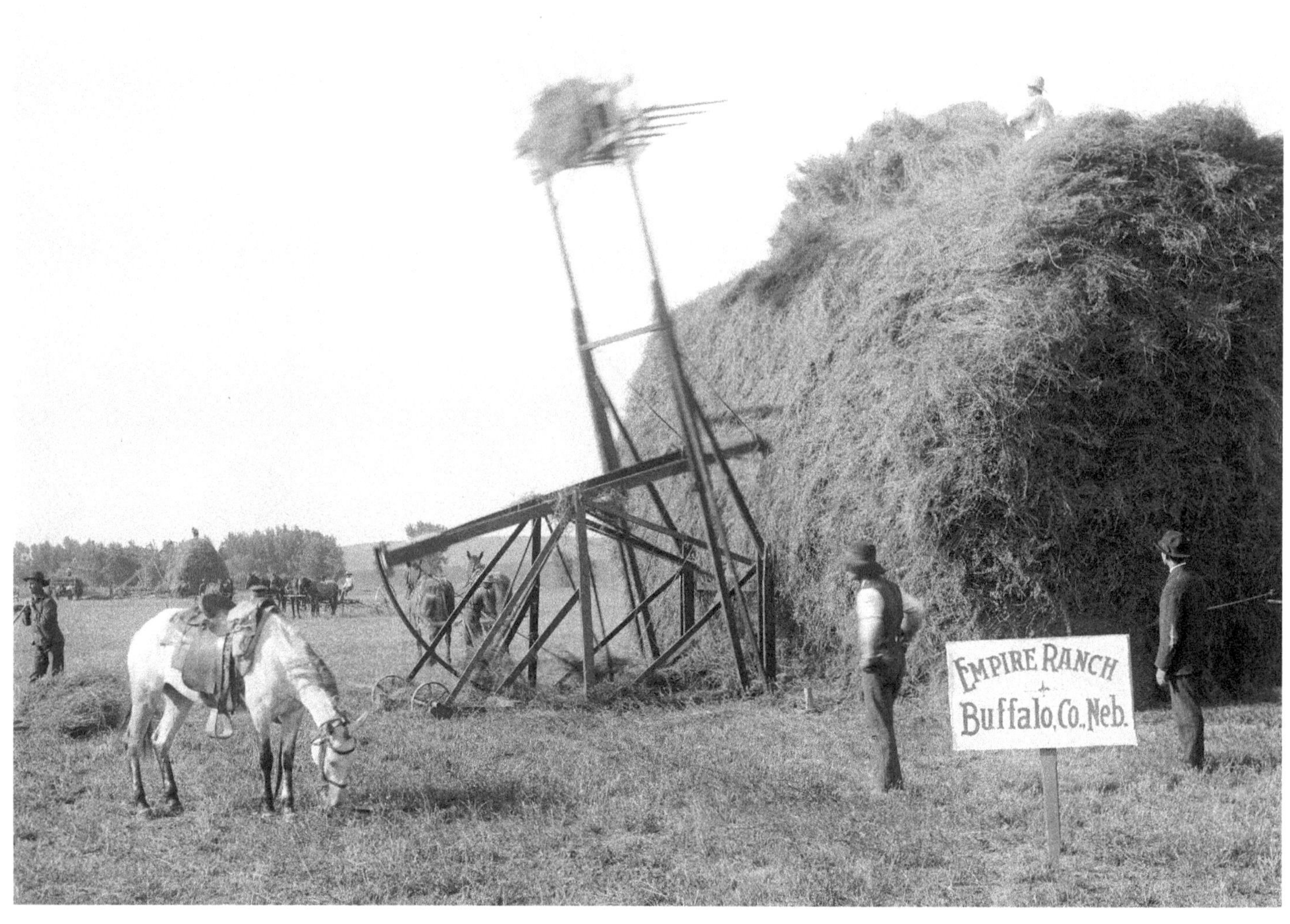

The Empire Ranch, established in the 1870s west of Kearney near Elm Creek, was a large horse farm that flourished during the late nineteenth century. This Solomon Butcher photograph shows a horse-drawn hay rake (in the distance) and a pivoting hay-stacking mechanism in use during the summer of 1905.

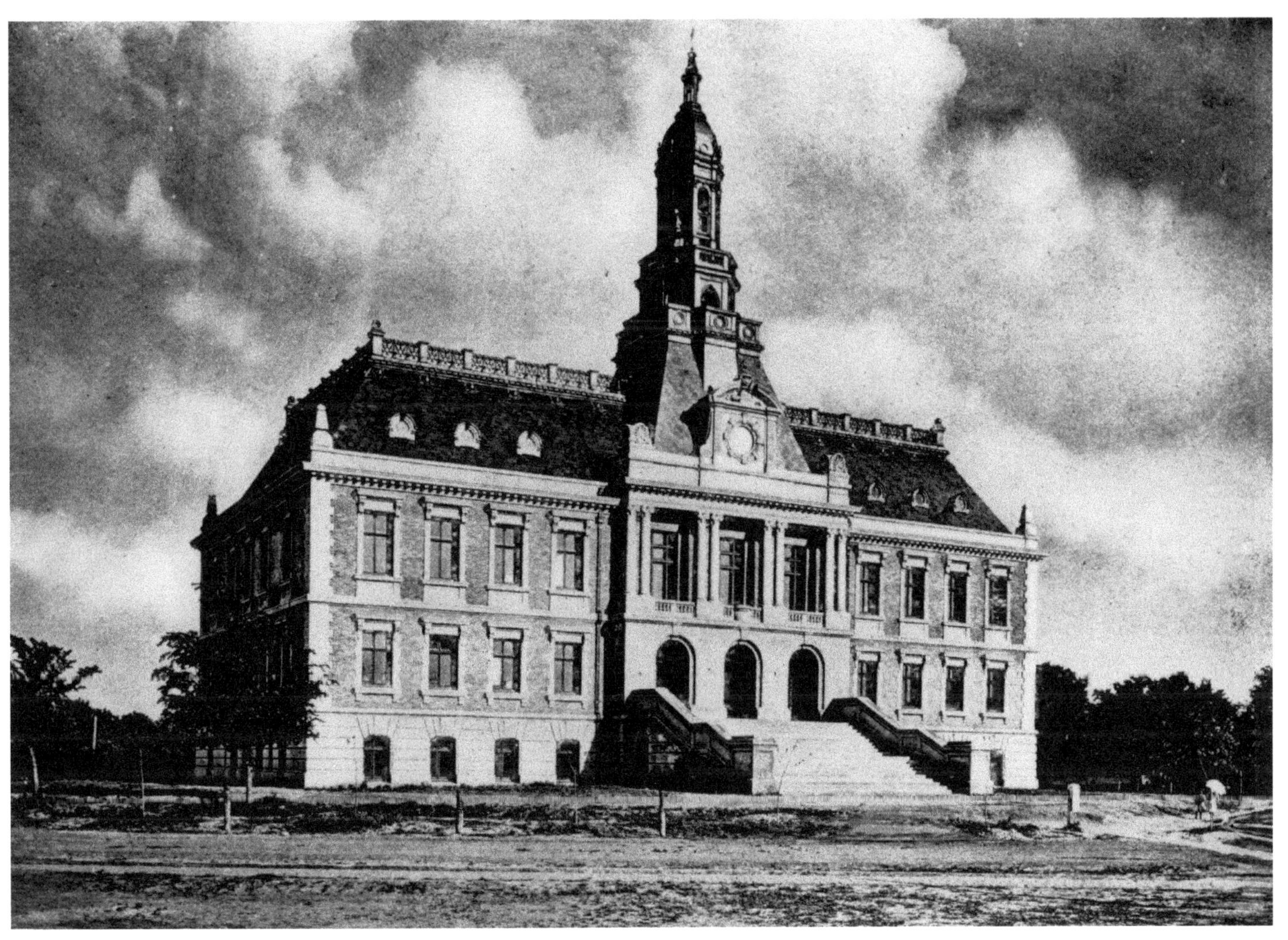

The Hall County Courthouse at Grand Island, located at First and Locust streets, began construction in 1901 and was completed in 1904. The courthouse remains standing today and is listed in the National Register of Historic Places.

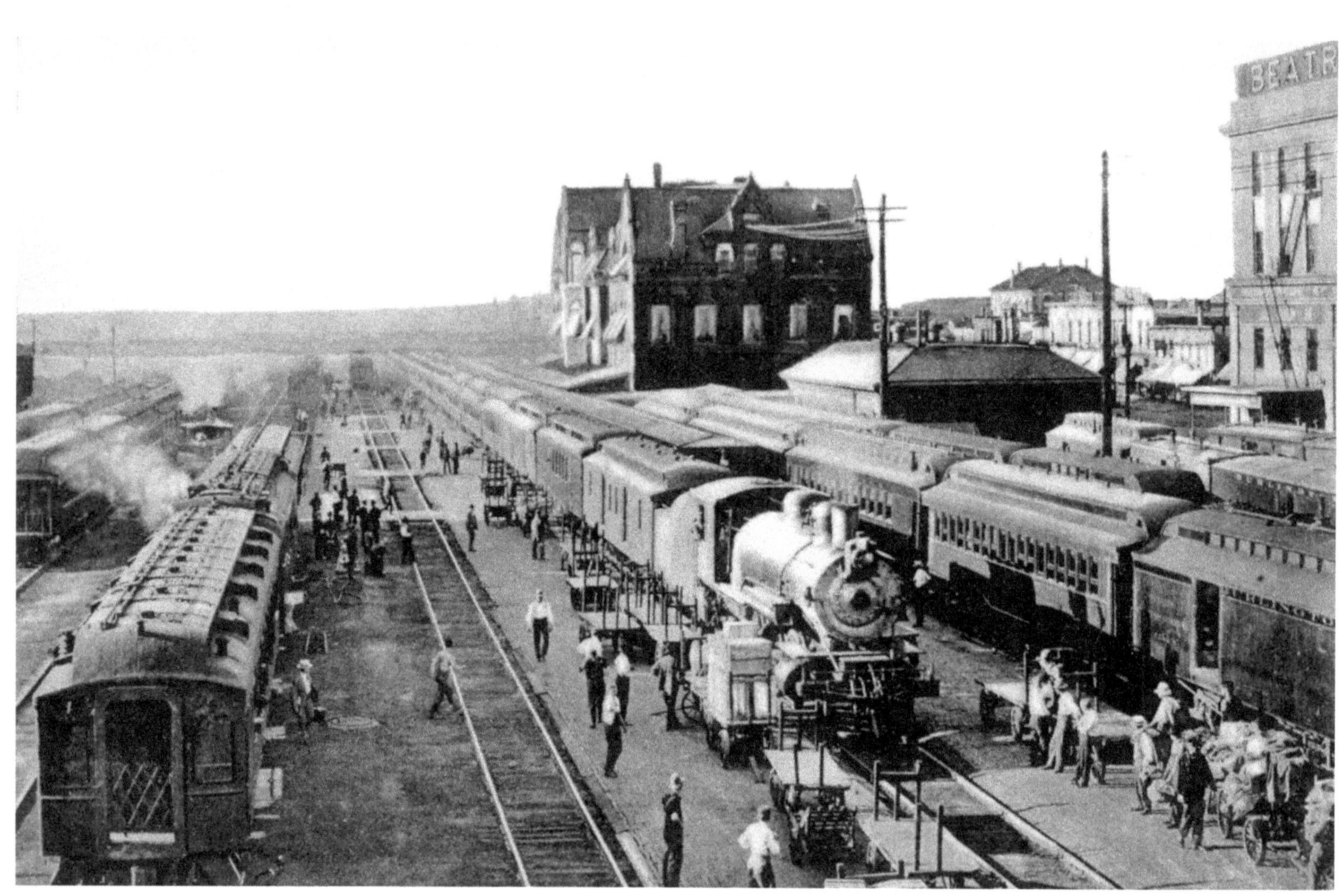

The Burlington & Missouri Passenger Station, located in Lincoln's Haymarket District, is shown here heavy with traffic.

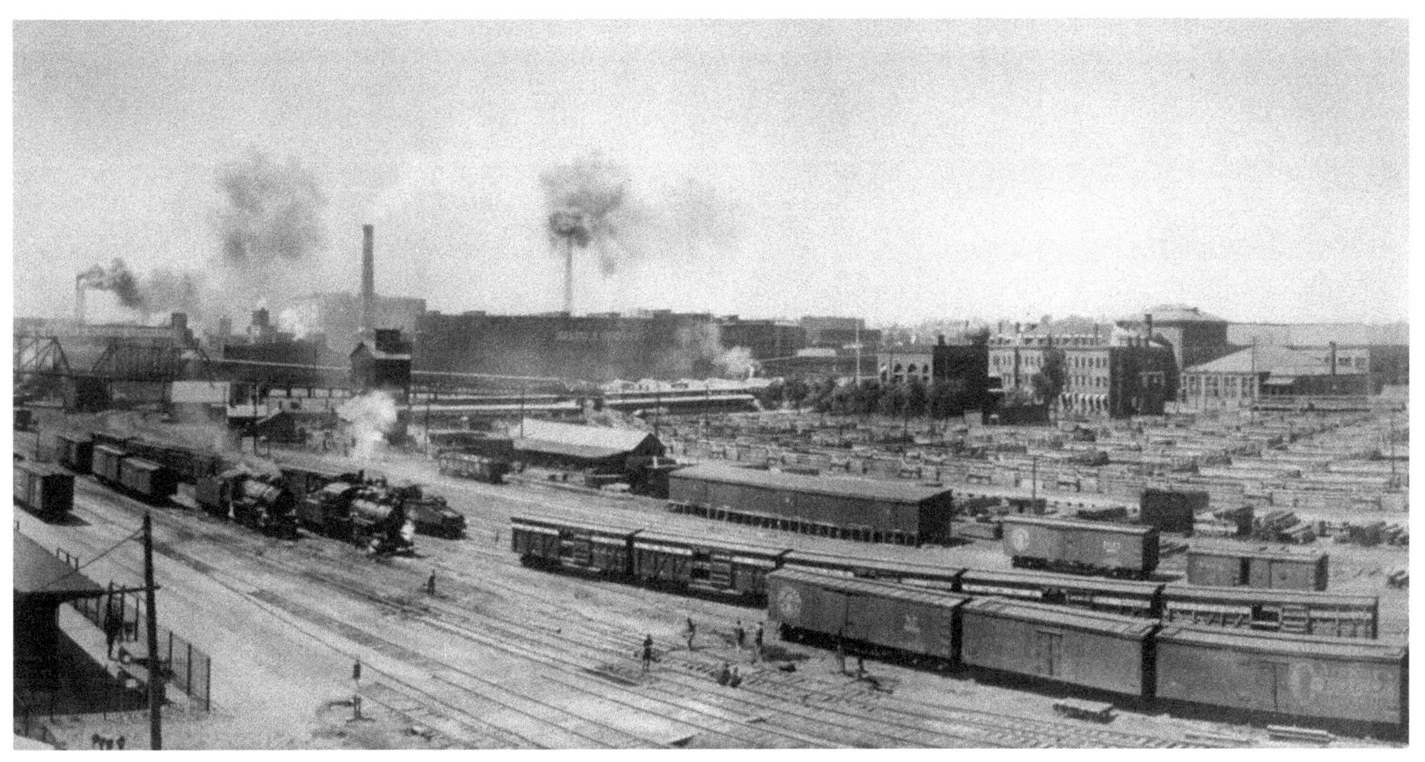

The Union Stockyards were established in 1883 and became the economic lifeline of Omaha for many years. The Armour plant here was the world's largest in the late 1800s, and during the mid twentieth century, the Union Stockyards were the world's largest meat-packing center. At their peak, six railroads hauled in livestock to be processed. The stockyards were closed in 1999 and became the site for the Stockyards Historic District redevelopment project.

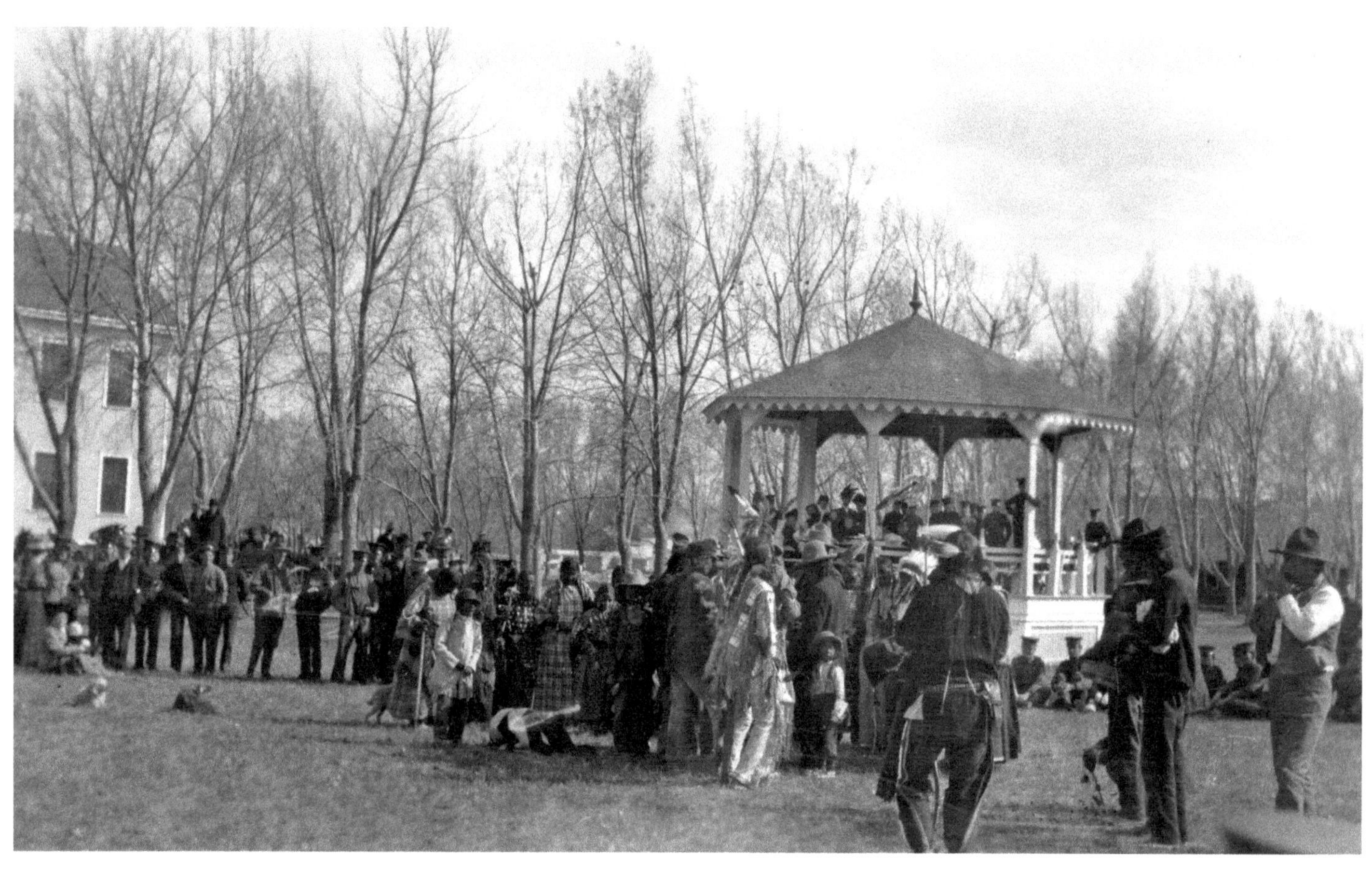

Oglala Lakota men, women, and children (likely from the Pine Ridge Reservation) are shown here gathered at Fort Robinson near Crawford. In 1906, military personnel at the post convened to watch various Lakota dances held in conjunction with a visit from the elderly Chief Red Cloud.

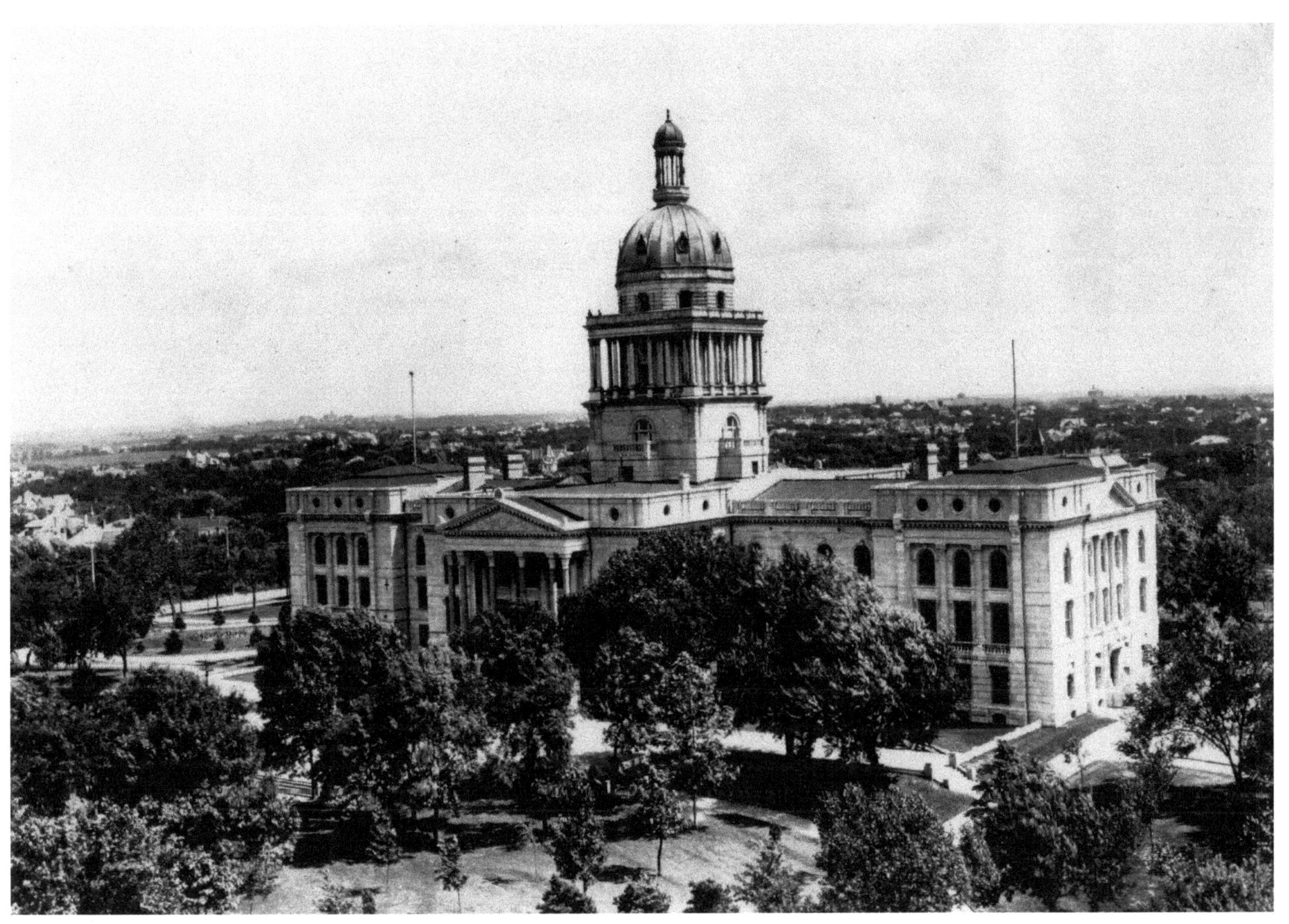

Nebraska's first state capitol in Lincoln was built in 1867 but soon began to crumble owing to its poor foundation and inferior quality of building stone. The second capitol (pictured here), built during the 1880s, lasted longer but eventually suffered the same fate. In 1919, the state legislature authorized the construction of a third capitol, which stands today.

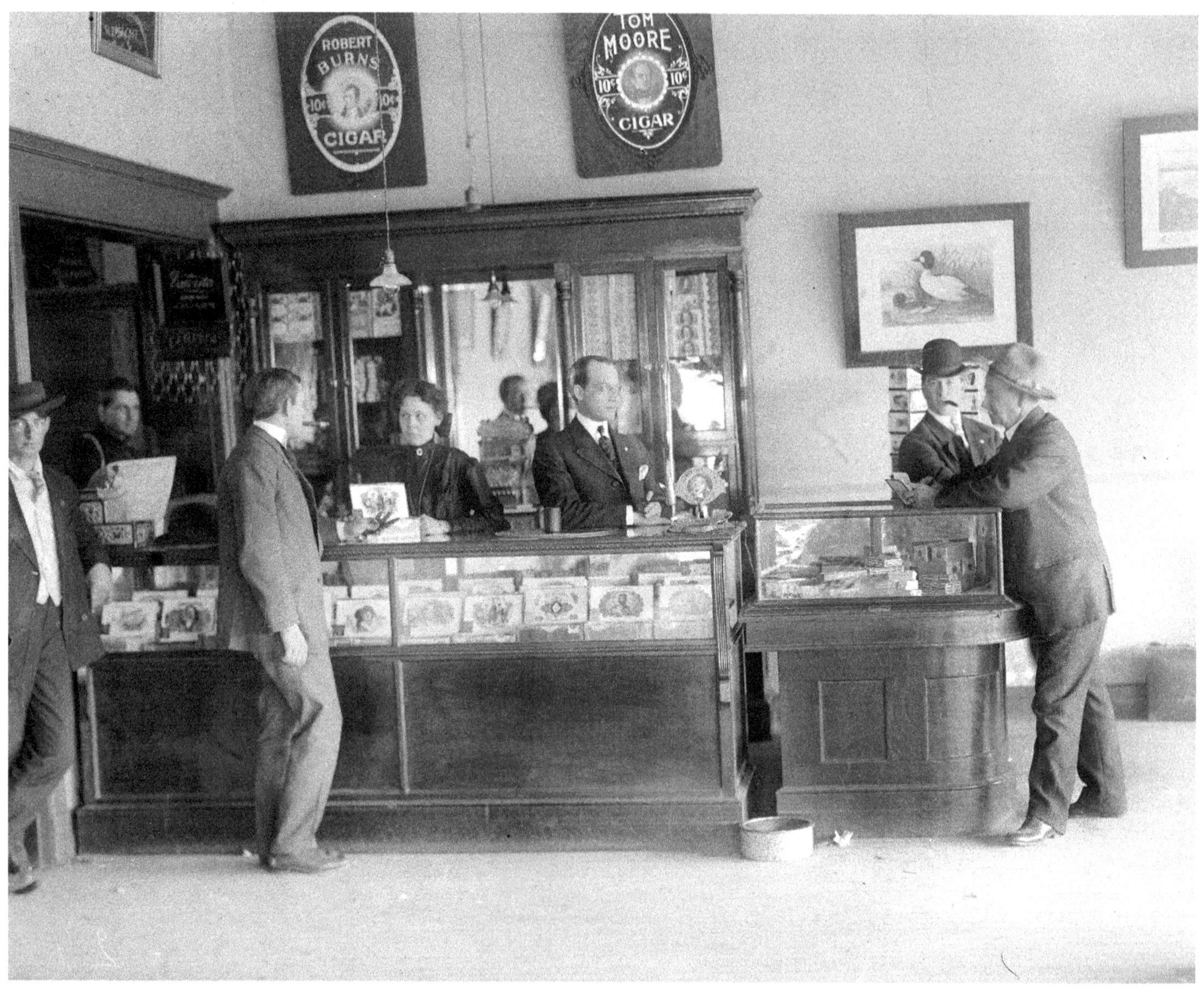

Kearney's Midway Hotel lobby boasted a cigar stand that was a popular place in 1907. Open boxes of cigars are on display inside the glass cases. This hotel, located at the busy intersection of 25th Street and Central Avenue, was known as one of the finest in the state. Its list of notable guests included Buffalo Bill and former president William Howard Taft.

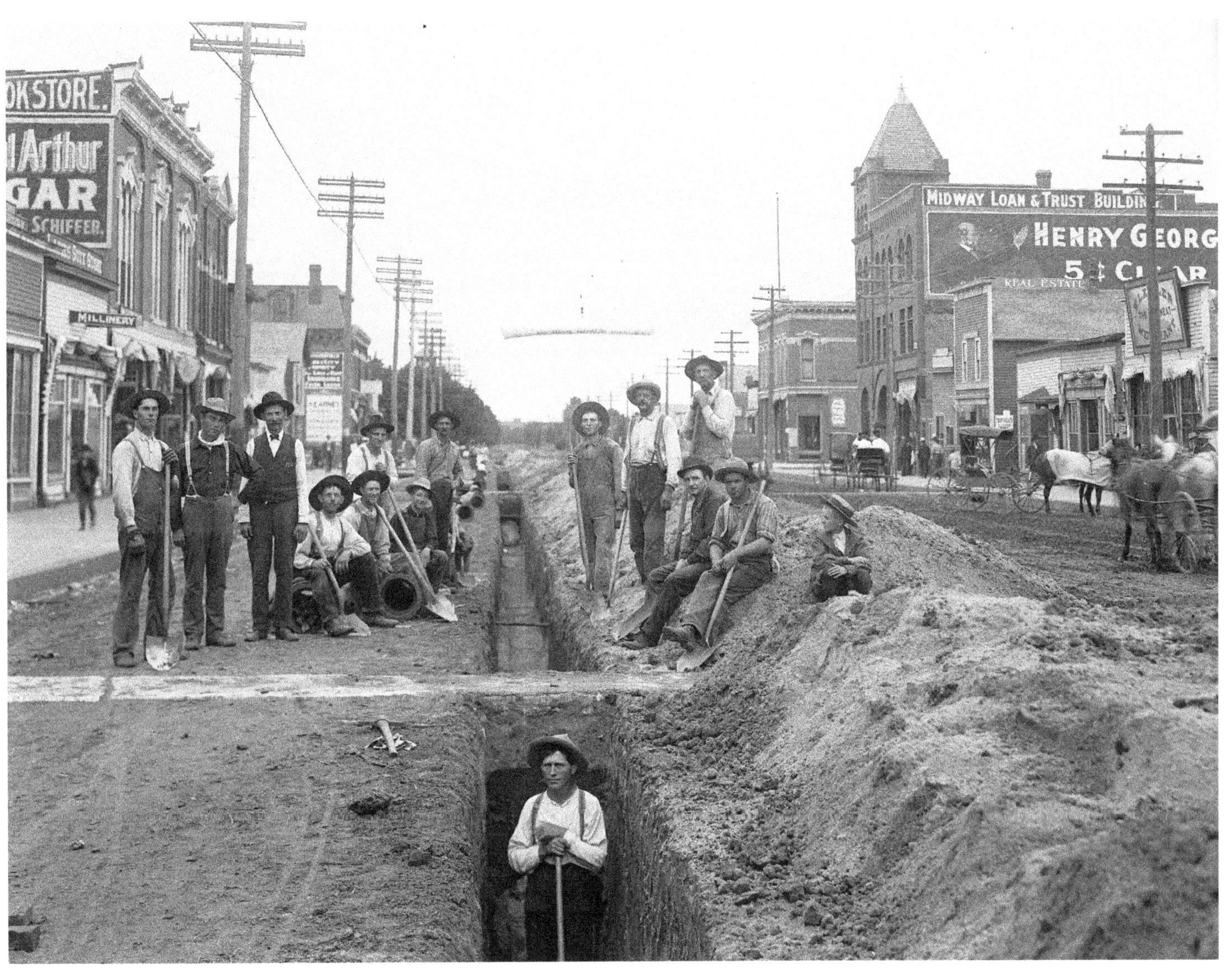

Long before the creation of the Occupational Safety and Health Administration, these laborers (and a small, well-dressed spectator) were busy digging a huge trench to lay pipe along the Kearney business district.

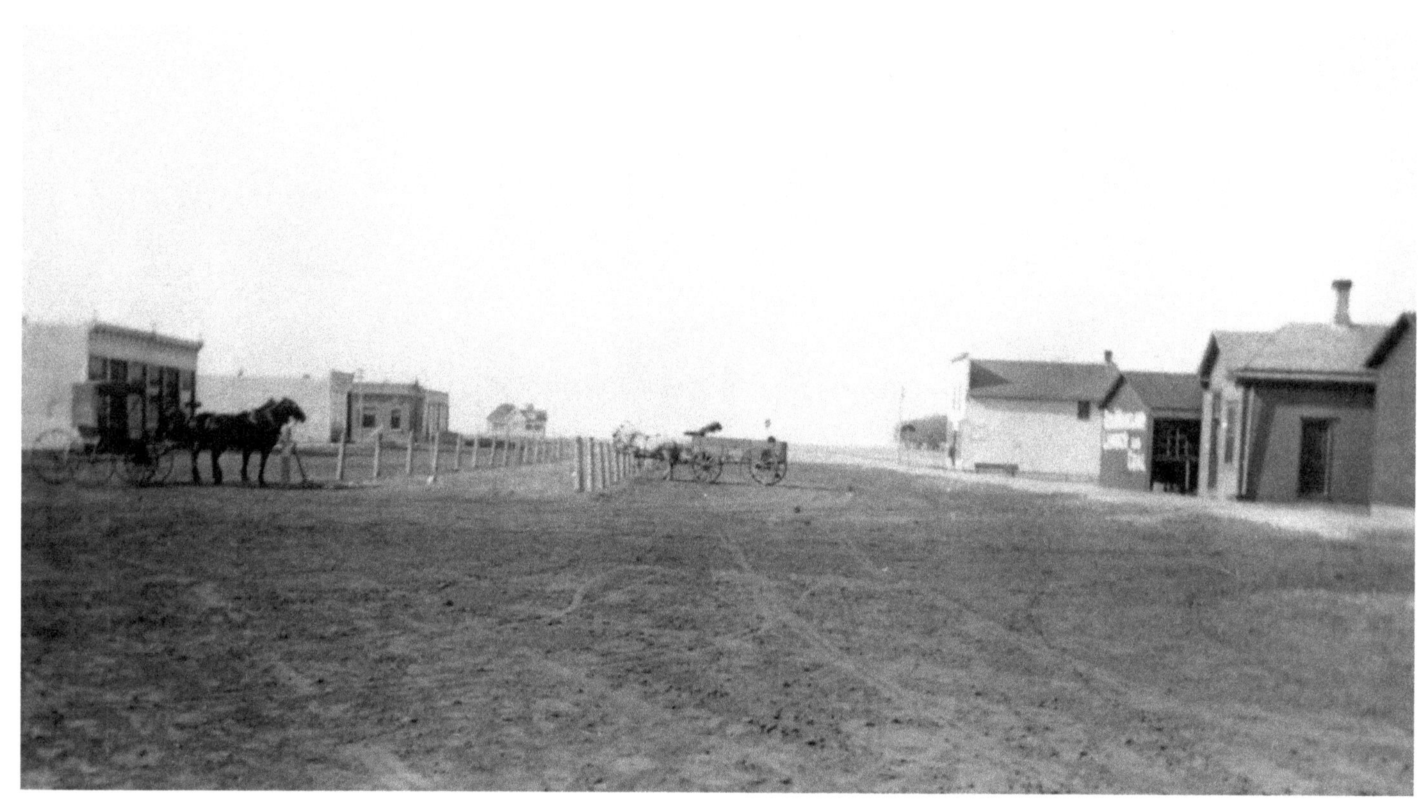

Two lonely looking teams of horses are tied up at hitching posts along Main Street in Hordville. The town, platted in 1906, was not always so quiet as this image suggests. At one point, Hordville had three doctors, four grocers, a drugstore, jewelry, hardware, and shoe repair stores, a photography studio, a garage, a blacksmith forge, a hatchery, a lumberyard, a barbershop, and several cafes in addition to a hotel and livery stable.

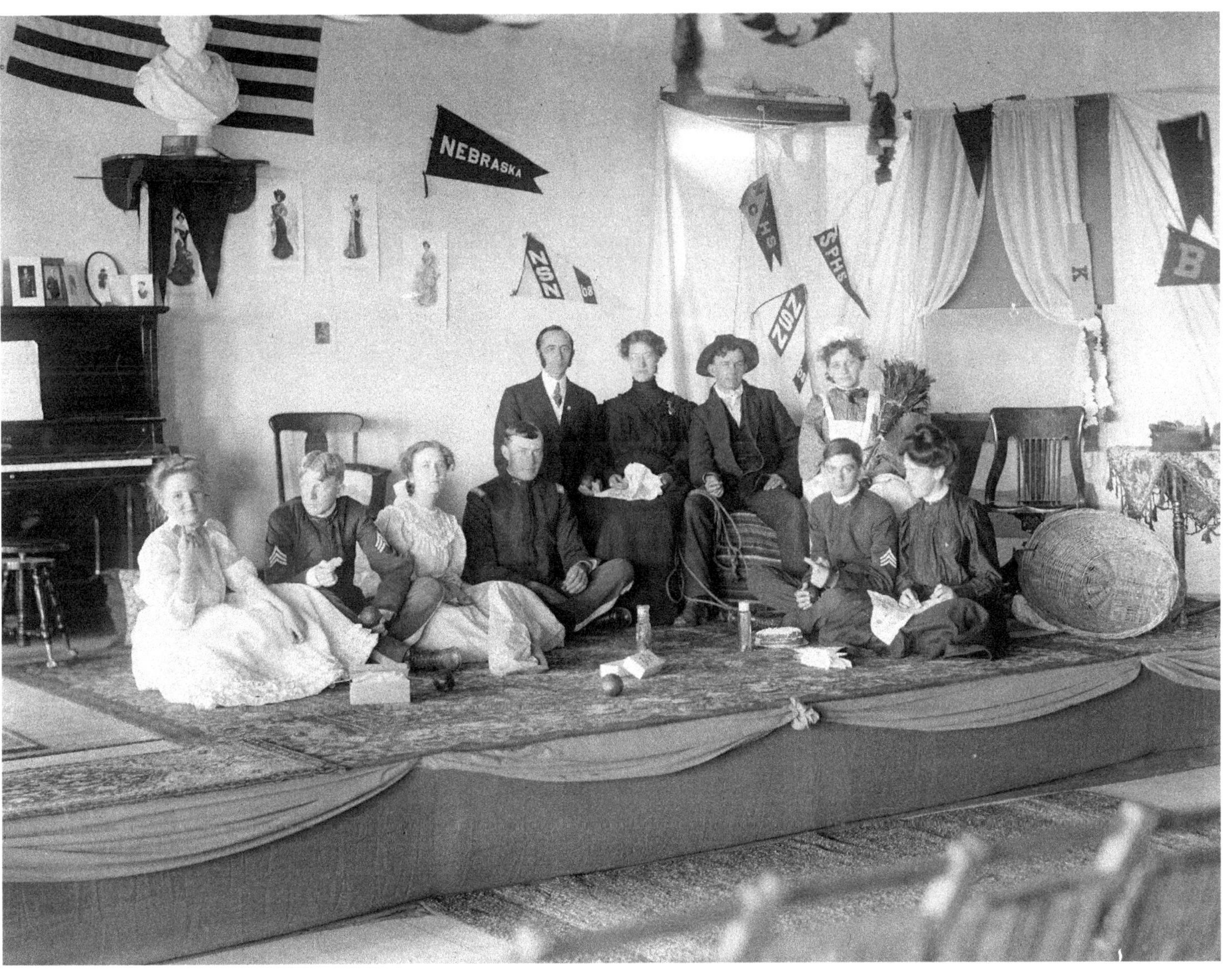

It's time for lunch at the Amherst School in 1907. The next year, a new building was completed, but it would be destroyed by fire in 1928 and replaced with a brick structure. By that time, Amherst had 16 businesses, 2 banks, and an opera house. The small town in Buffalo County has declined in population over the years.

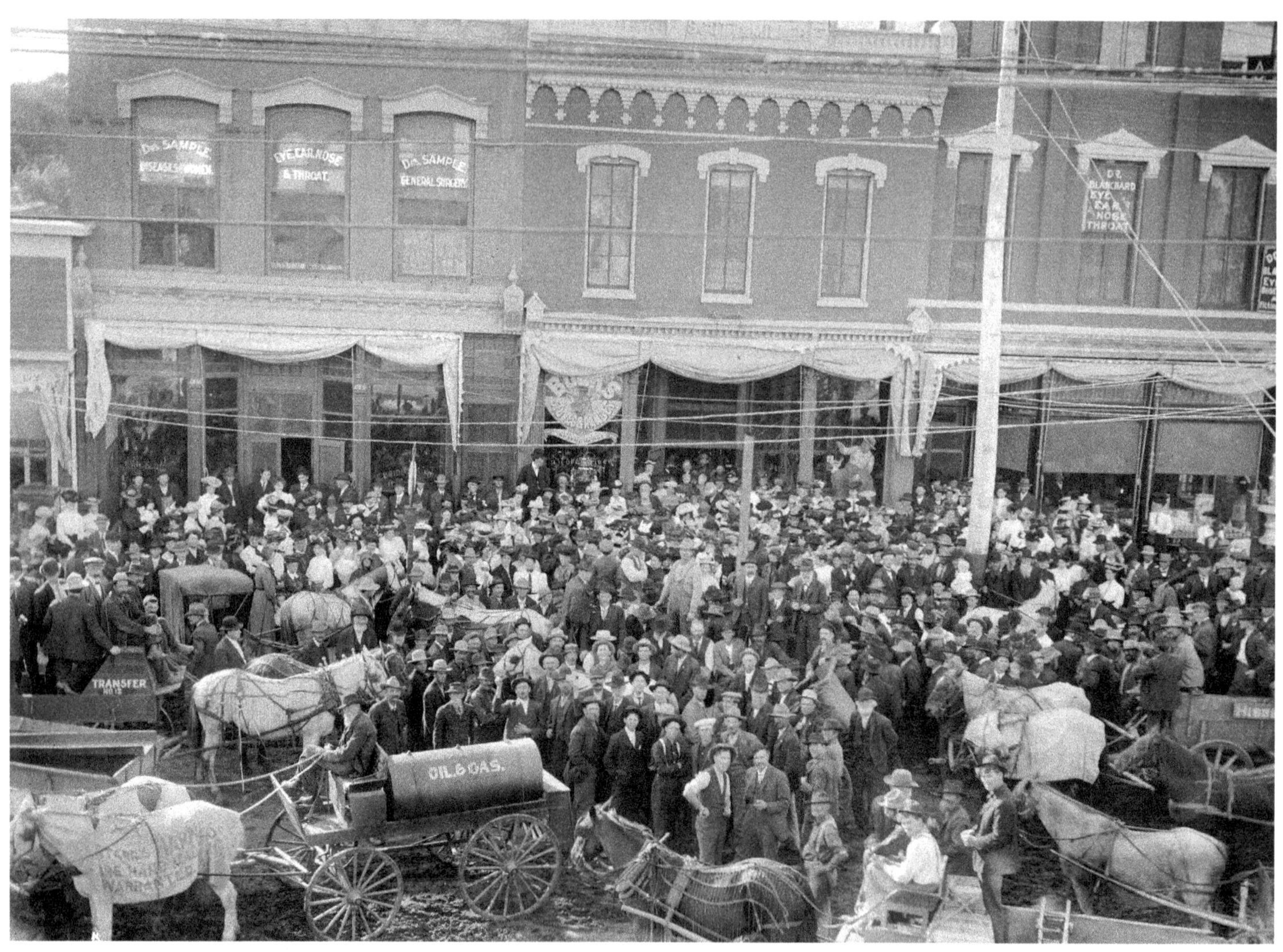

Nebraska's population was largely rural at the start of the twentieth century, but farmers came to town in droves on Saturdays, and small towns eagerly looked forward to the business they brought in. Here around 1908, the C. F. Bodinson Store in Kearney is sponsoring a lottery drawing to help lure customers.

Knowing that the Homestead Act would go into effect on January 1, 1863, Union soldier Daniel Freeman went to Brownville and persuaded the Land Office agent to open at midnight so Freeman could file a claim on 160 acres near Beatrice before he returned to duty that day. After the war, Freeman built a cabin there and never moved. Recognized as the nation's first homesteader, Freeman poses for a photograph four years before his death in 1908.

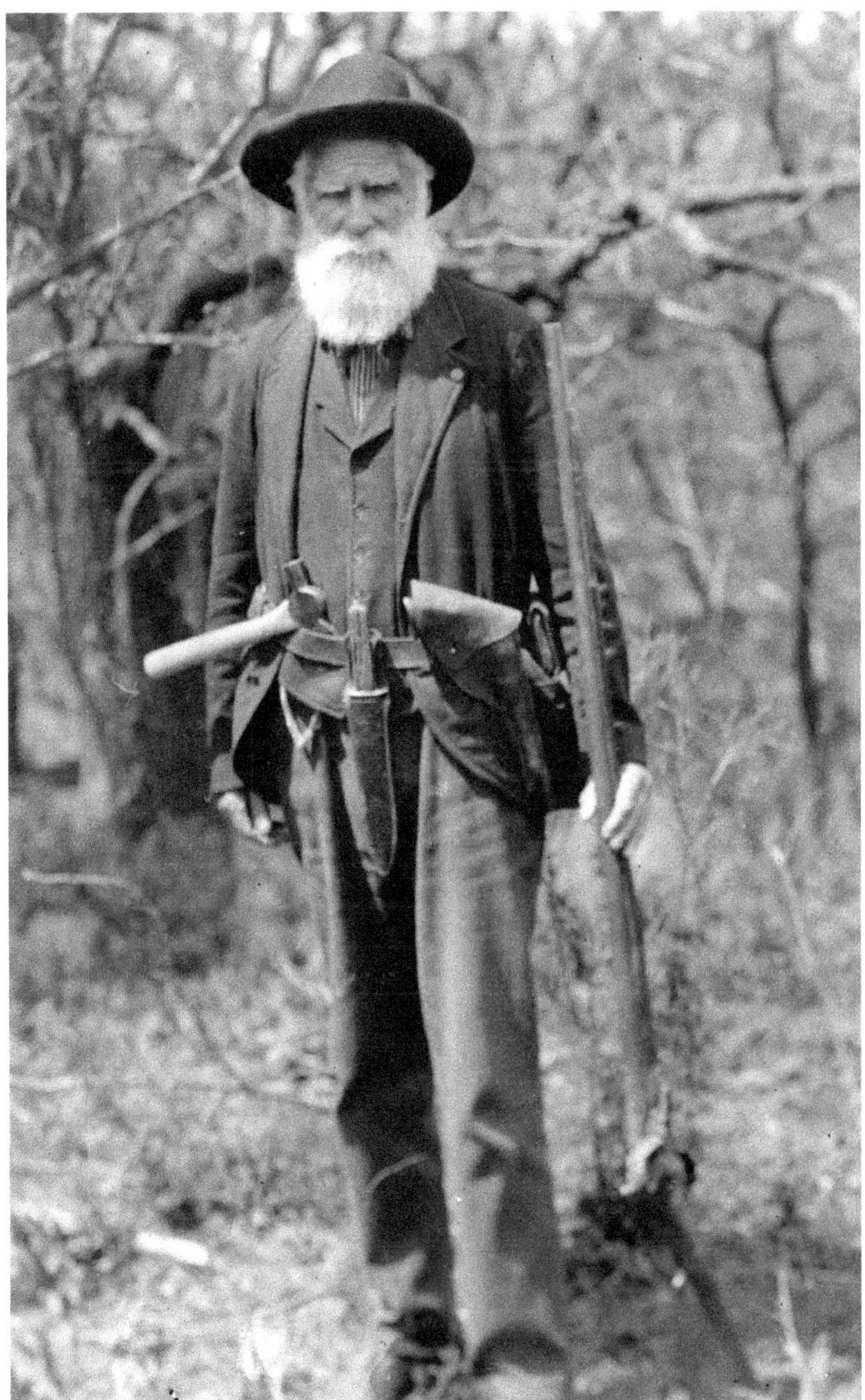

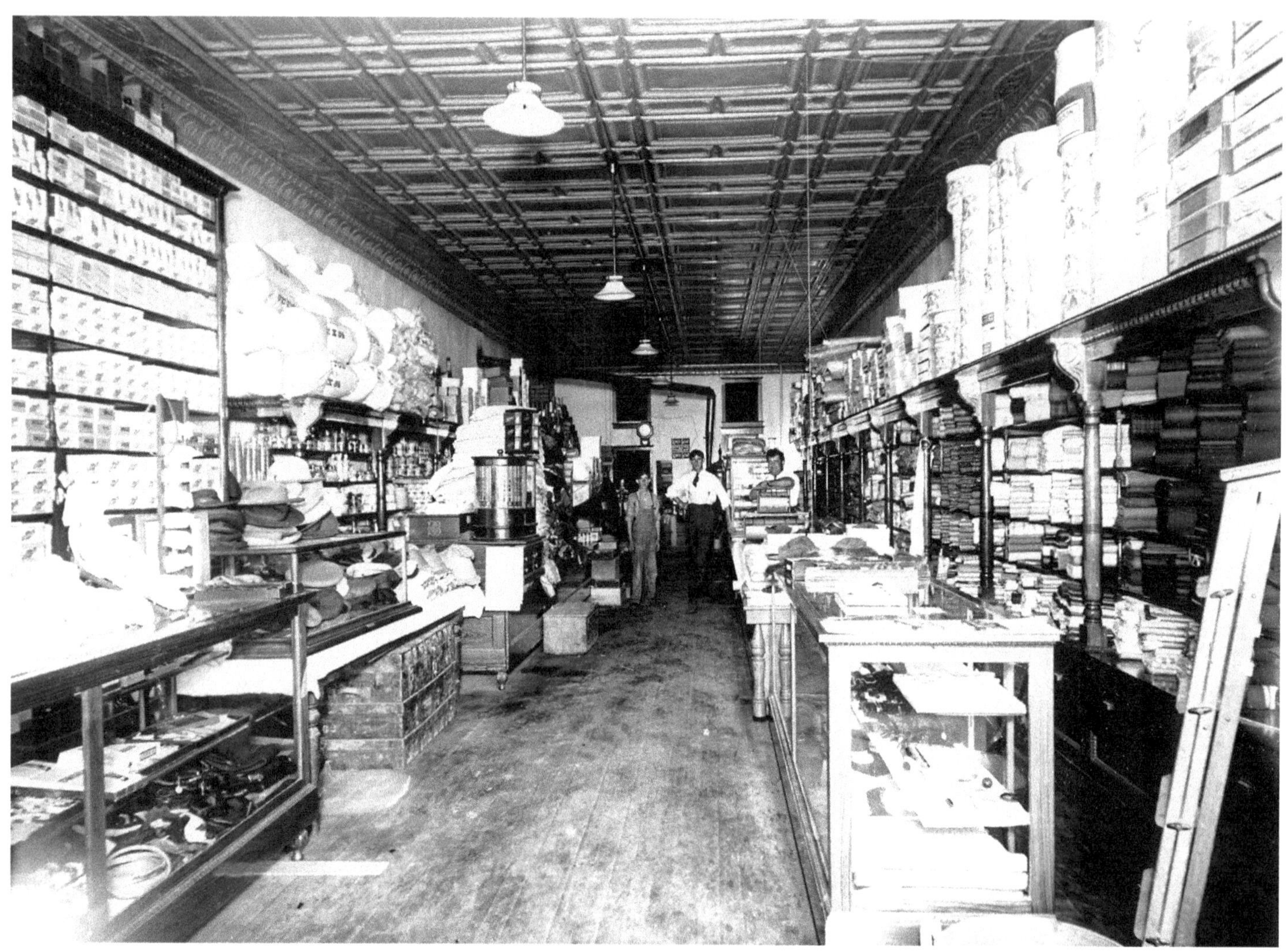

Intricately patterned ceiling and cornice tin adorns the Albert Pilger General Merchandise Store in Pilger in 1908. Bolts of cloth line the shelves and glass cases are filled with a variety of wares. Two men and a boy stand in front of the heating stove in the back of the building, where the "morning glory" speaker of a gramophone protrudes from the left.

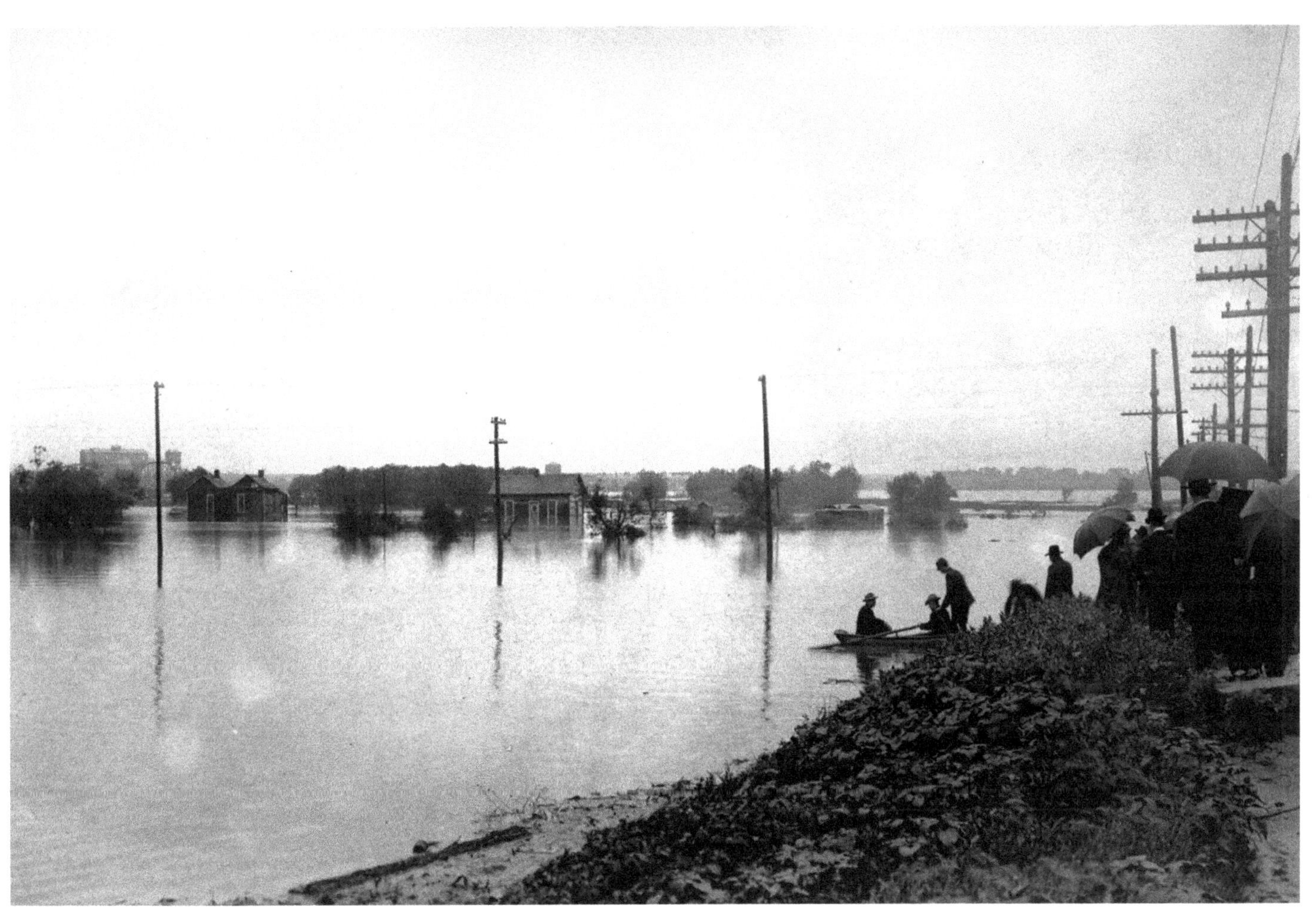

Floodwater coursed through the Salt Valley on July 6, 1908, devastating Lincoln and the surrounding area. Nine people were killed and approximately 10,000 left homeless by the floodwaters.

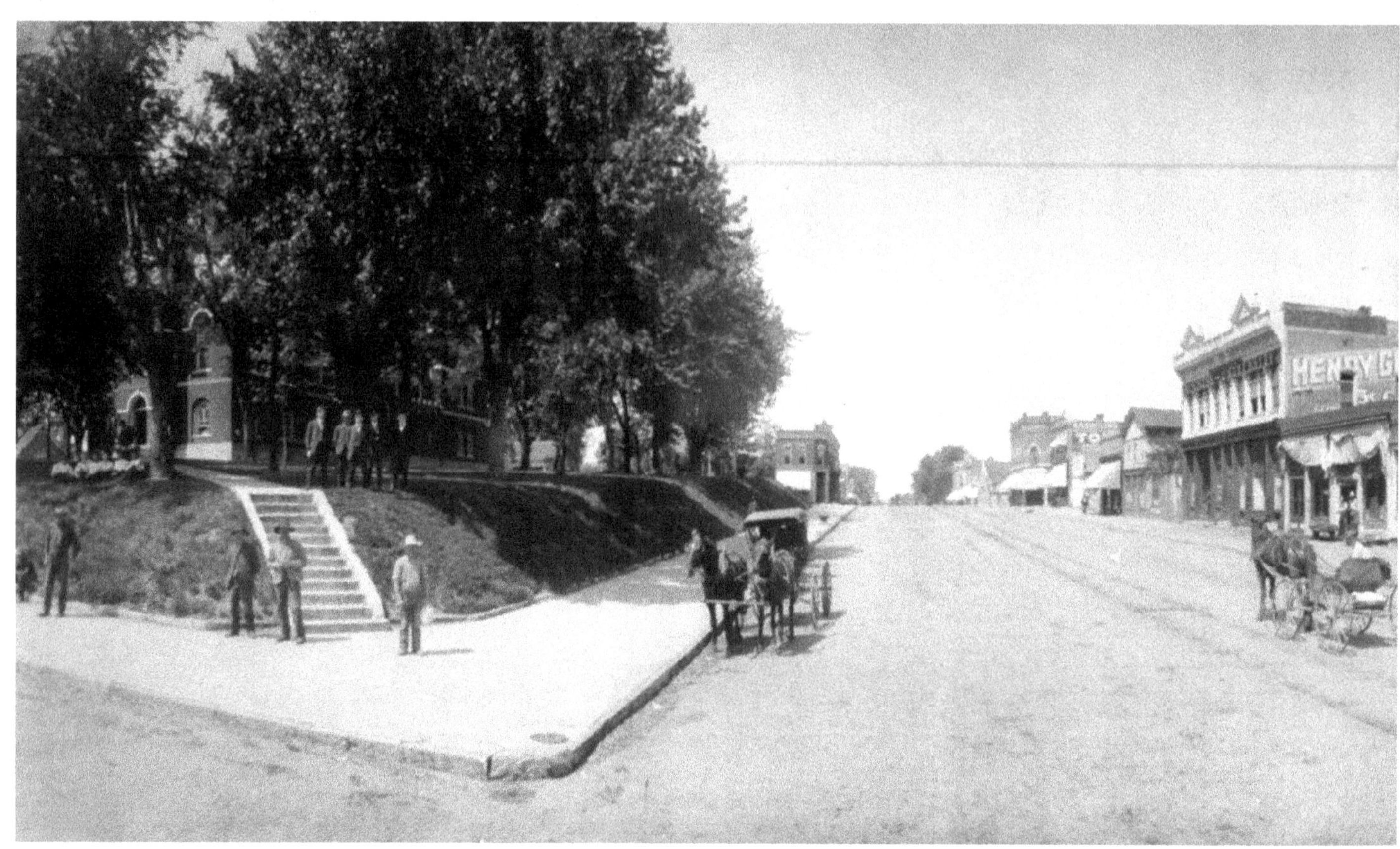

The state's earliest Missouri River ferry was located in Nebraska City, which became a launching point for overland freighters in the mid nineteenth century. In 1858, Russell, Majors, and Waddell secured a government contract to supply western forts with provisions, starting here. The town's most famous resident, J. Sterling Morton, established Arbor Day nationwide. Shown here in 1908, Nebraska City today is still home to the Arbor Day Foundation.

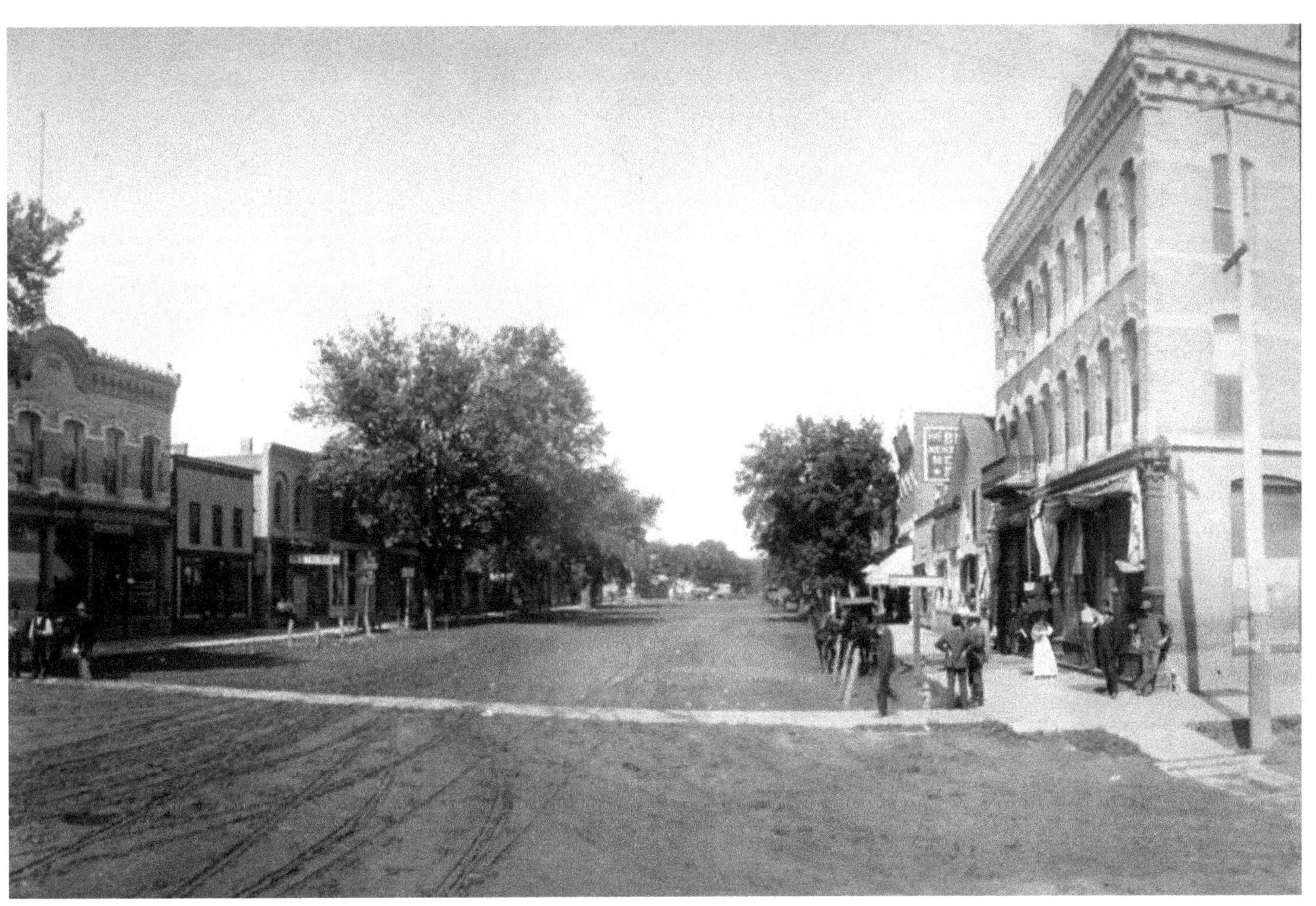

Platted in 1869 and named for the railroad official who purchased the area, Blair became the county seat of Washington County, where the forerunner of current-day Dana College was established in 1884. Blair served as national headquarters for two different Danish Lutheran denominations between 1884 and 1960. This photograph, one of several by Frederick J. Bandholtz included here, offers a glimpse of the town as it appeared in 1908.

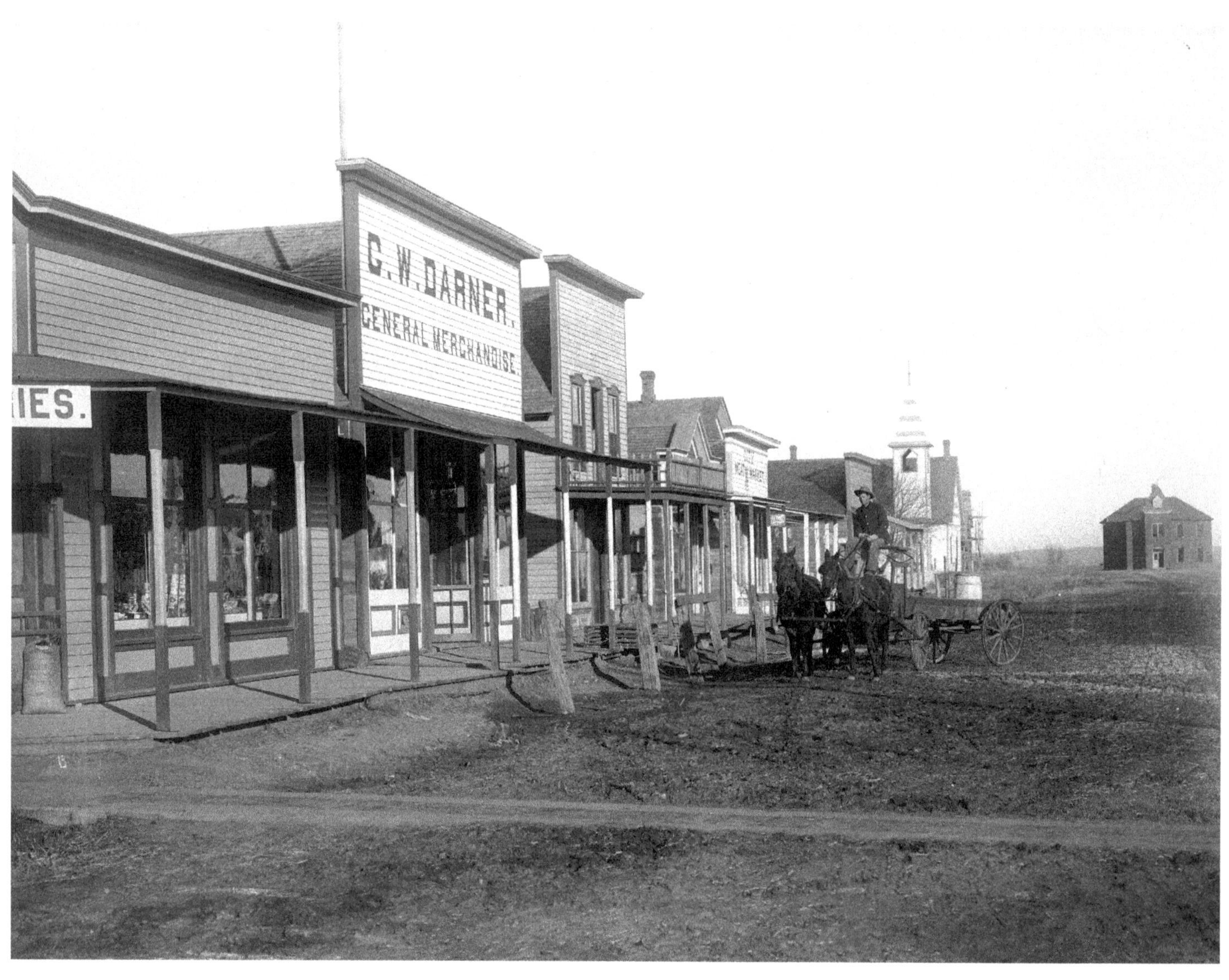

In 1908, residents of Overton, located in southeast Dawson County, could lay in provisions with a visit to the City Meat Market and C. W. Darner General Merchandise store.

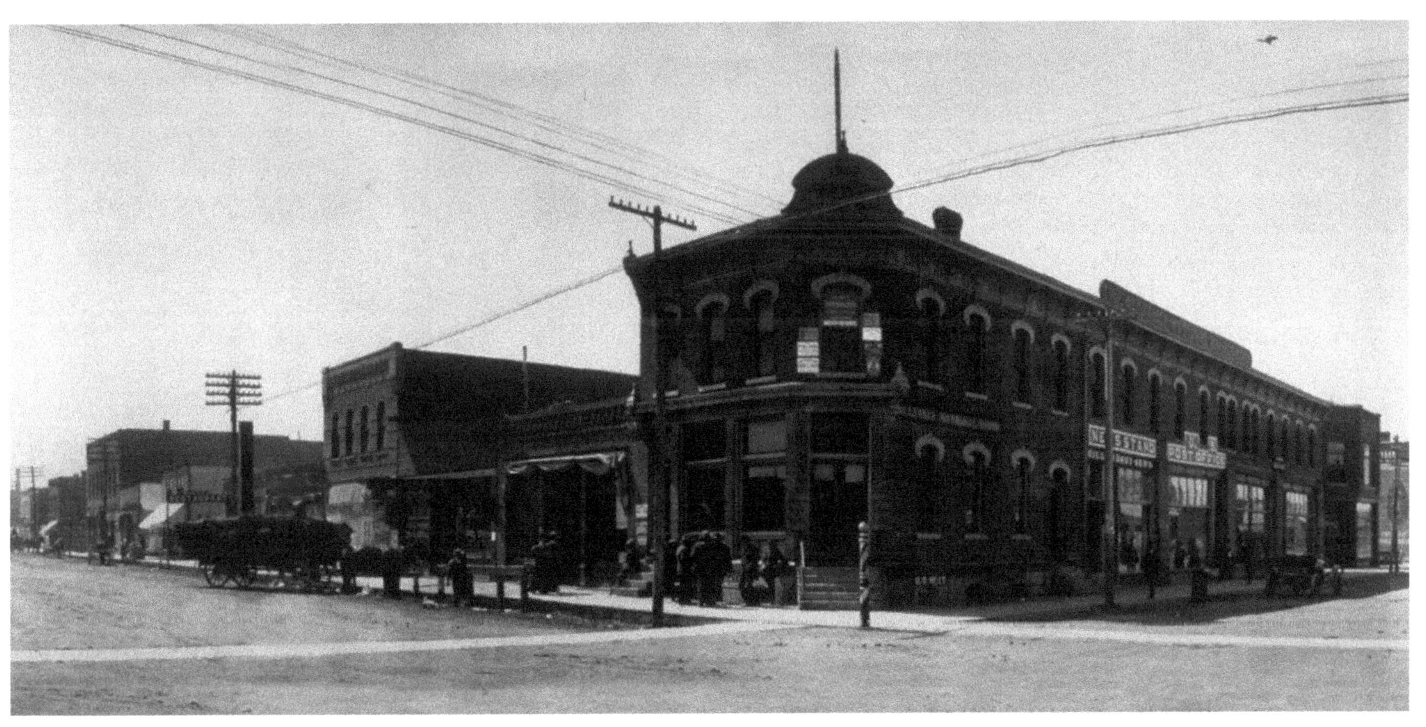

Founded in 1888 and photographed here in May 1908 by F. E. Taylor, Alliance had a population of 2,200 within a decade. Many of its settlers were Civil War veterans from Iowa and Illinois. The county seat of Box Butte County quickly became a main switching yard for the Burlington and Missouri Railroad. In the late twentieth century, Alliance would become famous as the home of "Carhenge," a sculpture north of town made of old automobiles.

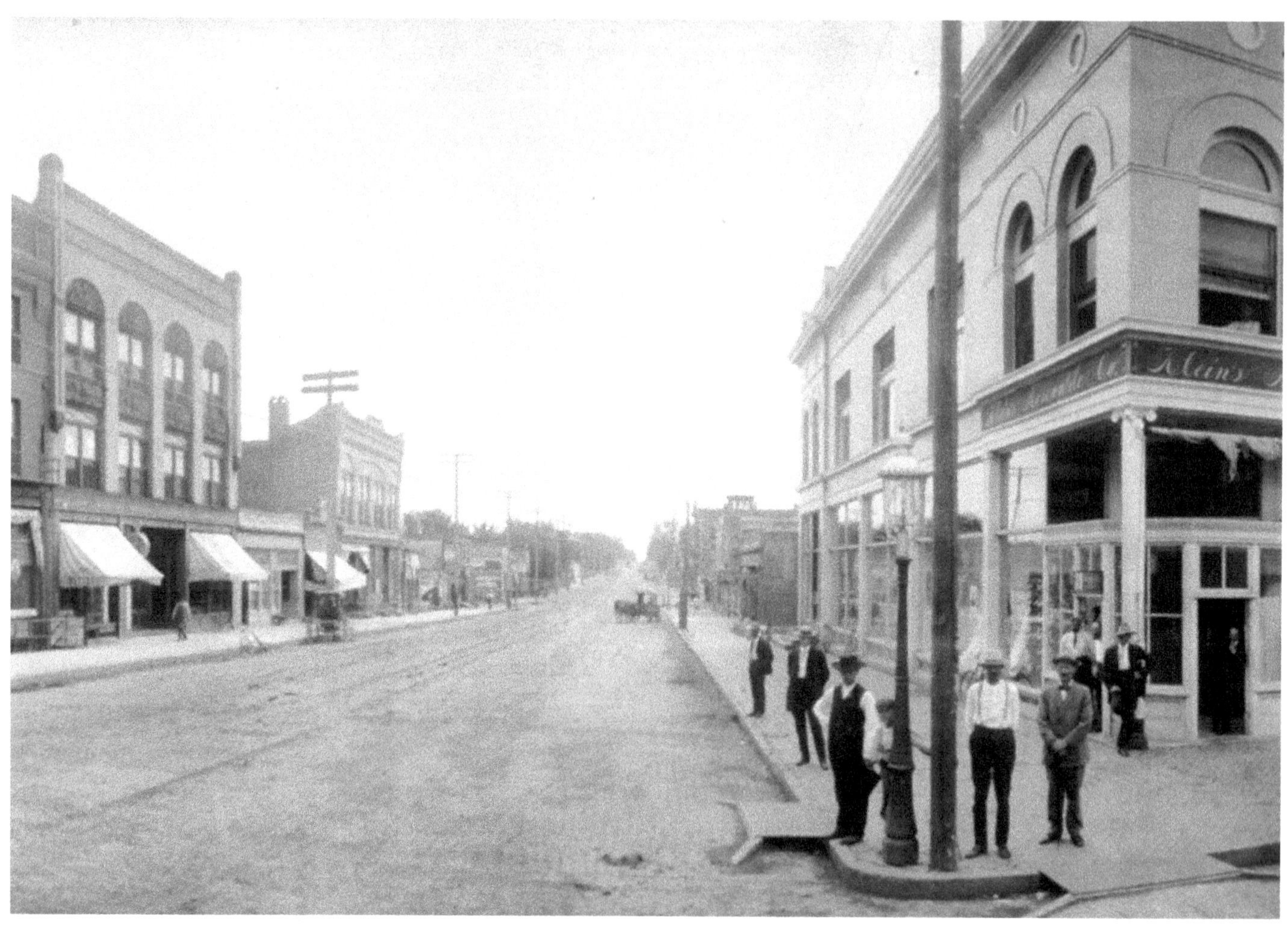

Beatrice was incorporated in 1871, and its population had increased to nearly 8,000 by 1900. This 1908 photograph by Frederick J. Bandholtz shows the intersection of Sixth and Court streets. Daniel Freeman, who was recognized as the first homesteader in United States history, settled near Beatrice, and the Homestead National Monument of America is located there.

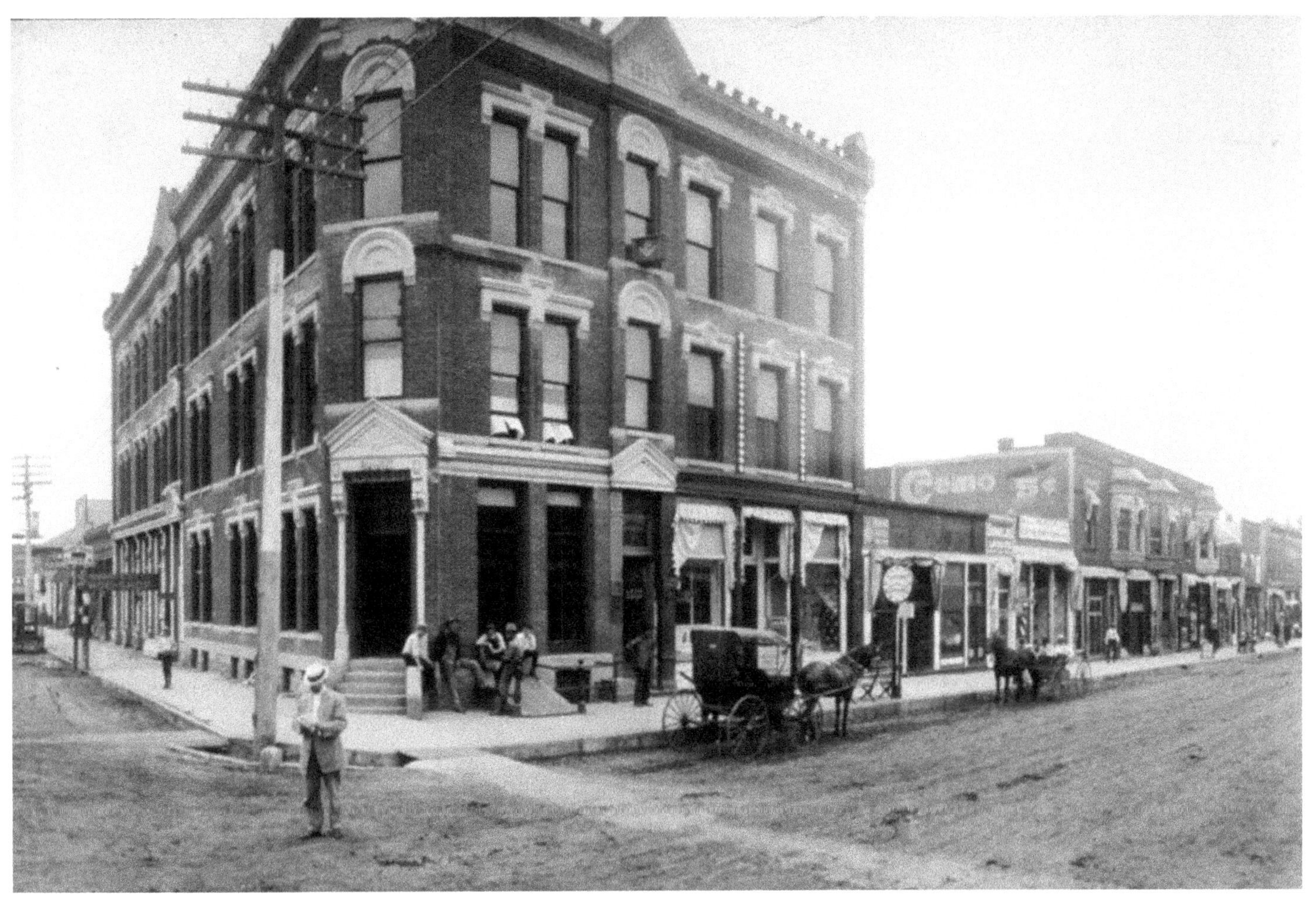

Founded in 1857 and shown here in 1908, Falls City was the Nebraska base on the "Lane Trail," which funneled free-state settlers from the Northeast and Midwest into Kansas in the 1850s and 1860s. Located in extreme southeast Nebraska, Falls City became county seat for Richardson County as the result of a series of highly controversial elections culminating in a gun battle that killed two men.

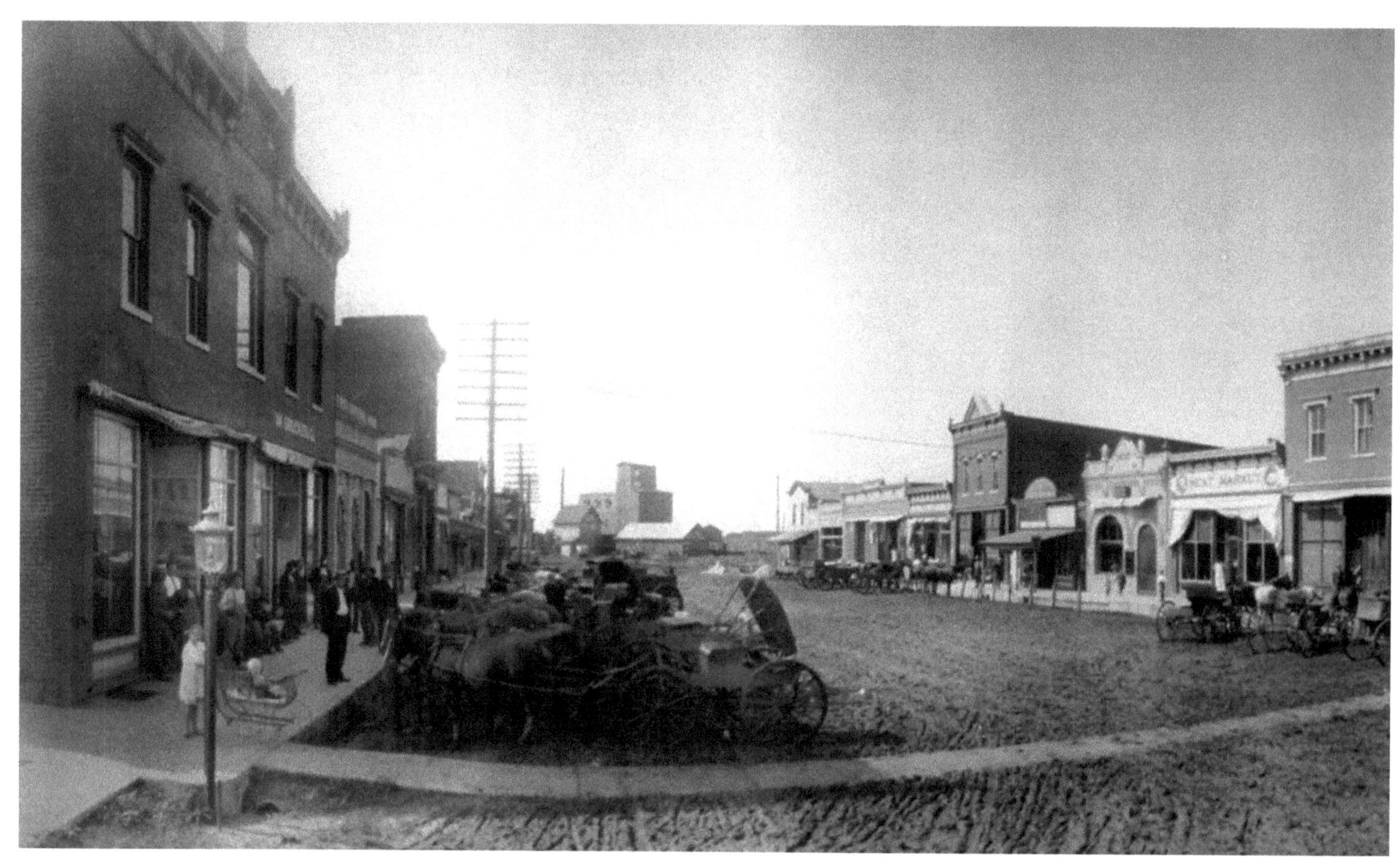

A group of people, including a little girl pushing a baby buggy, were gathered in the muddy business district of Scribner in 1908 for this photograph by Frederick J. Bandholtz. Scribner lies just 25 miles from the Missouri River.

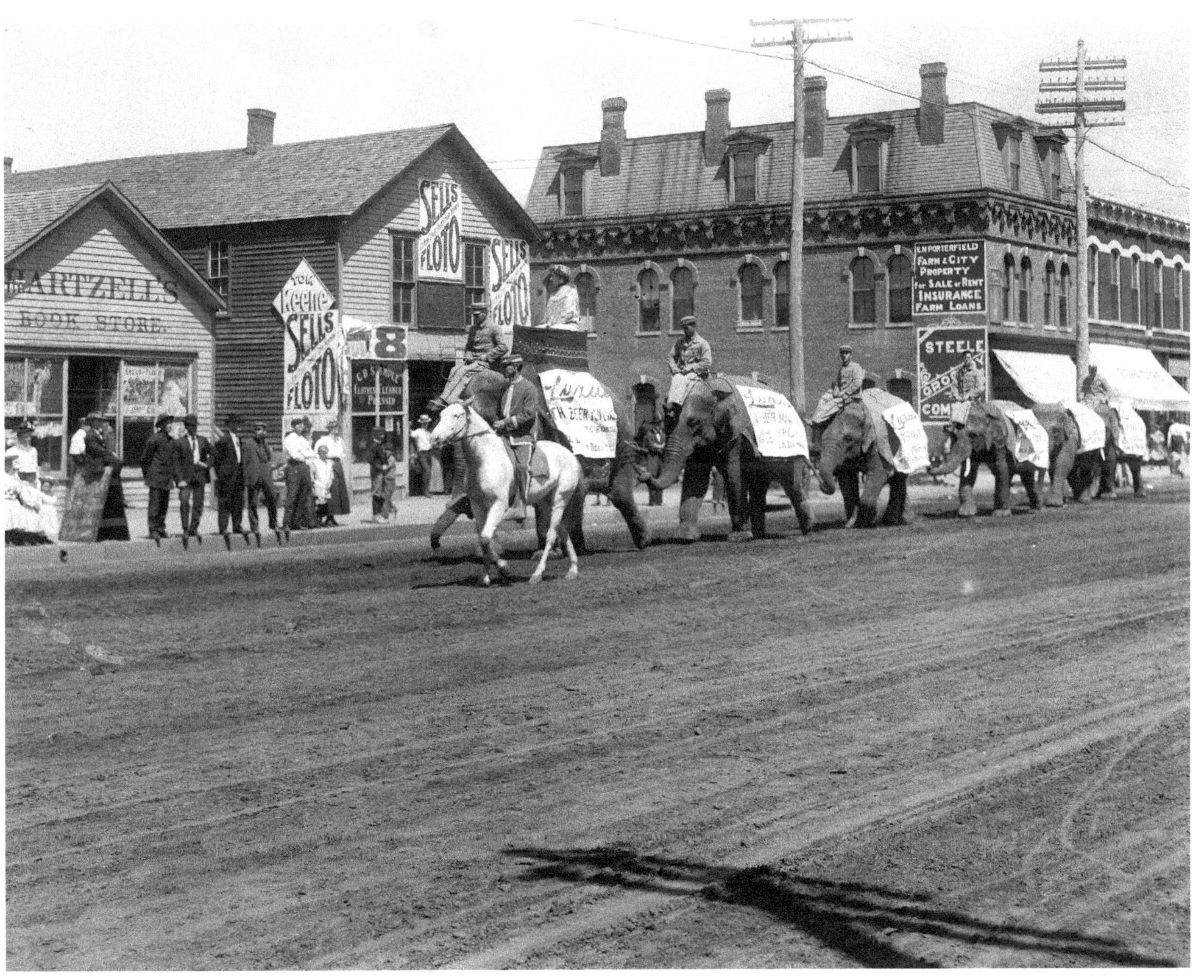

The Sells-Floto Circus filled Kearney with advertising posters as it came through town in 1908, and many of the residents saw elephants for the first time as the circus parade marched down the dirt streets.

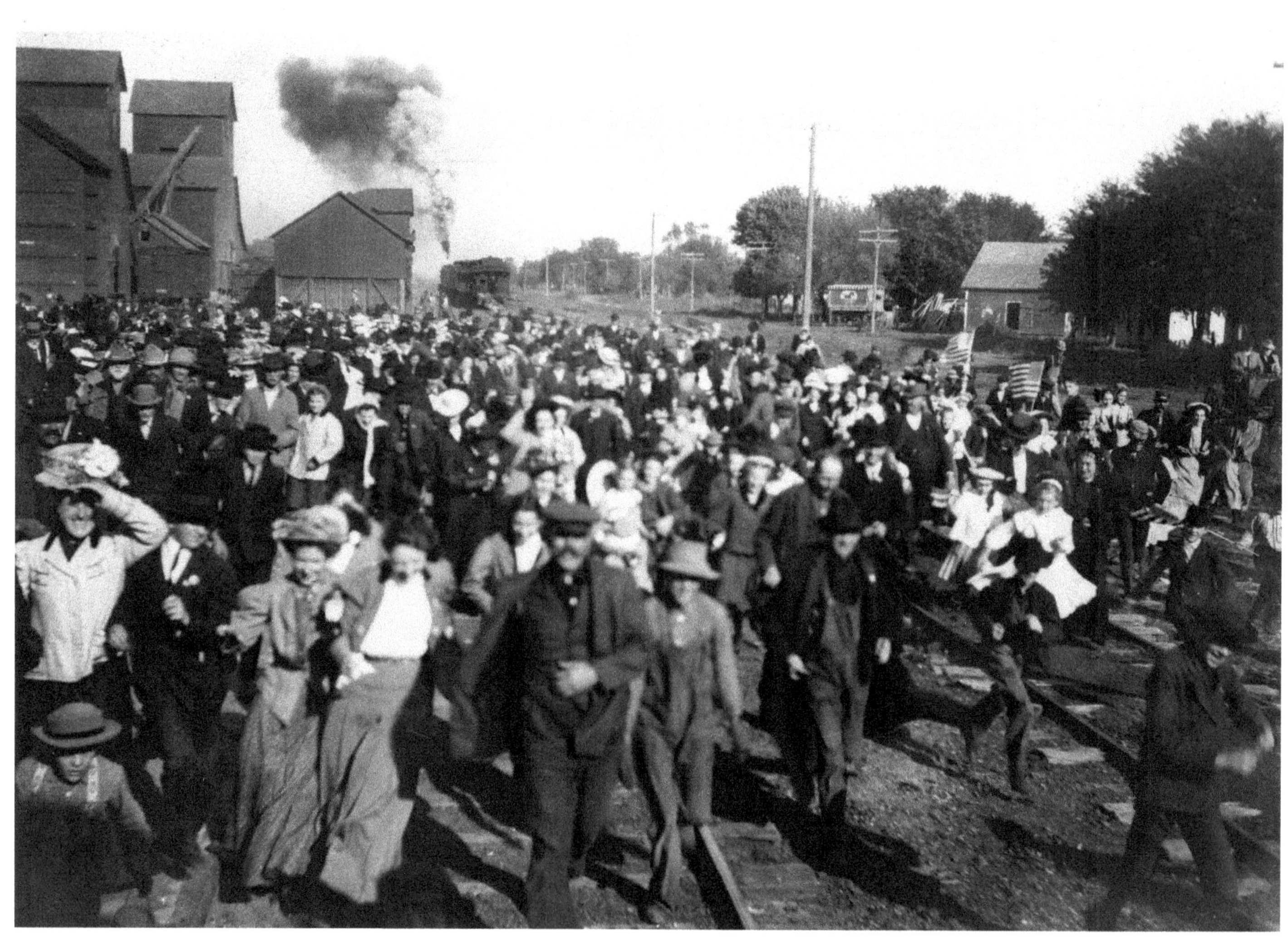

In 1908, the Republican candidate for president, William Howard Taft, made a campaign swing through Nebraska, which was the home state of his opponent, William Jennings Bryan. Here, a crowd eagerly rushes toward his train in DeWitt. Bryan tallied the most votes in Nebraska, but Taft won the election by a wide margin nationwide.

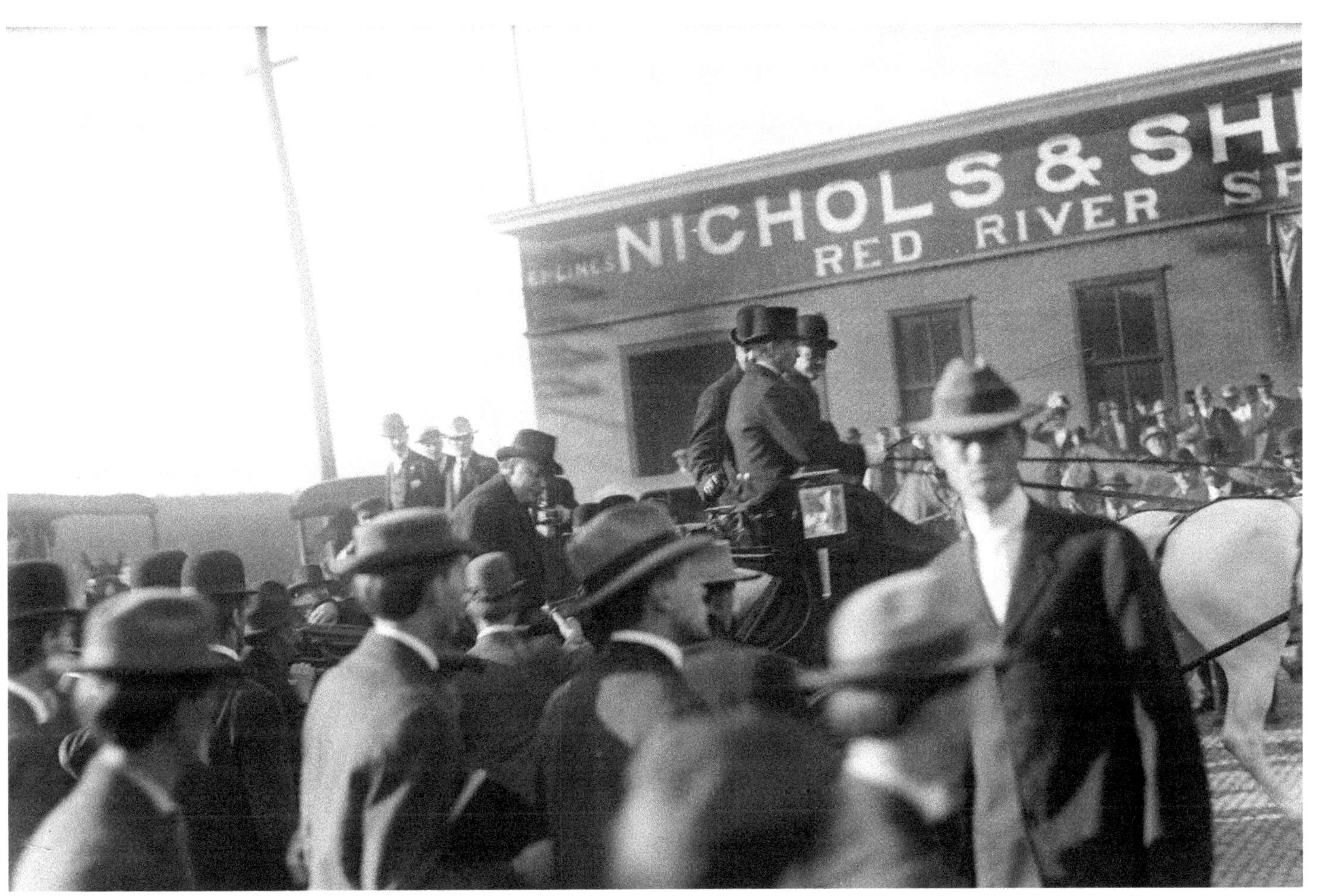

Presidential candidate William Howard Taft (seated behind the drivers) rides through Lincoln in the back of an open carriage on September 30, 1908, during his campaign against Lincoln resident William Jennings Bryan. Taft handed Bryan his third and final defeat in a presidential race.

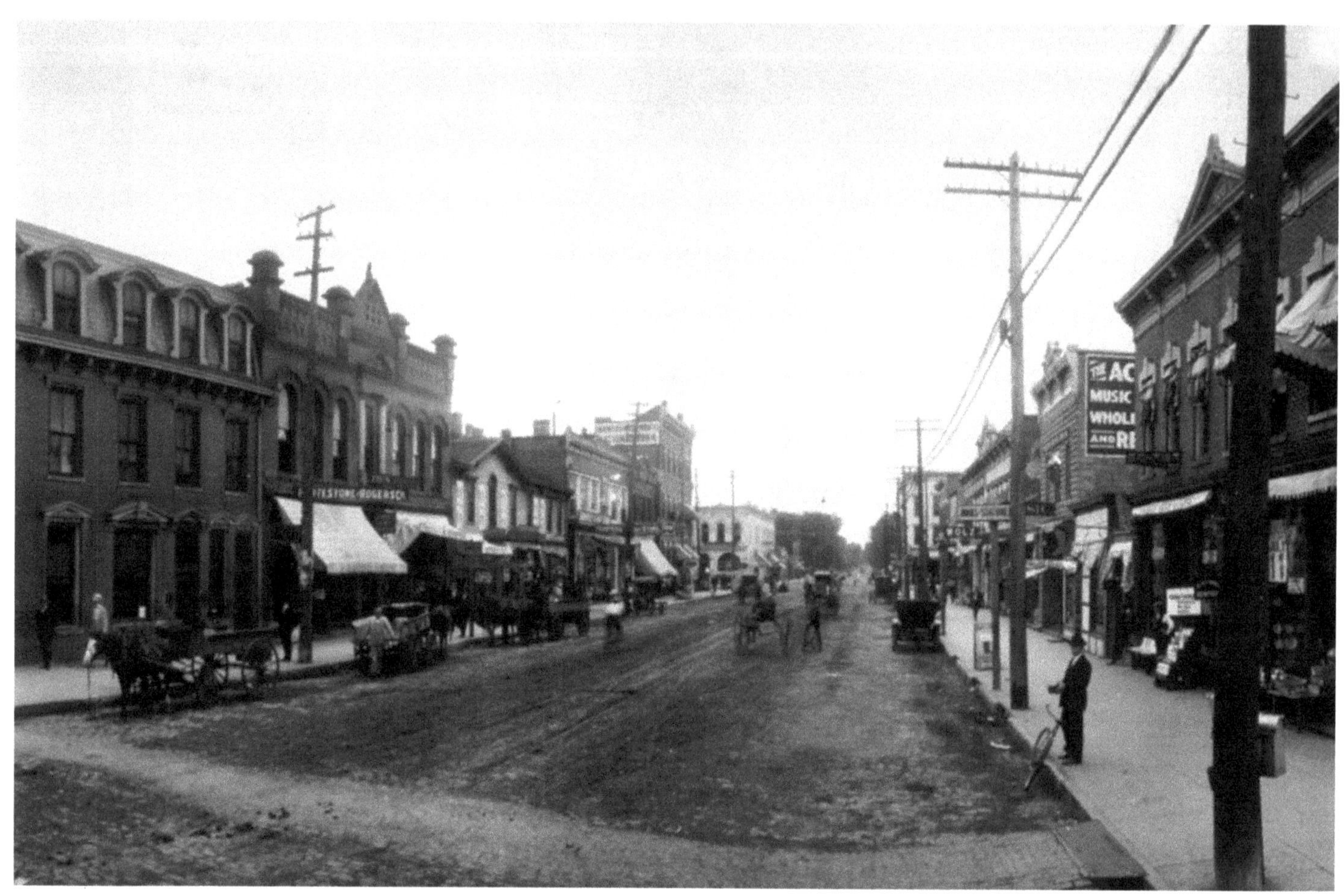

Fremont, the county seat of Dodge County, was founded in 1856 and named after John C. Fremont, the explorer, politician, and future Civil War general who was the Republican presidential candidate that year. Here in 1908, the main street is cobblestoned, but horses are still very much in demand.

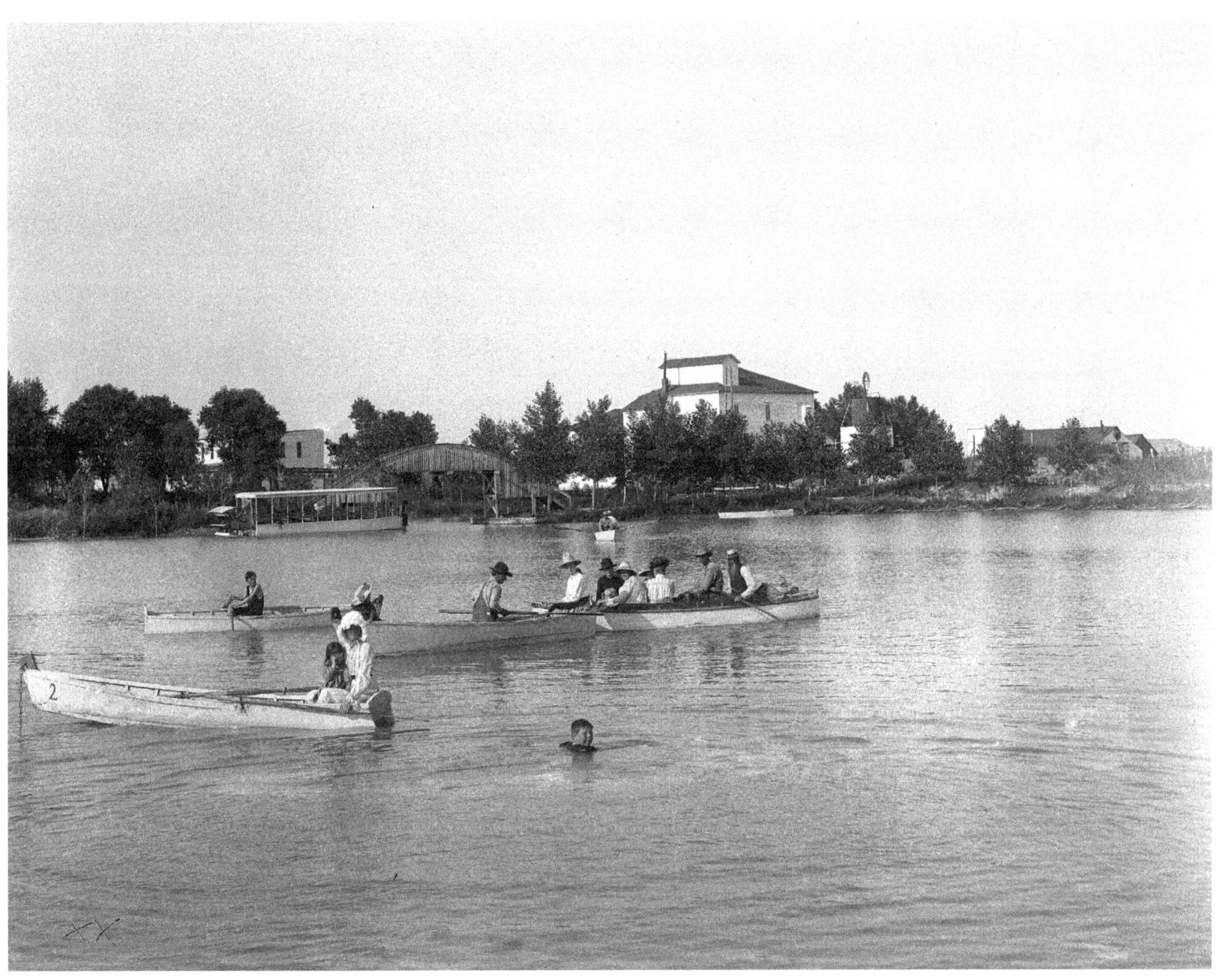

Boaters and swimmers enjoy a small reservoir on the Middle Loup River known as Lake Doris here in 1909. The lake was created by Rufus G. Carr, who began diverting water from the Middle Loup in the late 1880s for a flour mill. Lake Doris became a popular resort, and was known for its memorable Fourth of July fireworks displays before it became the site of a controversial—and short-lived—hydroelectric power plant.

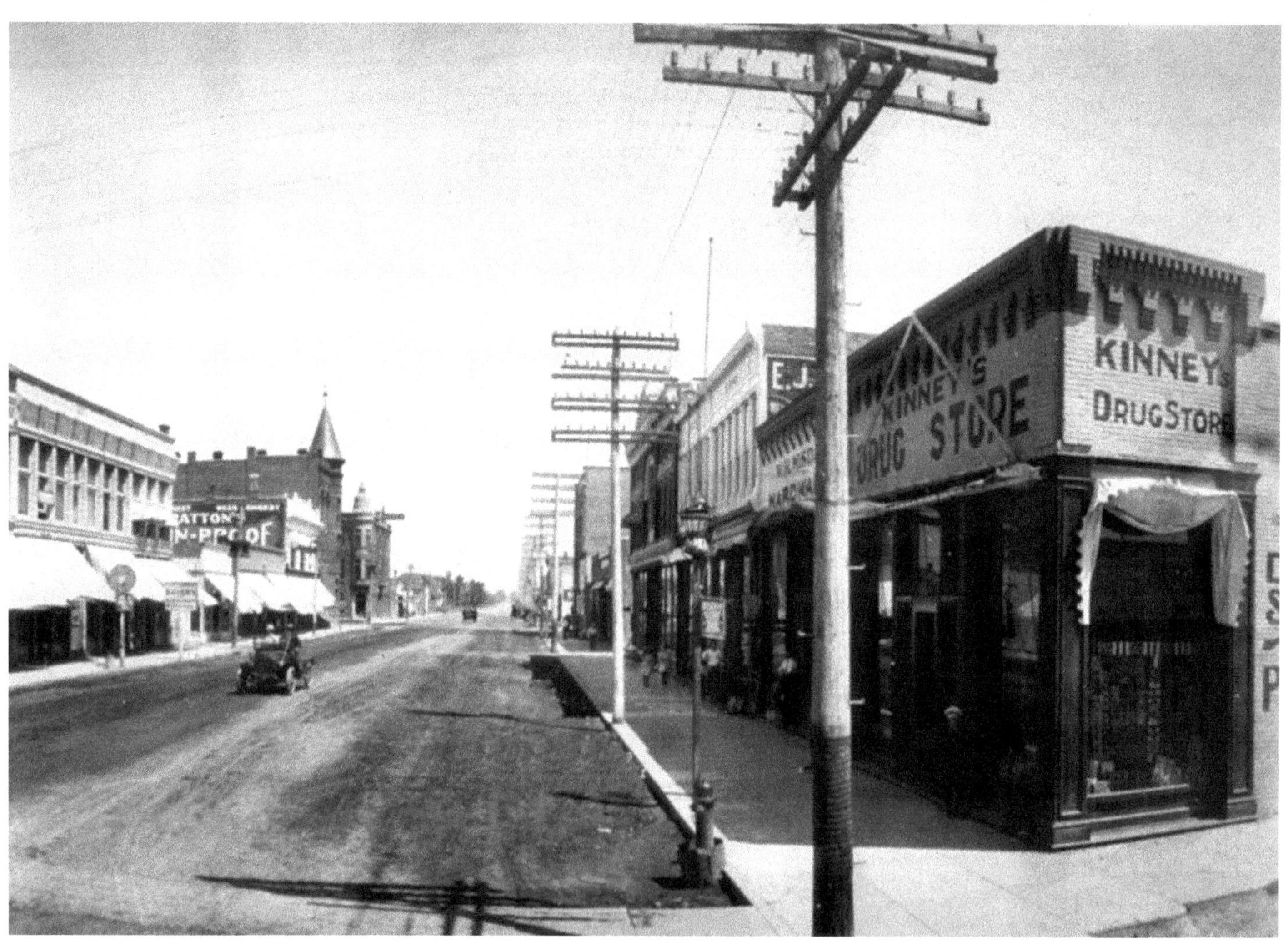

This 1909 Frederick Bandholtz image of Lexington reveals plenty of growth and development in the Dawson County seat when compared with the Solomon Butcher image already shown. An early automobile scurries up the street, scant evidence of the automobile age soon to explode across the nation.

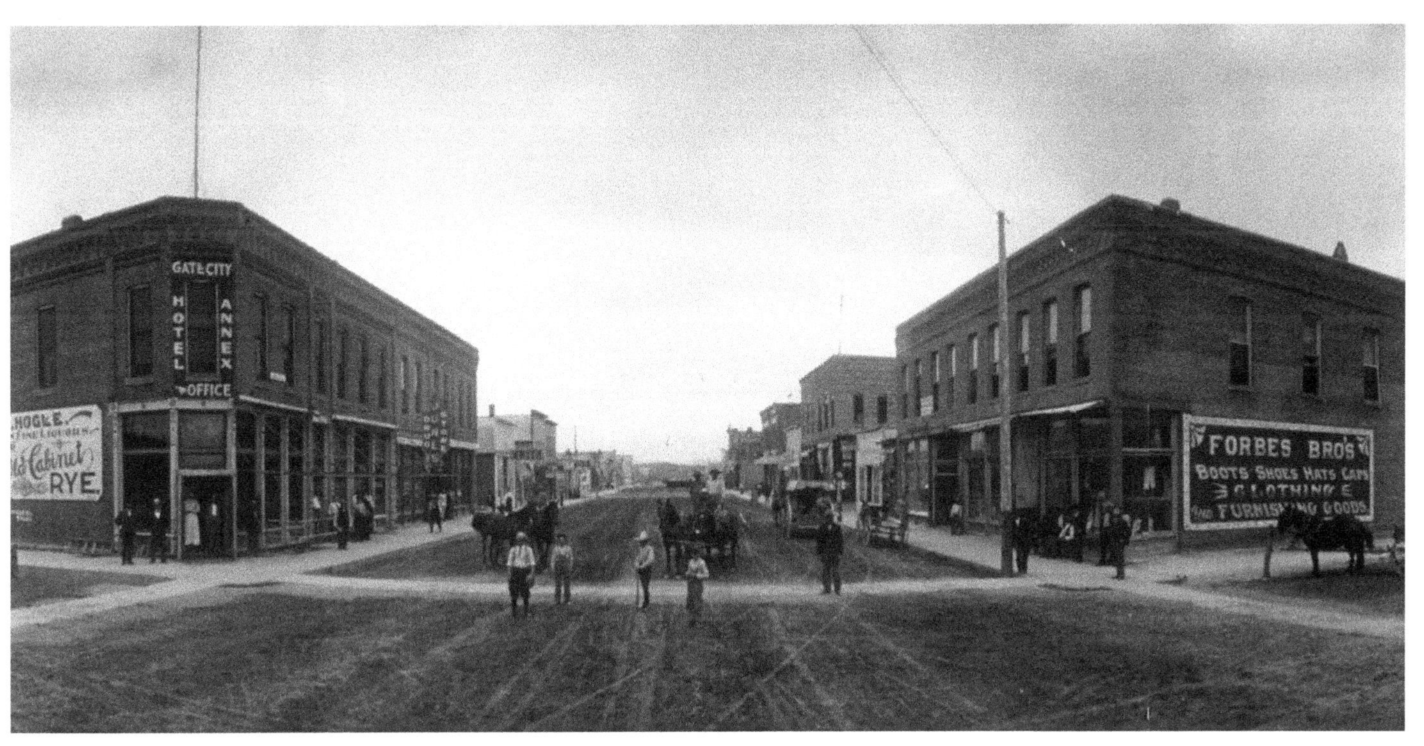

Pine Ridge rock formations lurk in the far distance and businesses like the Gate City Hotel and the Forbes Brothers clothing store are prominent in the foreground of 1909 Crawford.

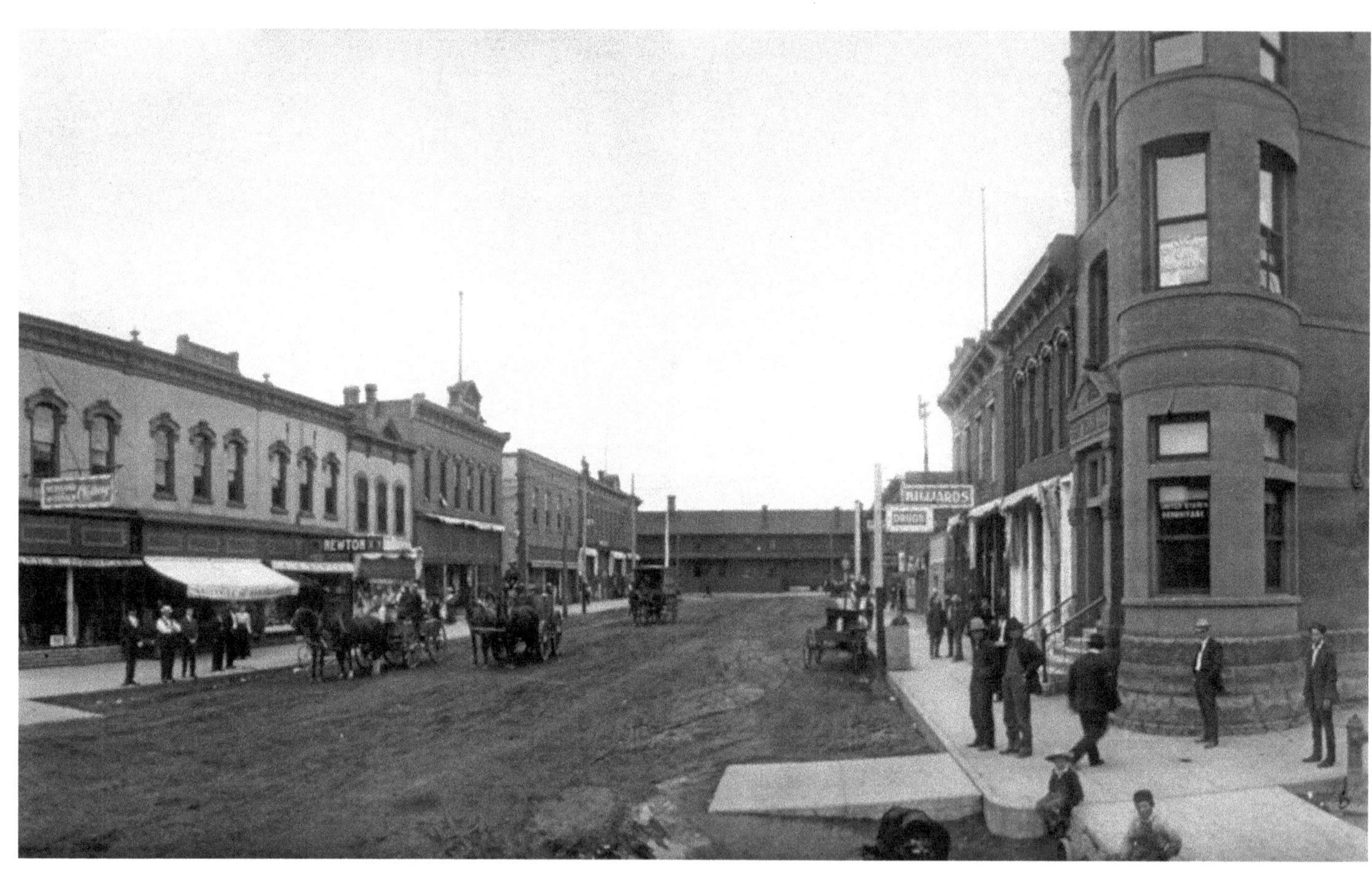

This is the corner of Sixth and Dewey streets in North Platte in 1909, after "Buffalo Bill" Cody had moved on to Cody, Wyoming, and during the period of North Platte's rapid growth as a railroad town. The Union Pacific's Bailey Yard at the west edge of town would become the world's largest classification yard for routing freight cars.

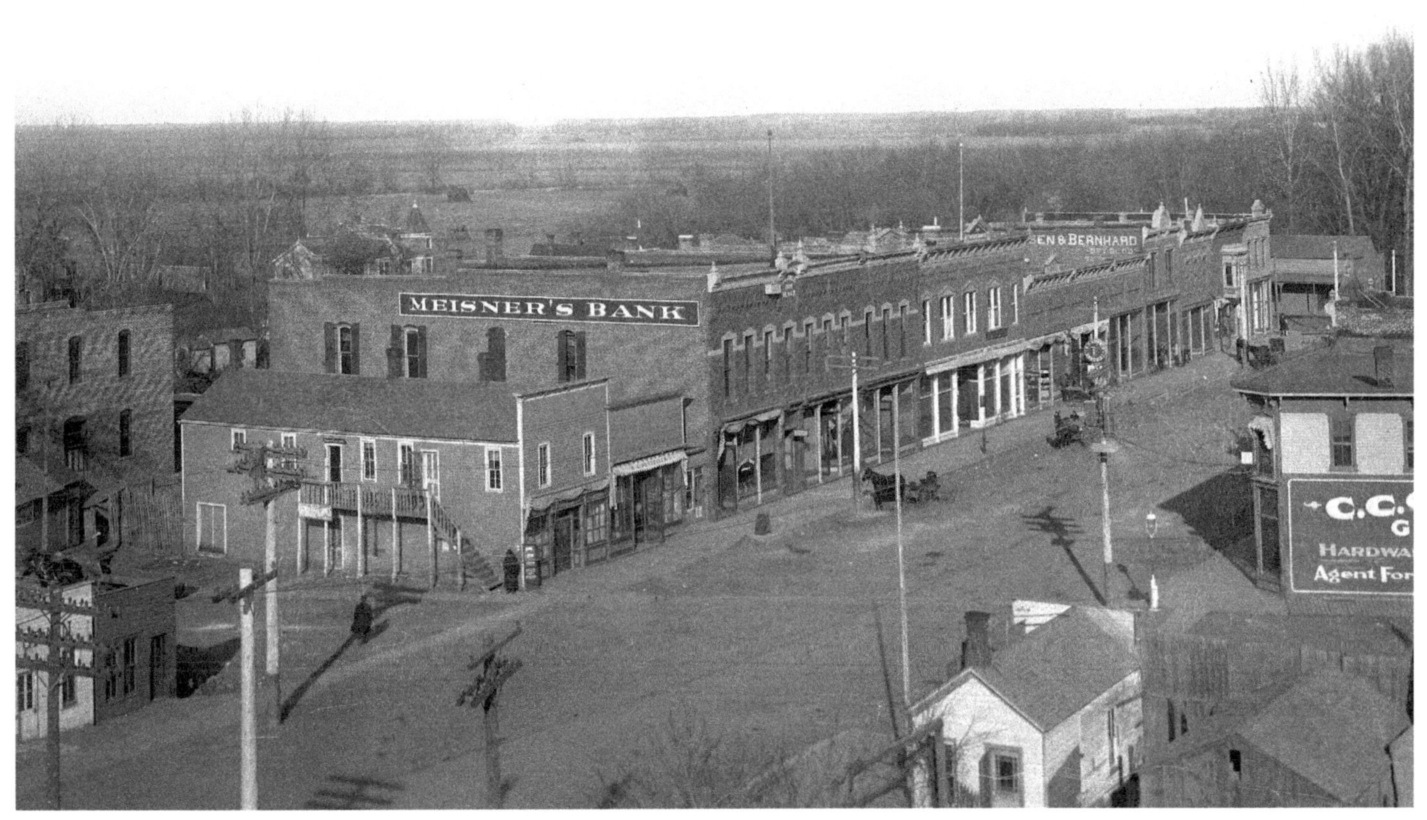

Meisner's Bank, the A. H. Morris Drug Store, and a dry goods store were some of the enterprises open for business along this street in Shelton in 1909.

Following Spread: The Eighth U.S. Cavalry lines up in formation at Fort Robinson on June 30, 1909. The fort was an important animal processing station for horses used in military combat, then served as a remounting center for transferring horses from the military to civilians. Fort Robinson would later serve as a Civilian Conservation Corps camp under the Franklin D. Roosevelt administration.

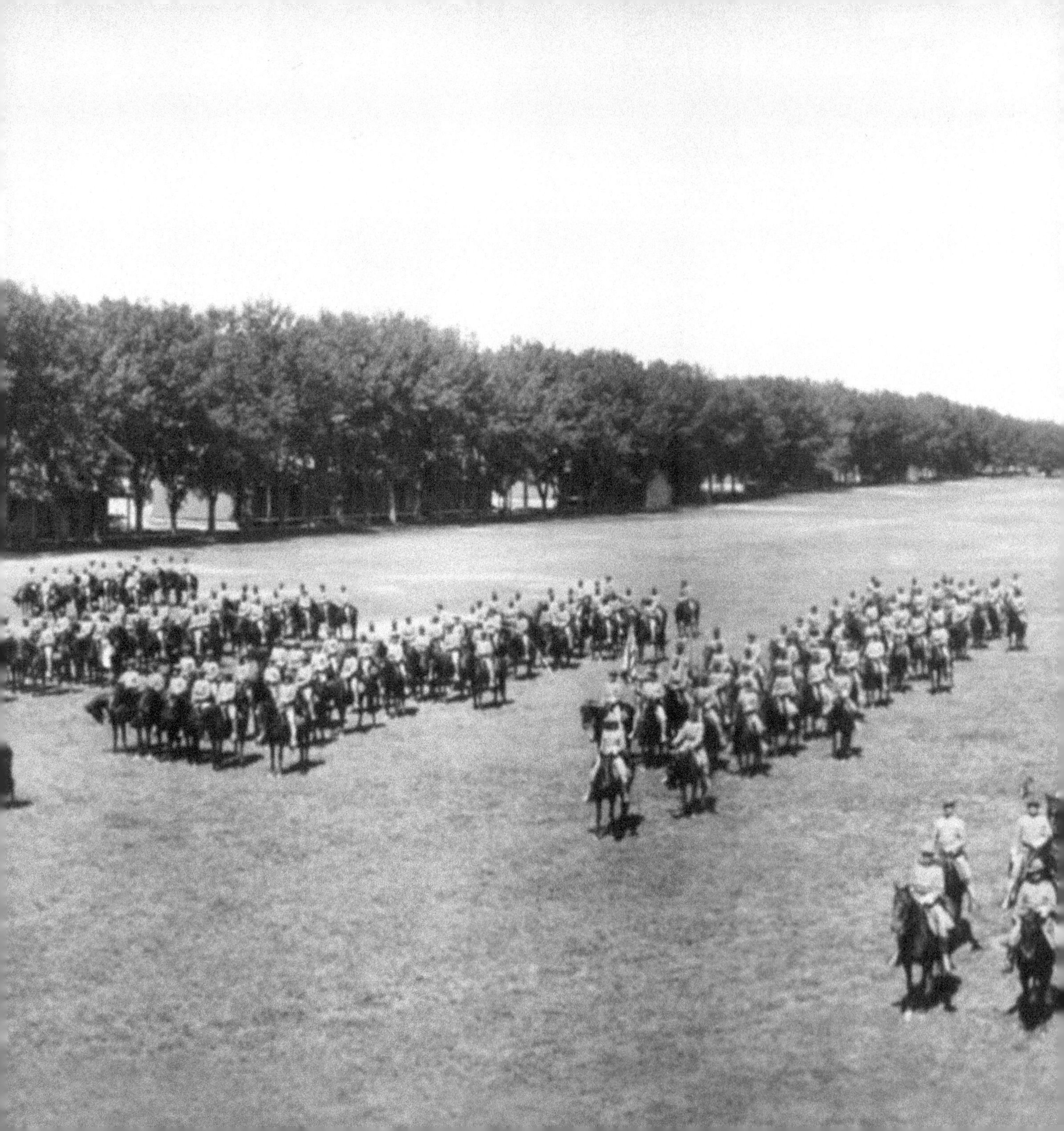

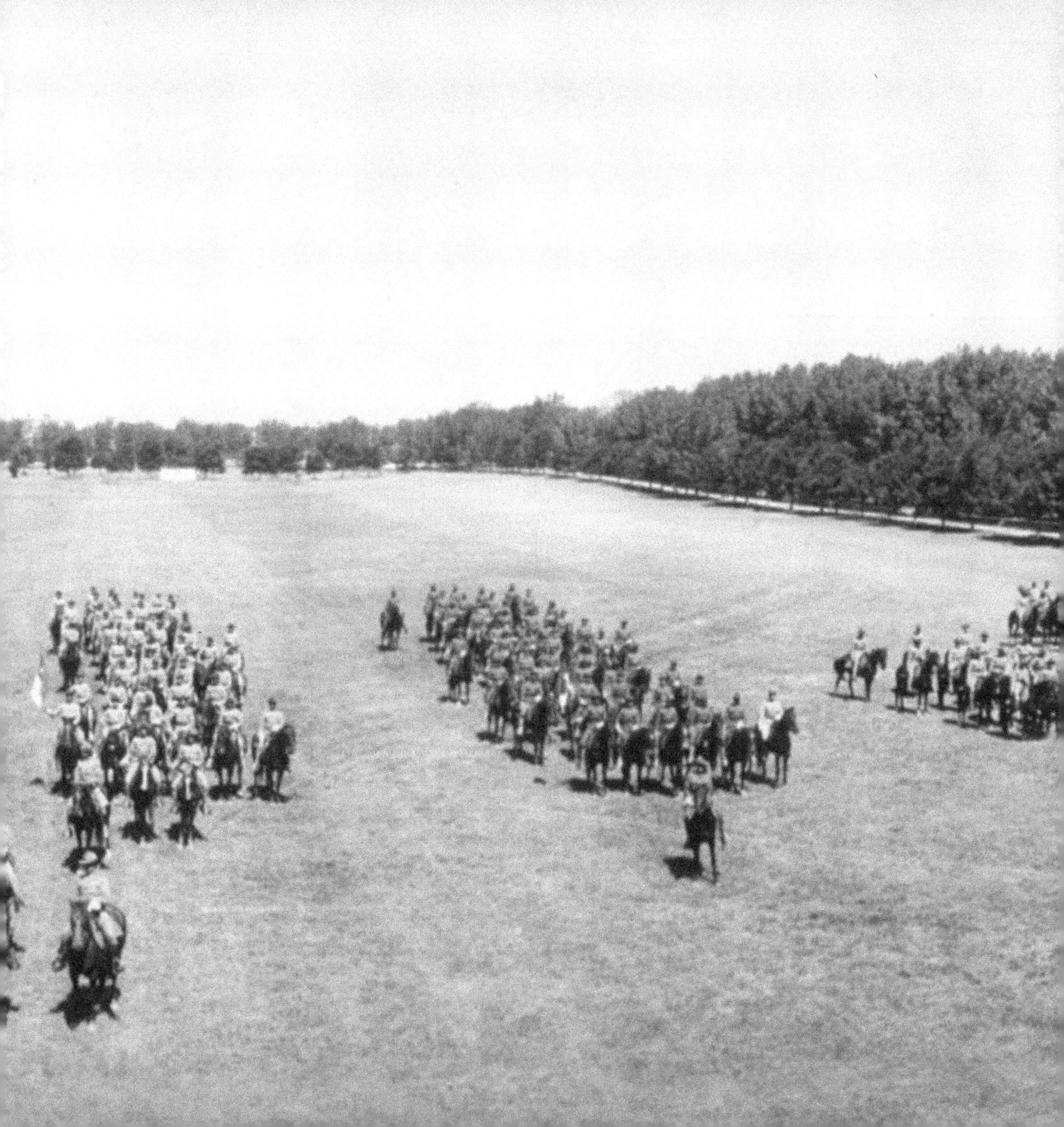

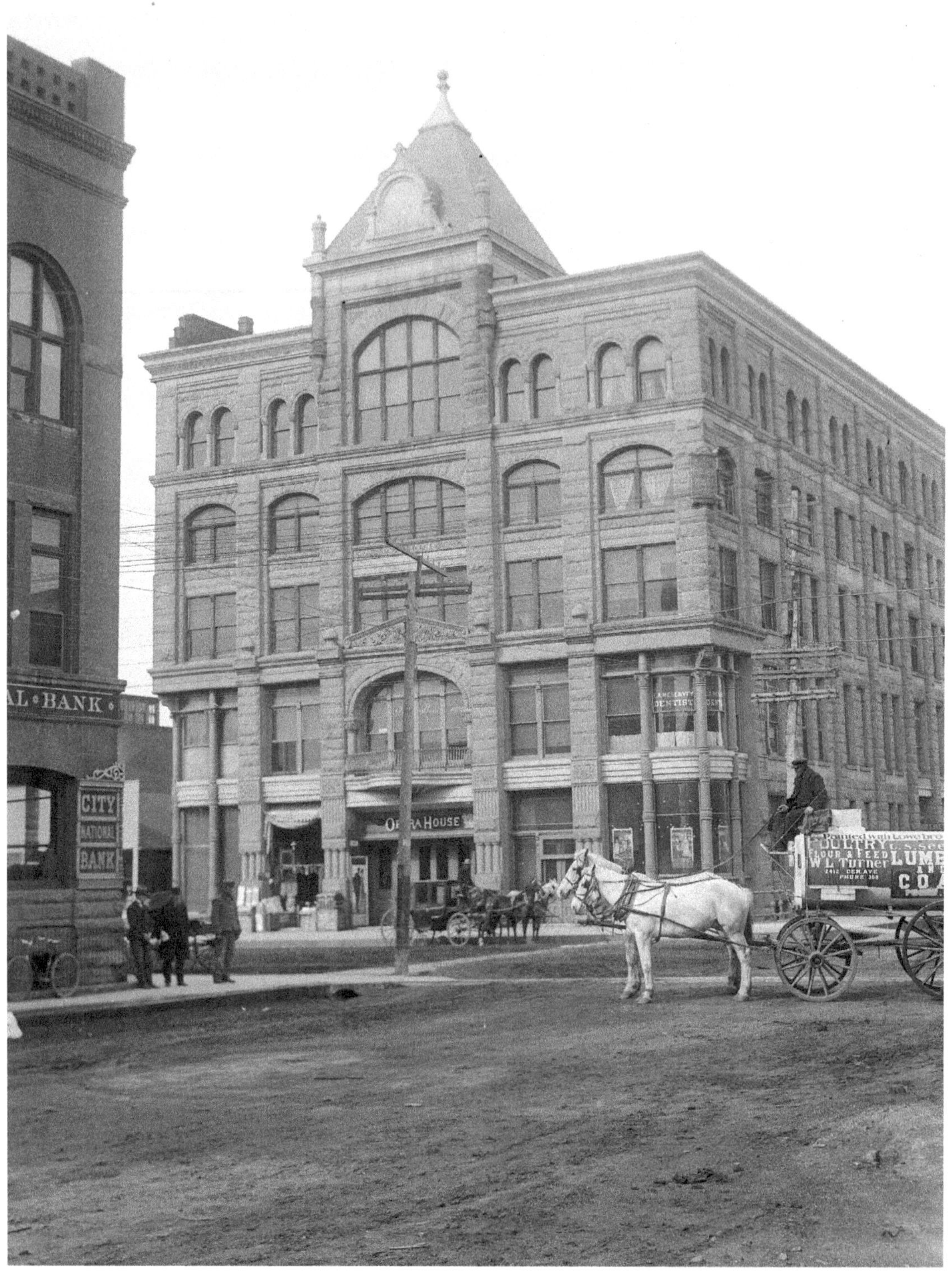

Kearney enjoyed an economic boom during the 1880s, and just before the crash of 1893, the city was able to build an opera house at the corner of 21st Street and Central Avenue for $140,000. Lavishly finished with marble tile, oak trim, and plush leather seats, the opera house was a community centerpiece until it closed in 1932. John Philip Sousa, George M. Cohan, Harry Houdini, and Carrie Nation were among those who appeared there.

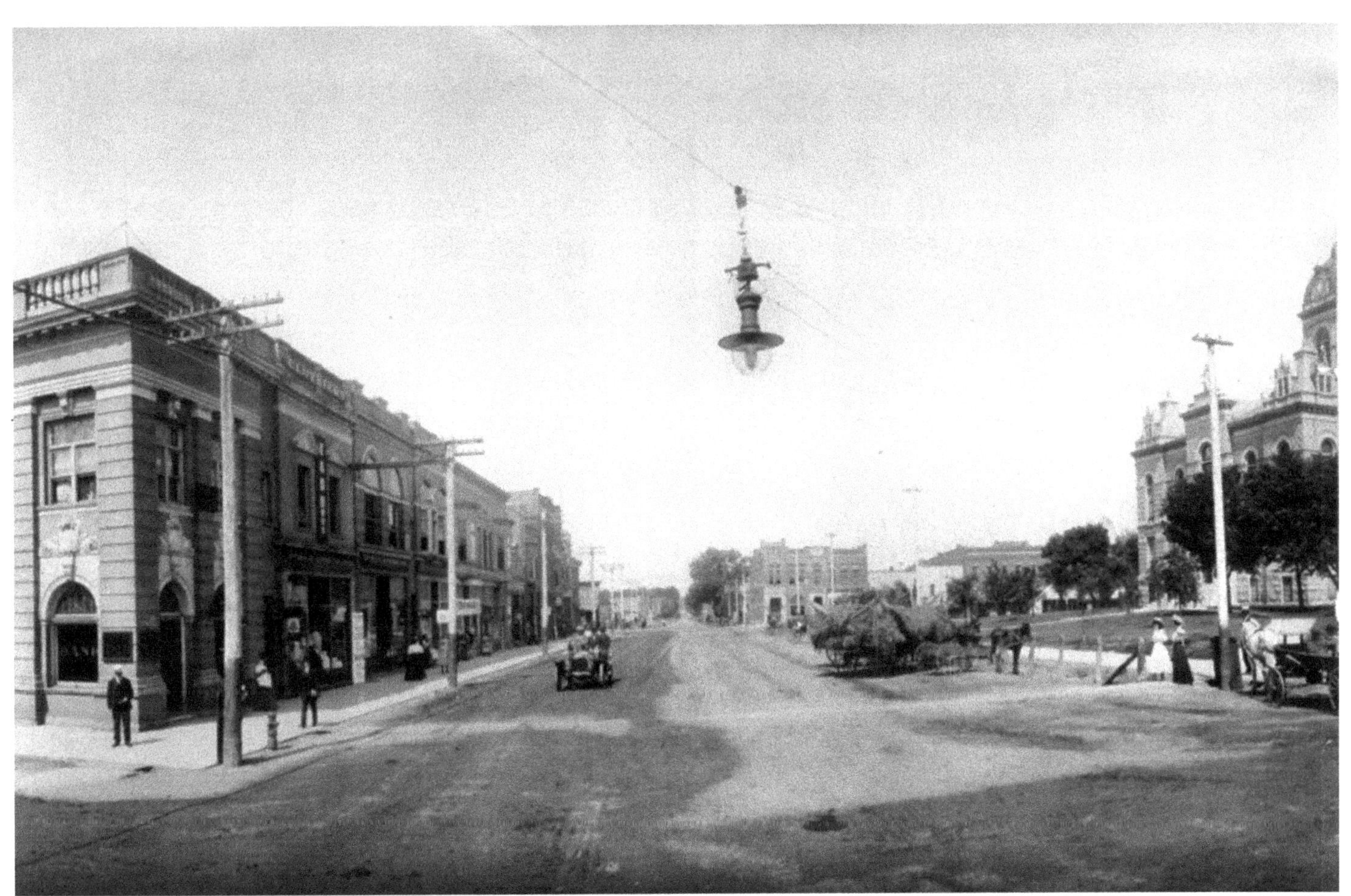

The Jefferson County Courthouse (at right) dominates Fairbury's 4th Street cityscape, where an automobile scoots within range of the camera to compete with the horses and carriages that typically filled the street. From 1885 to 1913, the Campbell Brothers Circus (second-largest in the world at one time) used Fairbury as its winter quarters. Despite its population of less than 5,000, Fairbury has preserved nearly 100 of its historic downtown buildings, including the Rock Island Railroad Depot, now open as a museum.

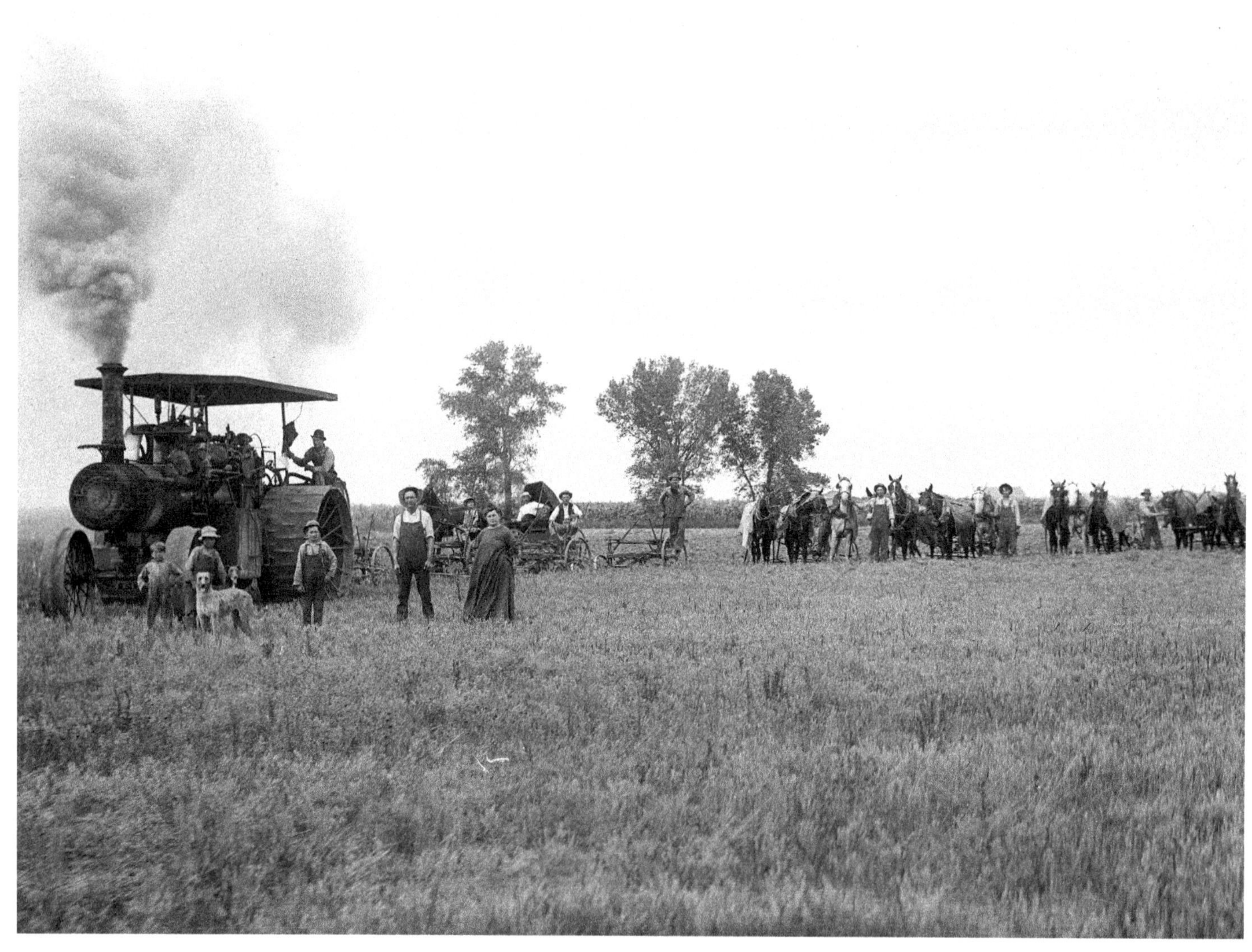

Ike Buck, his children and pregnant wife, and half the neighborhood lined up for this 1910 Solomon Butcher photograph on Buck's farm near Gibbon. Just who owned the large steam-powered tractor at left is not known, but the farmers were taking advantage of its pulling power. The machine tows a rigged five-gang plow.

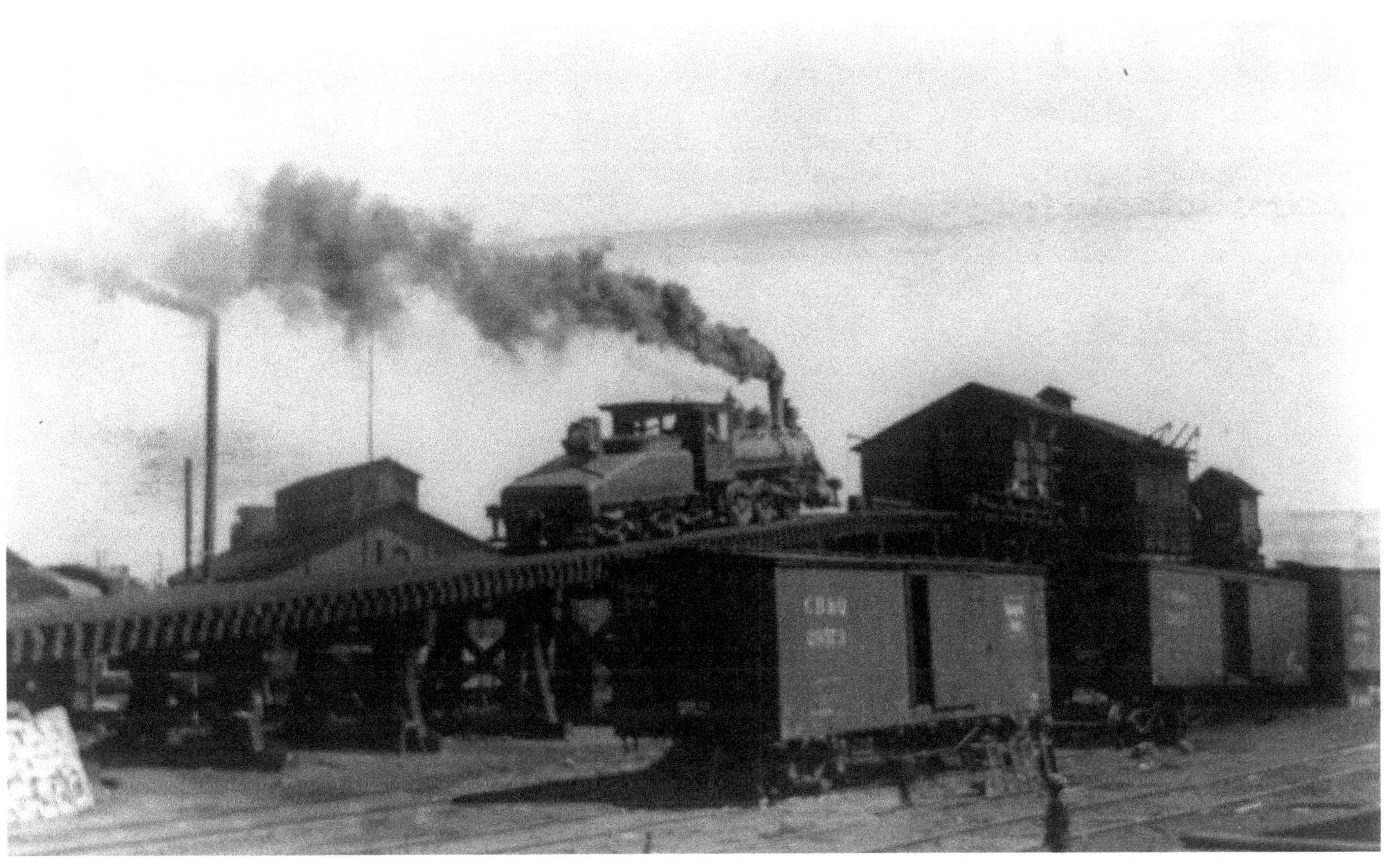

This 1910 image of a coal chute at Wymore is a reminder of the important role that coal-fired, steam-powered locomotives played in the railroad industry a century ago. Switch engines like the one climbing the trestle here were used in railroad yards to assemble freight cars into a train.

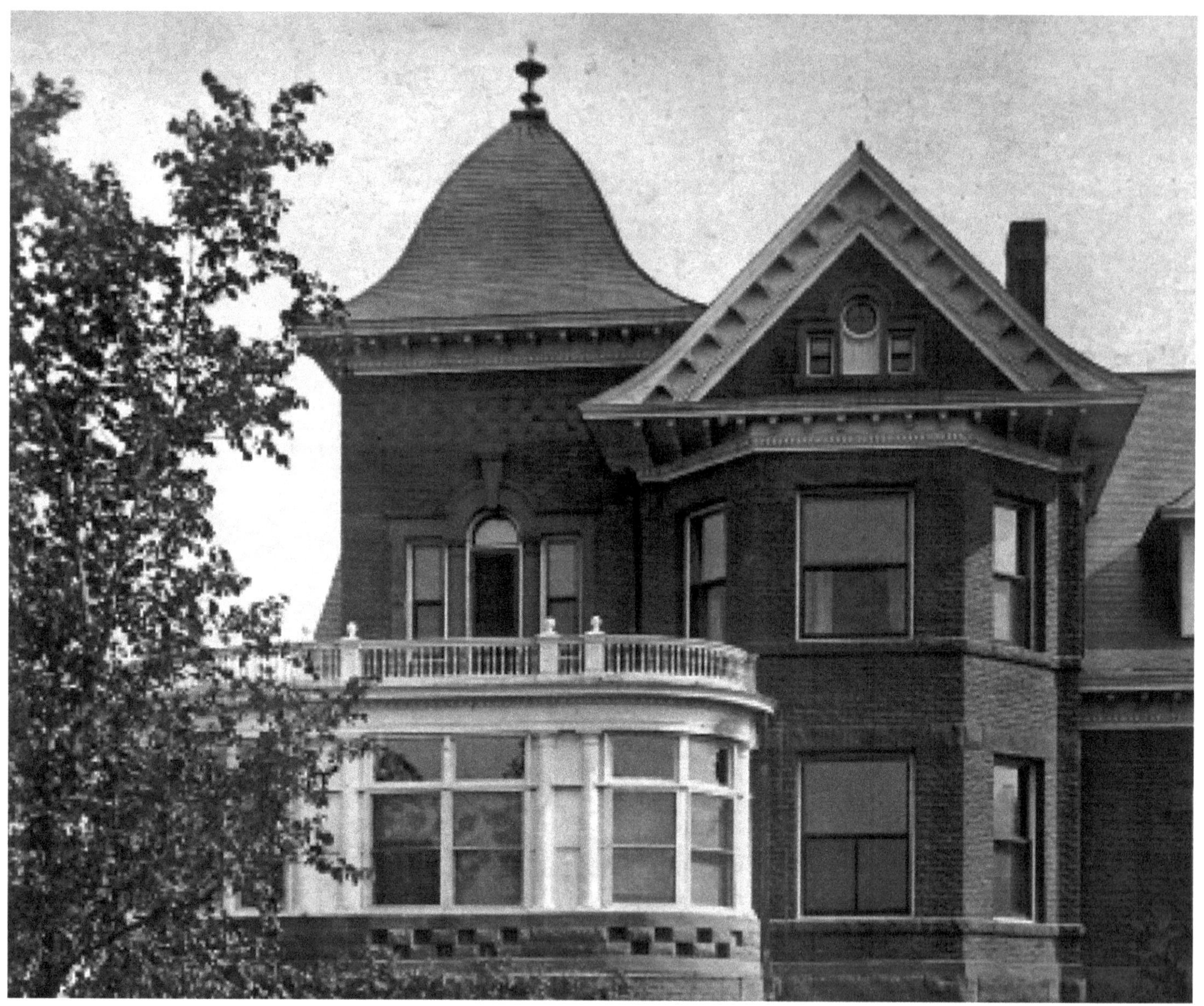

William Jennings Bryan's Fairview, his home at 4900 Sumner Street in Lincoln. Today the house contains the William Jennings Bryan Institute and the Bryan Museum. Although the "Great Commoner" lost presidential elections in 1896, 1900, and 1908, he is recognized as one of America's all-time most gifted political orators.

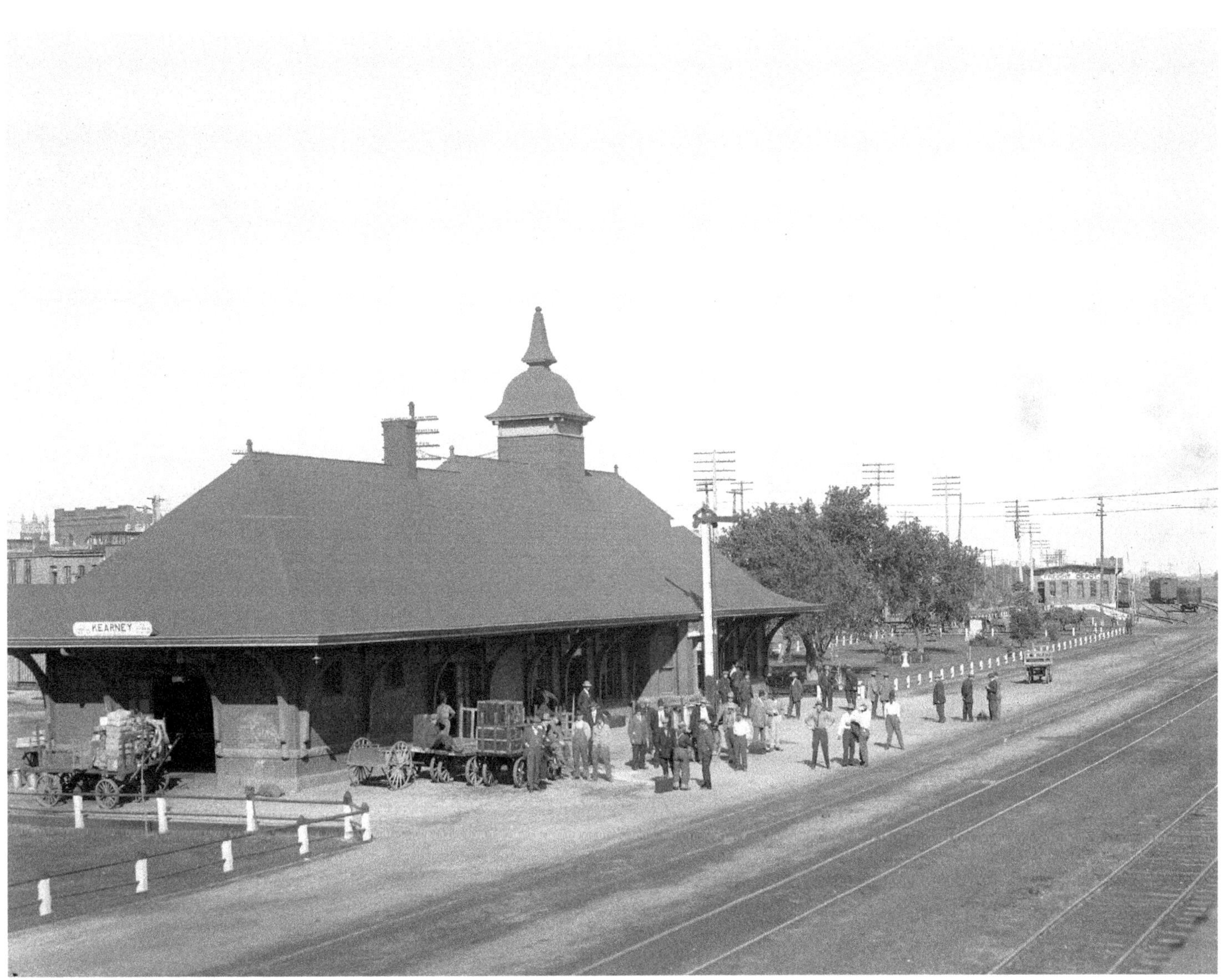

Baggage carts and a group of people milling about in front of the Union Pacific depot is a sure sign that another train was about to pull into Kearney here in 1911.

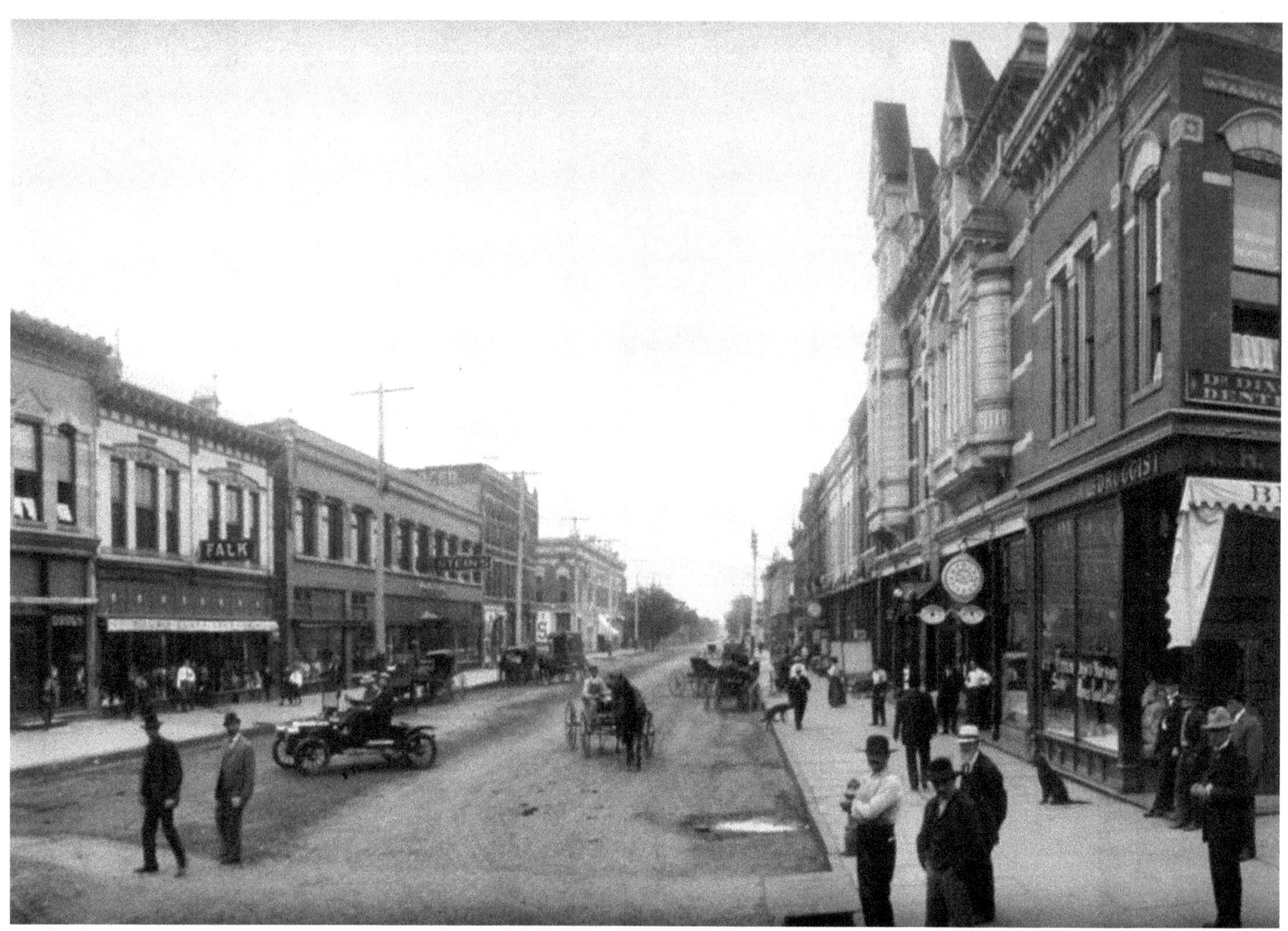

Incorporated in 1874, Hastings became the county seat of Adams County. During World War II, the Naval Ammunition Depot in Hastings produced almost 40 percent of the Navy's ammunition supply. Shortly thereafter, Tom Osborne starred as a football player for Hastings High School and Hastings College before going on to make his mark as a College Football Hall of Fame coach. At the University of Nebraska, Coach Osborne chalked up 255 wins and three national championships.

Practical Nebraska

(1912–1937)

Nebraskans are a frugal bunch and looking for bargains is a way of life. So when Senator George Norris proposed a one-house state legislature to save money and political maneuvering, Nebraskans approved it in 1934 as an amendment to their state constitution. The model had never been tried anywhere else in the nation. In 1936, Norris delivered something else dear to the hearts of his constituents—the Rural Electrification Act. It authorized the federal government to make low-interest loans to nonprofit farm cooperatives, which used the money to build electrical infrastructure. The act raised the standard of living in rural areas nationwide. Over the next decade, farmers began to acquire running water, clothes-washing machines, refrigeration, and even a radio in the living room. Some thought it was extravagant, but gramps and grandma soon decided they didn't miss running out to the privy in the middle of the night.

Two men who became friends at the University of Nebraska in the early 1890s went on to achieve fame in World War I. General John J. Pershing, a former military instructor at the university, led the American Expeditionary Force in Europe and became the only man ever to earn the Army's highest rank during his lifetime. Charles Dawes was a brigadier general under Pershing before serving as U.S. budget director, and then vice-president.

Omaha became increasingly multiracial, largely because of the employment opportunities at meat-packing plants that moved into the Union Stockyards. Blacks and Eastern Europeans settled various large districts of the city. Willa Cather, Mari Sandoz, and John Neihardt wrote about their Nebraska roots—mainly concentrating on rural themes. Many of their books and poems surprised readers because they were sympathetic to American Indians, and some became classics.

Severe weather, always a threat in Nebraska, struck with a vengeance. The Easter Sunday 1913 tornadoes killed more than 150 people in and around Omaha, which nearly a century later is still the highest number of storm fatalities in state history.

In the aftermath of World War I, the taxpayers of Nebraska embarked on their most symbolic and beautiful building project ever, demolishing their poorly constructed second capitol and raising a towering stone monument to the state's heritage. Being thrifty folk, they built it over a span of 10 years, pay as you go, and completed it debt-free.

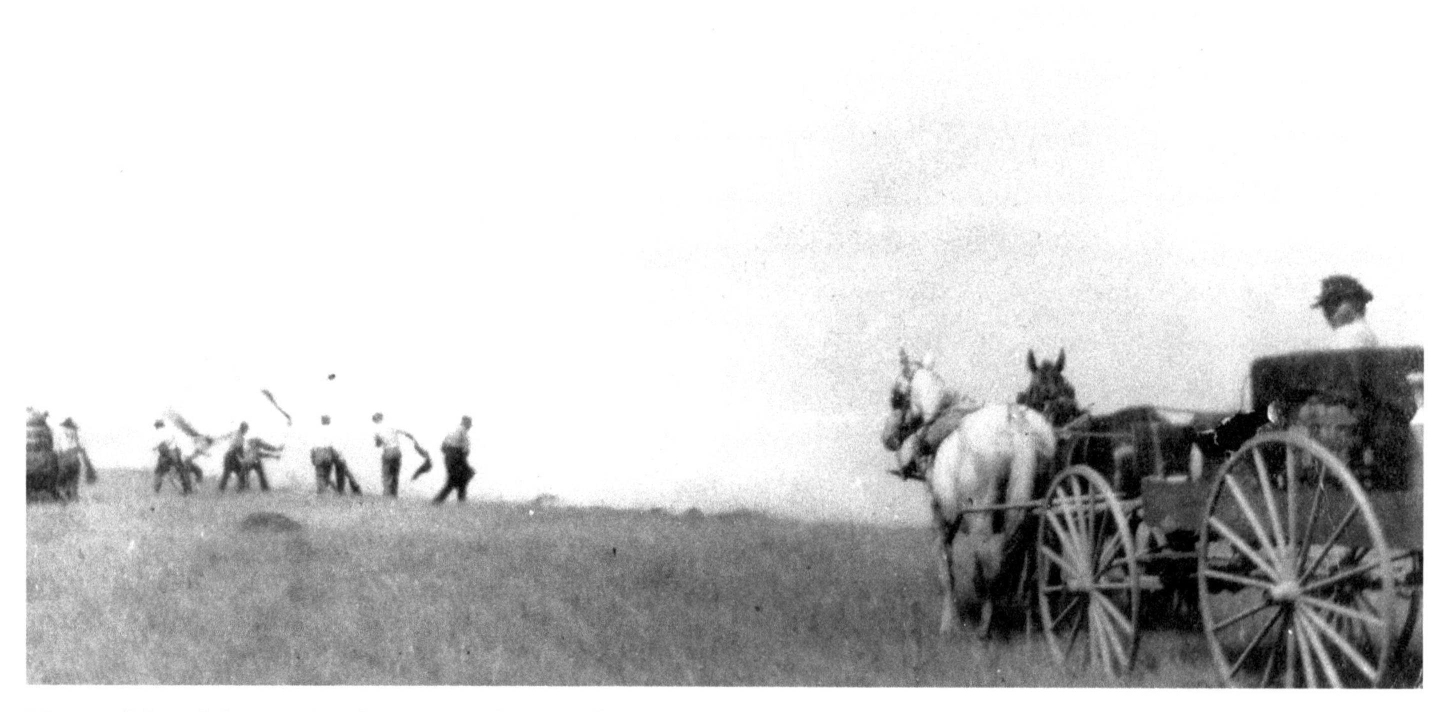

Men use flails and shirts to slow the progress of a prairie fire on June 30, 1911, while a woman waits in the foreground with a team and wagon. Gale-driven prairie fires once ravaged the grassy plains of Nebraska, threatening the lives and livelihood of settlers, and can still pose a hazard today

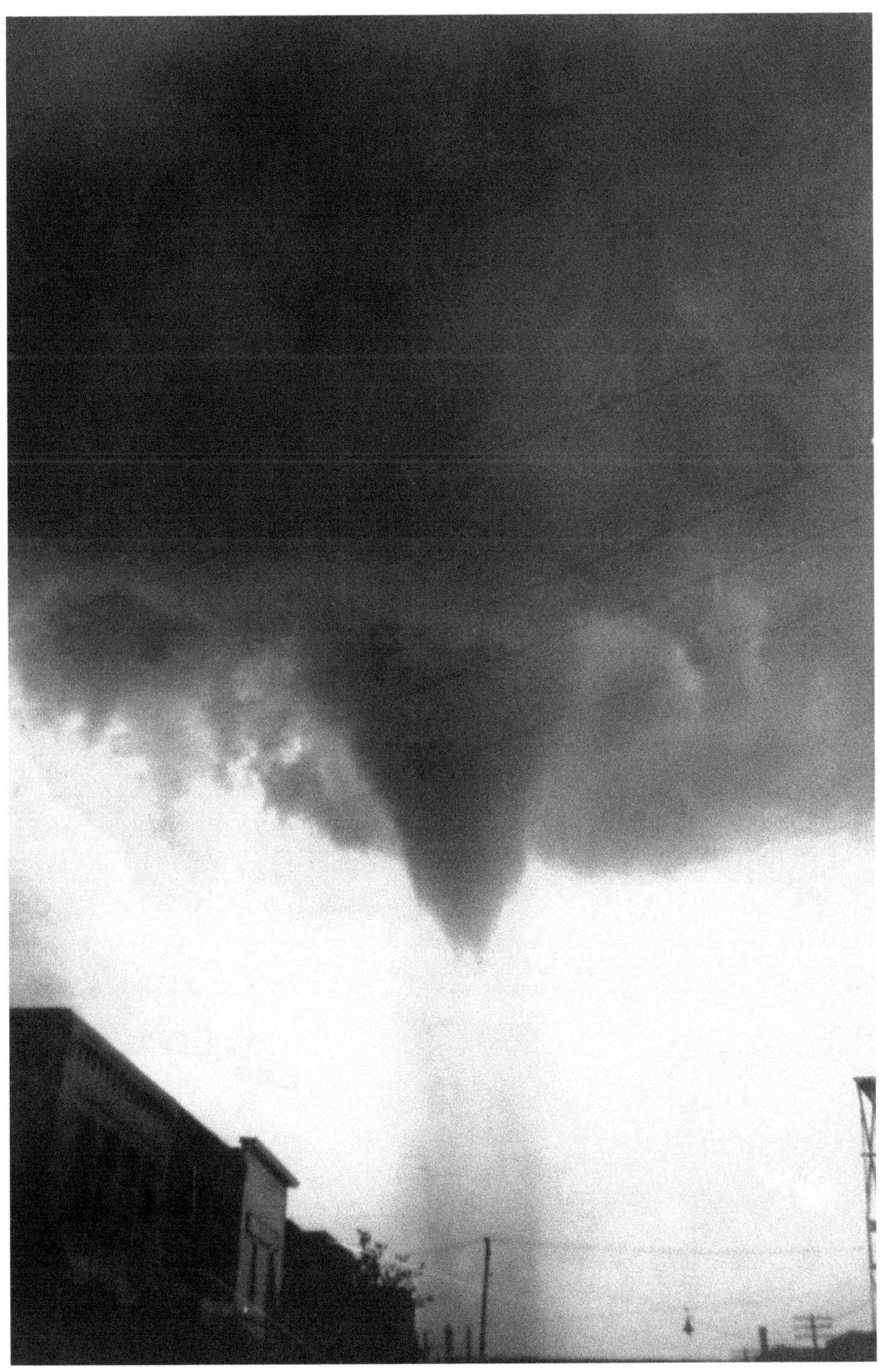

Located squarely in Tornado Alley, Nebraska typically experiences several dozen twisters every summer, although few of them do significant damage. This tornado approaches Alliance on August 4, 1911, caught on film by photographer Harvey Myers.

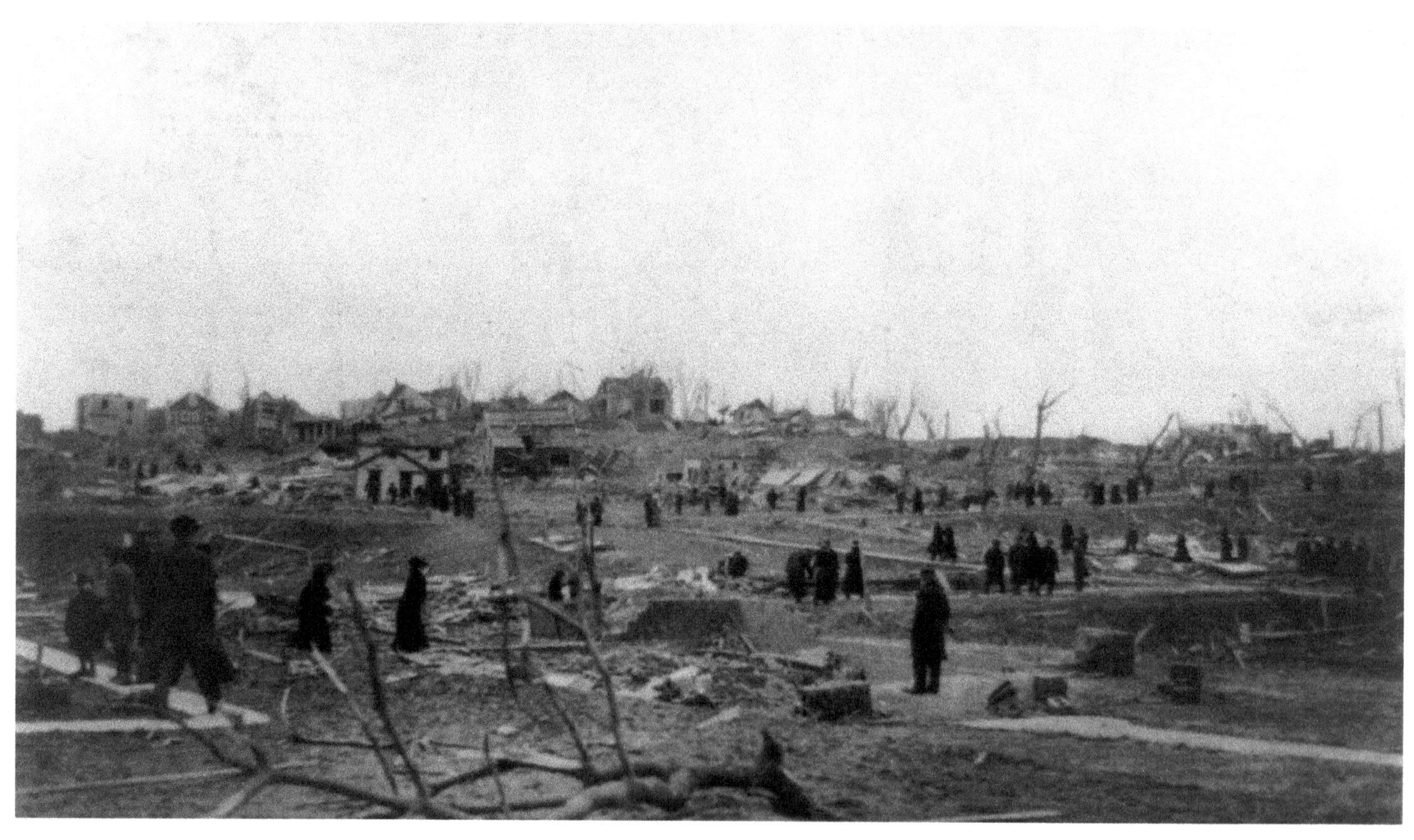

On Easter Sunday, March 23, 1913, a series of tornadoes struck Omaha and surrounding towns with catastrophic effect. In Omaha, the tempest was five blocks wide, indicative of a mesocyclone. Nearly a century later, the storm still ranked as easily the deadliest in state history. There are various listings of fatalities, but all agree that more than 150 people were killed in Omaha and outlying areas. This is the scene at 30th and Hamilton streets on April 26, more than a month after the storm.

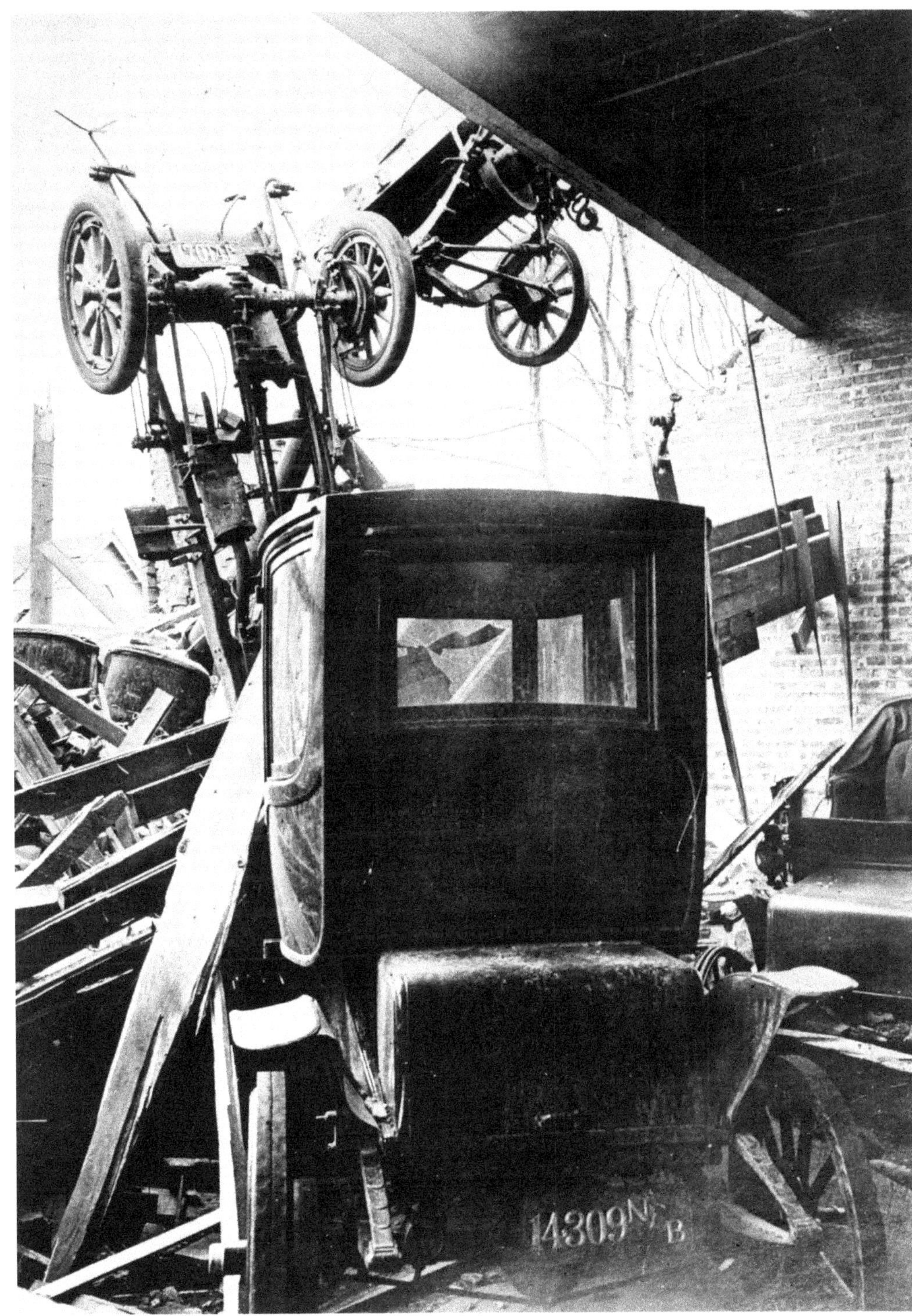

Property damage in the wake of the Easter 1913 tornado was profound and pervasive—not only in the Omaha region, but in a widespread area including Fremont, Yutan, Valley, Tekamah, Craig, Mead, and Plattsmouth, to the tune of at least $8.7 million. Making matters worse, a cold front swept through soon after and dumped snow on the region.

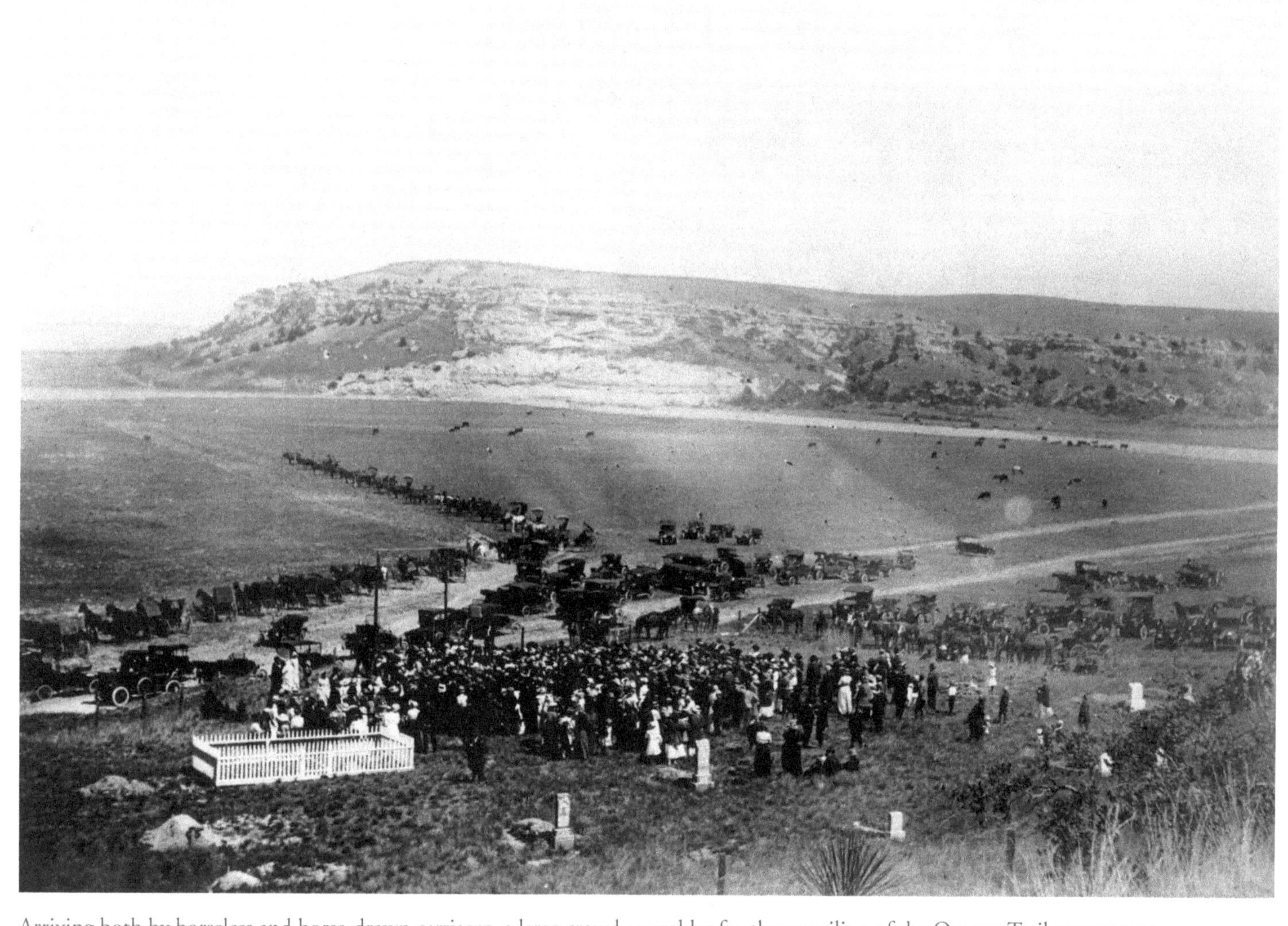

Arriving both by horseless and horse-drawn carriages, a large crowd assembles for the unveiling of the Oregon Trail monument in the Ash Hollow Cemetery near Lewellen. Many of these markers were erected by the State of Nebraska in 1912 and 1913. Although it required a risky descent of Windlass Hill, Ash Hollow held a fine freshwater spring which made it a desirable camping site for mid-nineteenth-century pioneers.

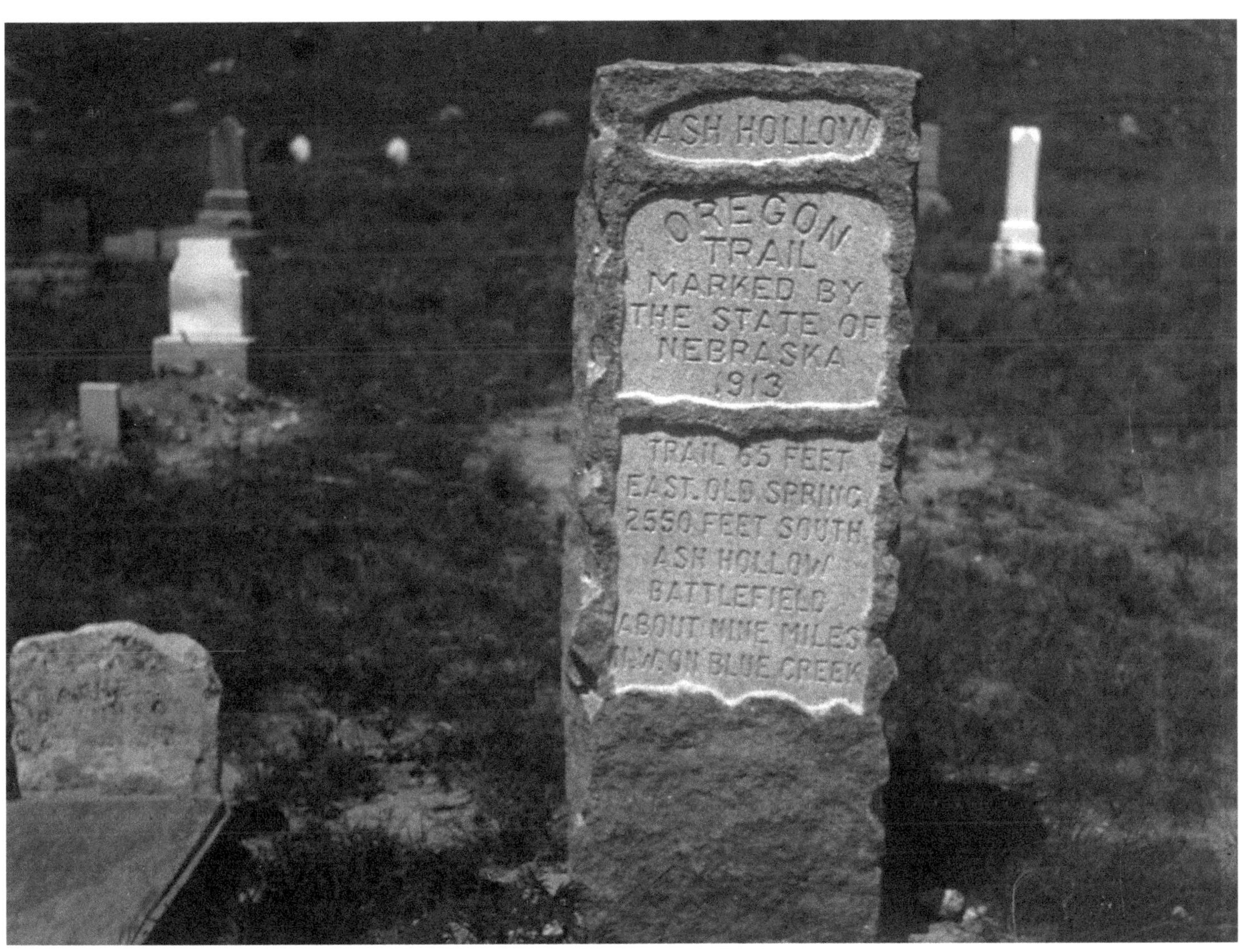

The marker at the Ash Hollow Cemetery is detailed here in 1916. Tourists regularly retrace the route of the Oregon Trail throughout the state in search of markers like this one.

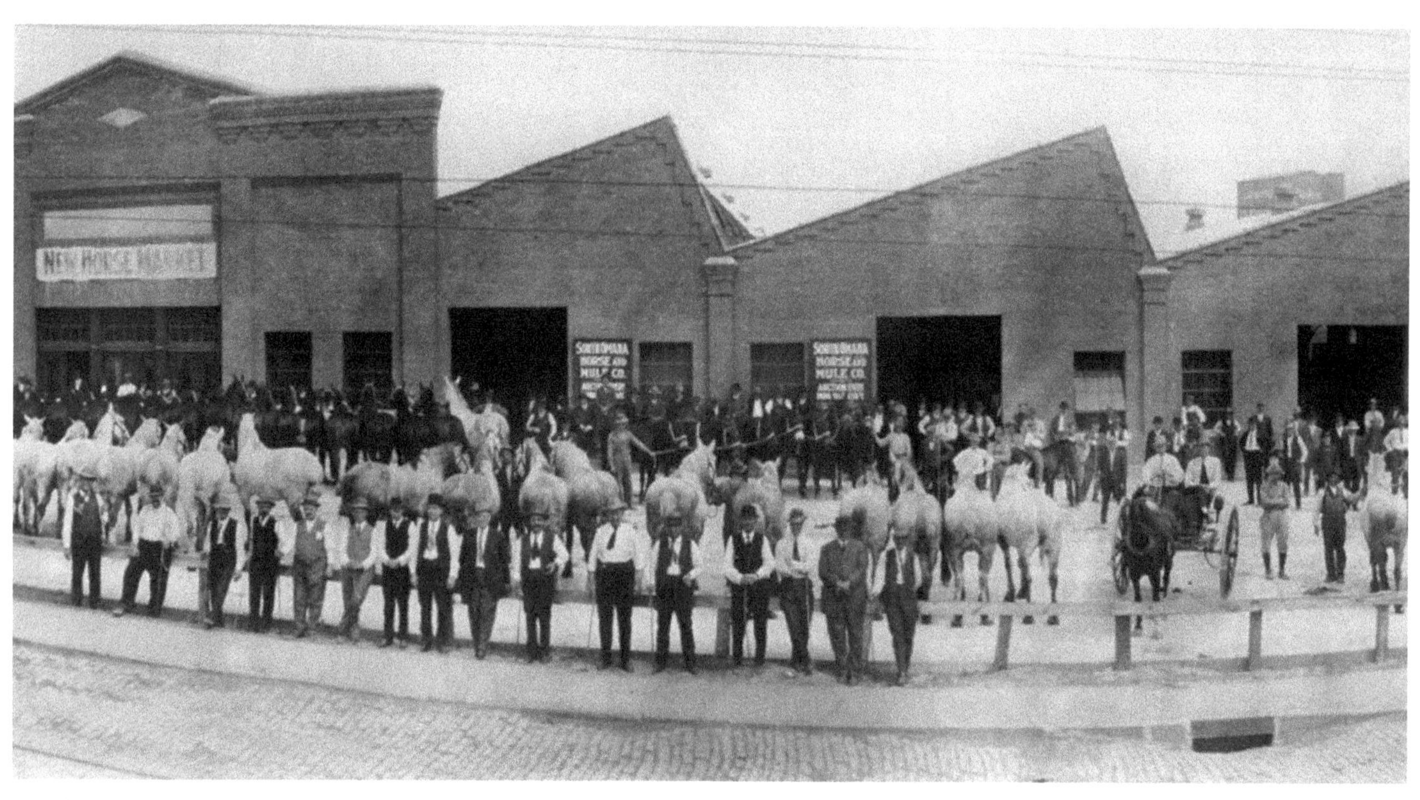

This 1914 photograph by the *Omaha Bee* (a regional newspaper based in Omaha from 1871 until it merged with the Omaha *Daily Herald* in the 1920s) shows the two-block horse and mule barn at the Union Stockyards, which at the time was the largest ranch horse market in the world.

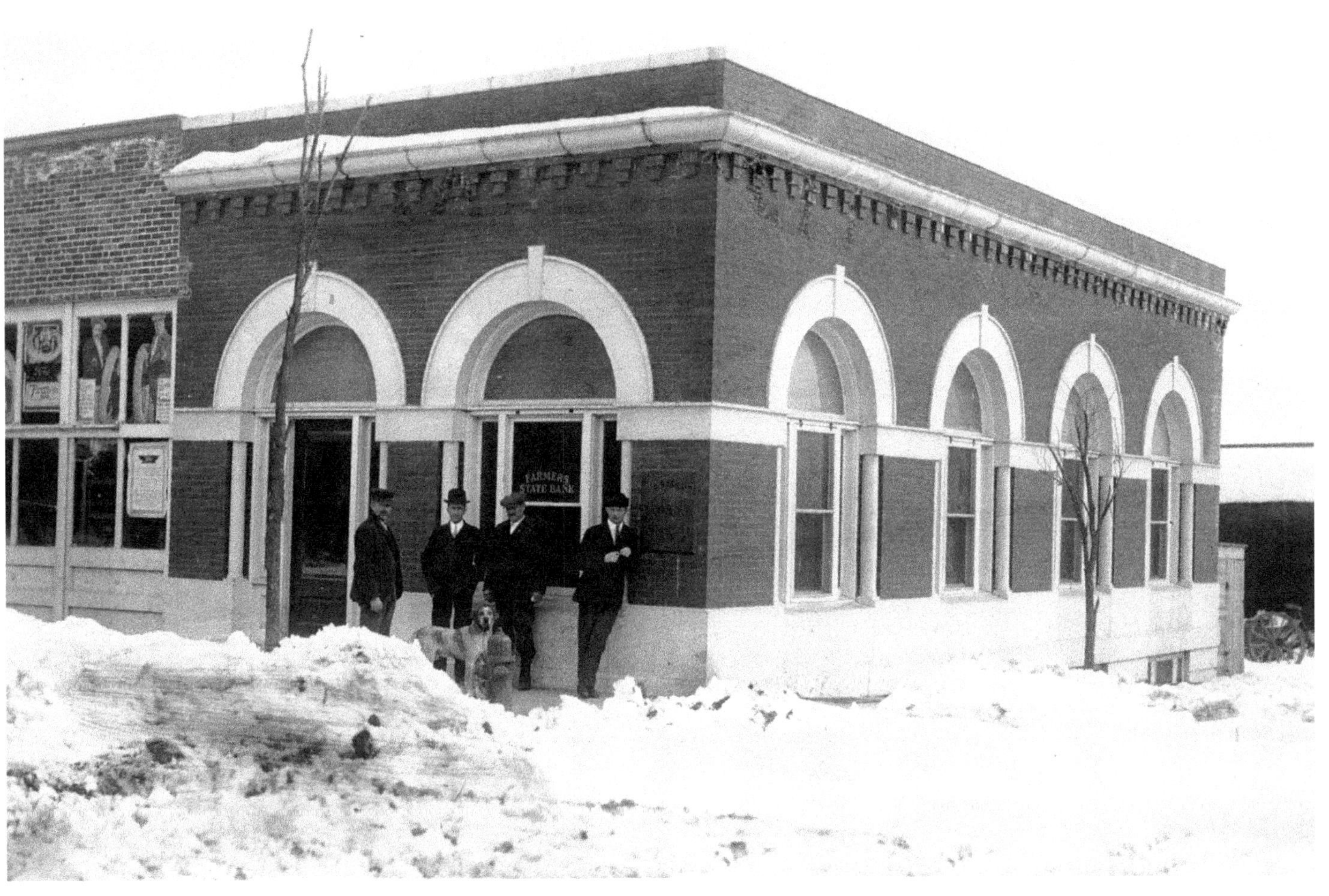

Four men and a dog stand in front of the Farmers State Bank of Talmage on a snowy March day in 1915. Next-door is a Ford automotive outlet. Talmage was founded in 1882 when the Missouri Pacific Railroad extended its route through the area.

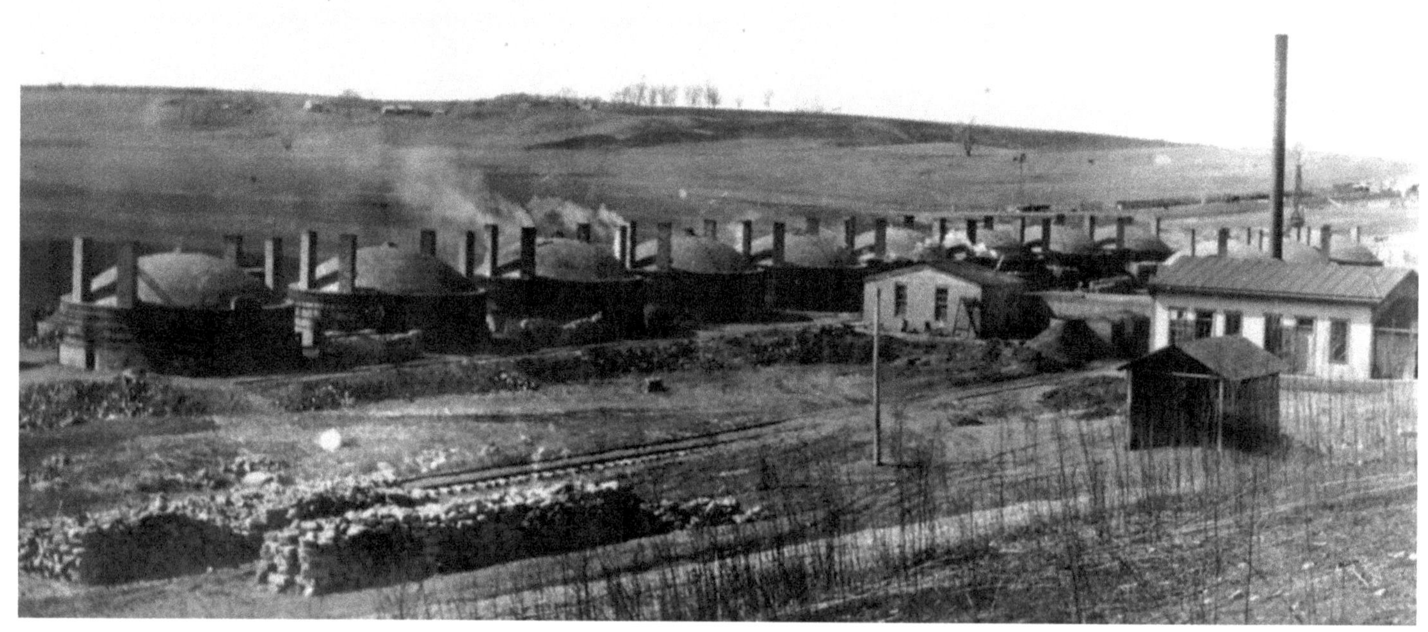

Nine round-top kilns belching smoke are evidence of an active brick-making operation under way in this photograph of the old brickyards at Humboldt, which was incorporated in 1875. Bricks fired here were used in many stations along various Burlington Northern Railroad lines.

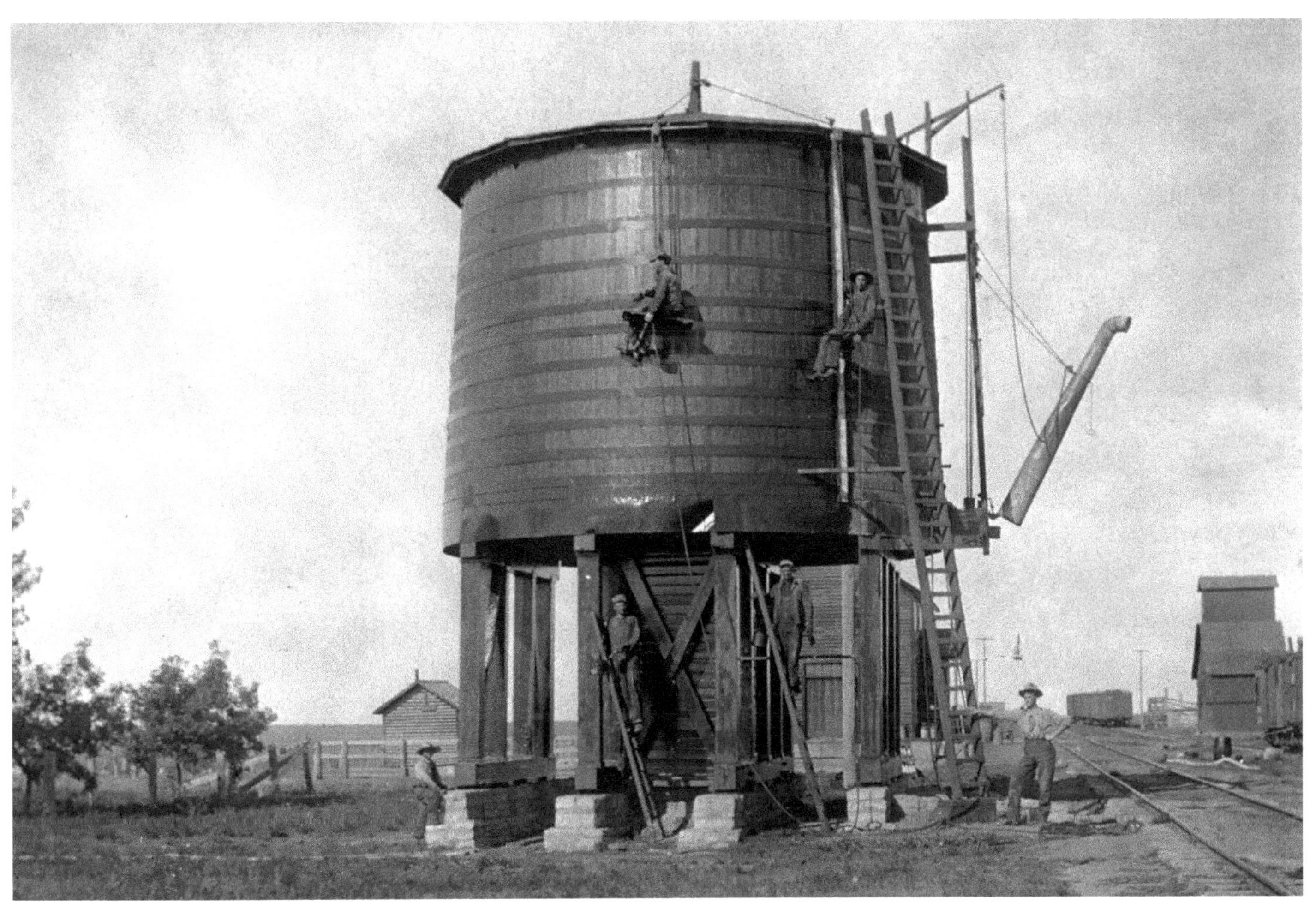

Steam locomotives required water to produce steam, and water towers like this one in Perkins County were once a common sight along the tracks. Originally part of Keith County, Perkins County was established in 1887, and three towns—Grant, Madrid, and Lisbon—vied for the financial benefits of being named county seat. After considerably more votes were cast in each of three elections than there were inhabitants of the county, a court ruling awarded Grant the victory. The village of Lisbon no longer exists.

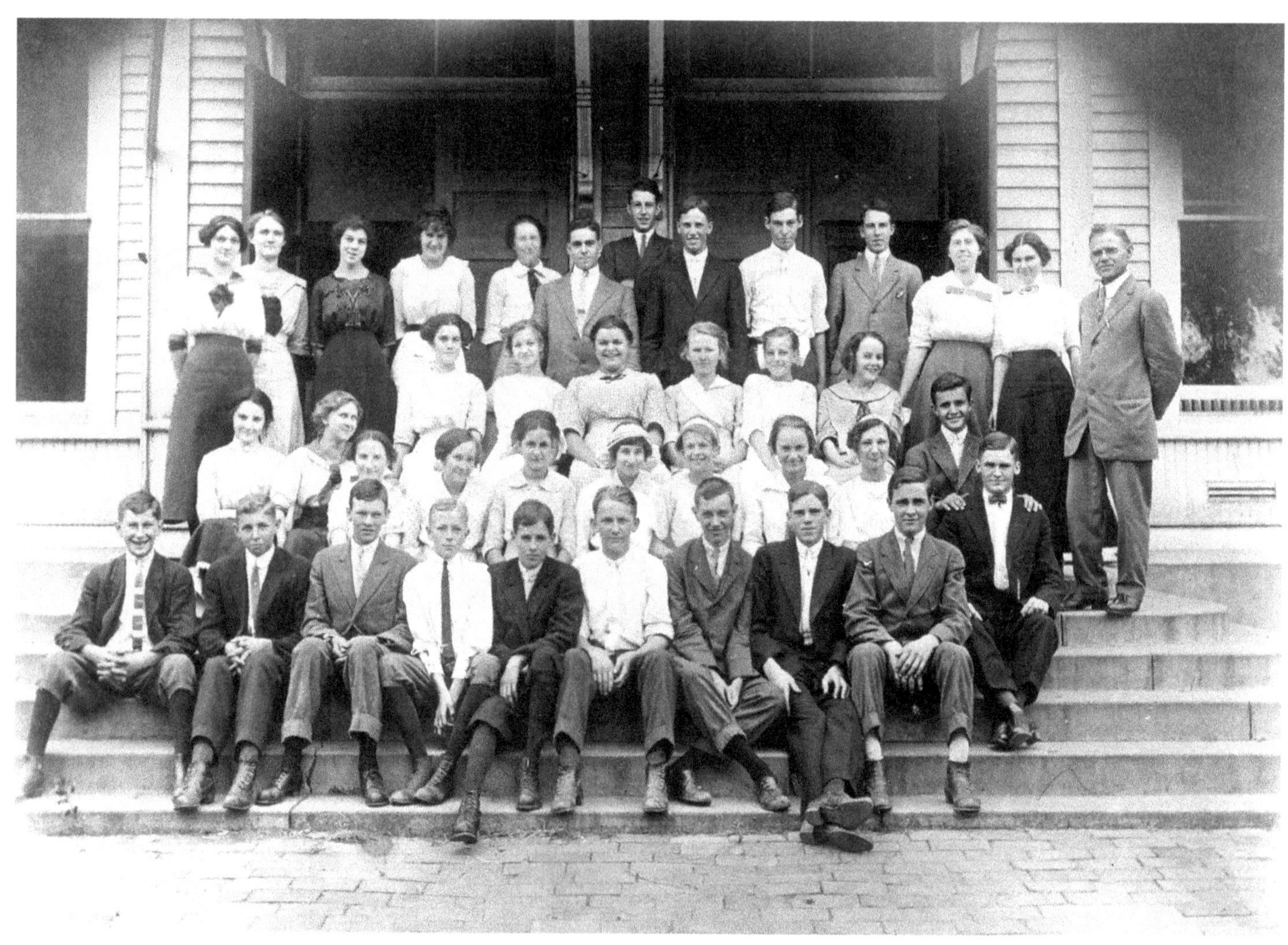

Students and faculty of Waterloo High School pose for a 1916 group shot on the front steps of the school. Located just west of Omaha, Waterloo for years was known as the world's largest producer of vine seed and seed corn.

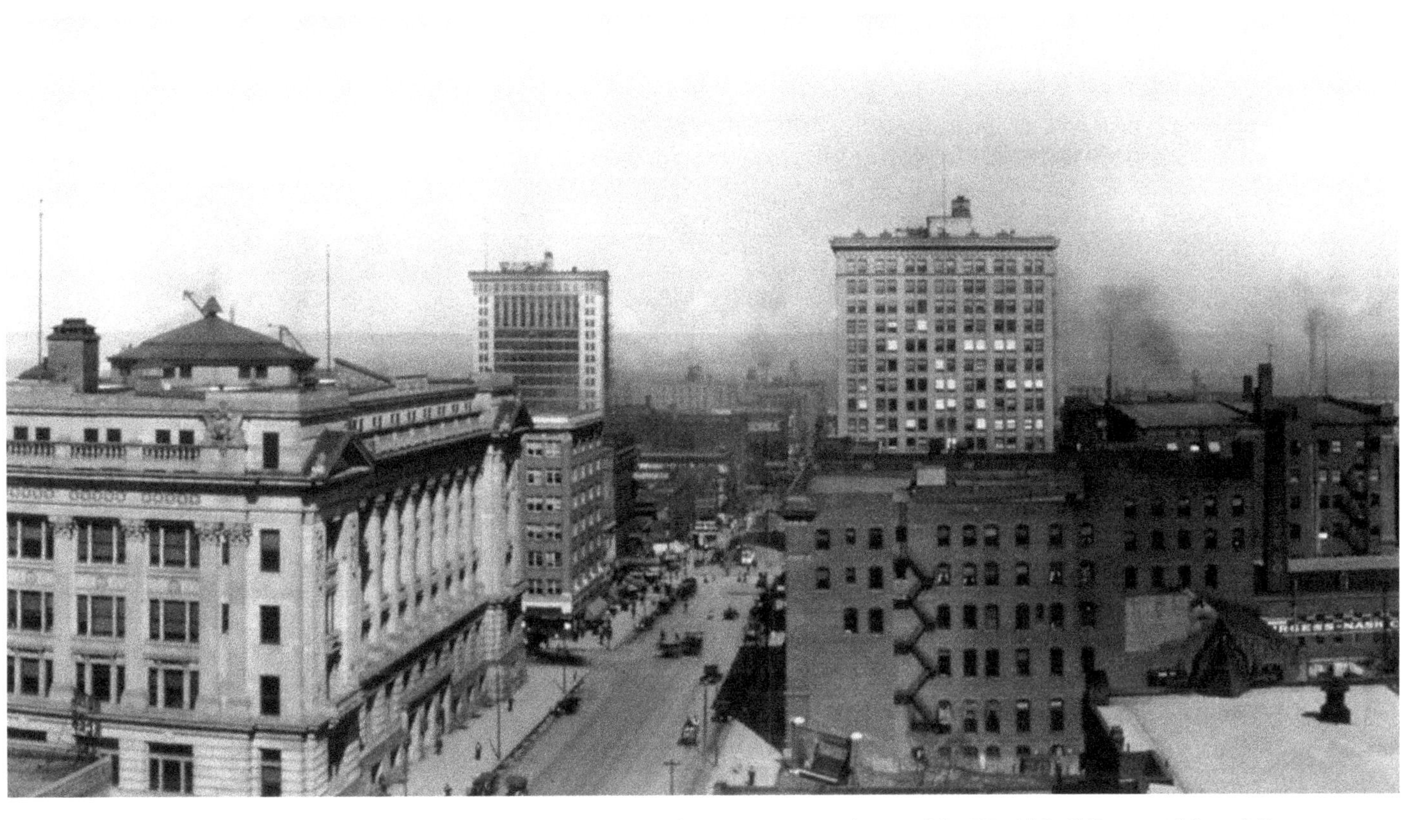

Downtown Omaha was growing in 1916. The 19-story Woodmen of the World Building at 14th and Farnam streets (center-right) was the tallest building between Chicago and the West Coast when it was dedicated in 1912. It would be replaced in 1969 by the 30-story Woodmen Tower.

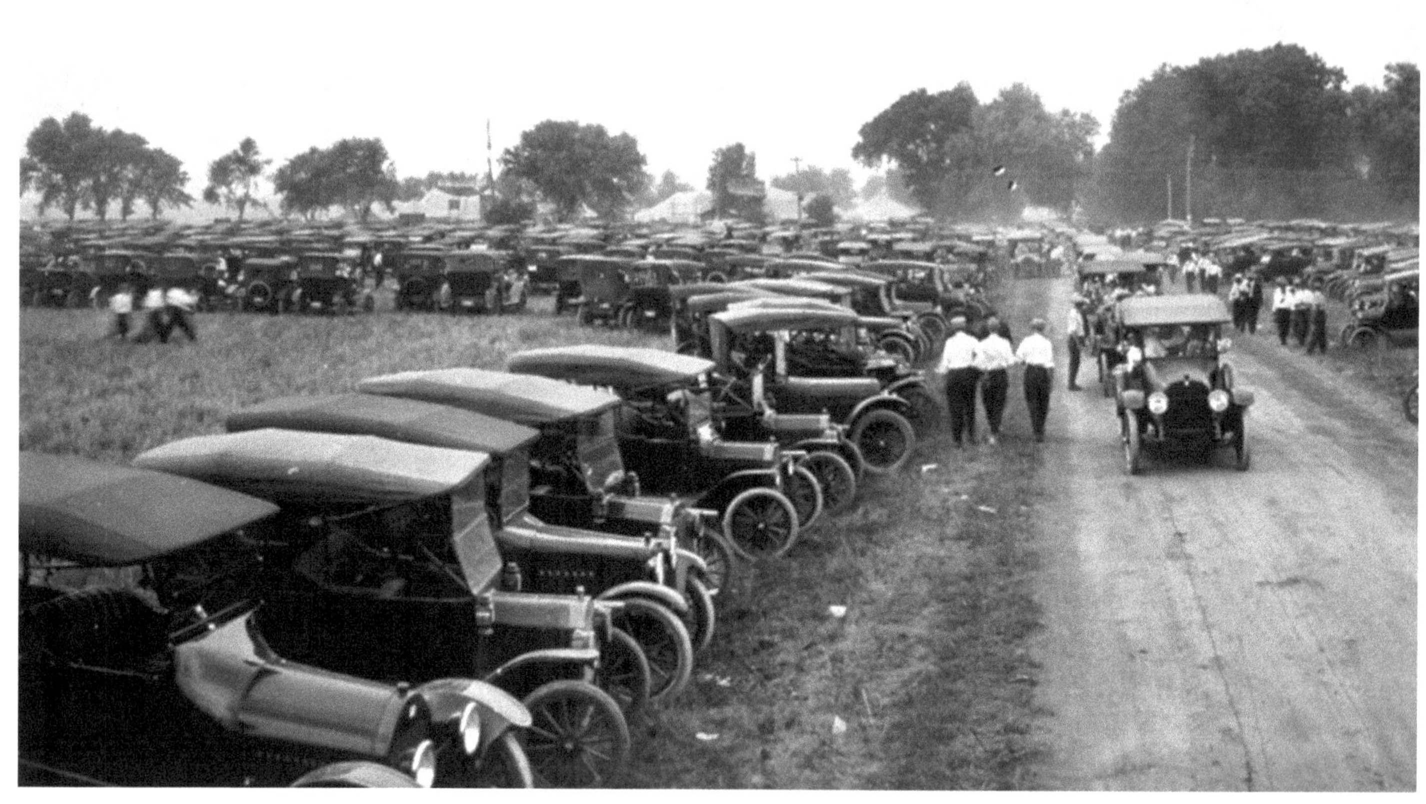

Fords aplenty were on hand in August 1916 at a widely publicized tractor show in Fremont as thousands greeted Henry Ford, who arrived with officials from his company (including his son, Edsel). The reclusive manufacturer spent much of his time trying to avoid the press. The show itself featured more than 250 tractors from 50 different companies and plows from 14 different companies. Farmers viewed an inventory of more than $1 million and purchased liberally.

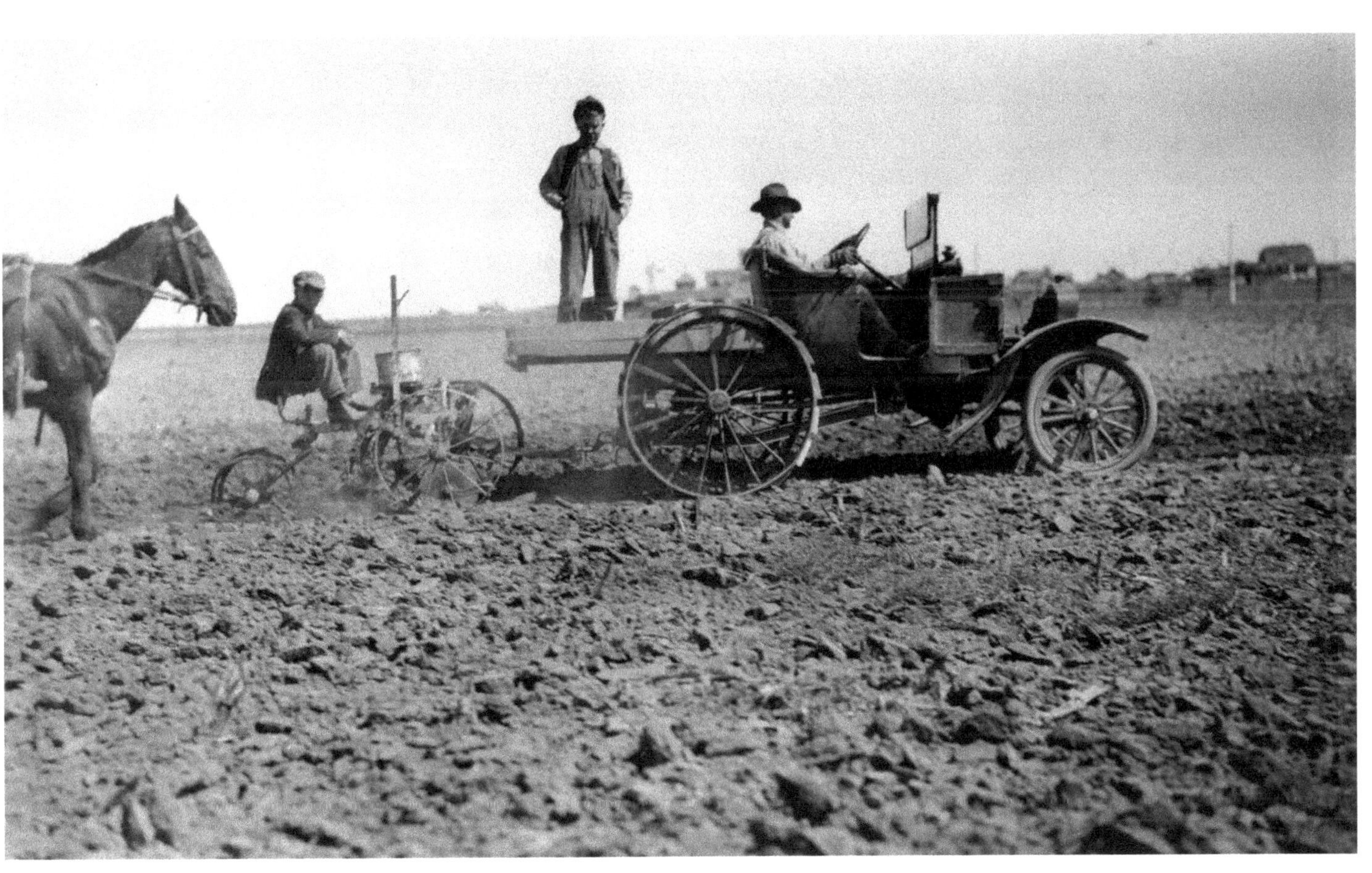

Why budget between a Ford or a farm tractor when a little ingenuity can give you both? At a farm south of Ogallala around 1918, these enterprising Nebraskans have found a way to remodel the family touring car to pull a seed planter.

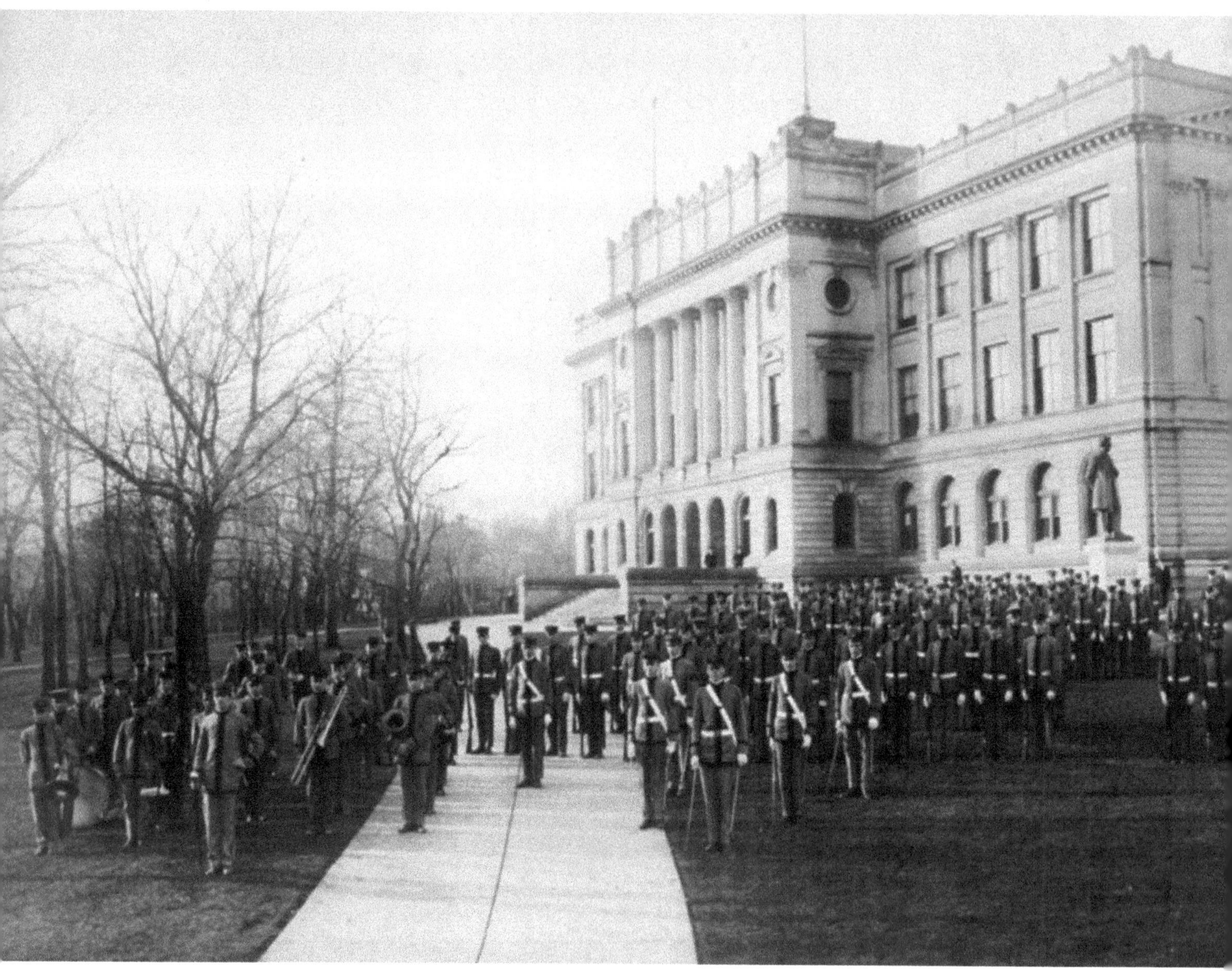

Omaha High School established a Reserve Officer Training Corps program during the 1892-93 school year, and every male student was required to become an active member. Despite its mandatory status, it was generally popular and the annual Military Ball was the social event of the year.

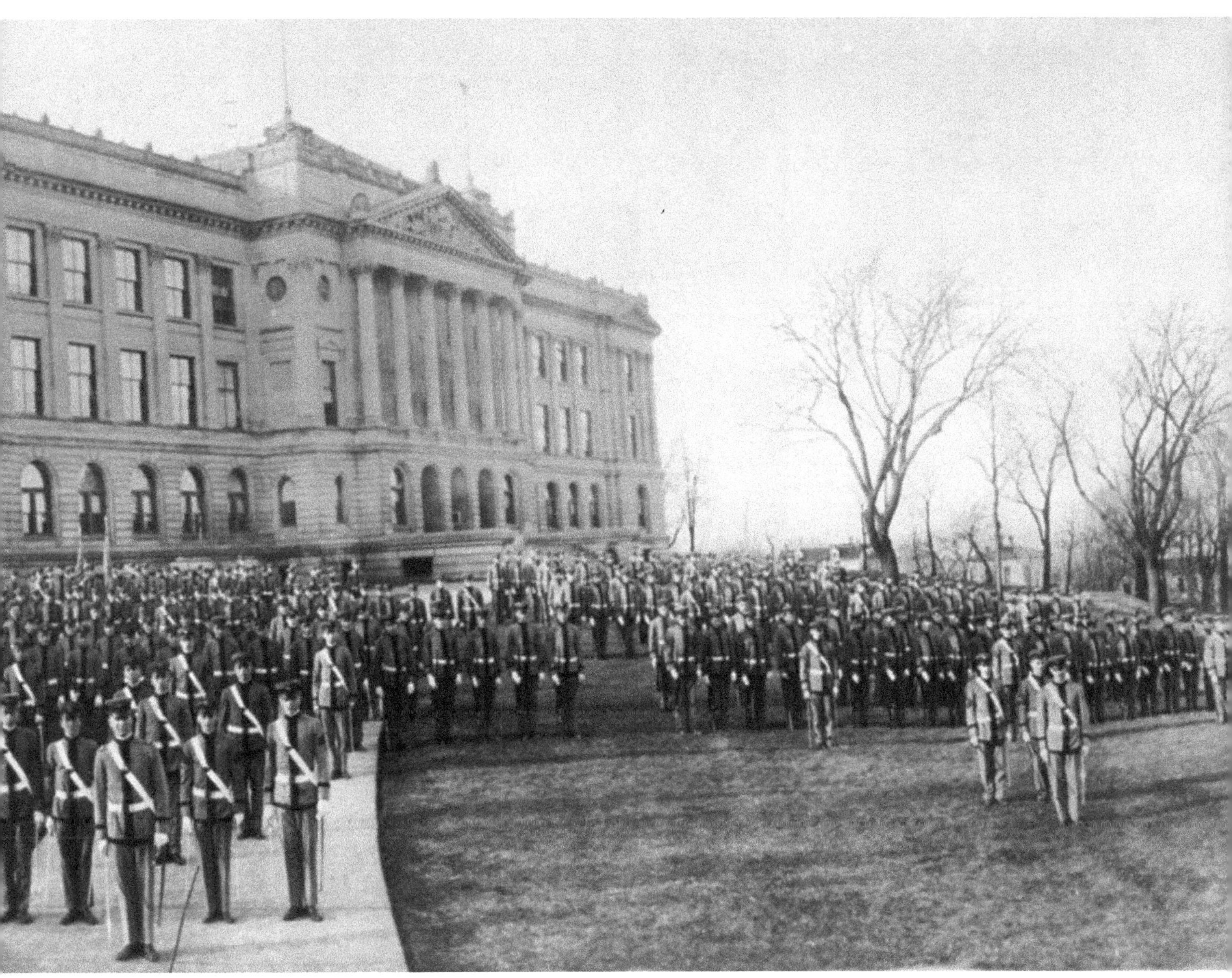

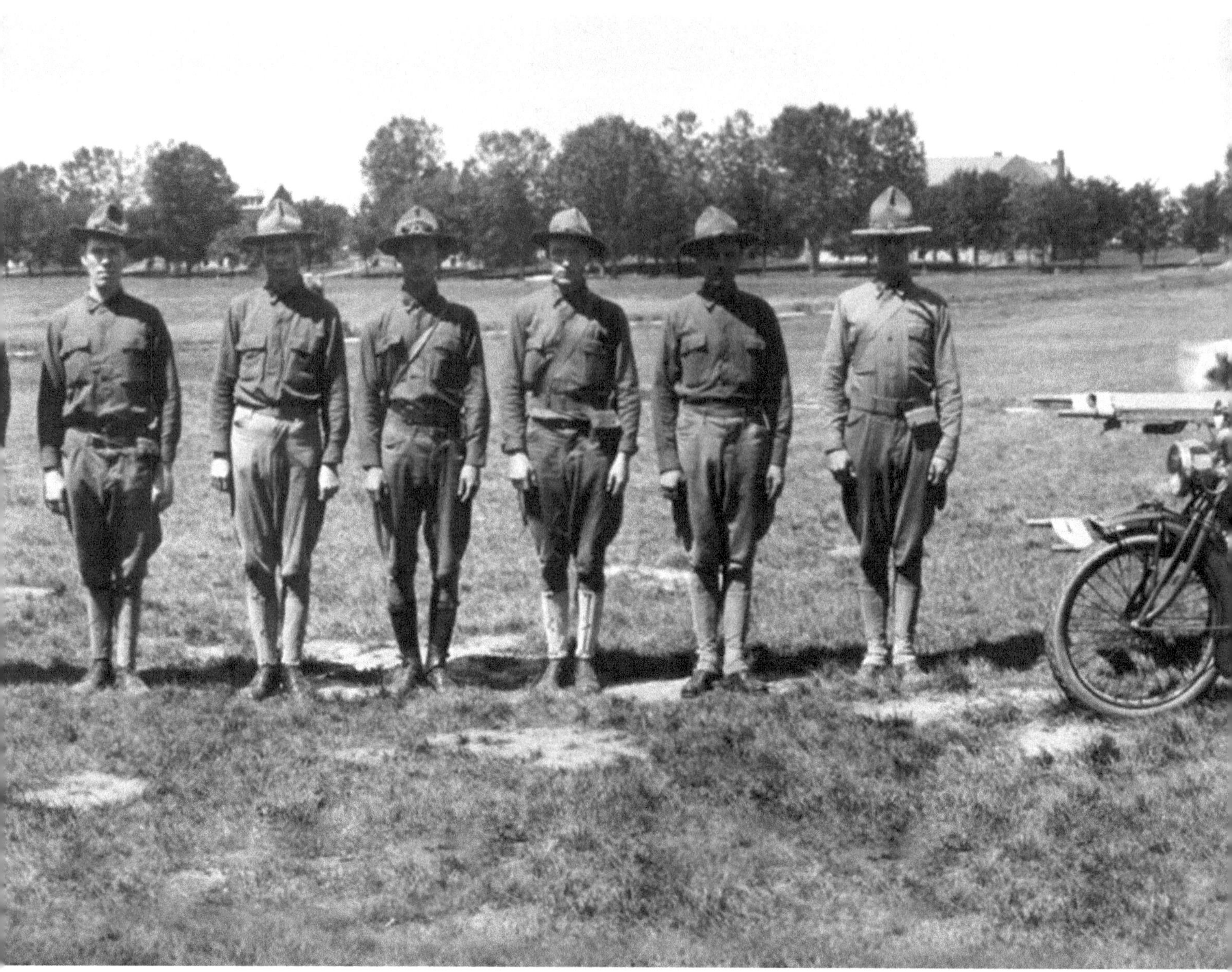

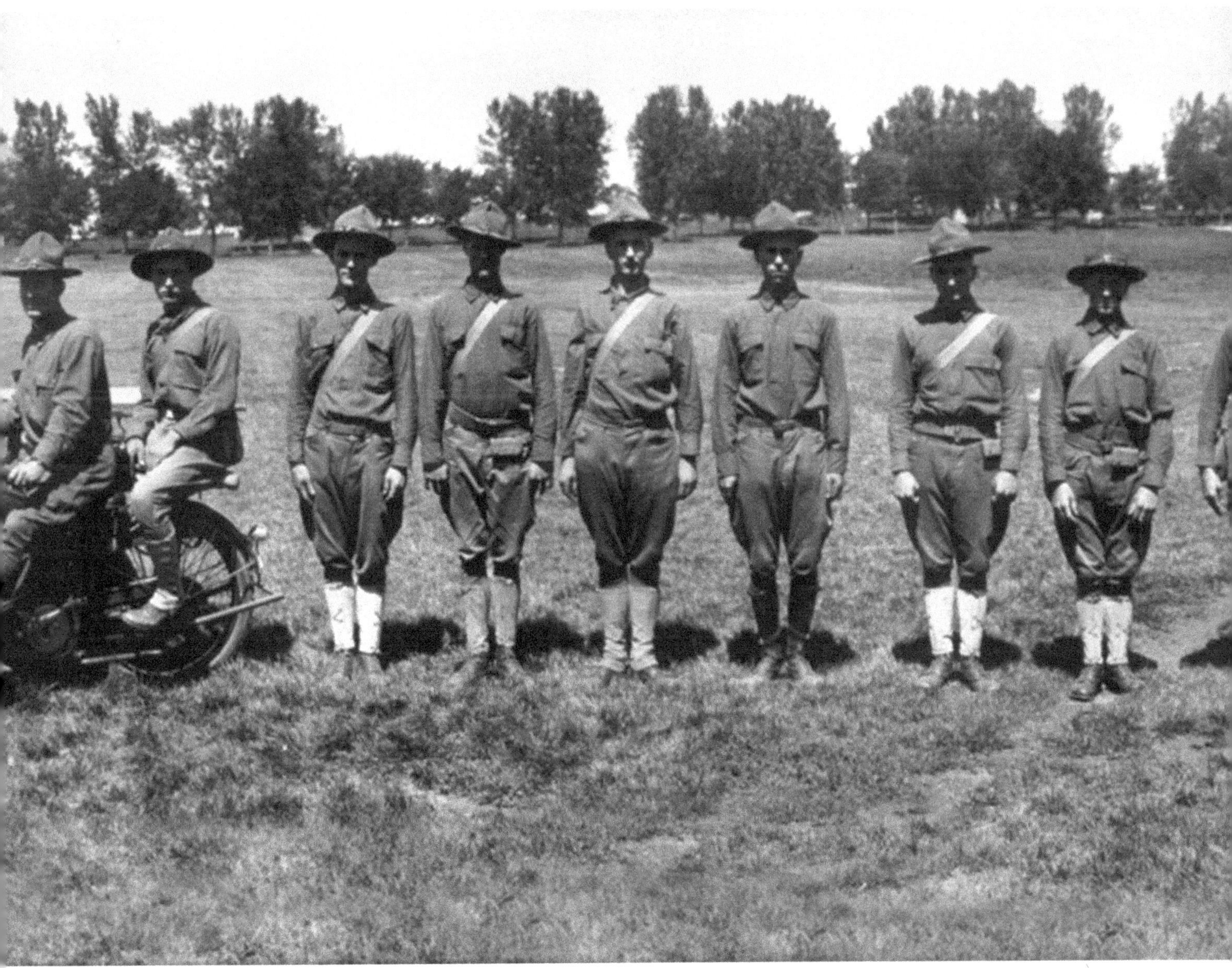

The Sanitary Company of the Fourth Nebraska National Guard is ready for duty with the onset of World War I. The Company lines up in September 1917 for this official photograph by P. J. McAndrews.

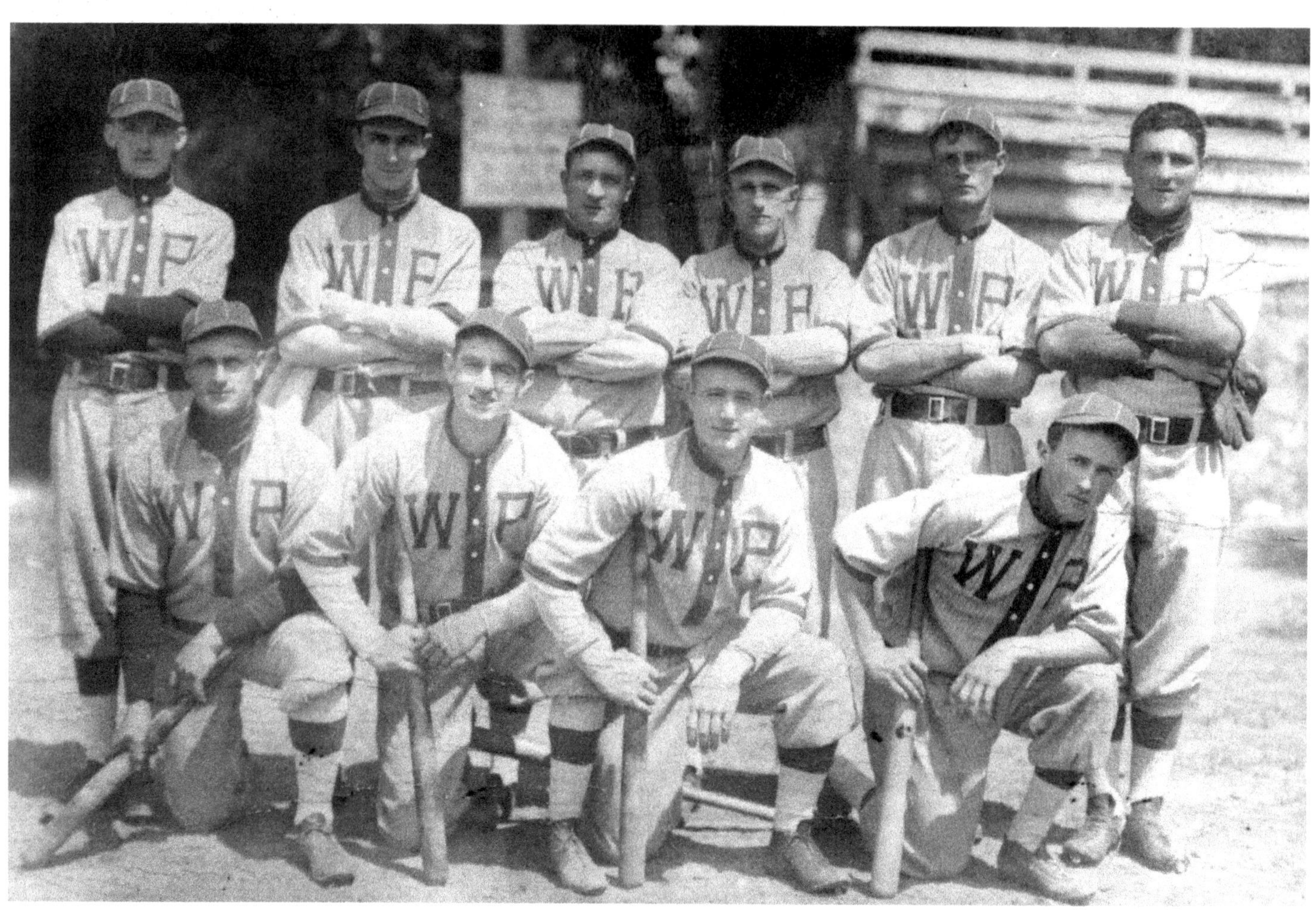

An Elkhorn Valley champion baseball team from West Point, Nebraska, poses proudly for this team photo. Minor league and semipro teams played in small towns throughout the state during the first half of the twentieth century. American Legion and kids' baseball remain popular statewide. Several Major League Hall-of-Famers were Nebraskans, including Grover Cleveland Alexander (born in Elba, died in St. Paul), Sam Crawford (of Wahoo), Richie Ashburn (of Tilden), and Bob Gibson (of Omaha).

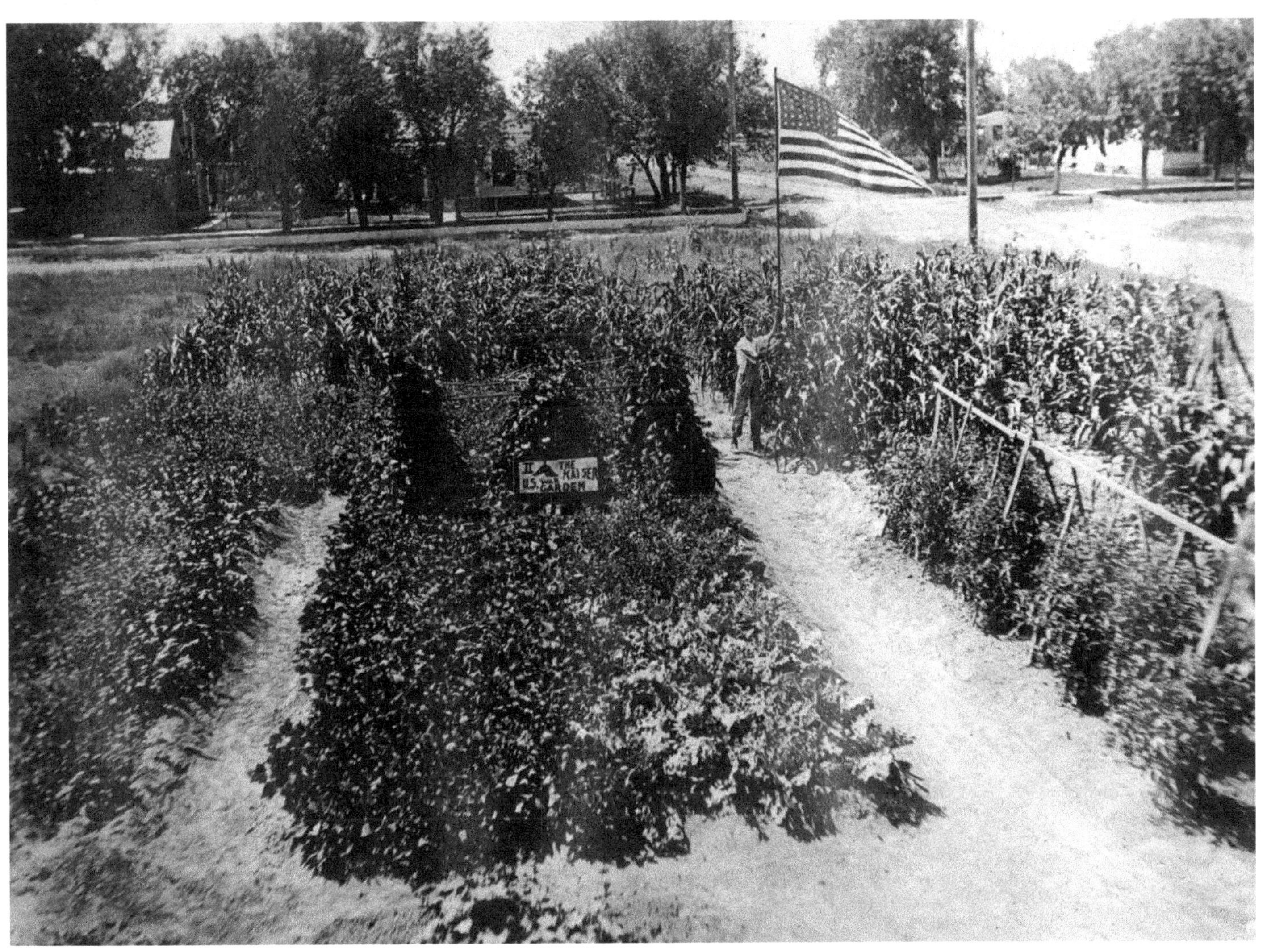

This World War I victory garden was tended by young Raymond Search of McCook (shown holding an American flag), who was applauded in the local newspaper for having one of the finest in the region. Ray's "To Hell mit the Kaiser" sentiments were shared by the majority of the nation, making it necessary for many German immigrants and Americans of German descent to downplay their heritage. Search would become well known in McCook as manager of the Fox Theater.

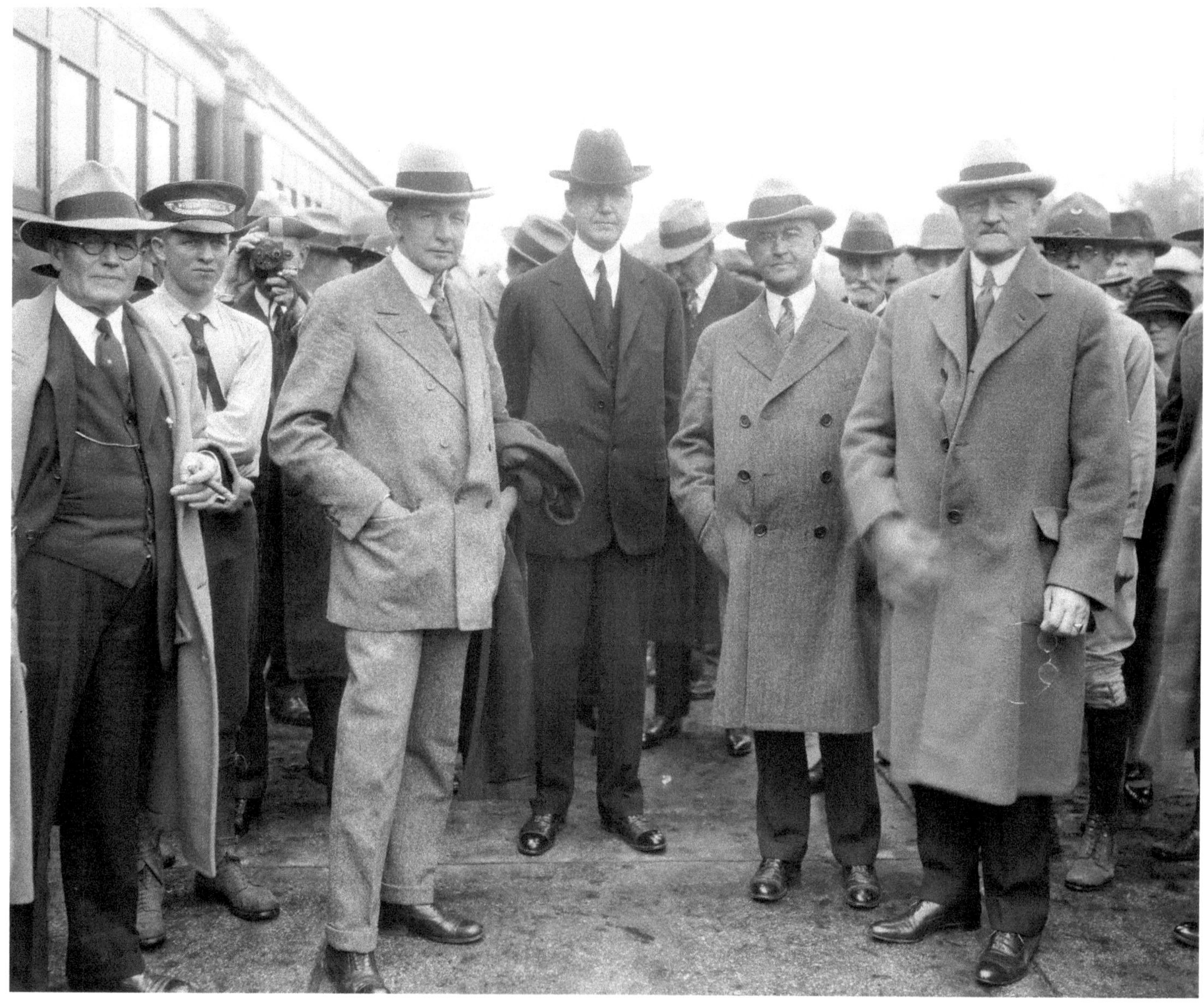

John J. Pershing was a professor of military tactics at the University of Nebraska from 1891 to 1895. More than two decades later, he became commander of the American Expeditionary Force during World War I and became the only man ever promoted to the Army's highest possible rank (General of the Armies) during his lifetime. (George Washington was promoted posthumously to that rank.) Pershing (at far-right) is returning to Lincoln to be honored after the war.

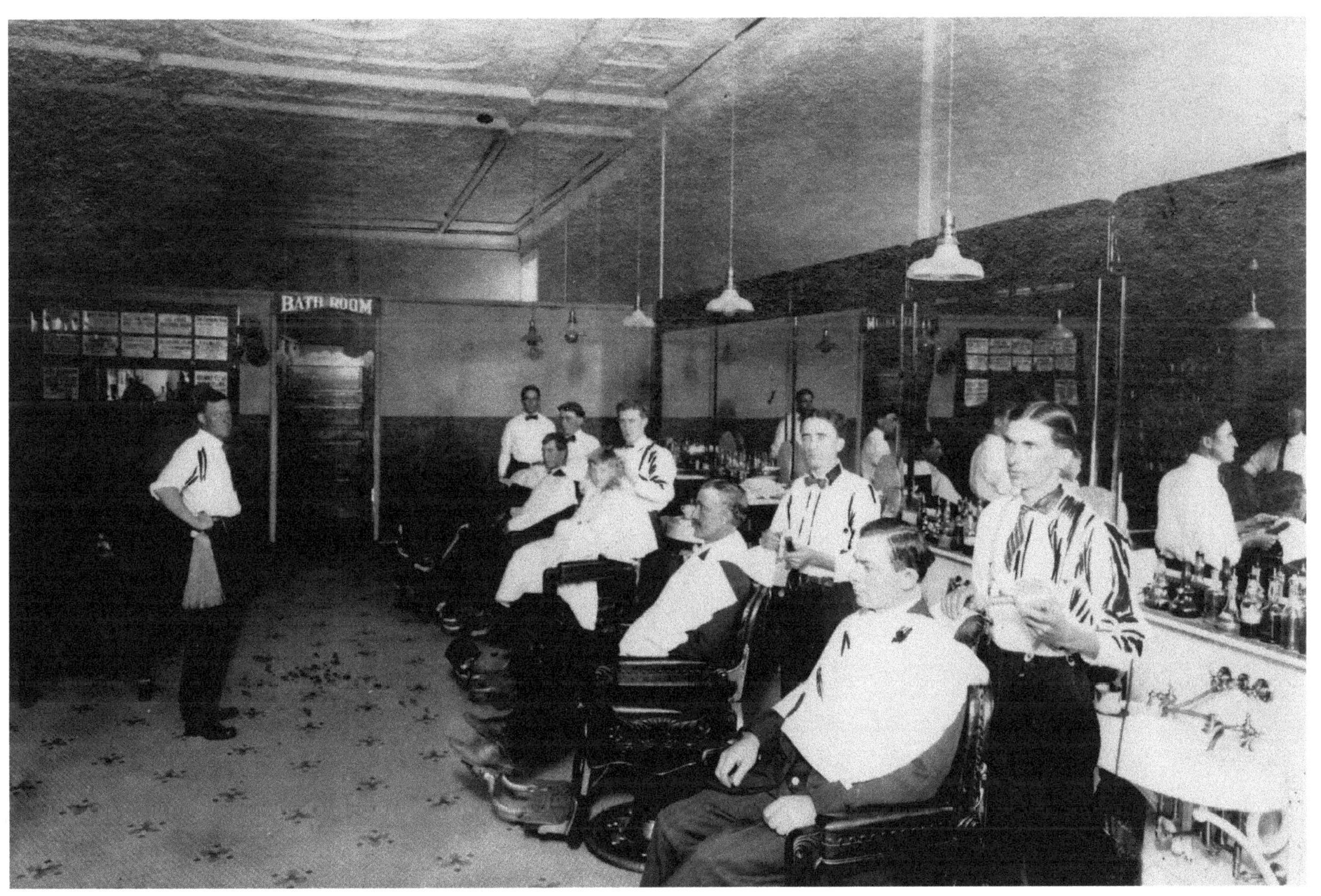

Four men at a time could get a shave and haircut in the Park Barber Shop at Columbus. Founded in 1858, Columbus would launch Buffalo Bill's Wild West Show in 1883 as the site of the show's first full-dress rehearsal. Boston-born George Francis Train, a shipping magnate, candidate for president in 1872, and prolific writer, made a fortune in real estate in Columbus through his associations with the Union Pacific Railroad.

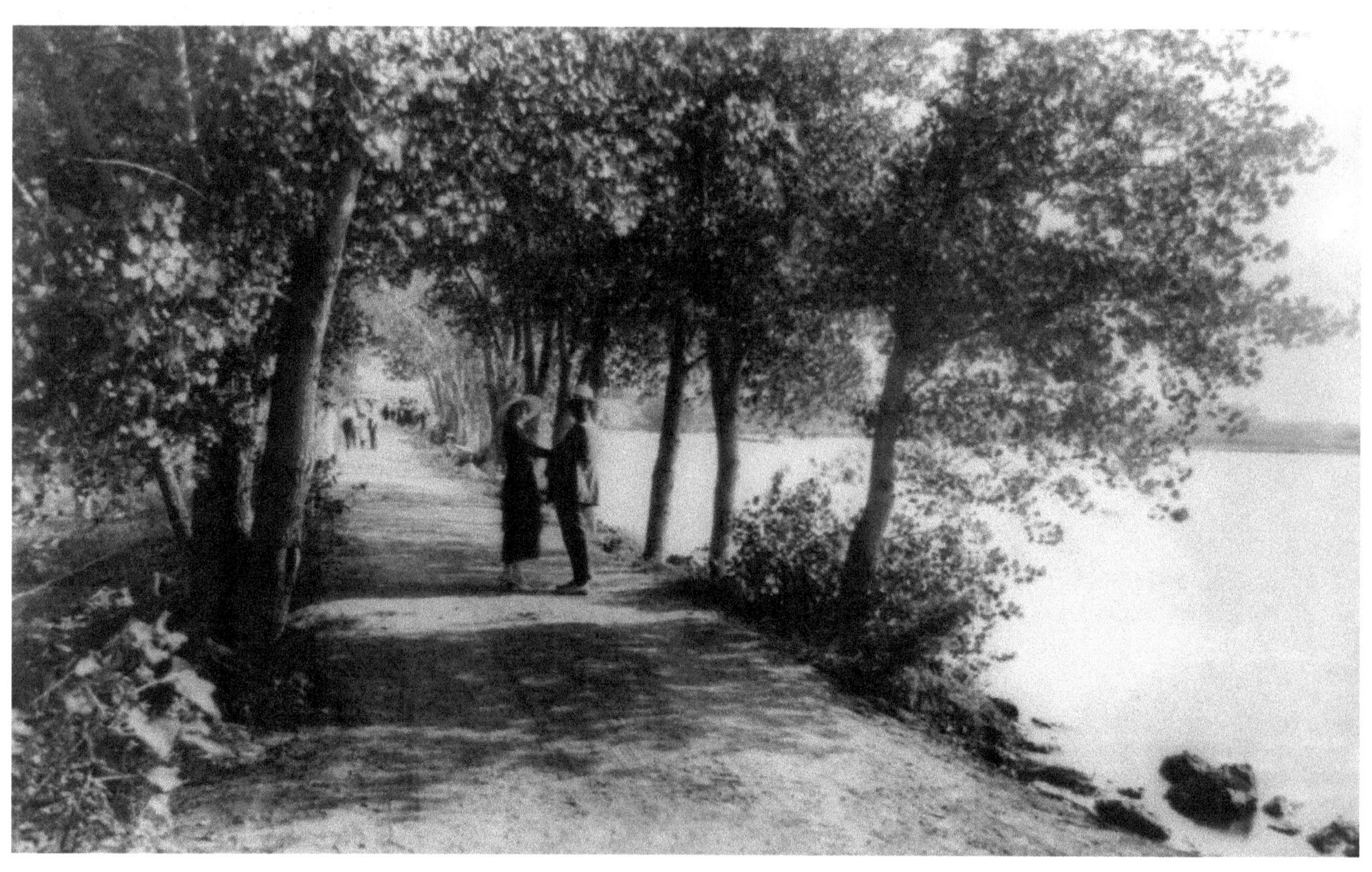

Photographer Martin A. Ellingson of McCook recorded this romantic image of Lovers' Lane in 1920 at Champion, located in Chase County, just a few miles east of the Colorado state line.

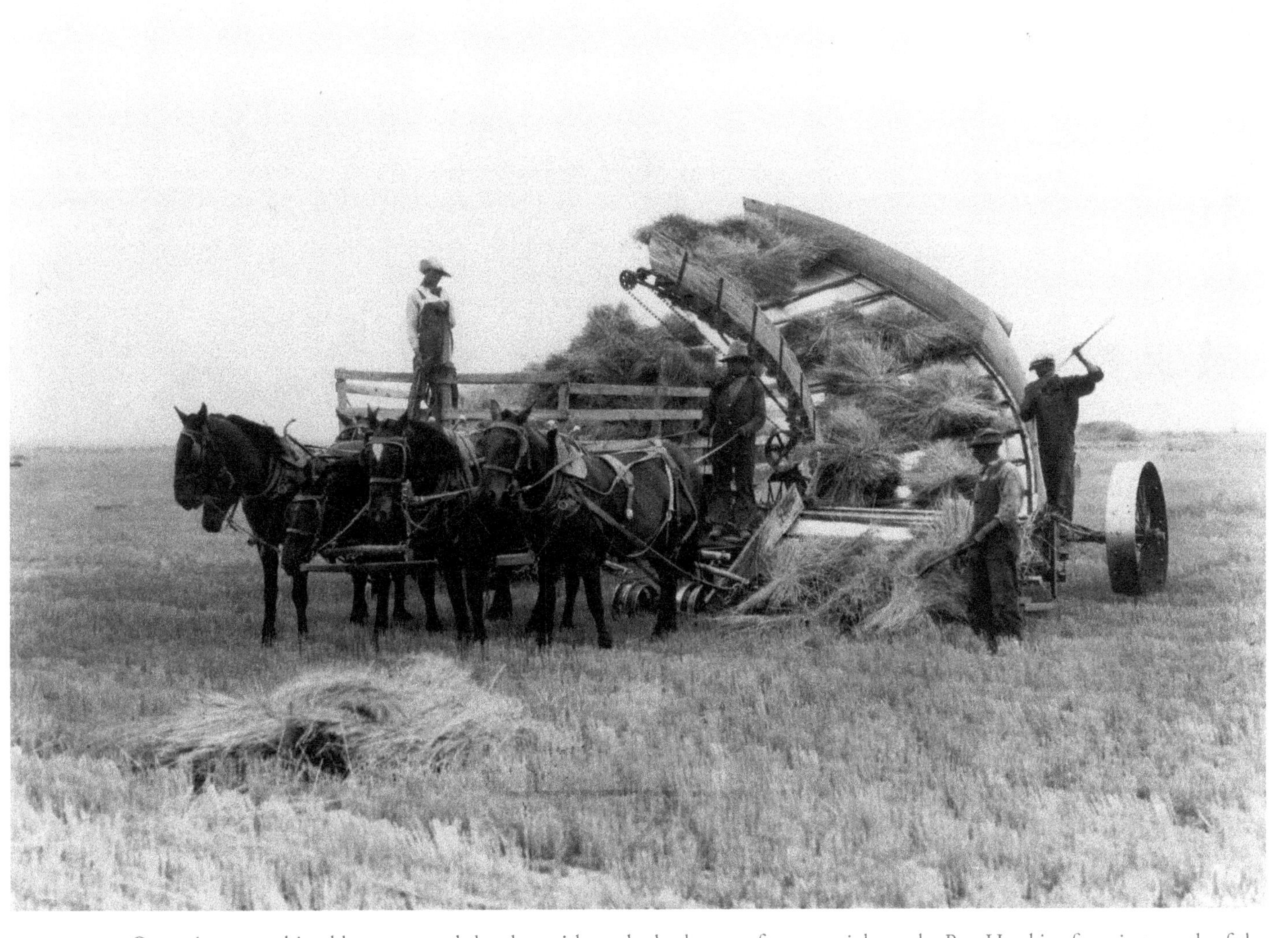

Operating a combined harvester and thresher with steel wheels was a four-man job on the Ben Hawkins farm just north of the Kansas border in Red Willow County. The original photograph includes a note that Hawkins averaged 20 bushels an acre from this field. Later versions of the "combine" would require only one operator.

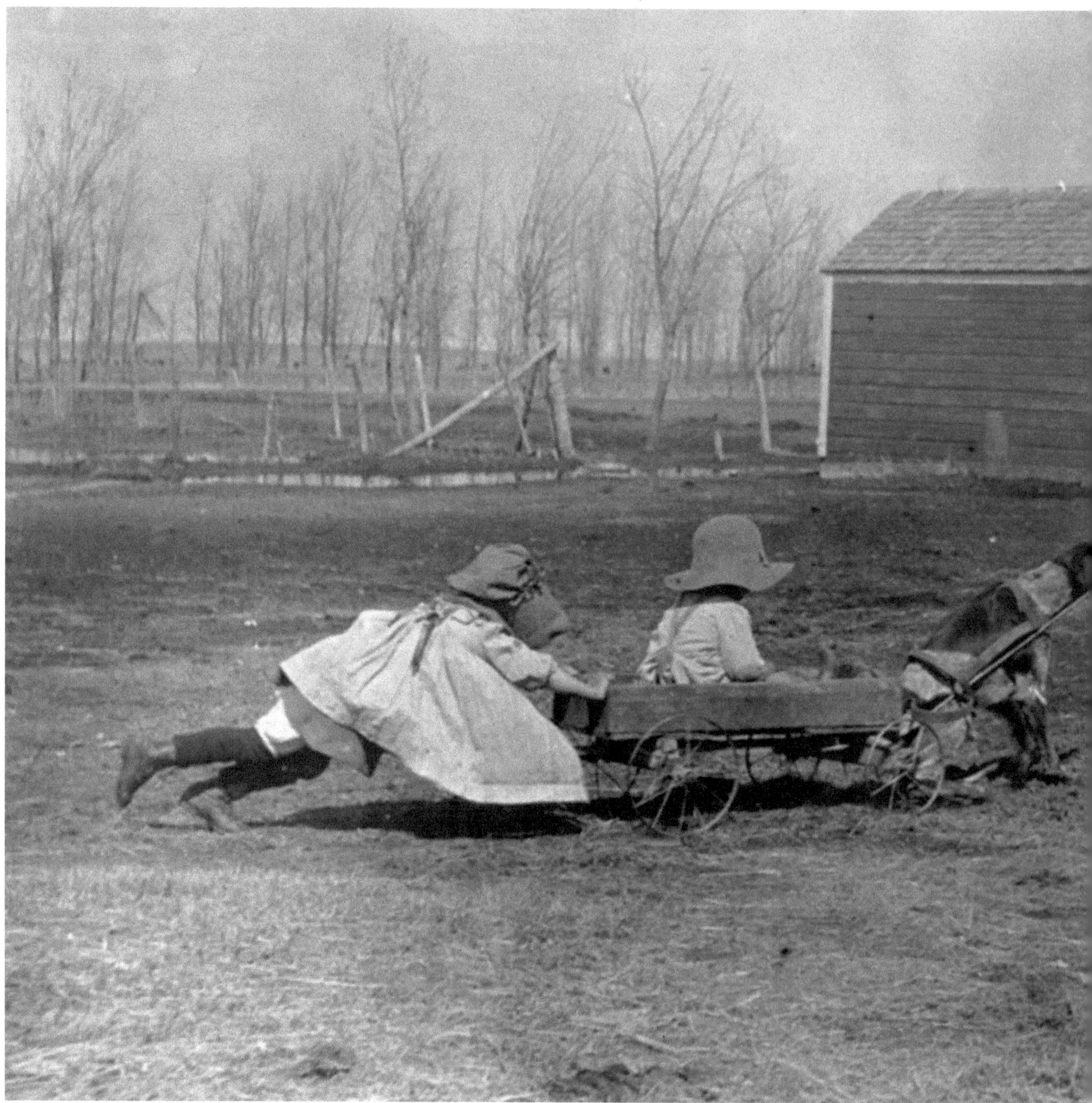

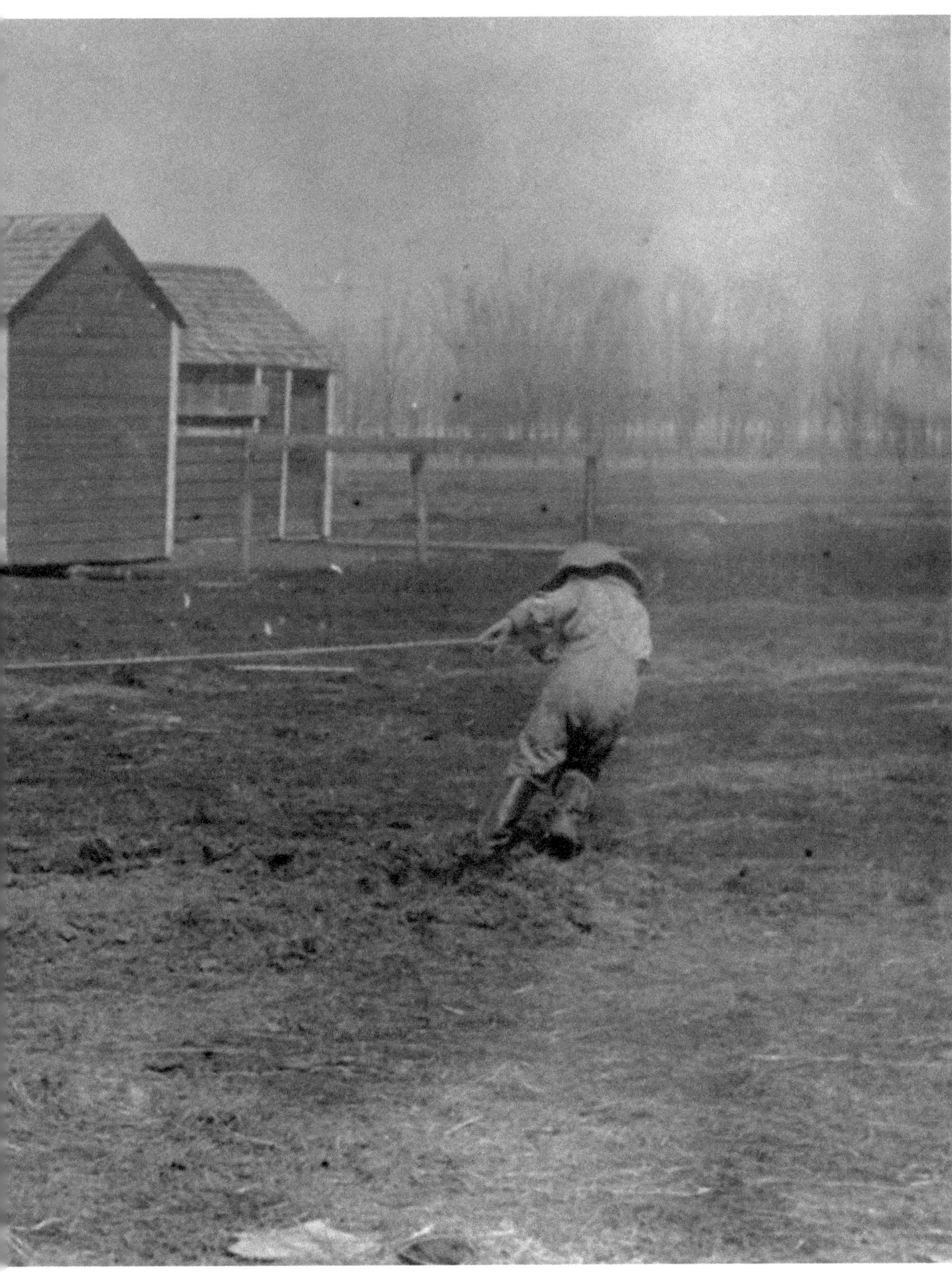

These three children are having a tough time convincing their reluctant dog to do his share of the work on their farm near O'Neill. The town was settled by Irish immigrant John O'Neill.

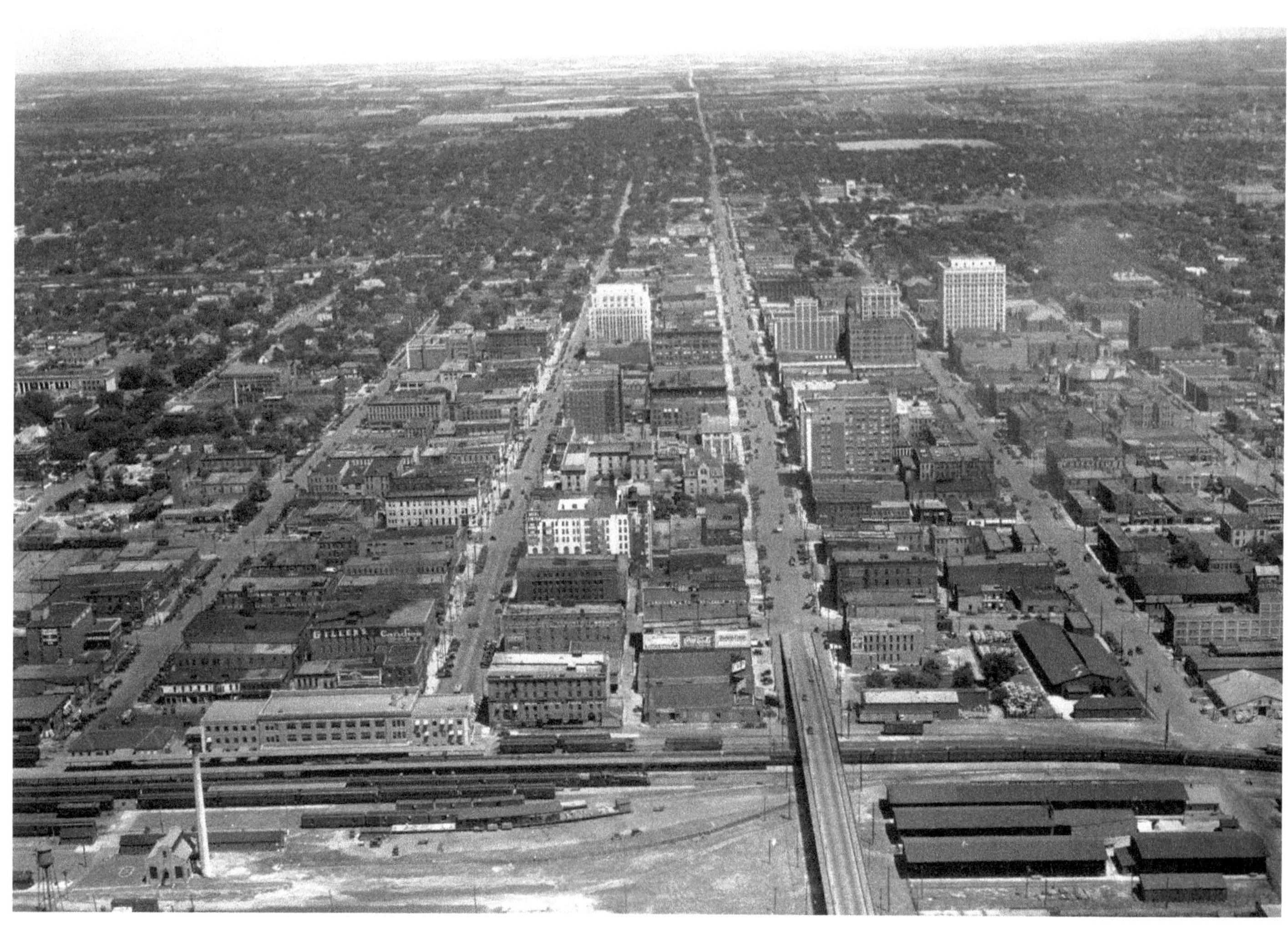

Facing east down O Street in 1920, this aerial panorama of Lincoln reveals that automobiles had by now replaced the horse-and-buggy as Americans' vehicle of choice.

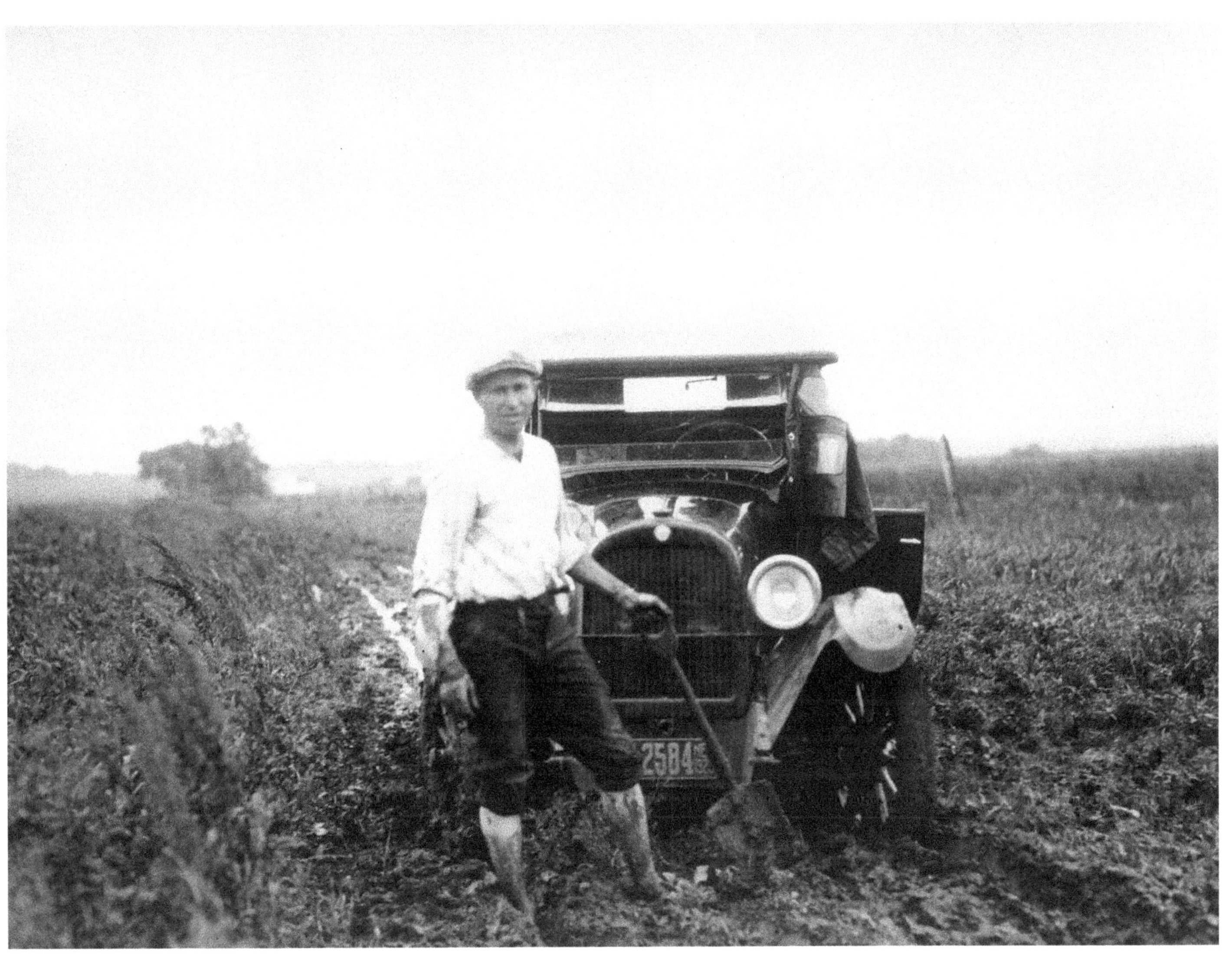

Digging out of trouble was a time-consuming ordeal when a car ventured into places it was not built to navigate, as this 1920 image illustrates. The scene was little different on wet Nebraska roadways, because very few of them were paved during the first half of the twentieth century.

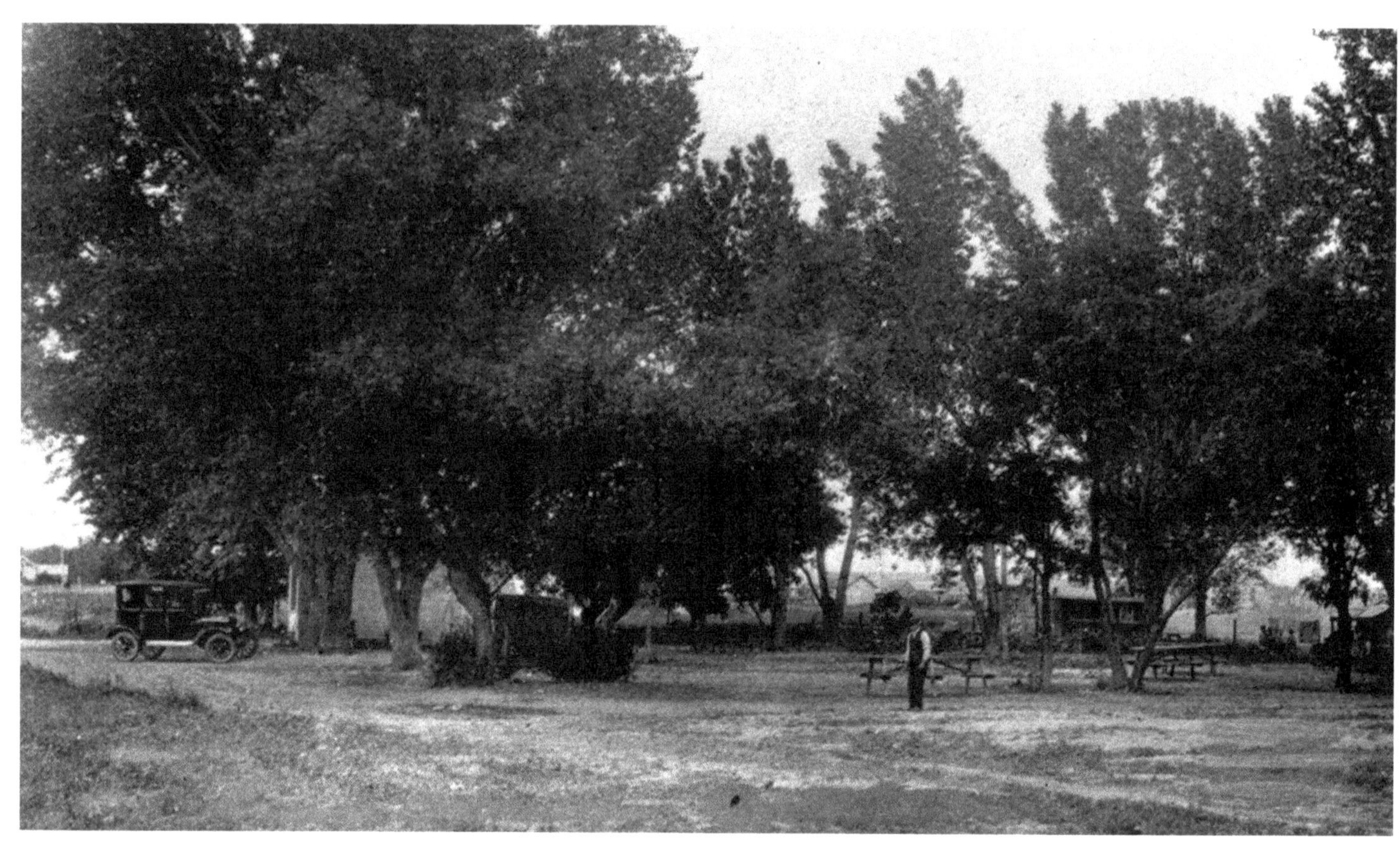

Campgrounds like this one in Ogallala were an inexpensive way for people to catch a night of sleep as they traveled cross-country in their automobiles, but they didn't have much to offer by way of amenities.

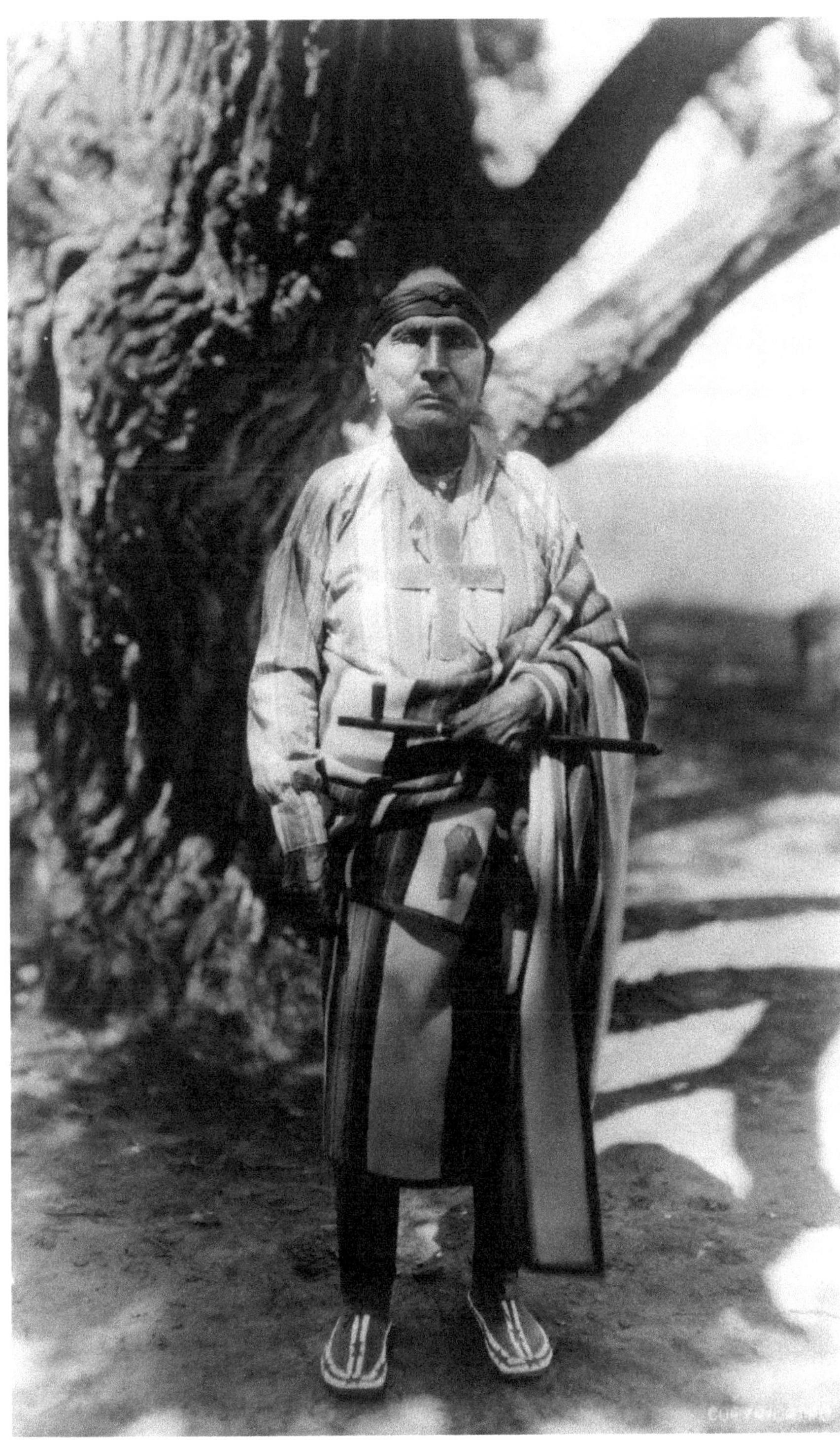

The Pawnee have a long history in Nebraska, living in large, dome-shaped earth huts along the Platte, Loup, and Republican rivers. They are thought to have numbered about 10,000 at their peak before being decimated in the nineteenth century by smallpox, cholera, and warfare. This man, holding a peace pipe, was photographed by Martin Ellingson around 1925 at Trenton.

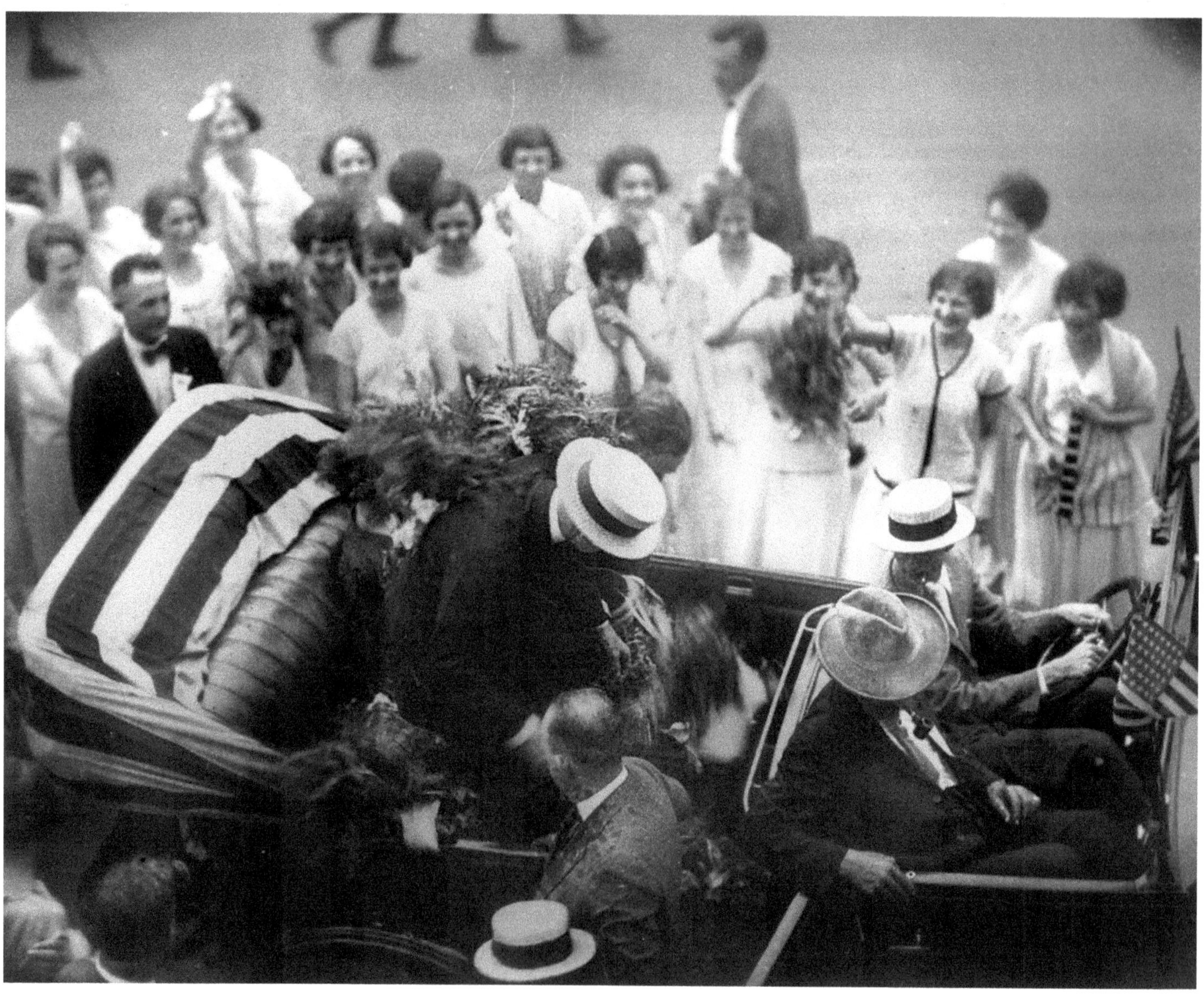

Charles G. Dawes, a former Lincoln lawyer and business leader, returned to be honored in a parade on August 22, 1924, while he was running for vice-president. He spoke at a Republican Party rally at Memorial Stadium that evening, and the following day met with Nebraska governor Charles W. Bryan (the brother of William Jennings Bryan, and who ironically was running for vice-president as a Democrat). Dawes was elected that fall and served with President Calvin Coolidge.

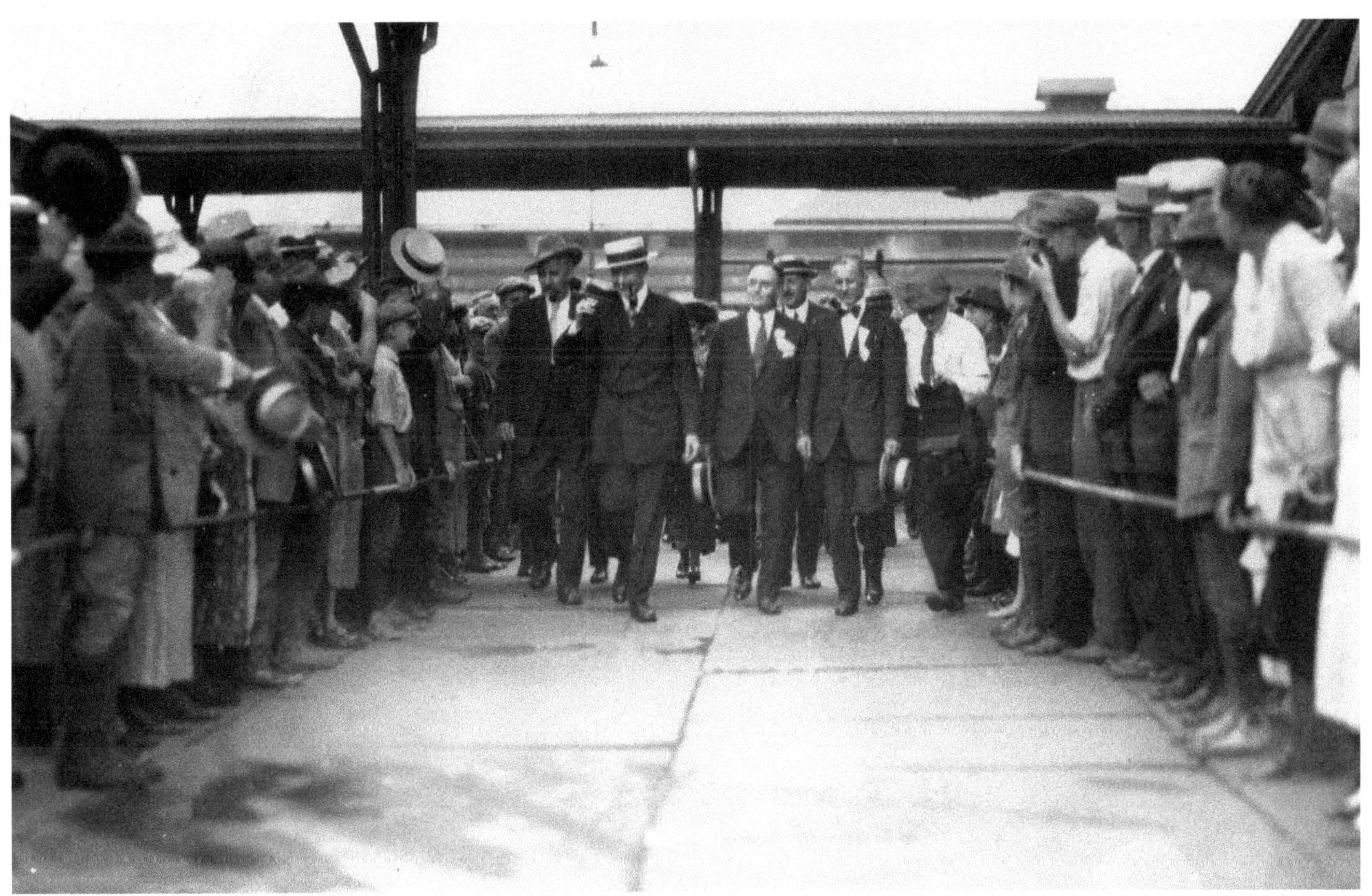

Charles G. Dawes (in the aisle, second from left) walks through a crowd of admirers in Lincoln on August 22, 1924. Dawes had served as brigadier general under his friend John J. Pershing during World War I, and then as the first director of the U.S. Bureau of the Budget before being elected vice-president later in 1924. He also won the Nobel Peace Prize for his plan to restore and stabilize the war-ravaged German economy.

Following Spread: The daring Jack Knight flew a DeHavilland-4 aircraft like this on the night segment of the nation's first transcontinental airmail flight in February 1921. A pilot flying from the west landed after dark at North Platte's Lee Bird Field (shown in this 1926 photograph by Otto C. Perry). Knight then took off for Omaha and points east. Lee Bird Field used fuel-burning barrels as torches to mark the perimeter for the planes on that flight.

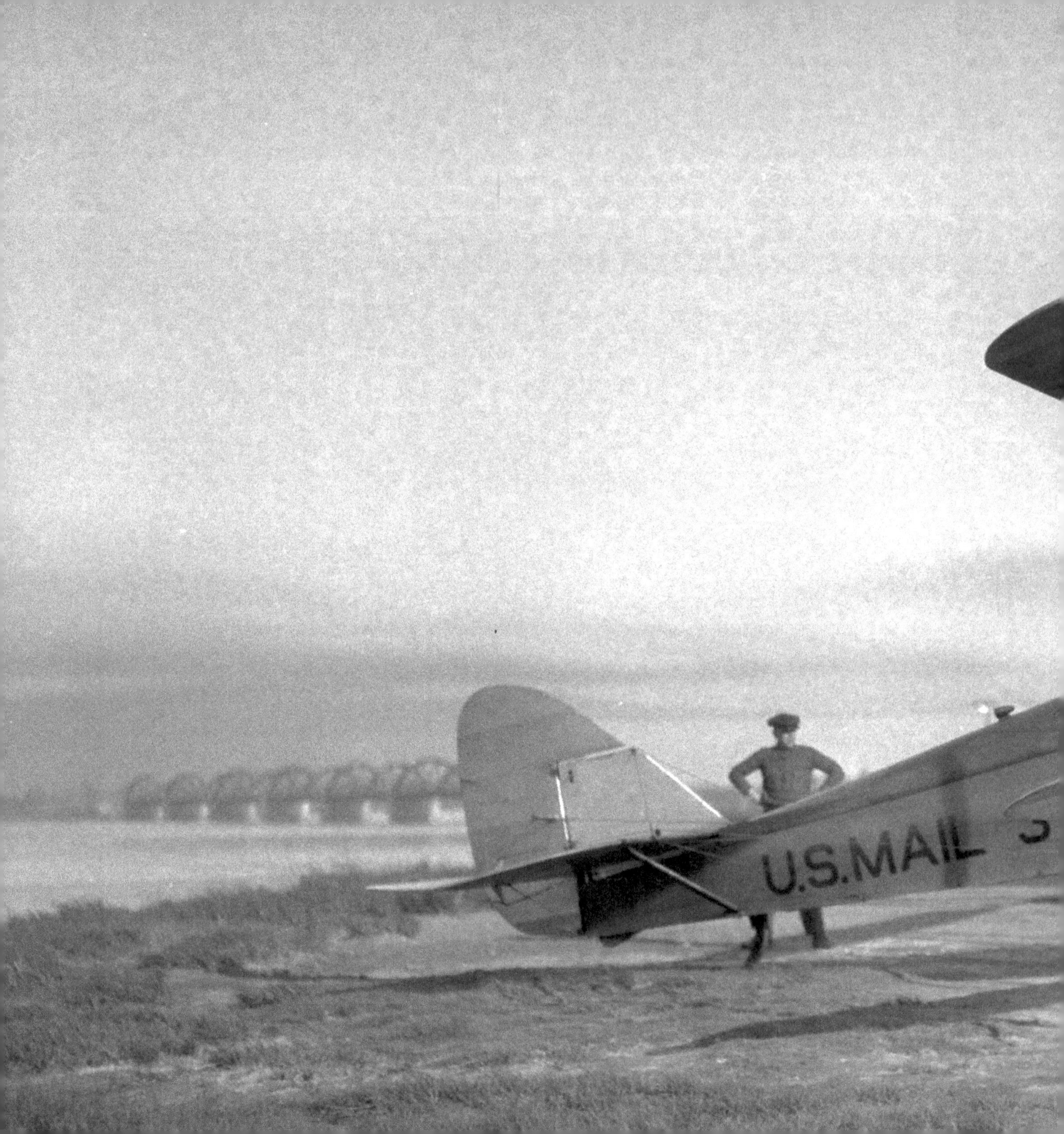
U.S.MAIL

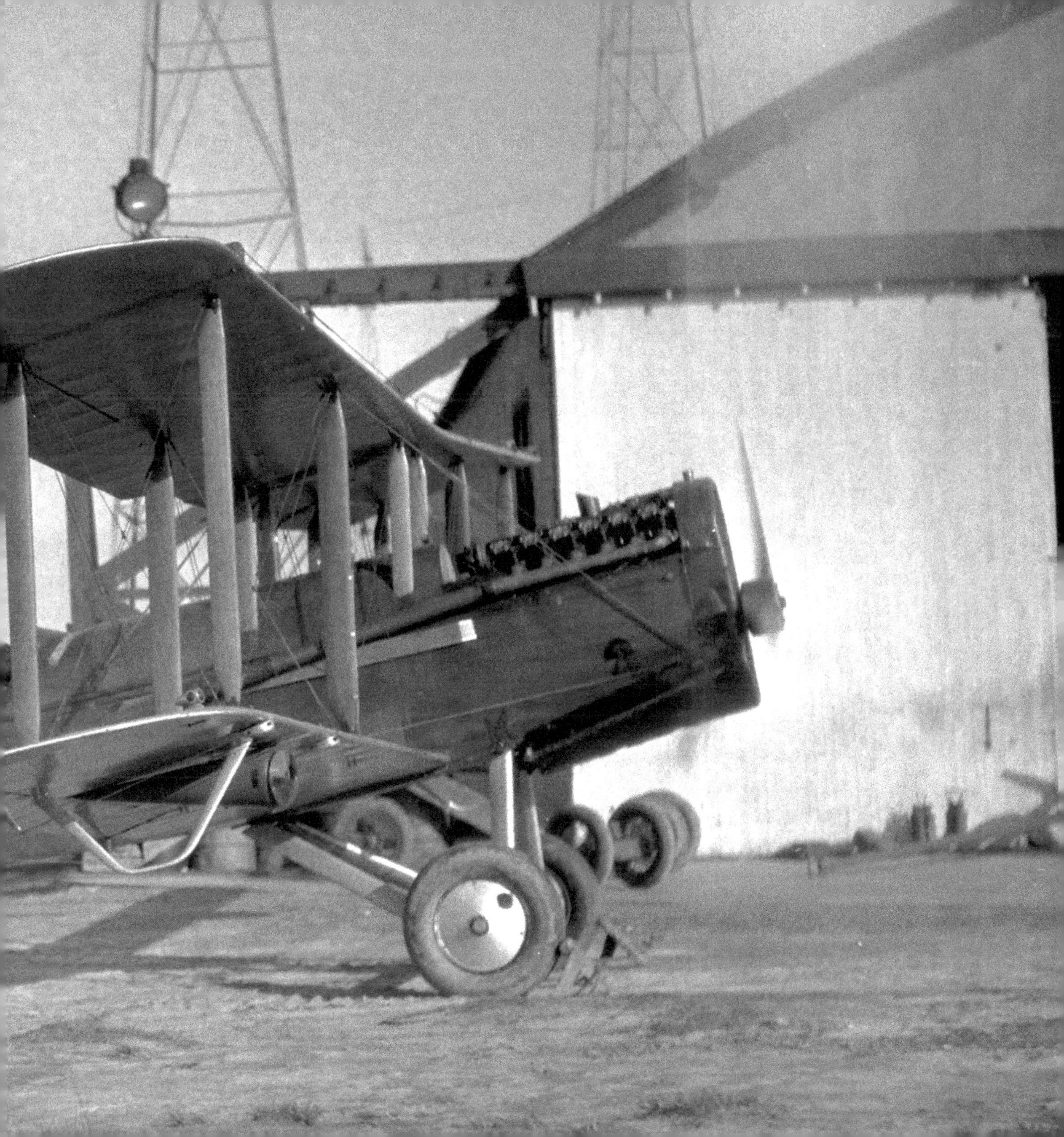

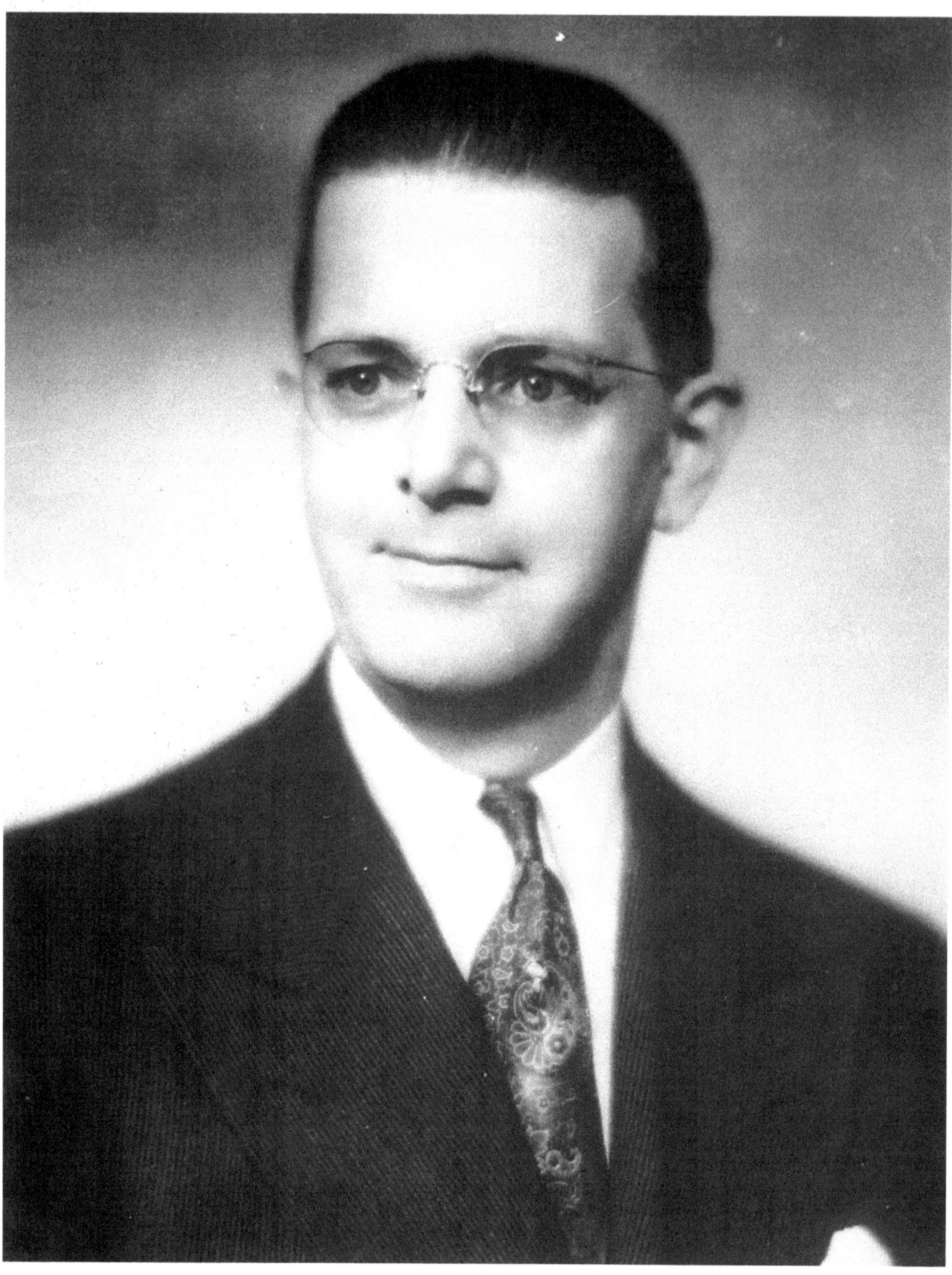

In the 1920s, Edward E. Perkins started experimenting with fruit-flavored drinks in his mother's kitchen in Hastings. He created a liquid concentrate he called "Fruit Smack." In 1927, to lower shipping hurdles and costs, he found a way to remove the liquid, leaving only a powder. Perkins started production of the original six flavors of what he named "Kool-Aid" (grape, orange, lemon-lime, raspberry, strawberry, cherry) in Hastings, but moved the operation to Chicago four years later.

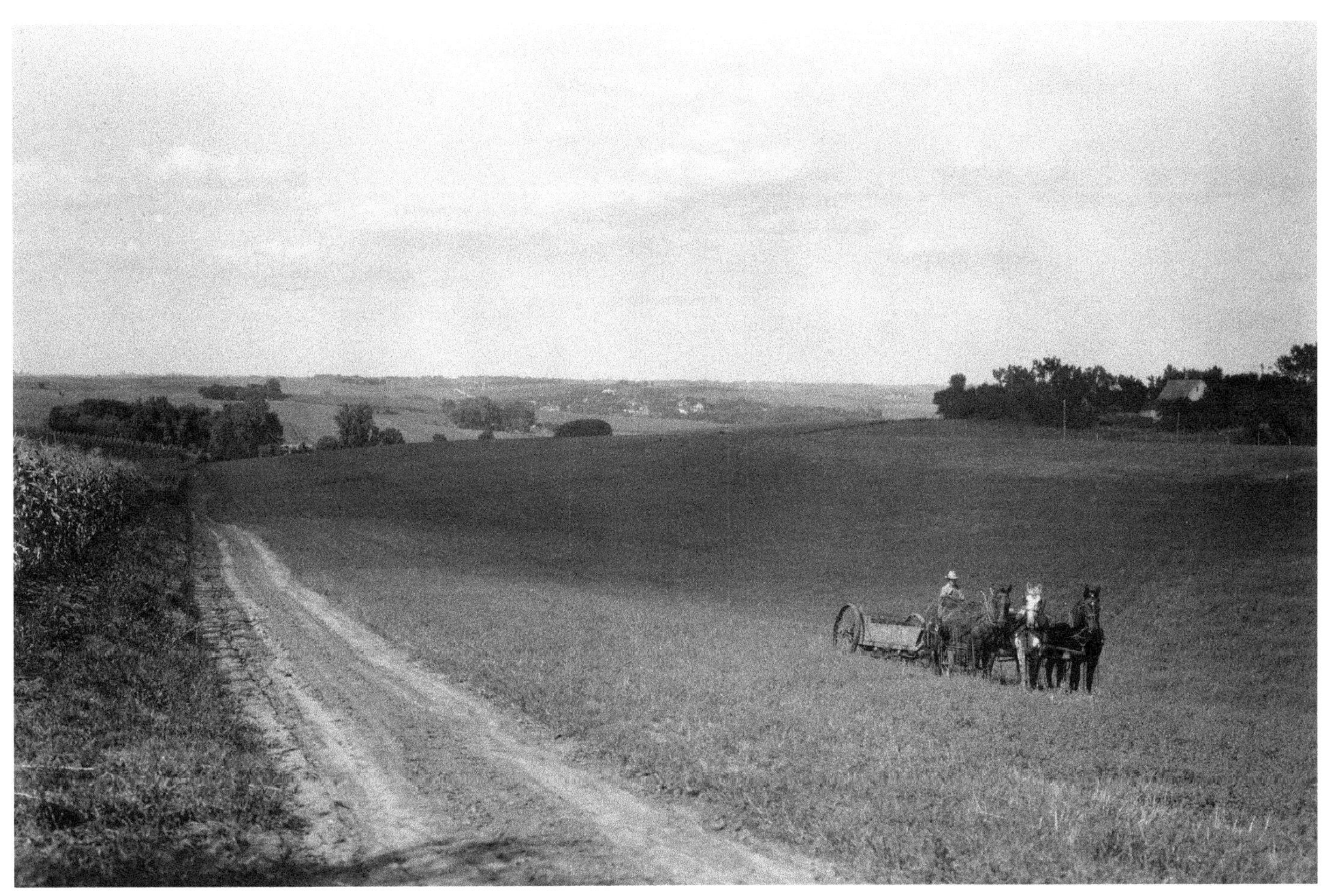

A pastoral scene recorded in August 1927 near Bennington. The maturing corn at left rustles in the breeze as a farmer uses a team of horses to pull what appears to be a manure spreader.

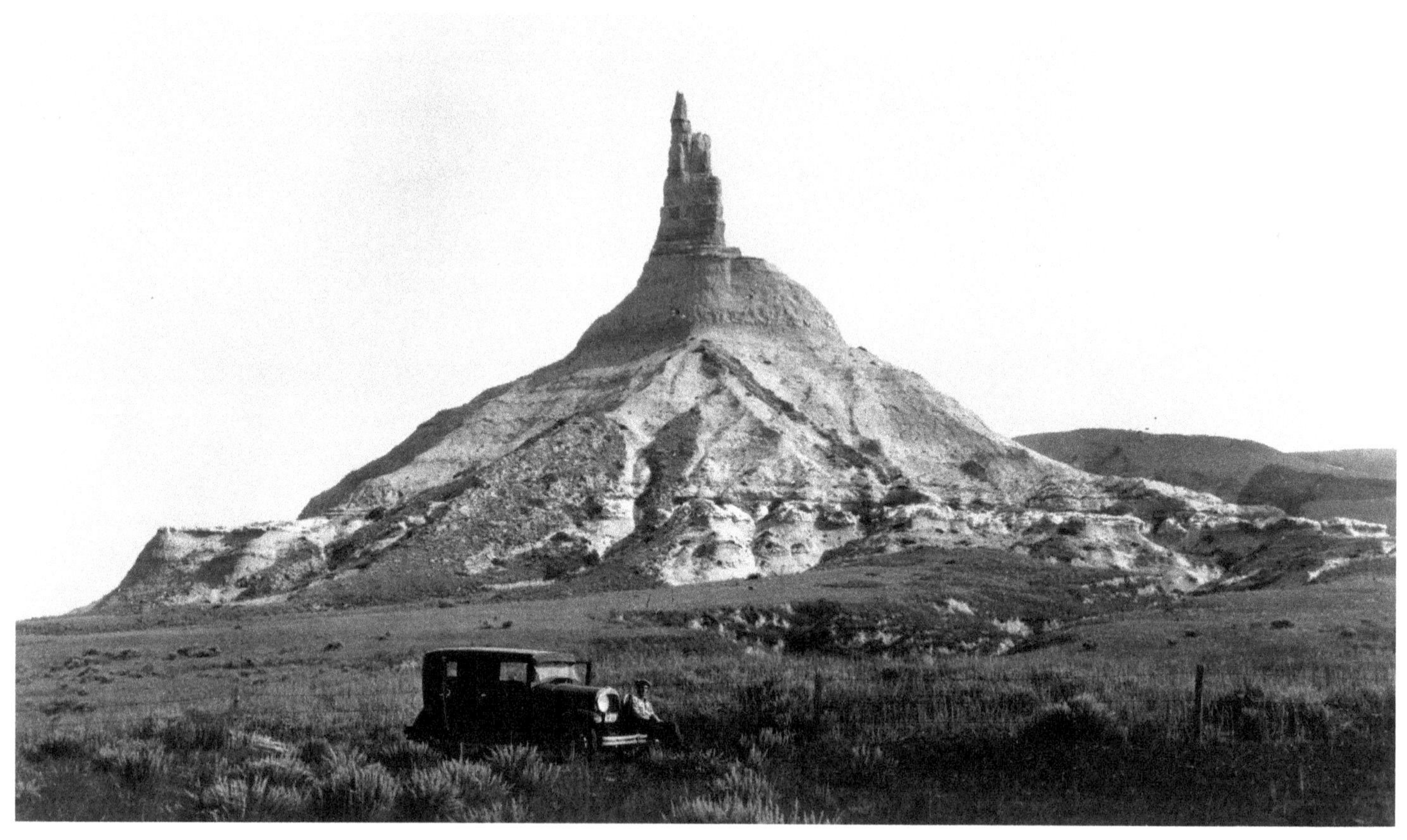

Chimney Rock, located along the Oregon Trail near present-day Bayard, is the most-commented-upon geological feature in the journals of those who traveled the trail in the mid eighteenth century. It is possibly the best-known landmark in Nebraska, and was featured on the Cornhusker State U.S. commemorative quarter in 2006. It's little wonder that this 1929 traveler found reason to pause beside a barbed-wire fence and gaze for a while.

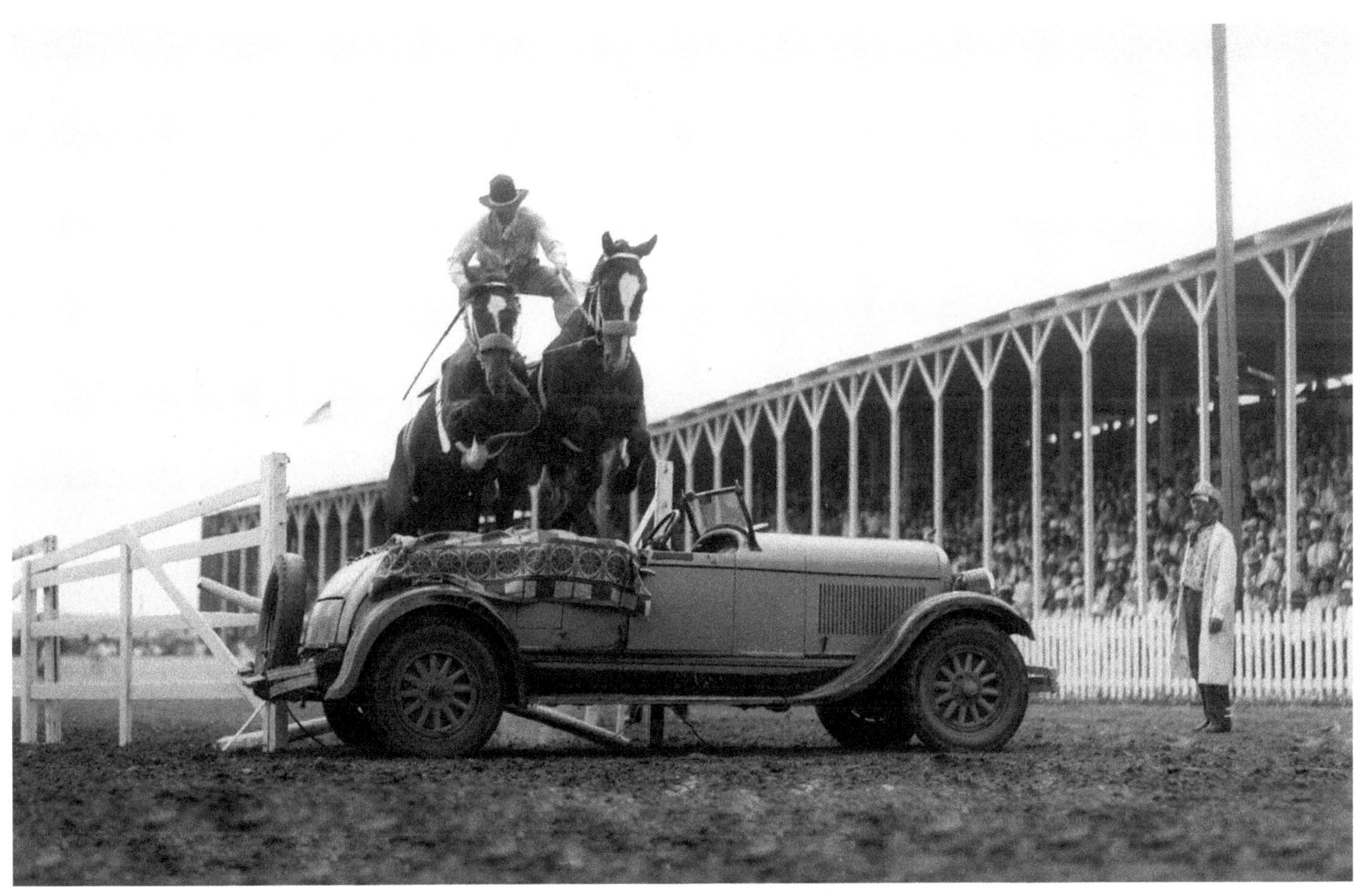

The crowd holds its breath as trick rider Red Breckinridge, with one foot firmly planted on the back of each horse, begins his leap over an open-cockpit roadster during one of the performances of Nebraska's Big Rodeo at Burwell. This scene from the 1929 rodeo was made into a postcard.

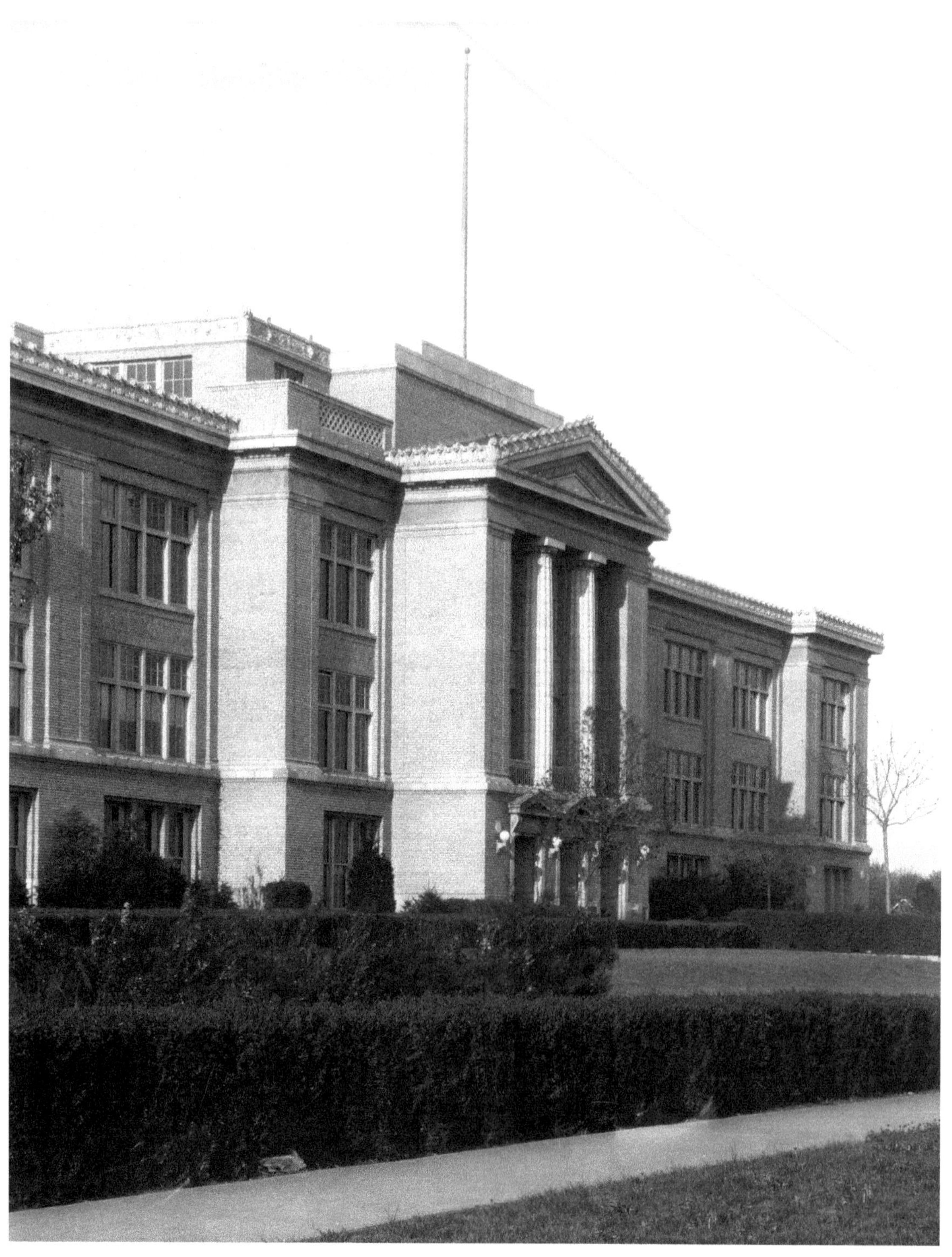

Founded in 1871, Lincoln High, shown here in 1929, is the oldest of Lincoln's high schools.

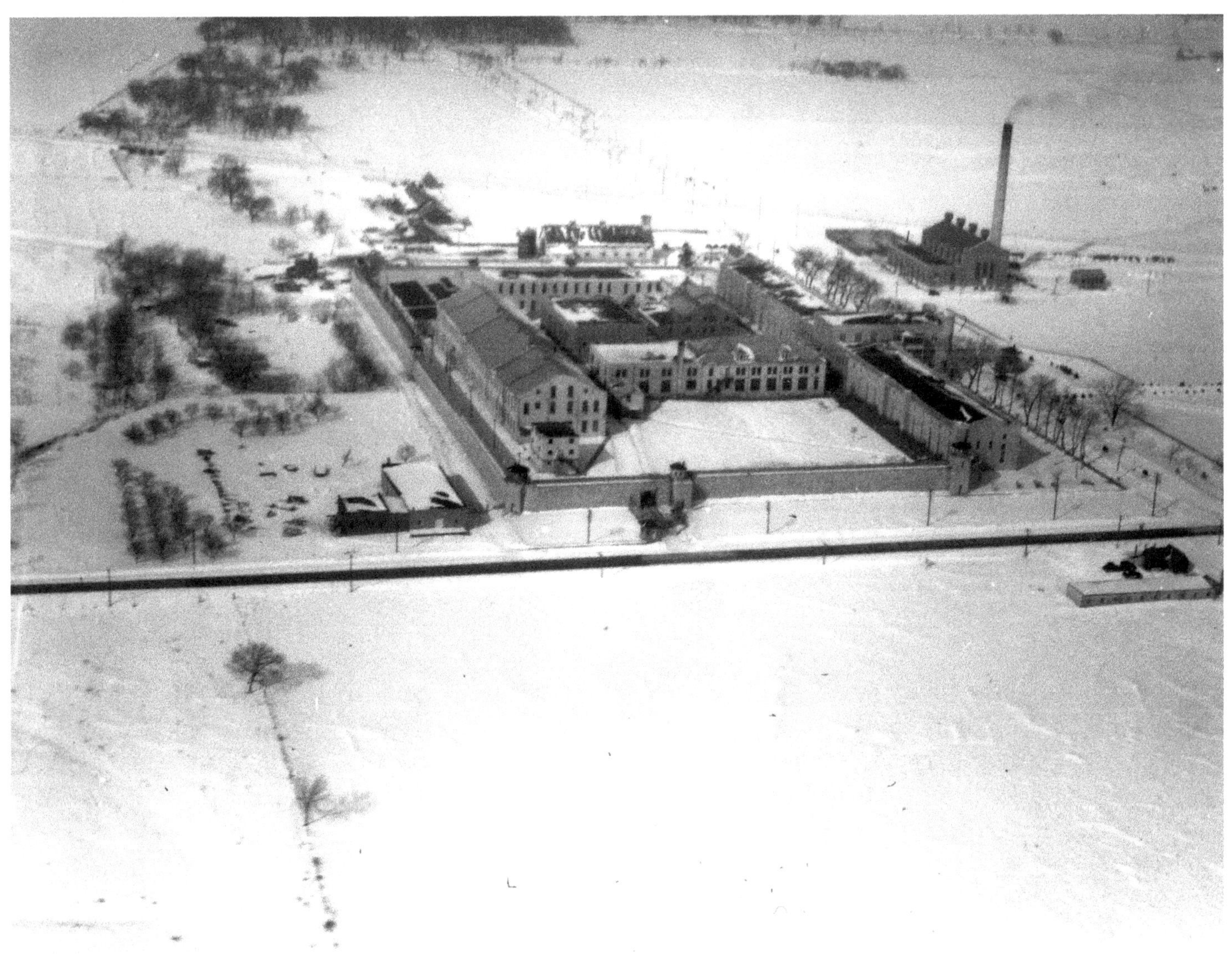

The Nebraska State Penitentiary, located in the southwestern part of Lincoln, is shown here around 1930. Its origins date from 1869, just two years after Nebraska joined the Union as the 37th state. Since 1903, all executions have been carried out at the penitentiary. Before World War I, it was the only adult correctional facility in the state.

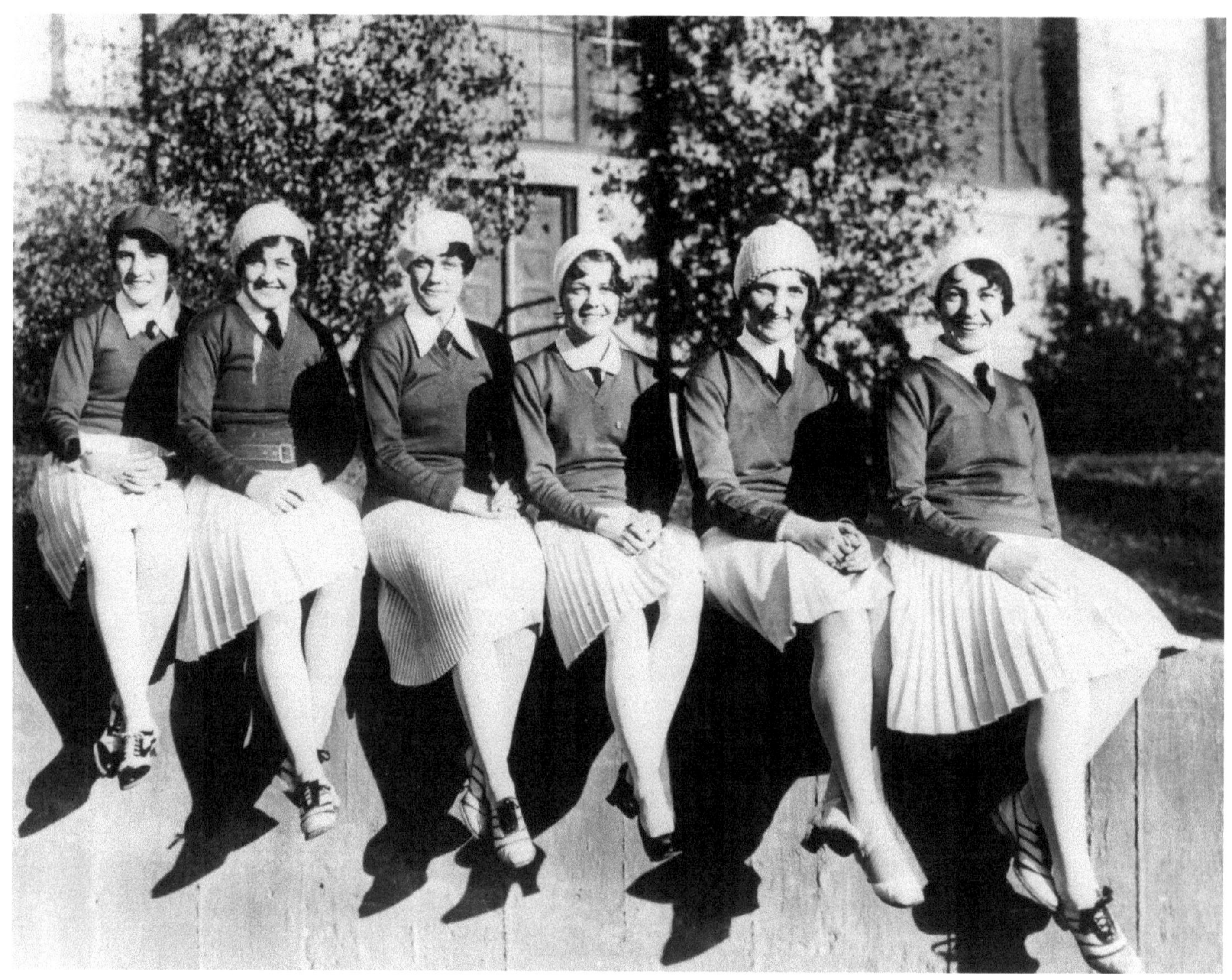

The University of Nebraska's football program was already nationally known in 1929, when these six cheerleaders helped stir up enthusiasm at games in Memorial Stadium. By that time, the Cornhuskers had defeated highly touted Notre Dame twice—in 1922, in the last year of old Nebraska Field, and in 1923, in the first season for new Memorial Stadium. Those two losses were the only ones ever sustained by coach Knute Rockne's famous "Four Horsemen" backfield.

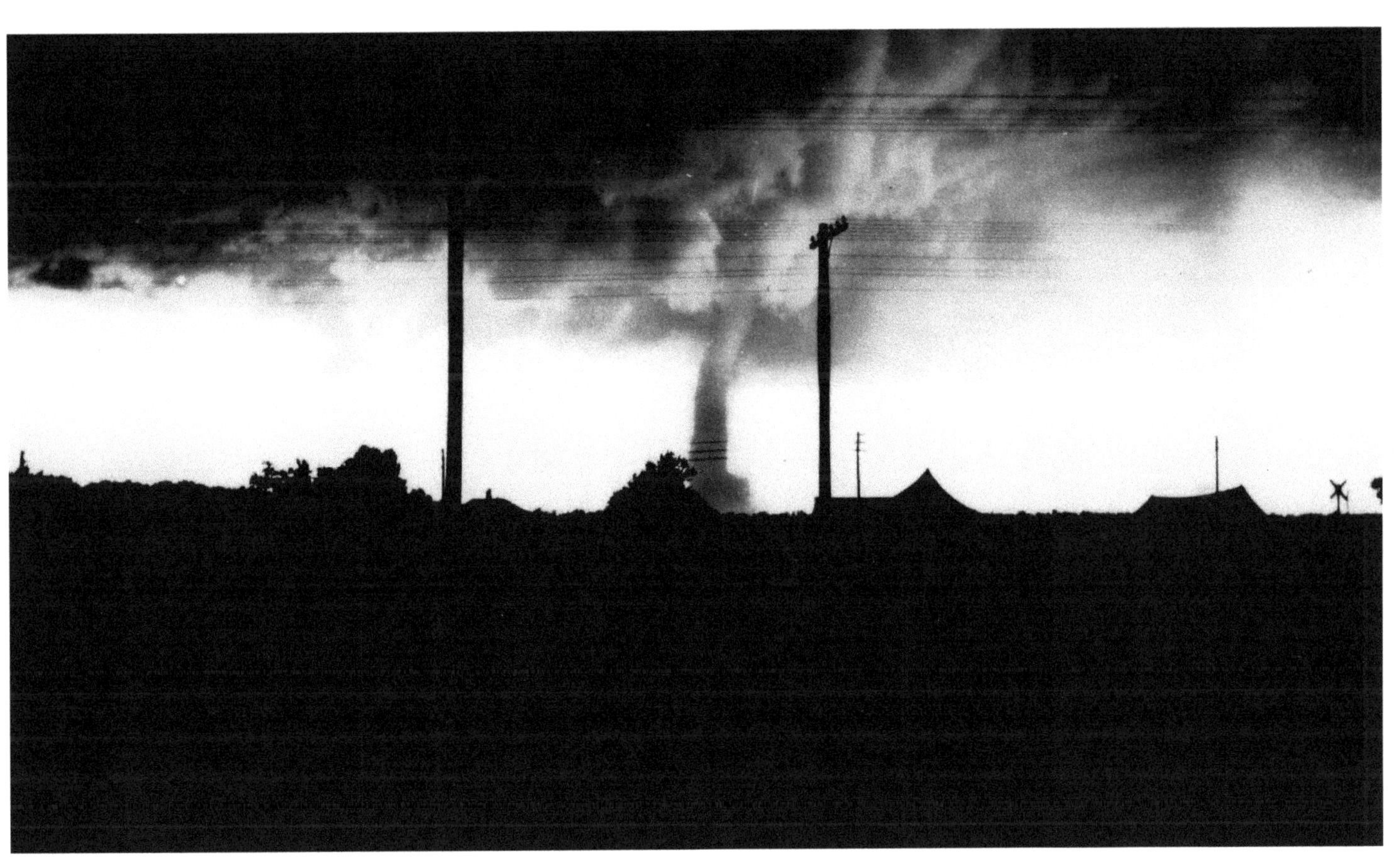

This tornado, shown near Gothenburg, was one of several to cause devastation in a wide swath through rural areas for 100 miles along the south side of the Platte River from Lincoln County across Dawson and Gosper counties into Phelps County the evening of June 24, 1930. The slow-moving storm caused more than $200,000 in property damage, but resulted in only one death and five injuries because people telephoned warnings to their neighbors.

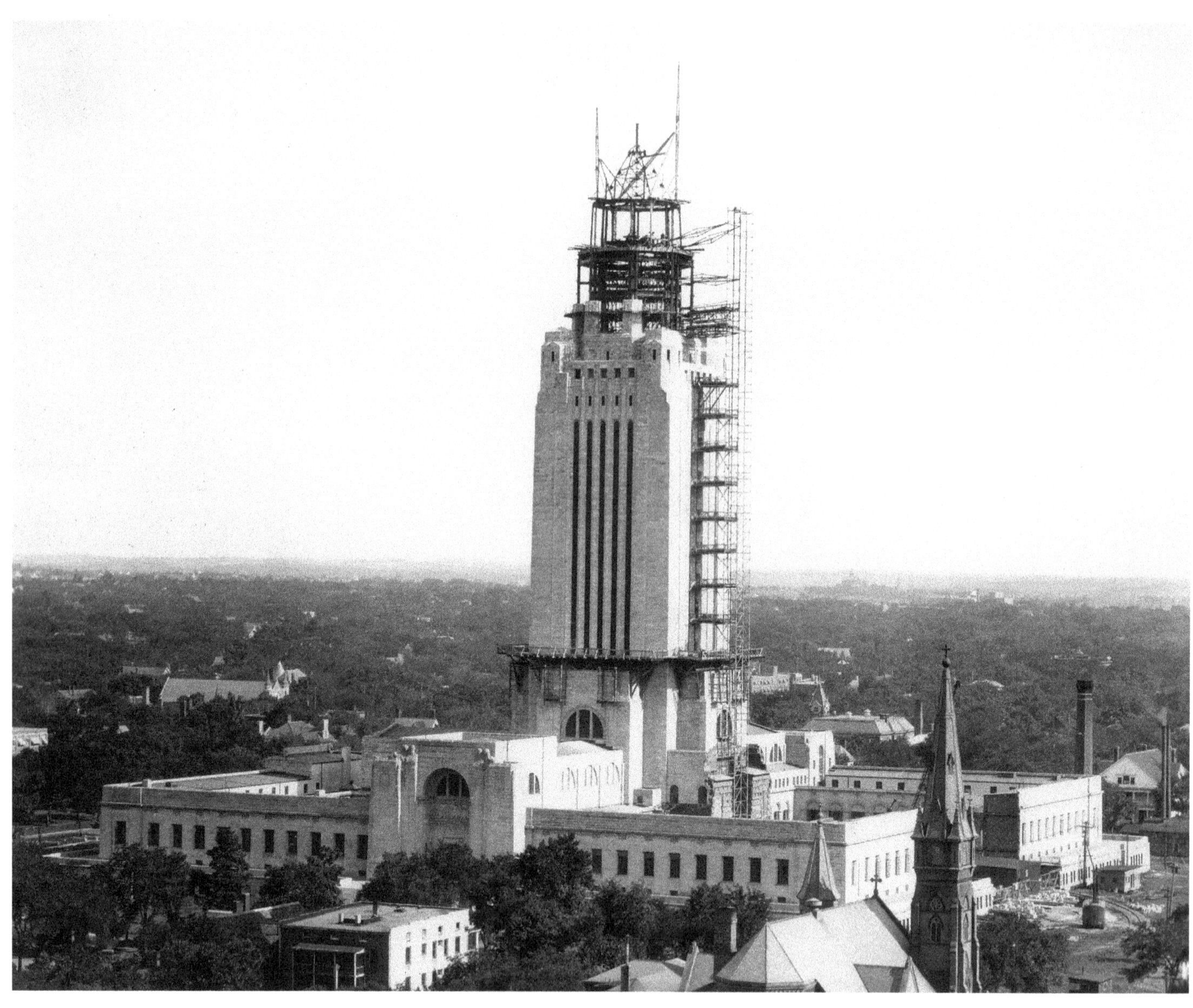

This bird's-eye view of the State Capitol was recorded in 1929, with its tower nearing completion. Construction advanced on a pay-as-you-go basis. The project began in 1922 and ended in 1932, for a total cost of $9.8 million.

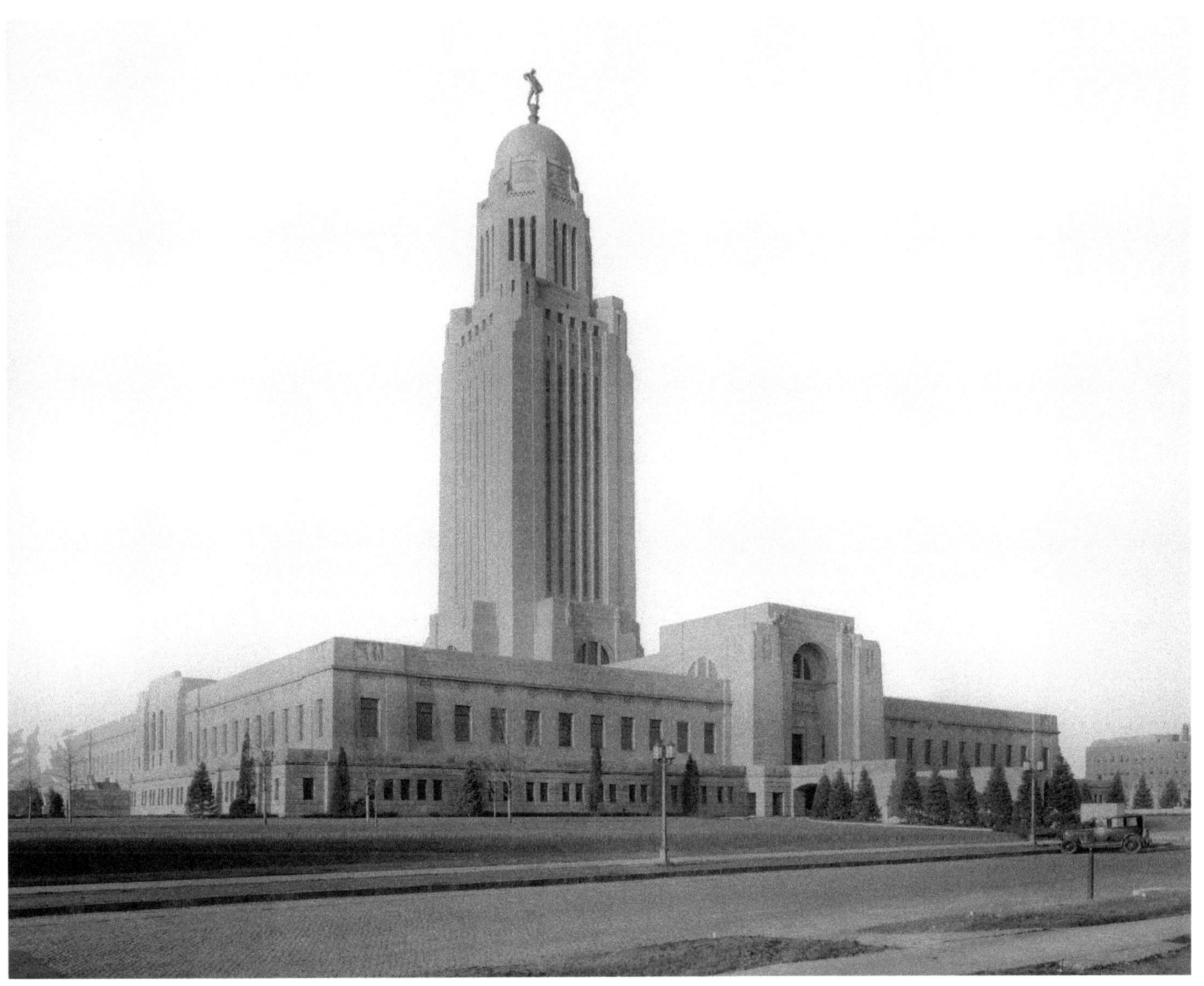

The third (and current) Nebraska State Capitol is recognized as one of the most significant buildings in the nation. Designed by architect Bertram Grosvenor Goodhue, it was built of Indiana limestone. The 437-foot-wide base was constructed around the second capitol, which, in turn, was dismantled to make room for the 400-foot tower. Sculptor Lee Lawrie created the bronze *Sower,* and his thematic carvings are evident throughout, as are inscriptions by native Nebraskan Hartley Burr Alexander.

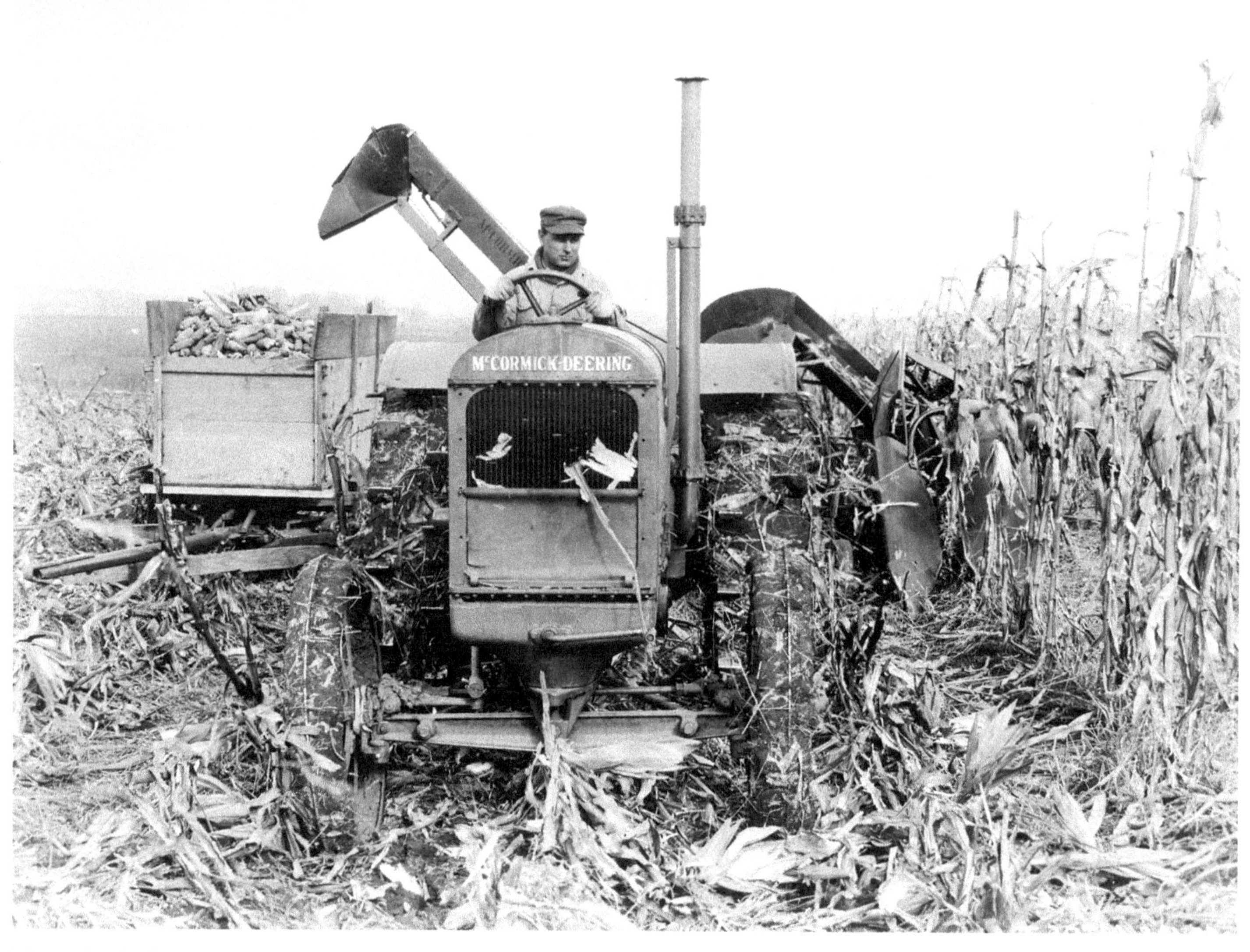

This Nebraska farmer is making good use of his McCormick-Deering single-row corn picker. The success of the annual corn harvest was important to the financial well-being of the Depression-era farmer, even if he planted other crops such as wheat or alfalfa.

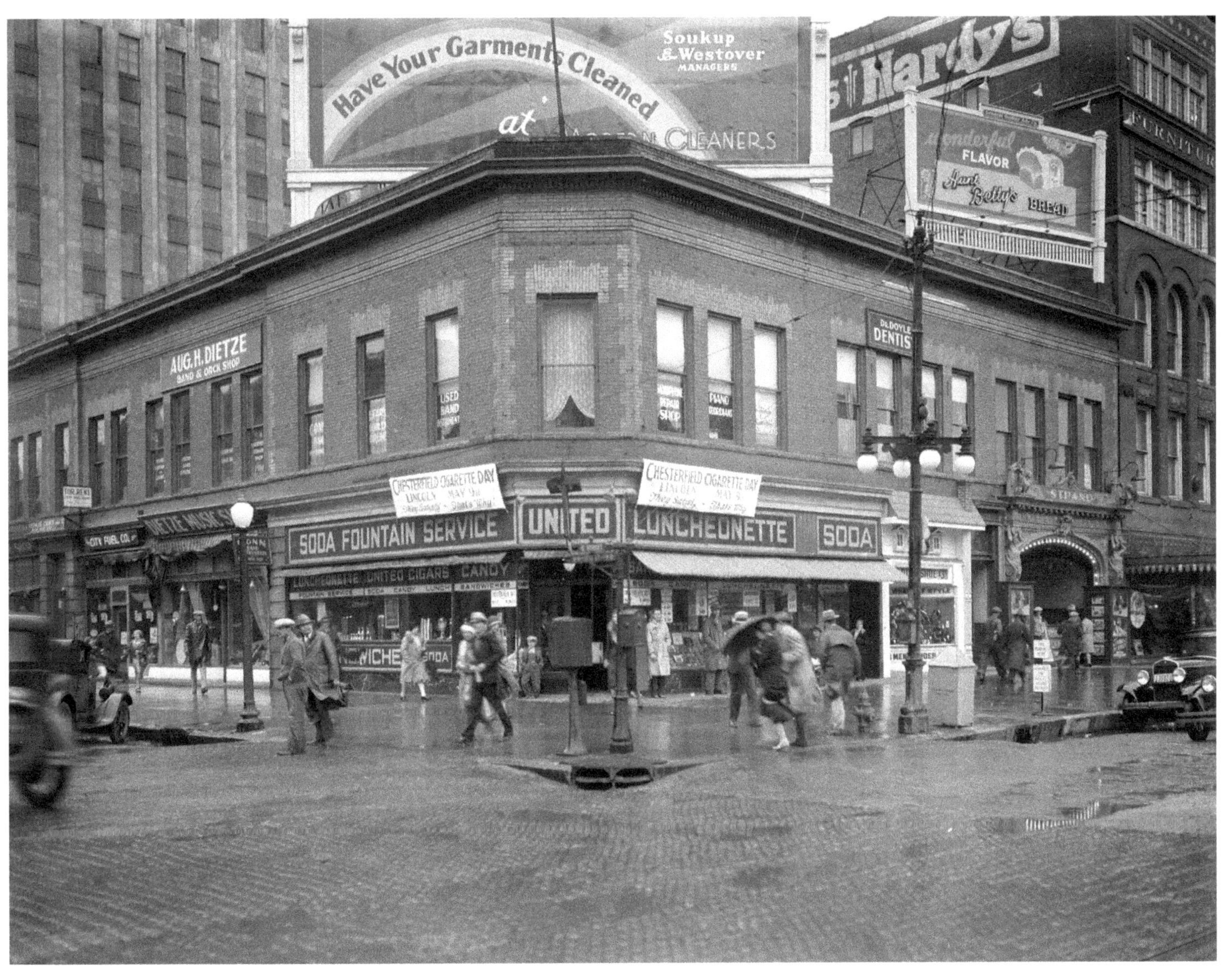

It's a wet and blustery day here in 1931 at the intersection of 13th and O streets in Lincoln. Dietze Music Shop, United Luncheonette, the Strand theater, and other businesses in view provided a handy escape from the rain.

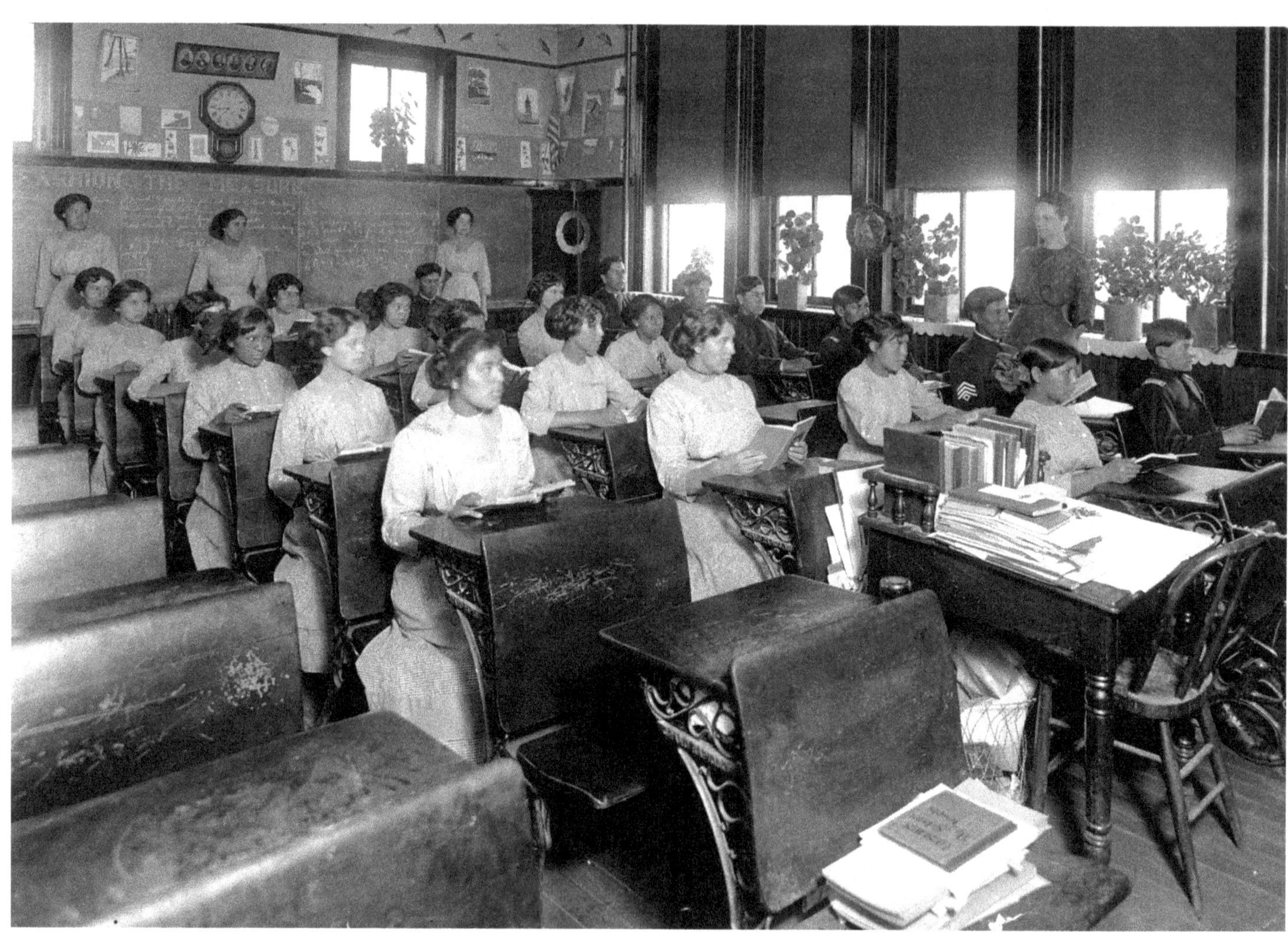

The Indian Industrial School was a boarding institution established in Genoa in 1884 by the Bureau of Indian Affairs in an attempt to "Americanize" a new generation of Native Americans by giving them an education and Christian training. The building had formerly housed a vocational school for Pawnee, who requested the school as part of a treaty with the federal government. At least 20 tribes from 10 different states were represented at the later school, which housed nearly 600 students at its high-water mark before closing in 1934.

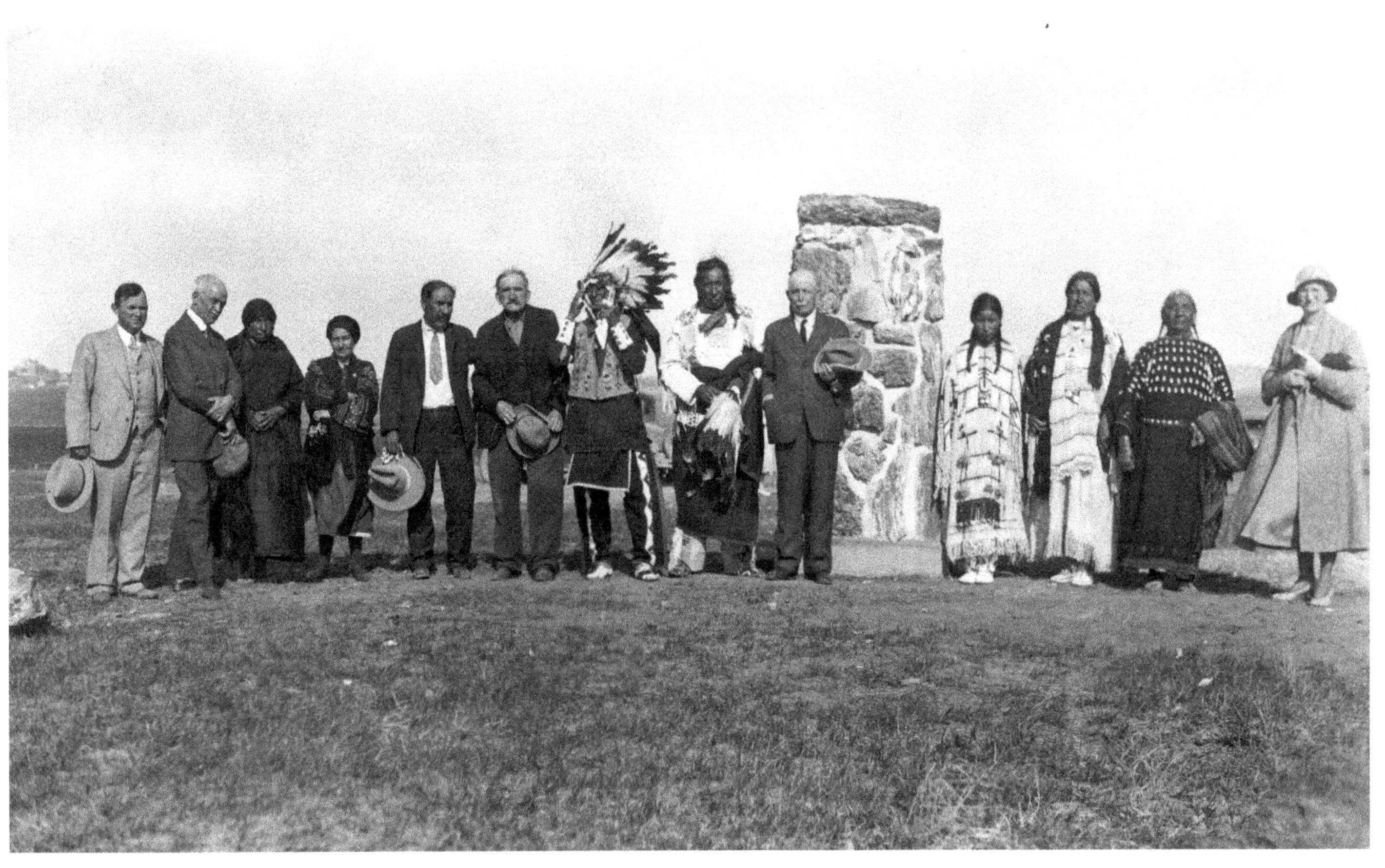

A group of dignitaries and relatives of the famous Oglala Lakota chief Red Cloud gathered May 9, 1932, for the dedication of a monument to the old Red Cloud Agency, a holding area for Lakota from 1873 to 1877. Following the killing of the agency clerk, troops were brought in and stationed nearby at Camp Robinson, which later became Fort Robinson. In 1878, the agency was moved to South Dakota and named the Pine Ridge Indian Reservation.

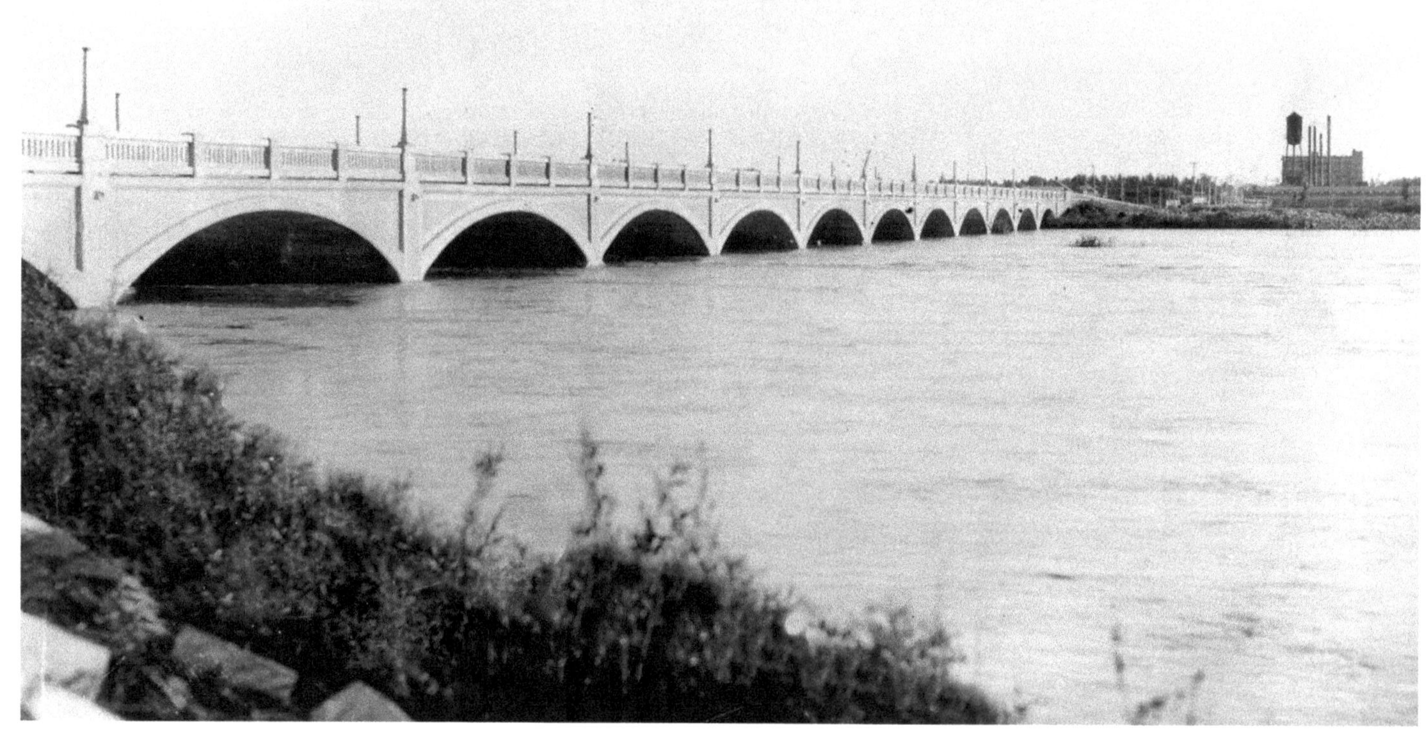

A factory with smokestacks and water tower is visible beyond the North Platte River Bridge, since razed, which spanned the North Platte River near Scottsbluff. The North Platte Valley is home to many huge rock formations that were mileposts for more than half a million Oregon Trail travelers. This image was recorded by O. W. Simmons.

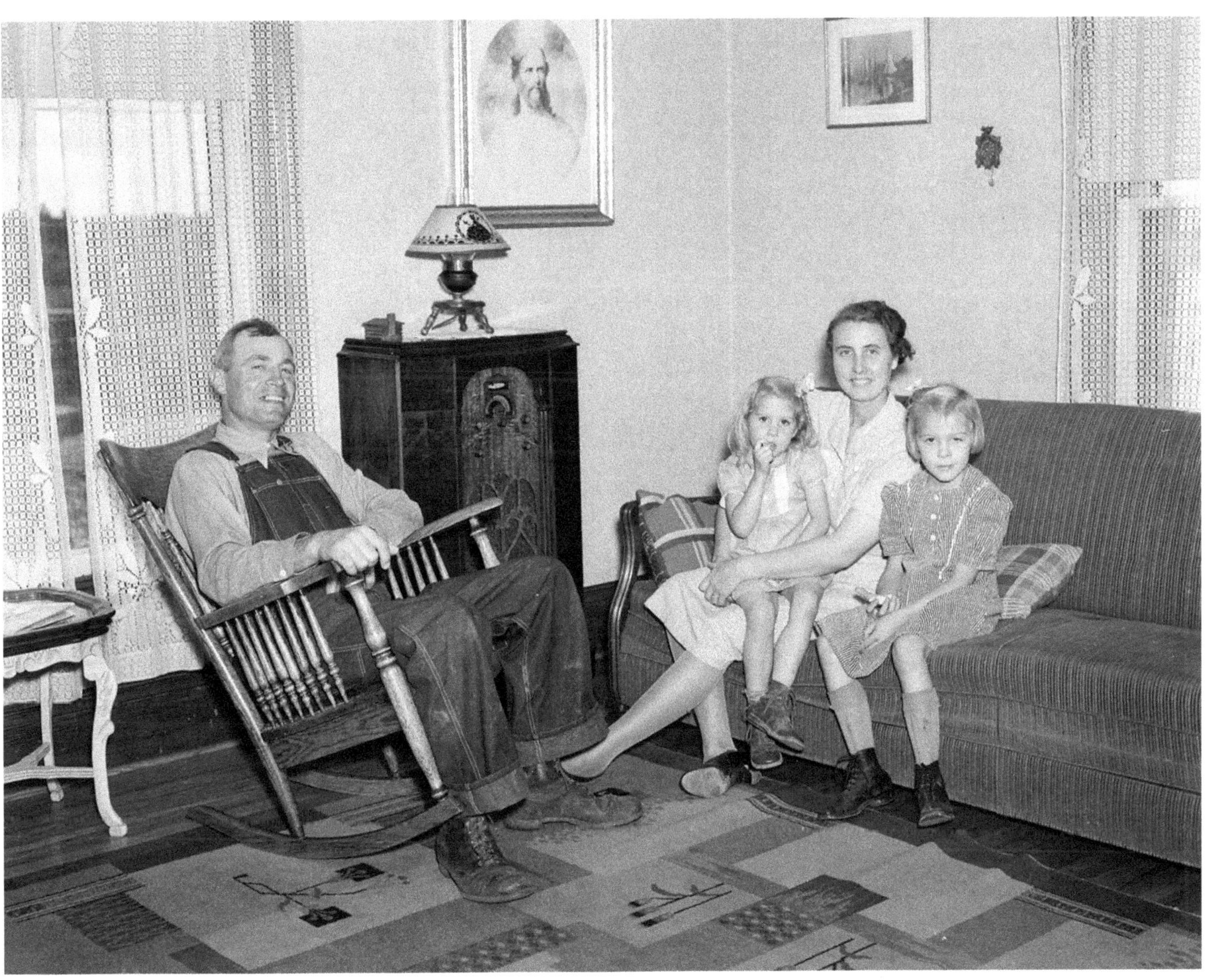

The big radio in the living room was one of the few creature comforts that Nebraska farm families could enjoy on a regular basis during the Great Depression. A framed picture of Jesus, hardwood flooring, lace curtains, and a miniature cuckoo clock complete the decor. This image is among those recorded by photographer Frederick Macdonald's Lincoln studio.

Known as a lawyer and judge in Beaver City before he moved to McCook, George Norris was elected to Congress, where he successfully fought his own Republican leadership to limit the power of the Speaker of the House. In 1912, he was elected to the Senate, where he served the next 30 years. By authoring the 20th Amendment, Norris helped reconfigure Congressional sessions and presidential terms of office so that they begin soon after Election Day.

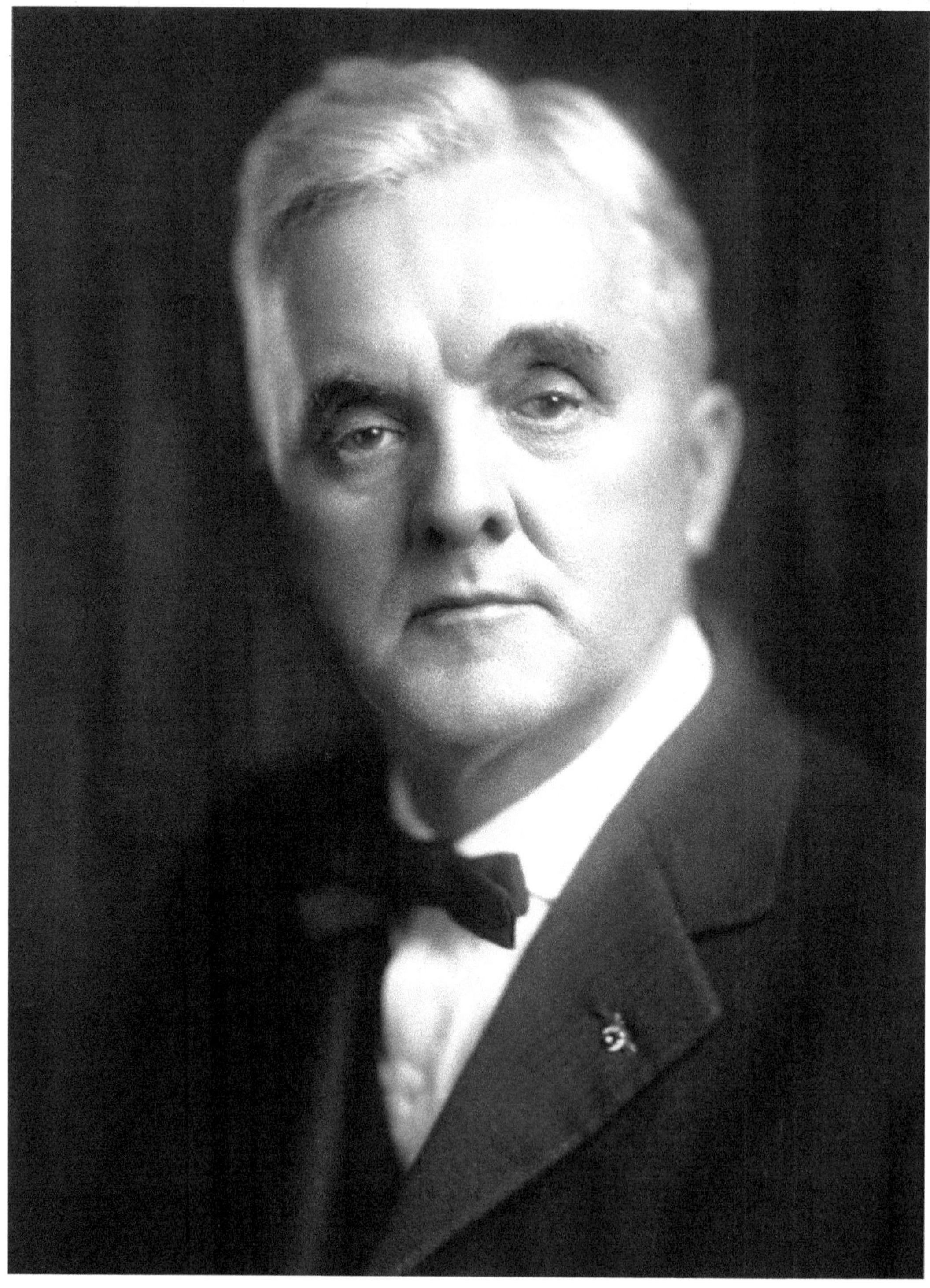

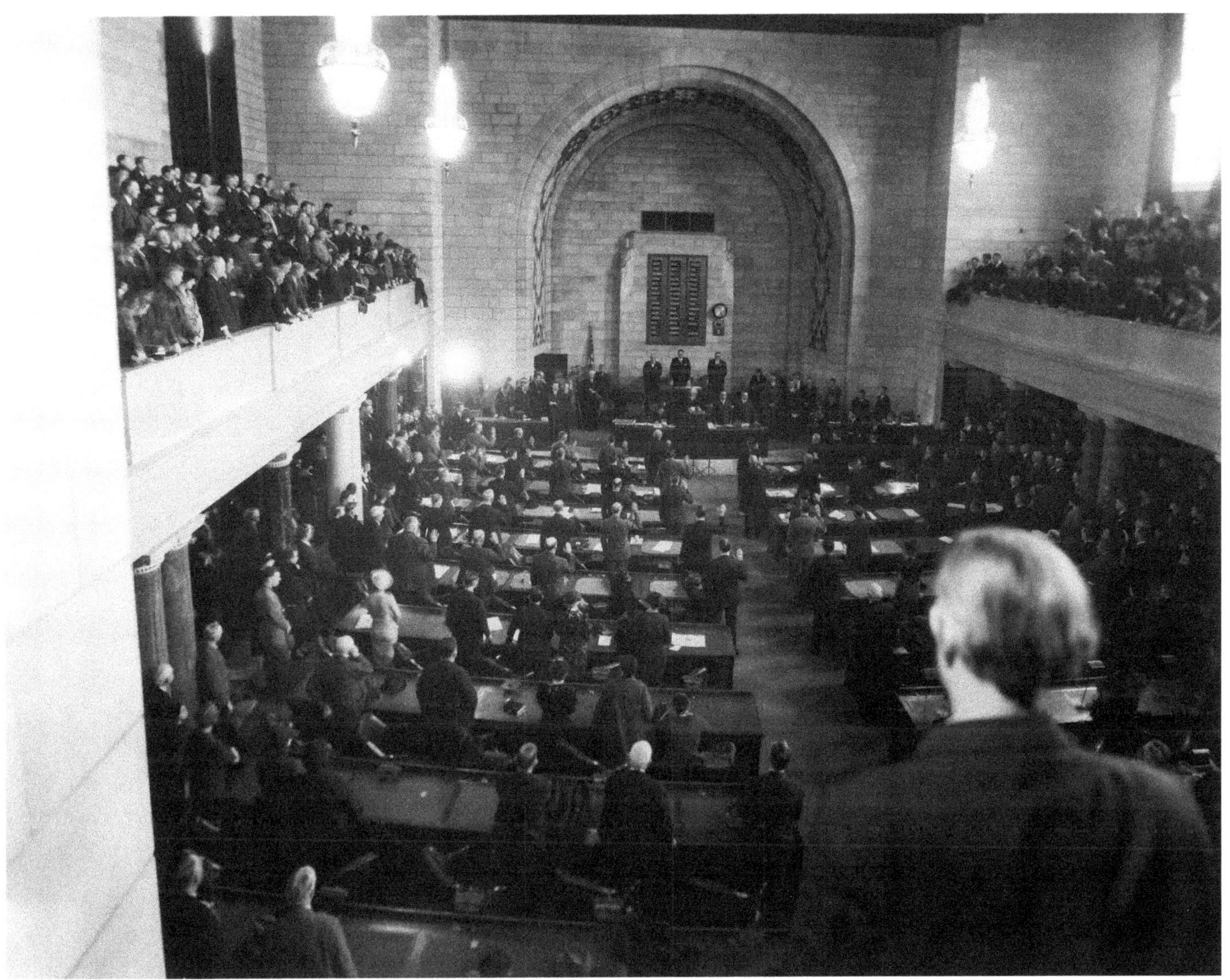

Known as a champion of liberal causes, George Norris continued to be elected by Nebraskans because of his reputation as a straightforward, independent thinker. Norris was instrumental in the passage of the Rural Electrification Act, and he proposed that all states adopt a nonpartisan one-house (unicameral) legislature to cut through political red tape and save money. In this image, Norris (at center podium) presides over the swearing in of the first such legislature—in his home state of Nebraska.

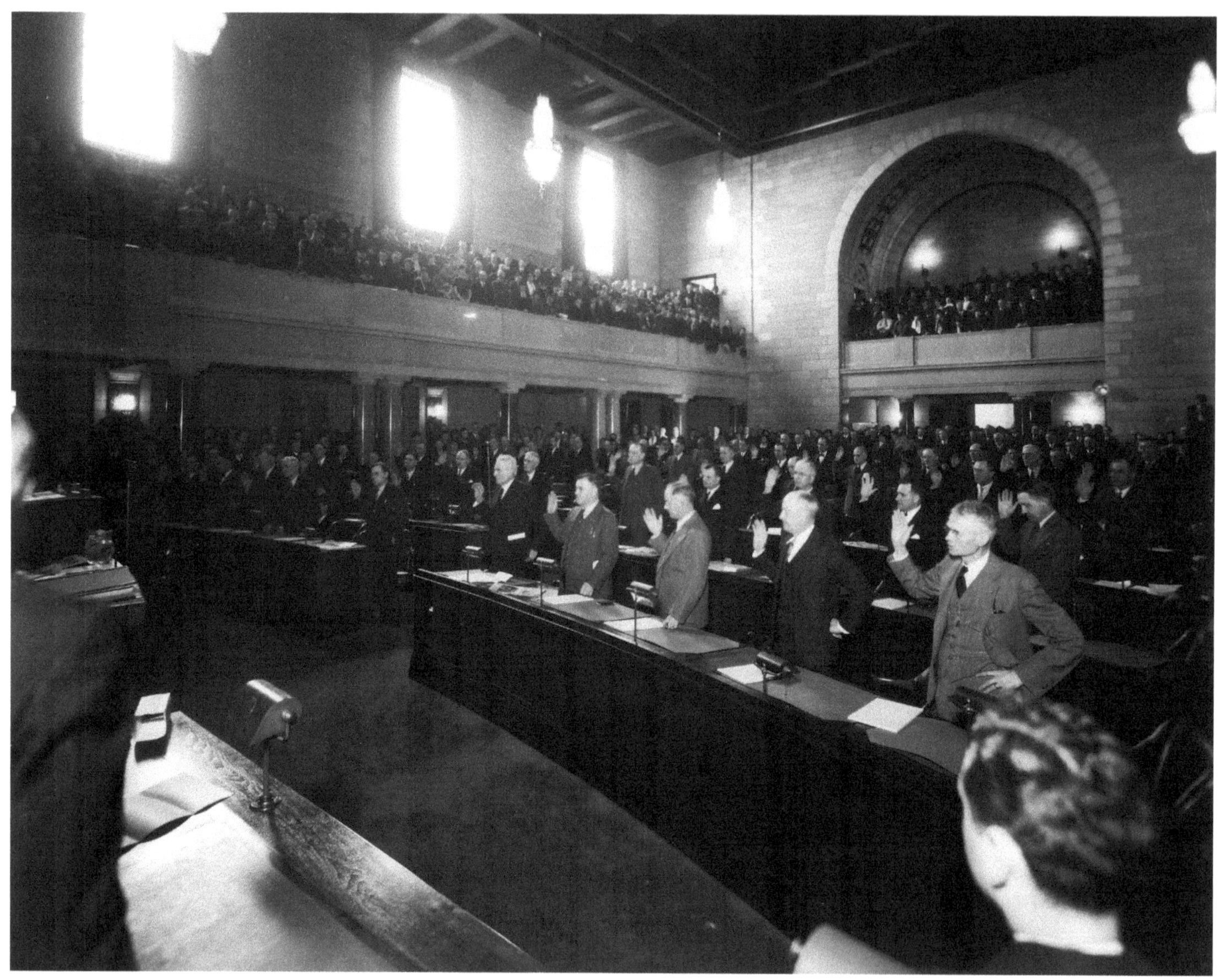

The first unicameral state legislature in the nation's history is sworn in on January 5, 1937, in the Nebraska State Capitol. Authorized by constitutional amendment in 1934, it was one of the most dramatic steps ever taken to shrink the size of a state's government. As of 2010, Nebraska remains the only state with a nonpartisan unicameral legislature.

ESTABLISHED NEBRASKA

(1938–1970S)

That old enemy, extreme weather, attacked Nebraska with a vengeance during the 1930s even as the Great Depression hit the entire nation. Extreme heat, drought, and dust storms made life miserable across the Great Plains, especially for those who did not yet have electricity.

Through tax dollars, the federal government employed many out-of-work Americans in Franklin Delano Roosevelt's myriad New Deal programs. In one of these programs, photographer John Vachon of the Farm Security Administration used his camera to capture Nebraska's response to the tough economic times. Many of his photographs are included in this chapter.

More than 2,000 German prisoners of war were held in confinement at Fort Robinson in the northern Panhandle as World War II brought testing and trials to the nation. Some of the war's many heroes were west-central Nebraska women—an absolute army of homemakers who met every troop train at the Union Pacific depot in North Platte with coffee, fruit, sandwiches, and birthday cakes for anyone in uniform. For decades afterward, countless numbers of thankful soldiers, sailors, airmen, and marines poured out their fond memories of the North Platte Canteen.

Always a highly regarded destination for hunting and fishing, the state became increasingly sports-minded after the war, with high school athletics gaining in popularity. Several Nebraskans achieved Hall of Fame status in football and baseball, both at the college and professional levels. Late in the twentieth century, the University of Nebraska built one of the most successful college volleyball programs in the nation, but the state is probably best known for its unprecedented 33-year run of dominance in college football from 1969 to 2001, during which the Cornhuskers never failed to win at least nine games or go to a bowl.

Nebraska constantly rates high on the national charts in quality of life, based on its friendly population, laid-back pace of life, relatively stable economy, low cost of living, and relative lack of crime. Thousands of tourists who visit the state each spring to watch the migration of Sandhill cranes realize that Nebraska is a place of durability and timelessness that celebrates the recurring themes of life.

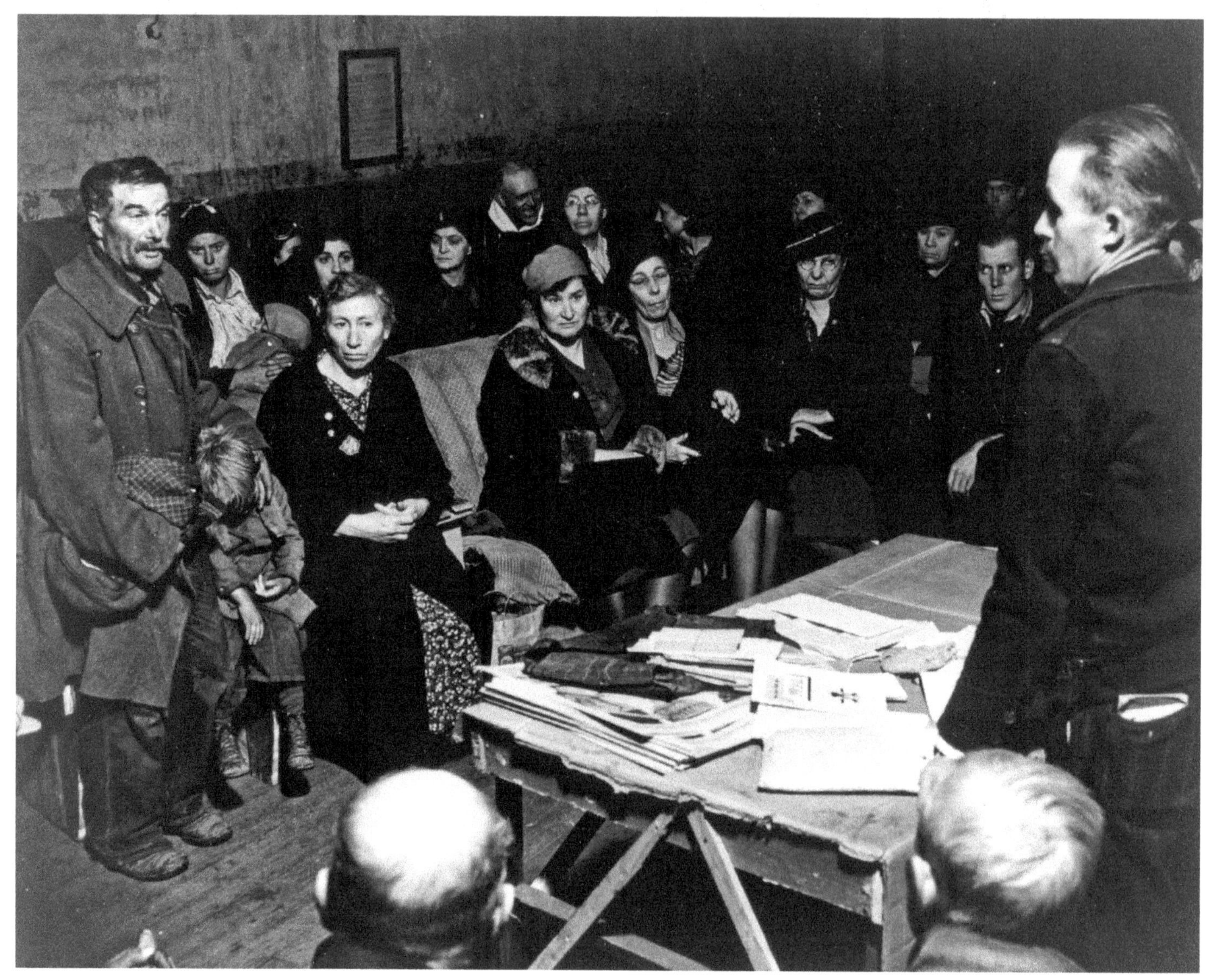

This photograph was taken by Hansel Mieth in North Platte at an organizational meeting of the Workers' Alliance of America, a national organization for the unemployed which was created in April 1936. Best known for her social commentary photography, Mieth was a German-born photojournalist who eventually worked for *Life* magazine.

This image of an unemployed father and son, recorded in the late 1930s at a Workers' Alliance of America meeting in North Platte, is one of Hansel Mieth's best-known photographs.

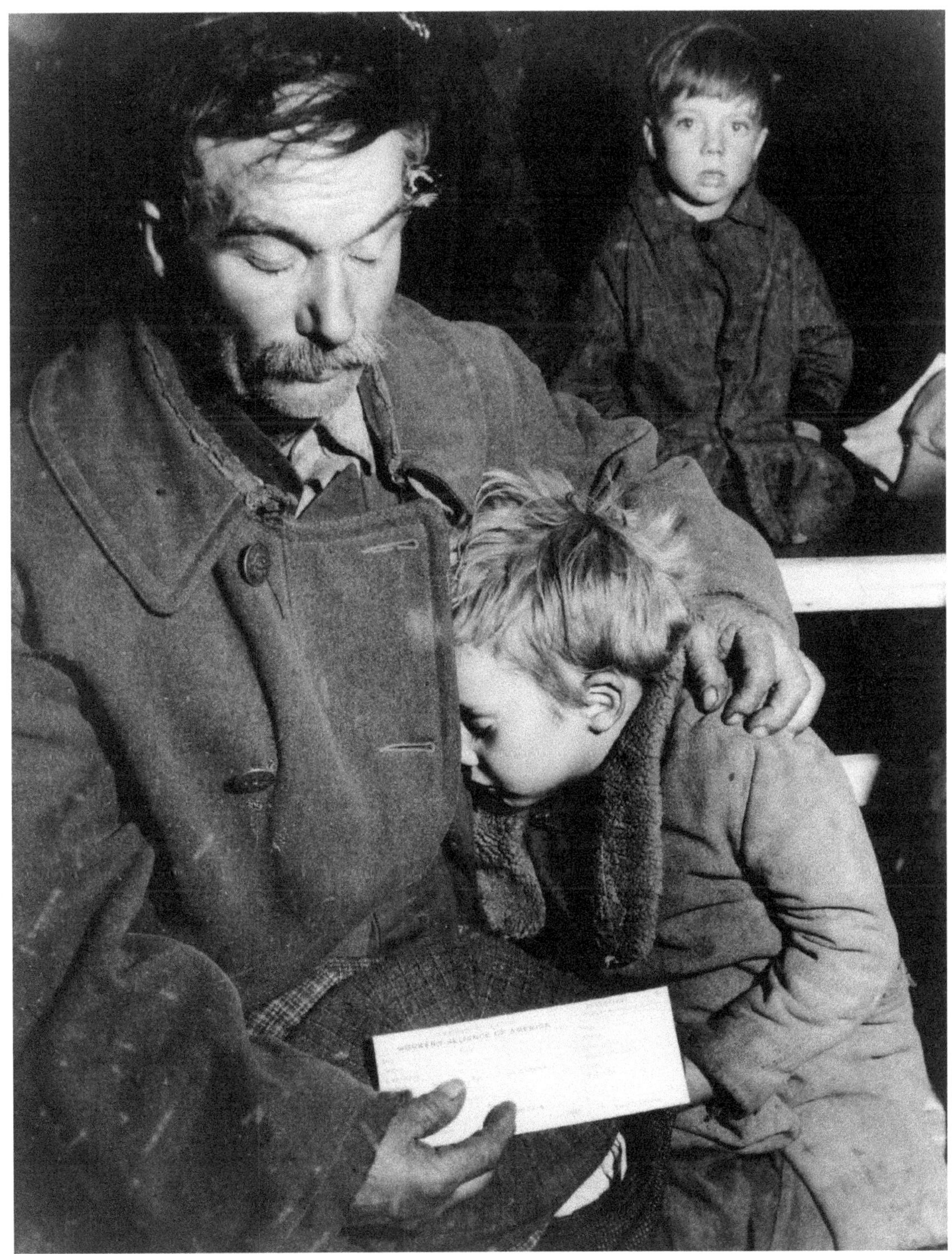

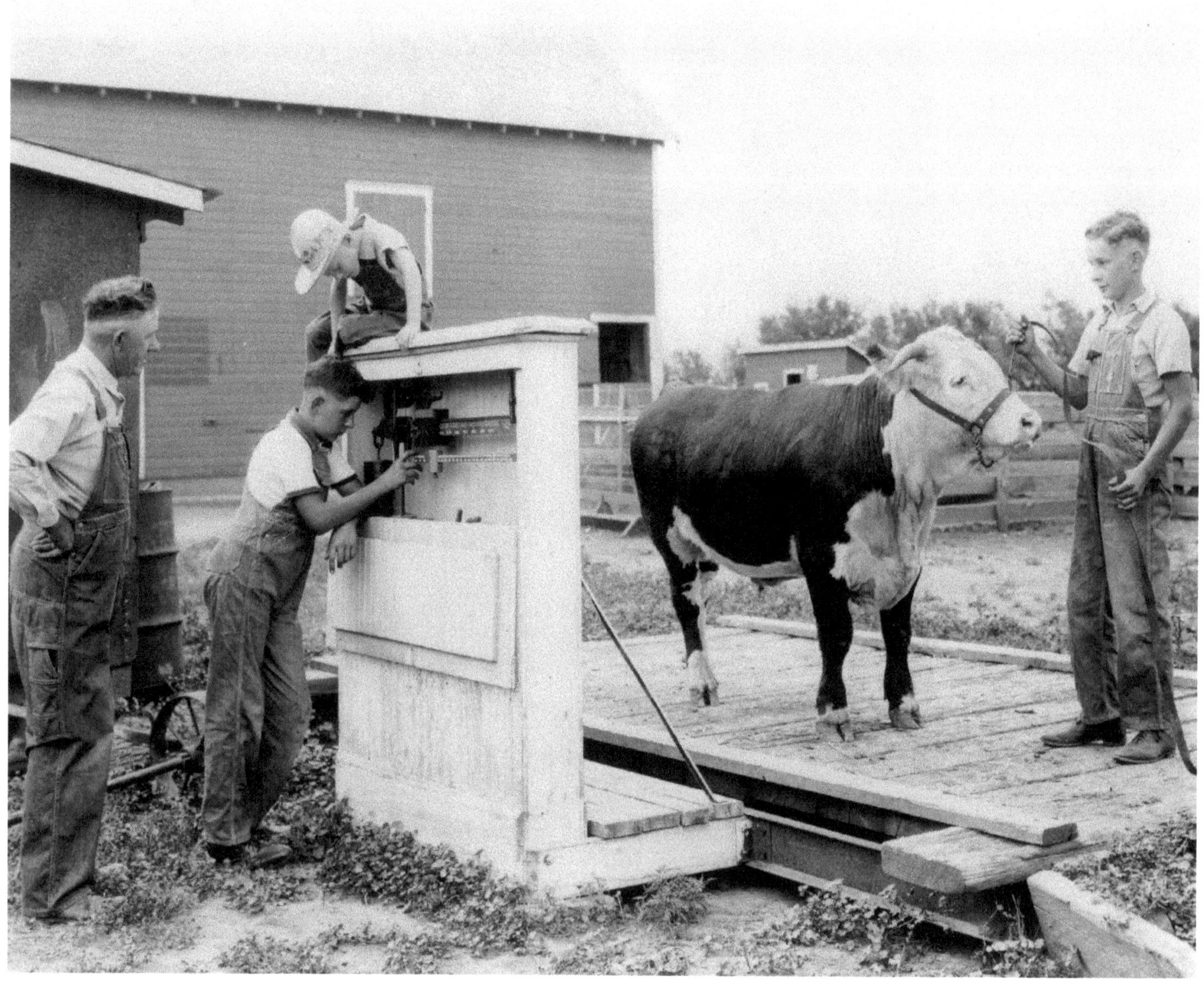

A 4-H member has his baby beef weighed as he prepares for the 1938 Seward County Fair. Nebraska youth have been learning responsibility, sharpening their skills, and pursuing their interests through 4-H since about 1905, just three years after the club's founding in the United States.

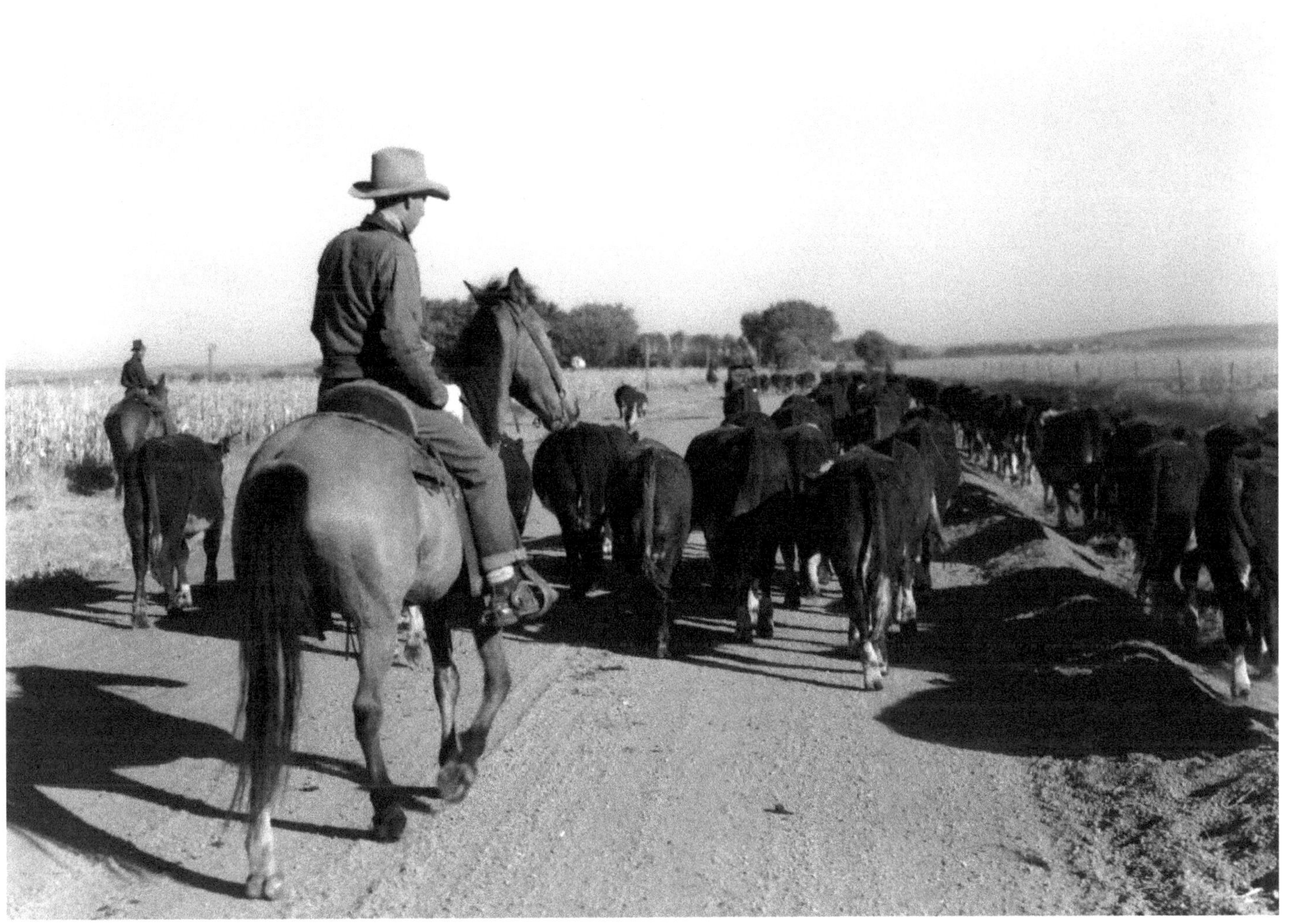

If you've ever driven your vehicle into the rear of a cattle drive on a rural road in Nebraska, you know you are in for a long wait. It's much better to meet one head-on. This 1938 photograph of a Dawson County cattle drive was made by John Vachon, who captured many images of the Great Depression on film.

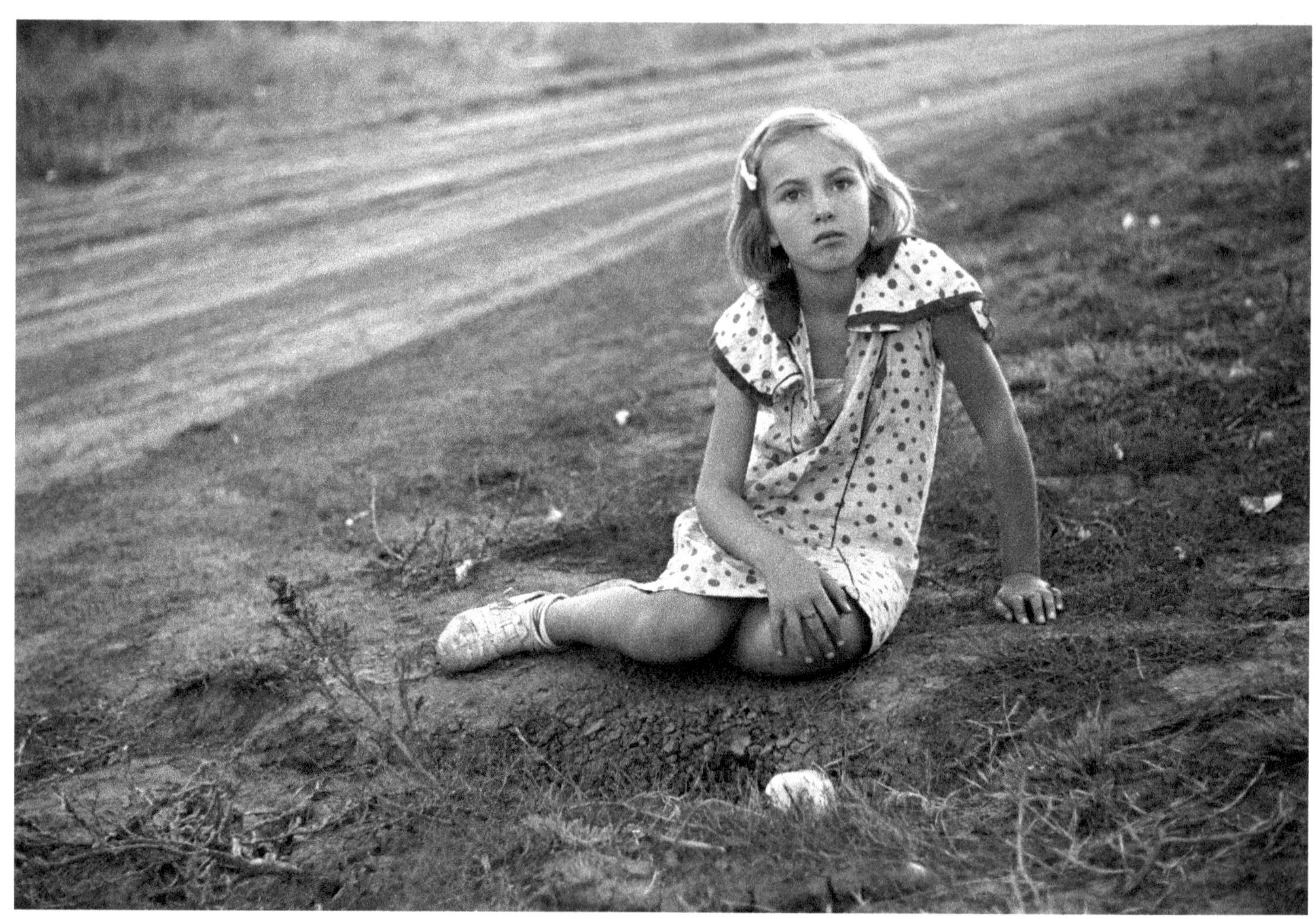

This photograph of a farm girl in Seward County was taken by John Vachon in 1938. Vachon was one of several photographers hired by Roy Stryker, who headed the Historical Section of FDR's Farm Security Administration. Stryker was charged with capturing a visual record of people hard hit by the Great Depression, and he sent some of the nation's best photographers on journeys across the nation to take the pictures.

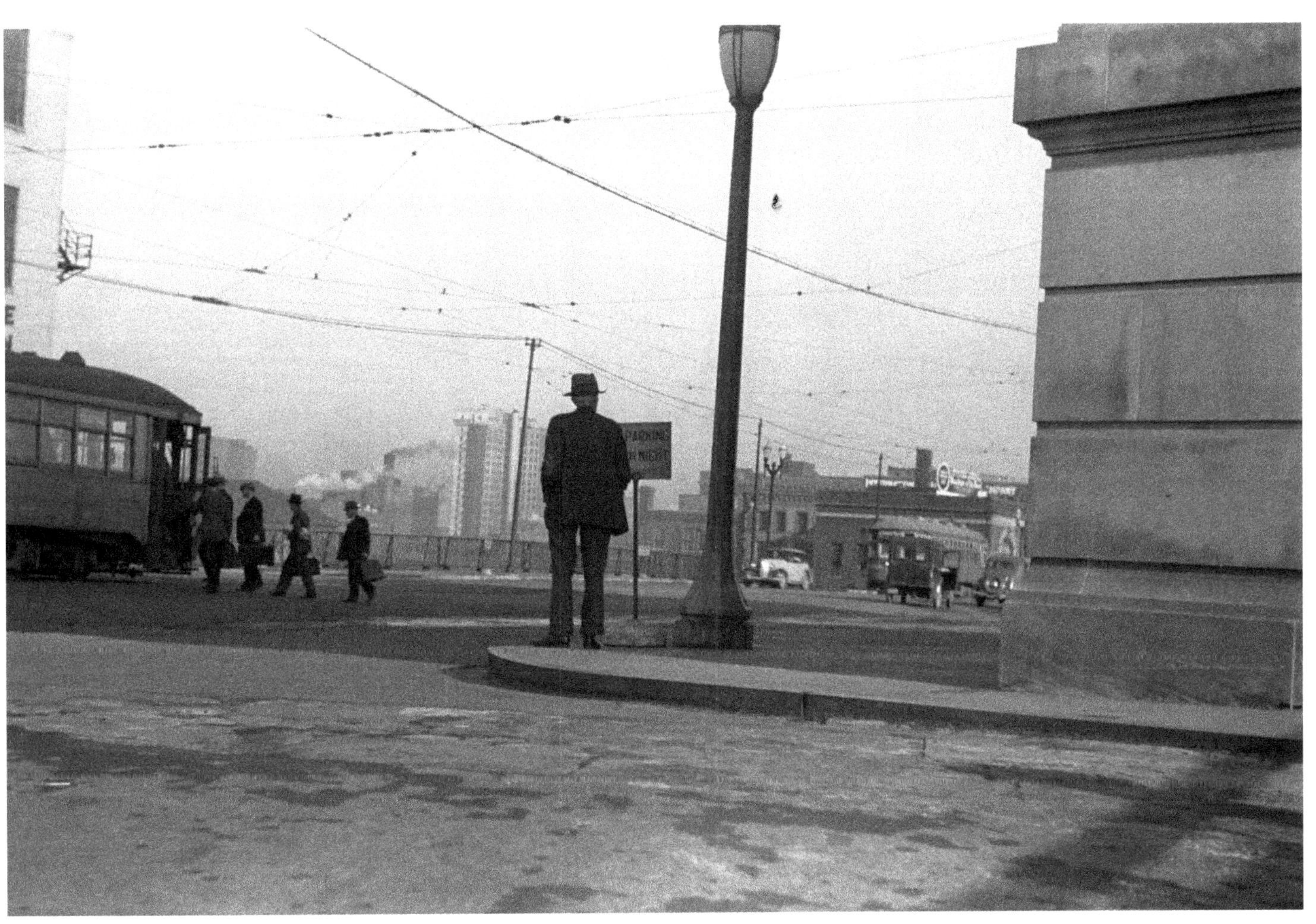

John Vachon traveled the United States from 1936 to 1943 as part of the Farm Security Administration's photography project. Vachon showed a nation in transition from the depths of the Great Depression to its mobilization for World War II. This 1938 photograph is titled "6:30 a.m. in front of Union Station, Omaha, Nebraska."

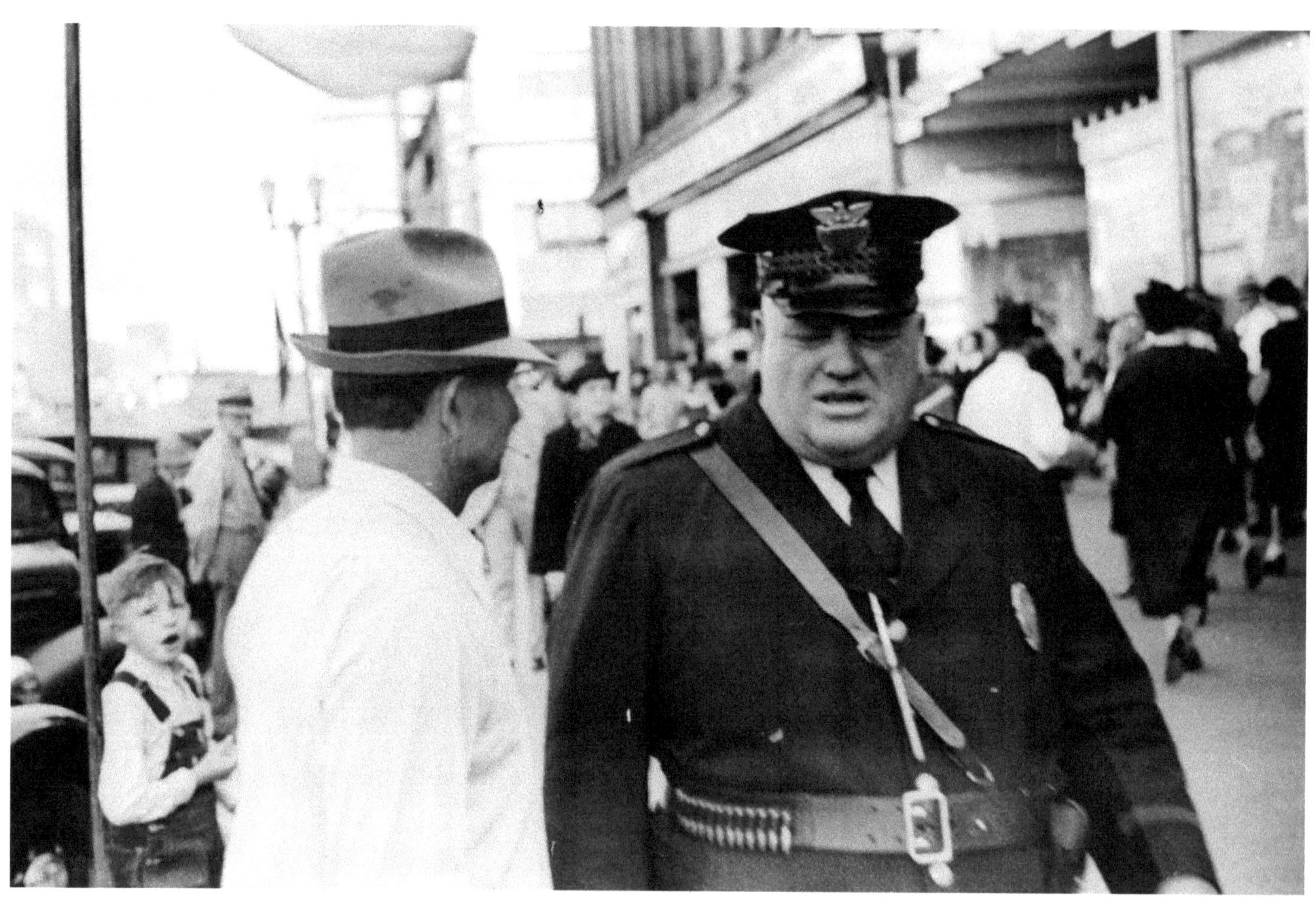

A policeman walks his beat on a crowded Lincoln street in October 1938. The Lincoln Police Department traces its history to its first three-man crew in July 1870.

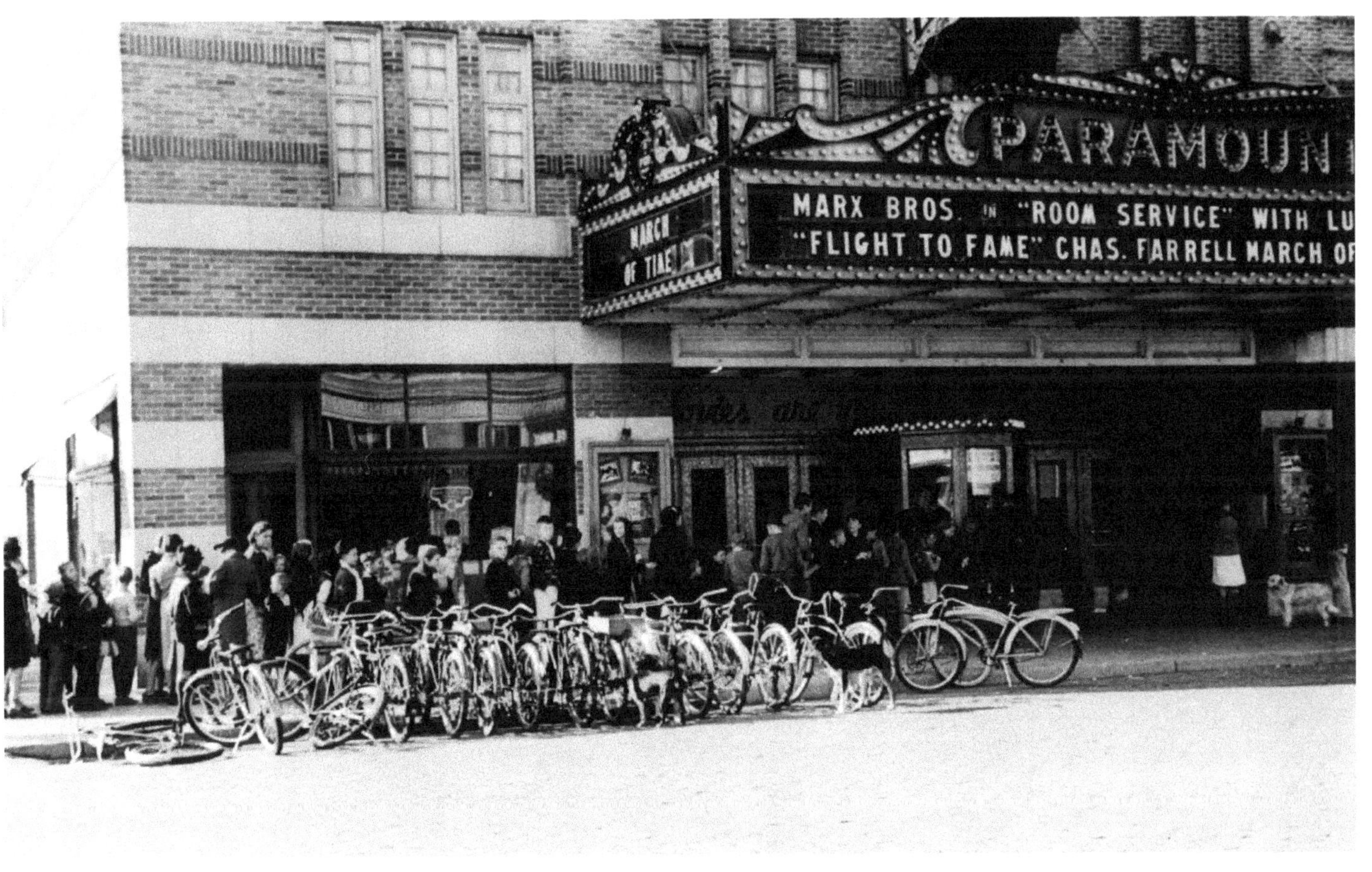

Glad to be out of school for the weekend, these kids park their bikes and line up on an October 1938 Saturday morning to see the Marx Brothers in *Room Service* at the Paramount Theater in North Platte.

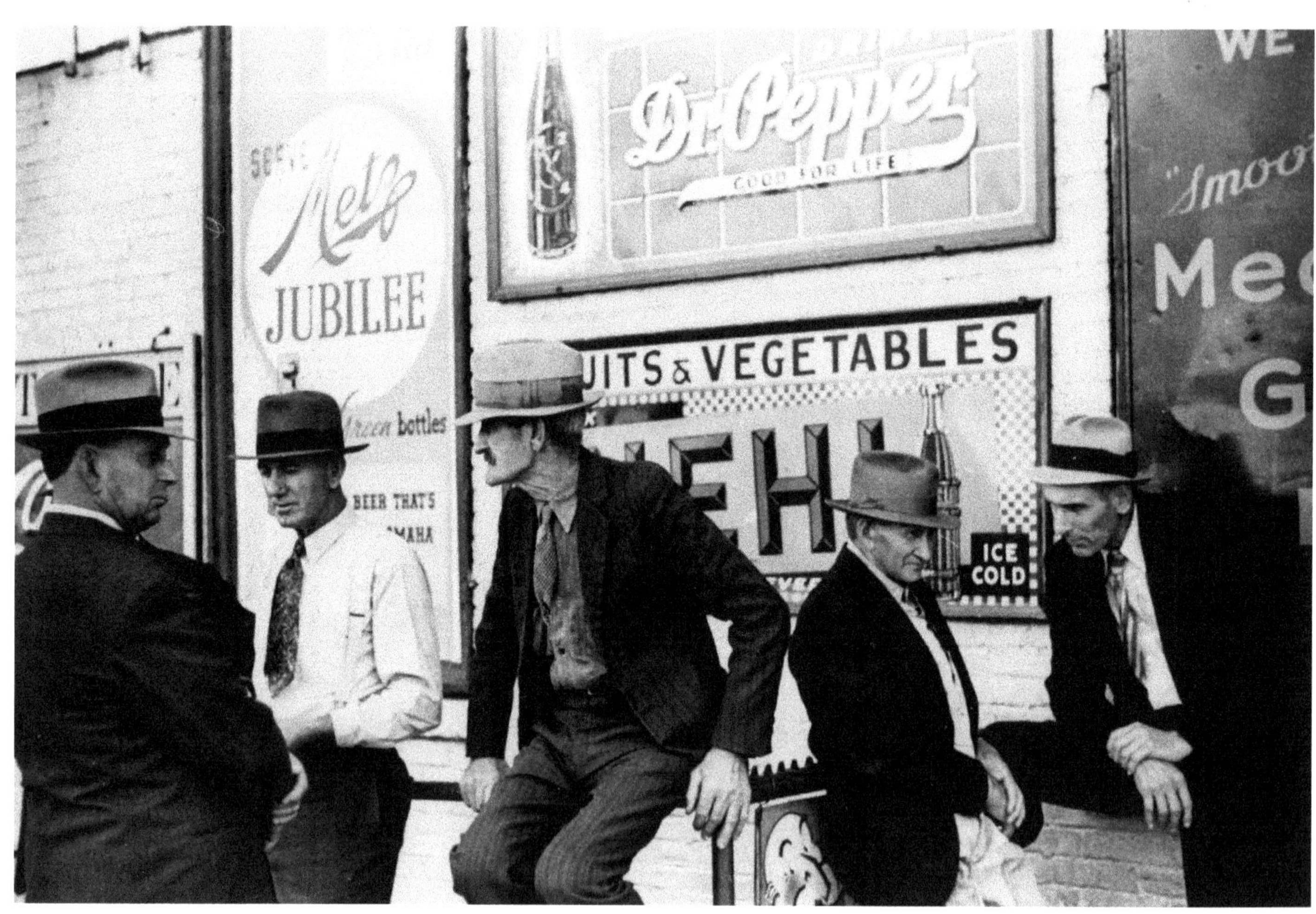

A group of men ponder their next move as they meet outside a Lincoln grocery store in the late 1930s. FDR's New Deal programs had been in force since 1932. Six years later and despite unprecedented levels of federal spending to relieve the symptoms of the Great Depression, in 1938 unemployment across the nation still hovered at an ominous 19 percent.

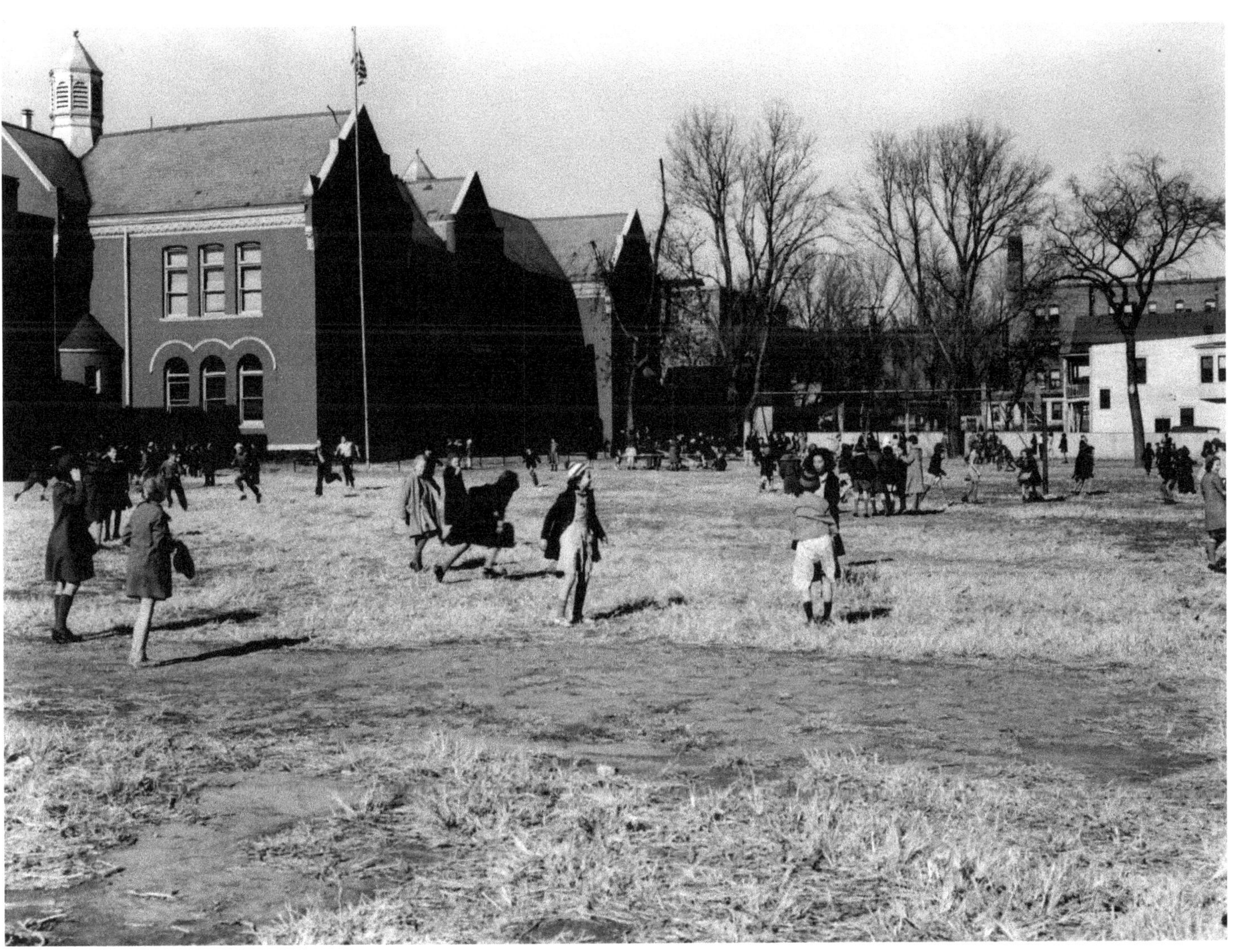

Students at an Omaha public school are bundled up on a chilly but sunny day in November 1938 in this photo by John Vachon, who had never used a camera before he was hired by the Farm Security Administration as an errand boy. Vachon borrowed one to use in his spare time, and within two years he was taking on FSA photo assignments. He eventually became a photographer for *Look* magazine.

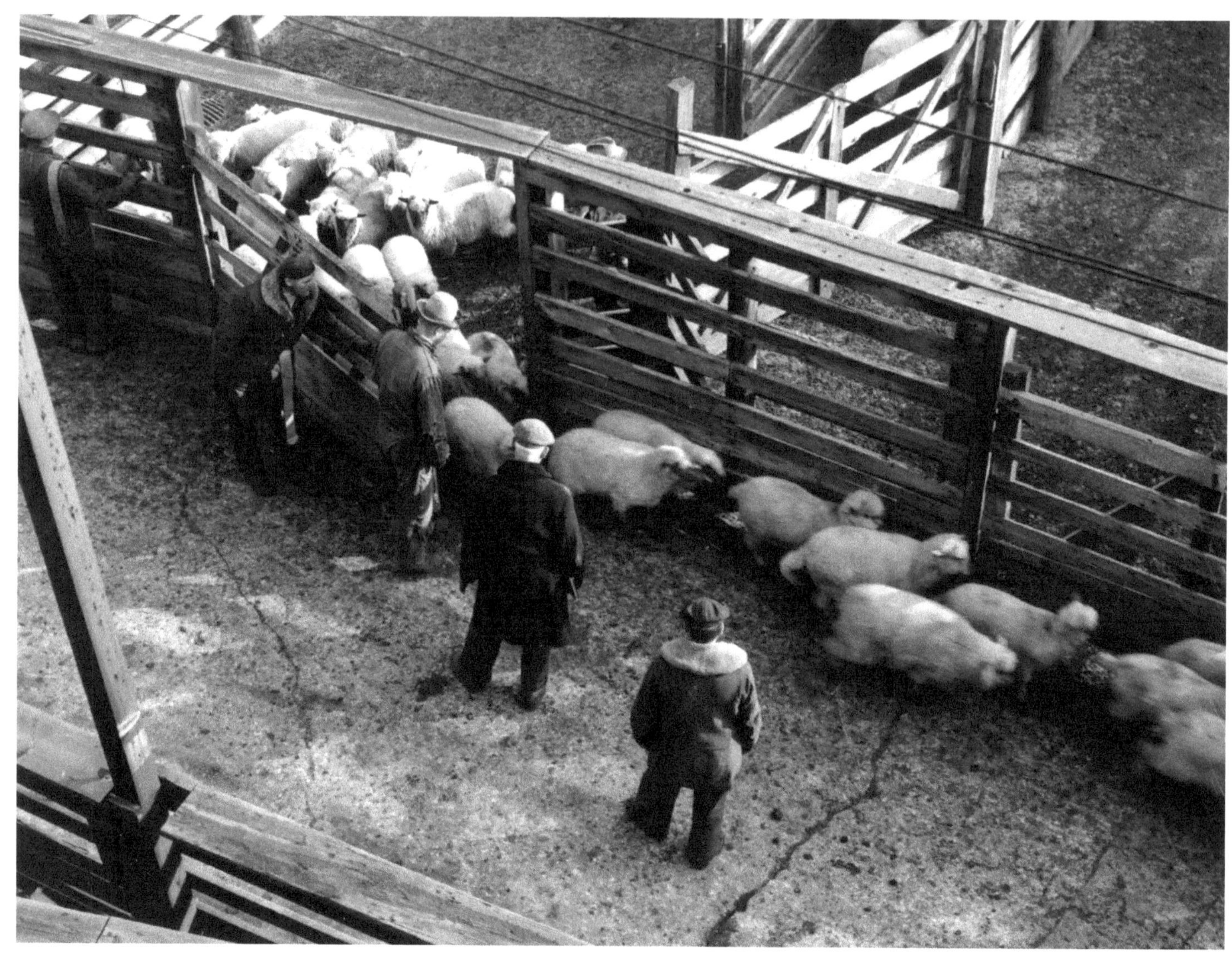

Sheep are counted and herded into Omaha's Union Stockyards in the late 1930s.

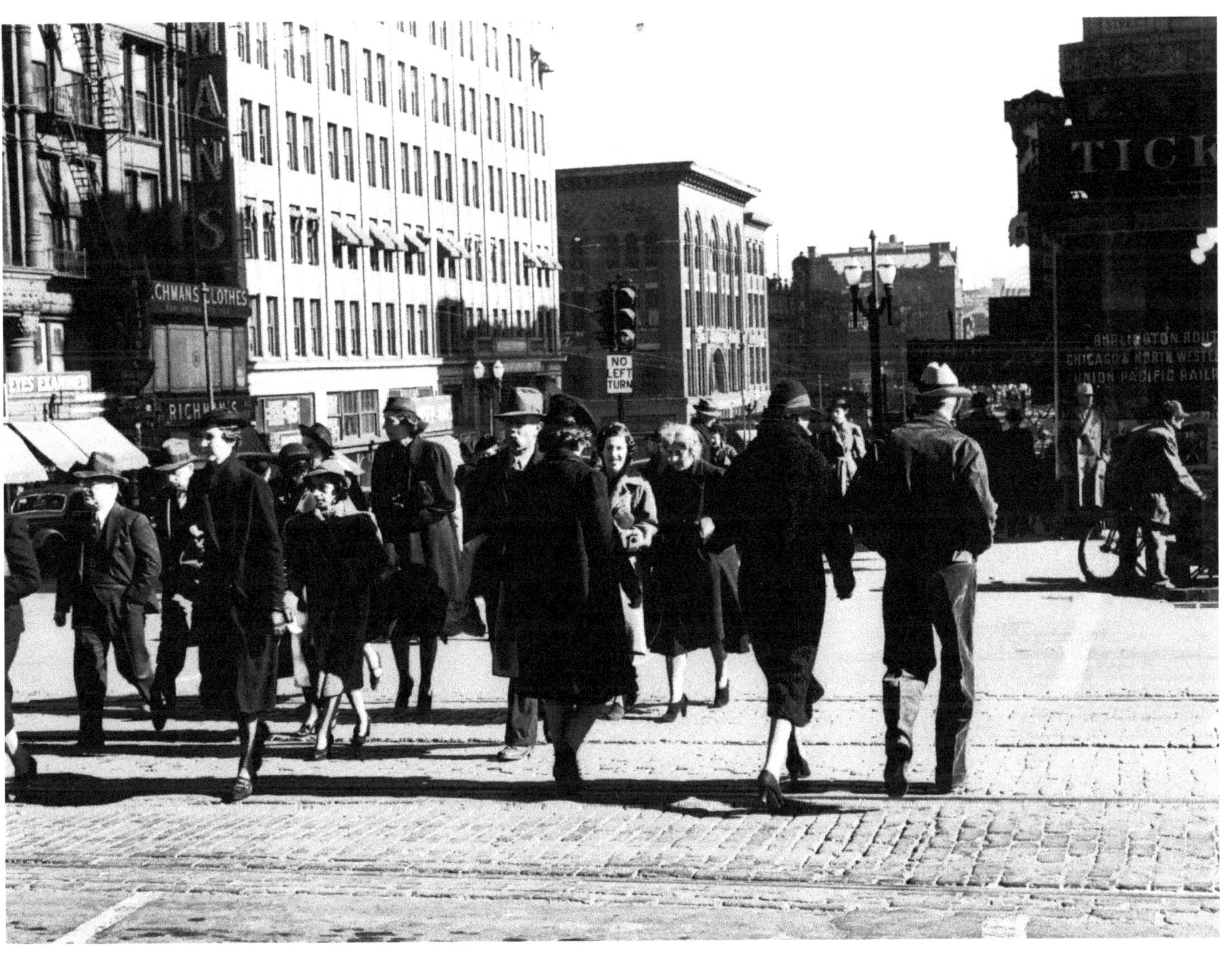

The scene in downtown Omaha on a cold and sunny late 1930s day. Pedestrians cross trolley tracks, bundled against the chill in coats and hats, some perhaps on their way to the railroad ticket office across the street at right.

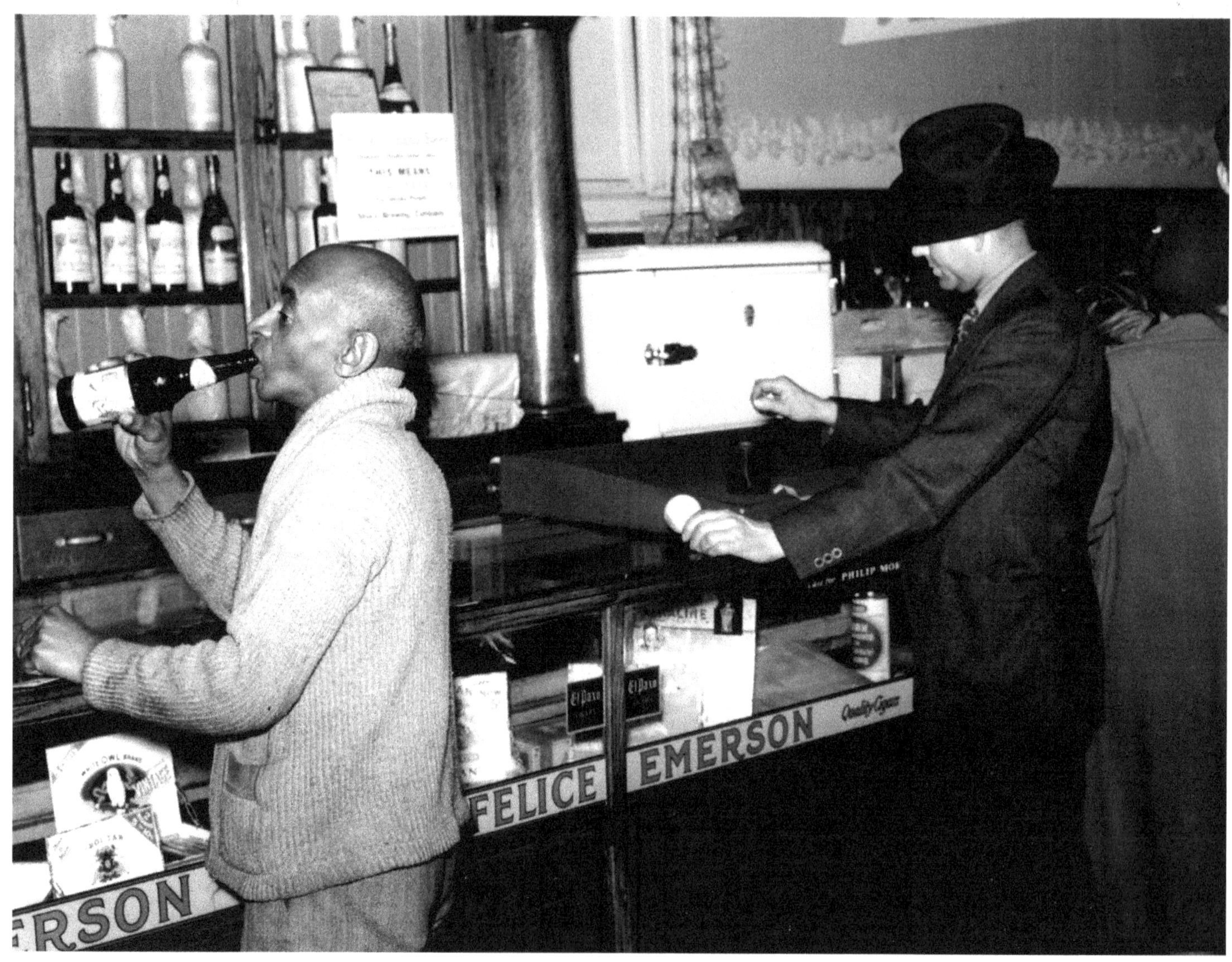

Probably relieved to have any sort of job during the Great Depression, these two Omaha fellows enjoy a quiet drink before heading home from work. Historically, Omaha has enjoyed lower unemployment than the national average and has tended to ride out economic storms better than many cities.

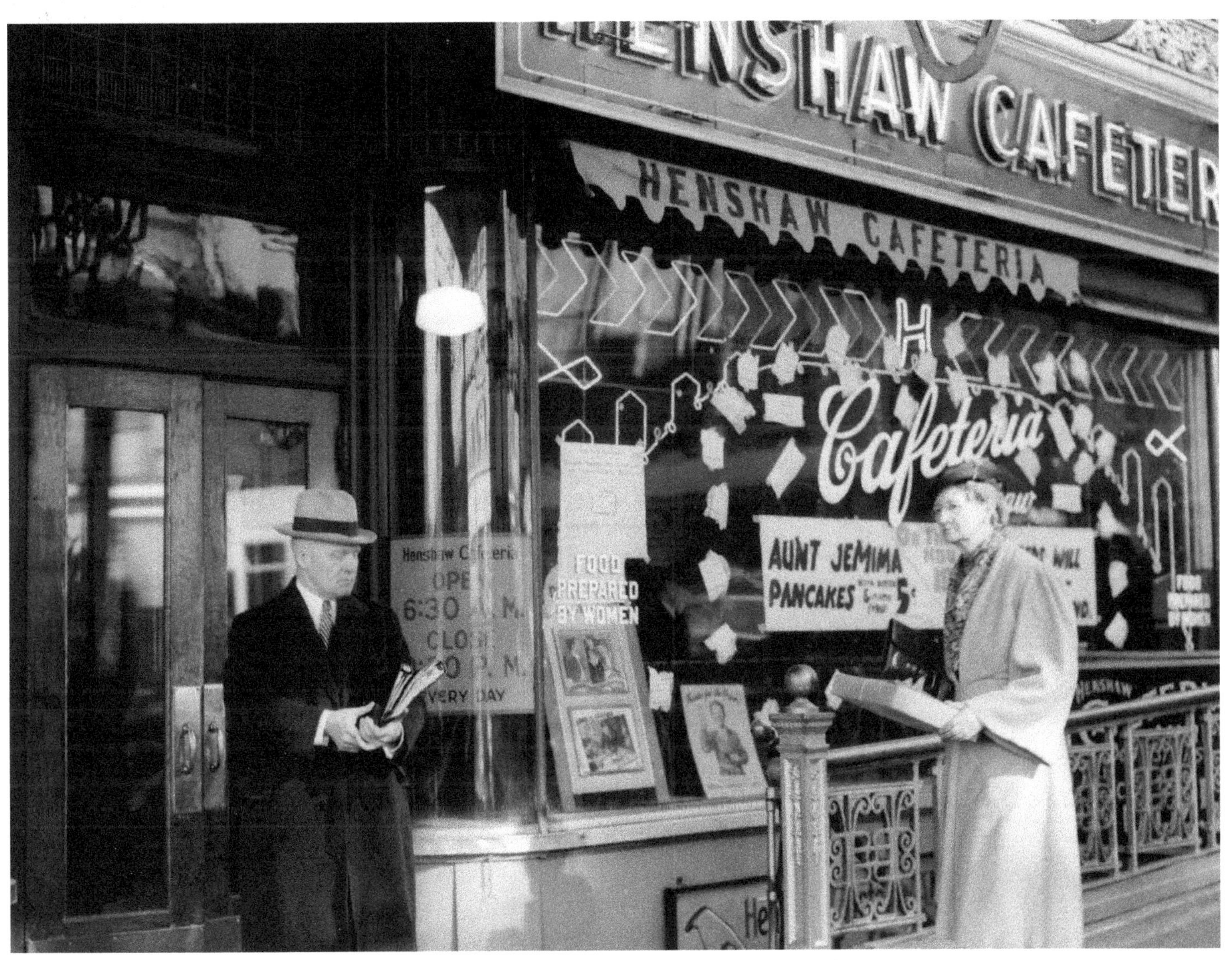

The Henshaw Cafeteria was one of Omaha's most popular dining establishments during the Great Depression. Hours were 6:30 A.M. to 8:30 P.M. "every day," and the food was "prepared by women," reads the window advertising.

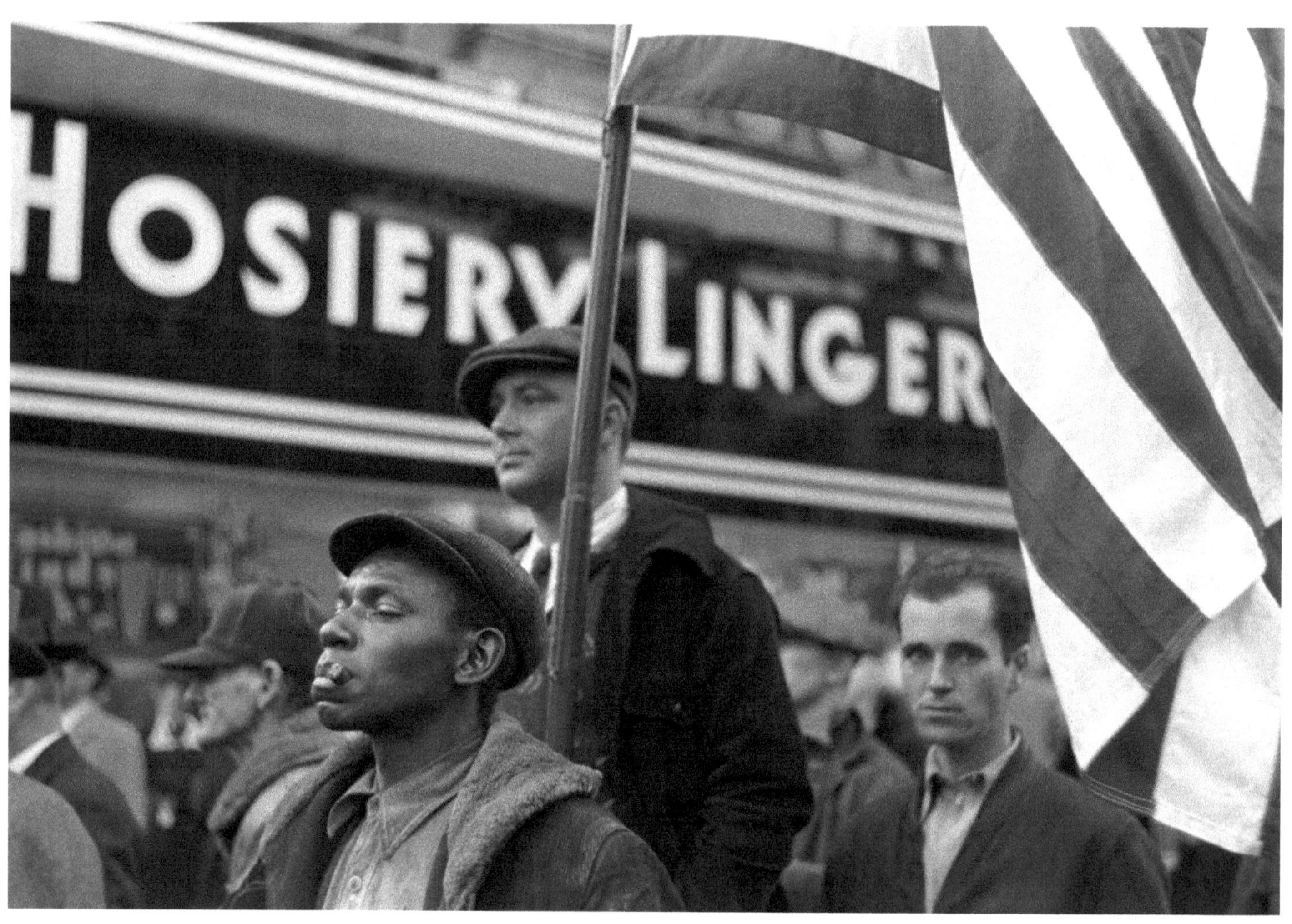

John Vachon recorded this image of a group of men watching the 1938 Omaha Armistice Day parade.

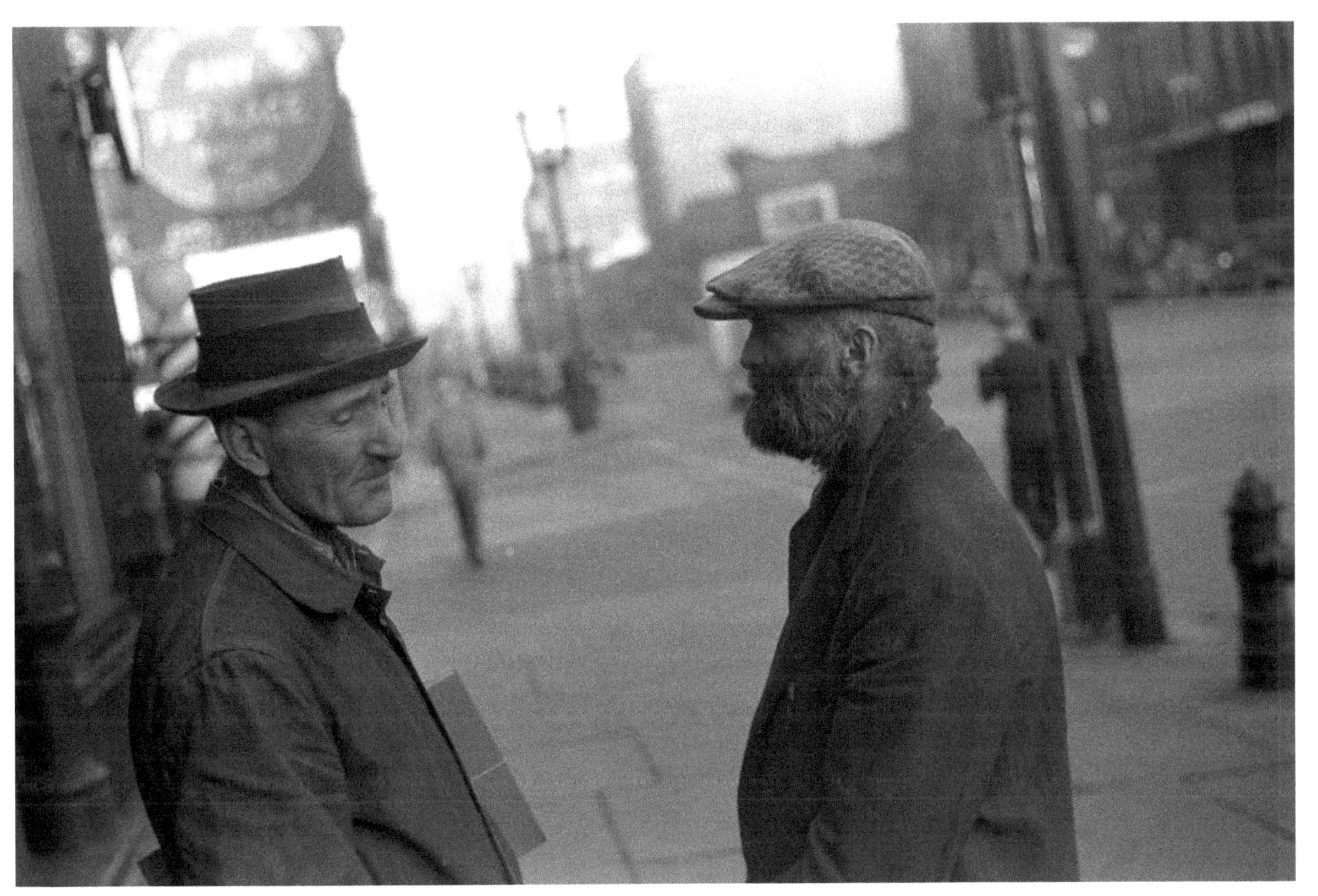

Two unemployed men share their stories on Lower Douglas Street in Omaha.

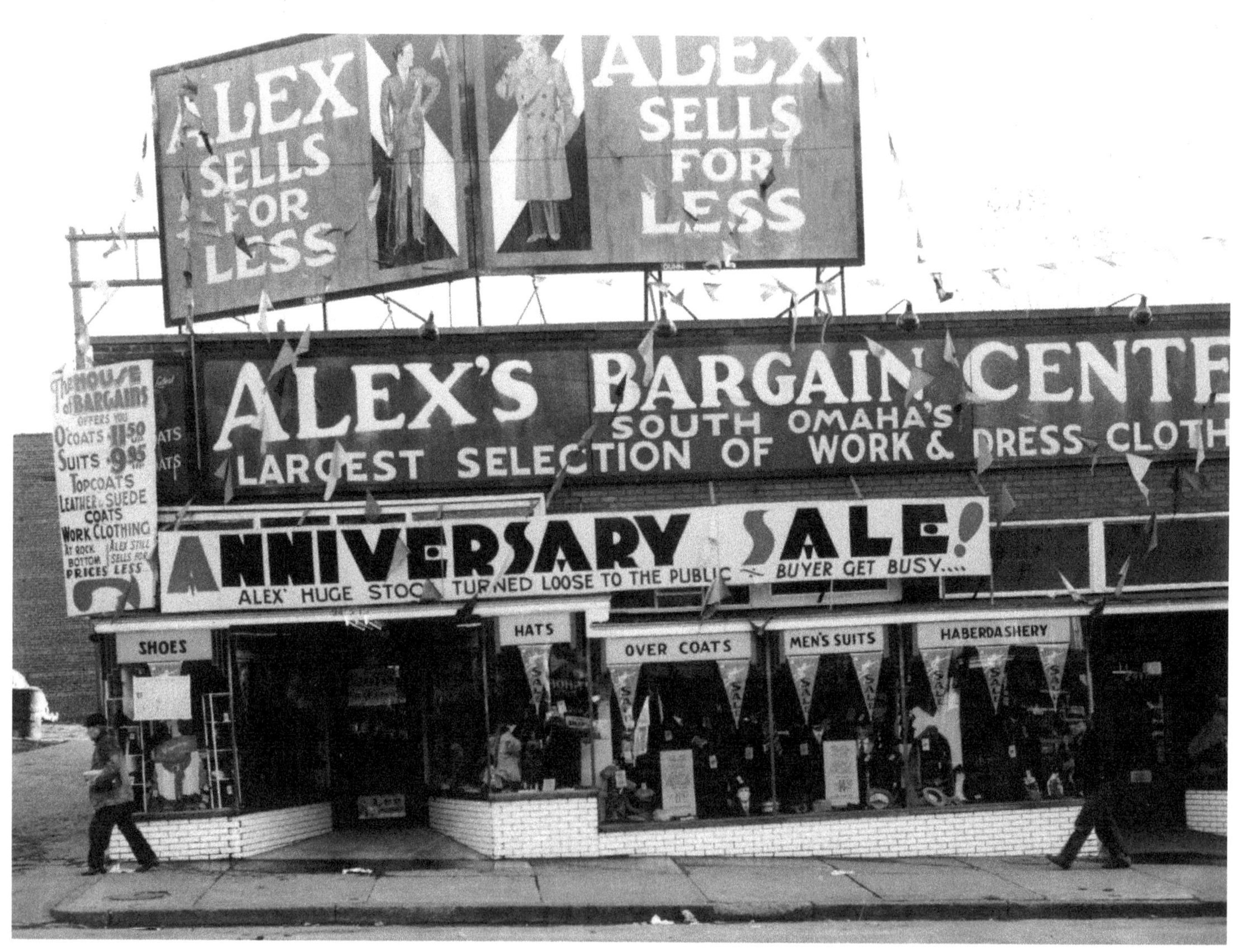

Alex's Bargain Center was a Depression-era discount clothing store in South Omaha that catered to farmers and many others looking for ways to stretch their money.

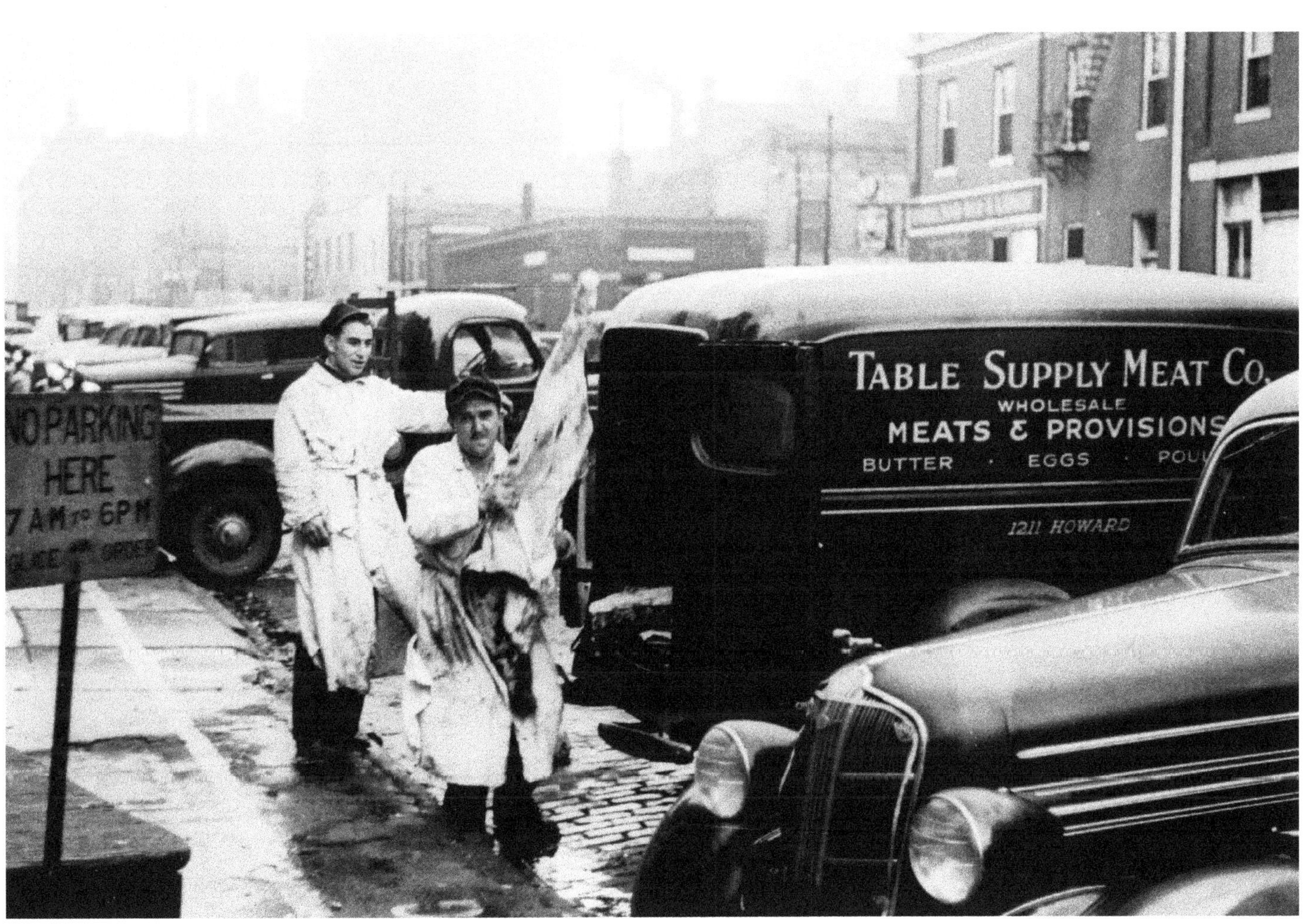

These men unload meat as they make deliveries in the wholesale district of Omaha in the late 1930s.

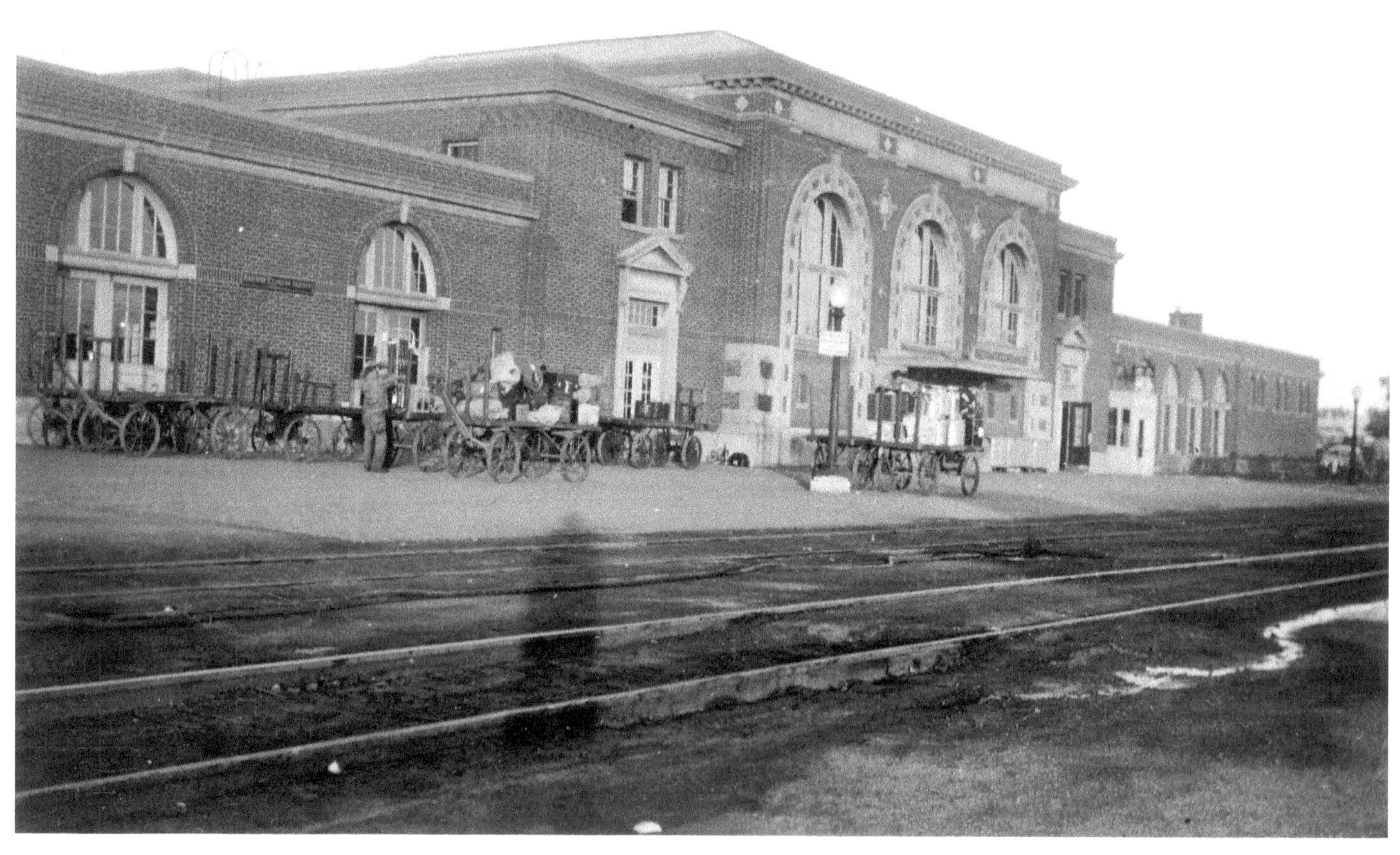

Photographer Joseph Schick casts an early summer evening shadow in 1938 at the North Platte Union Pacific depot, which would become the site of the world-famous North Platte Canteen a few years later during World War II.

The isolation of a Nebraska farmstead has been treasured by some and avoided by others, but there is little doubt that it was a quiet existence on the High Plains near Imperial in 1940. This photograph was taken by Arthur Rothstein, one of the many photographers sent out by Roy Stryker to capture Depression-era images for the Farm Security Administration.

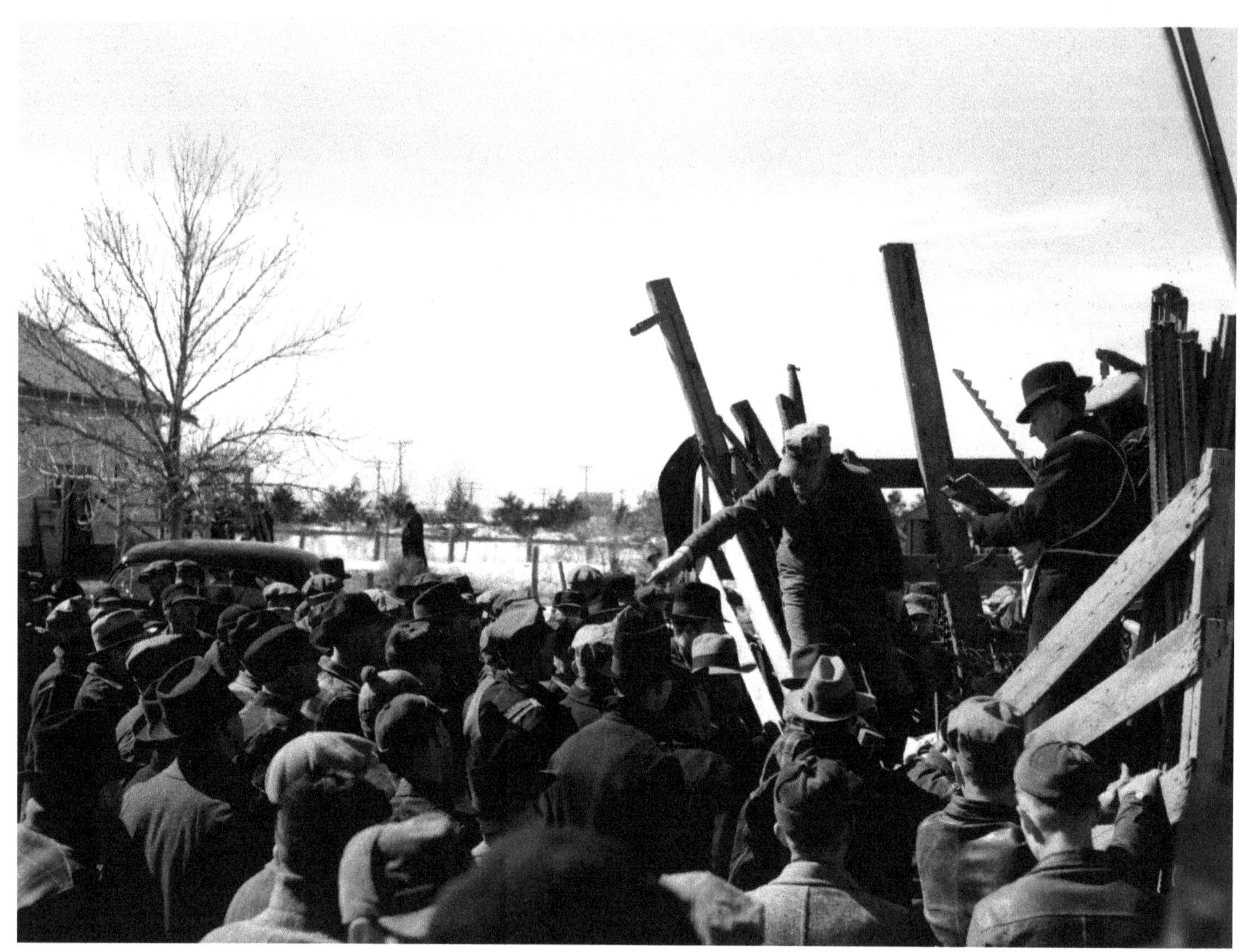

An auction can be a good source of bargains for the opportunist, but for the Zimmerman family of Hastings, their March 1940 farm auction was probably not a happy occasion. As the Great Depression wore on, scenes like this one would affect farms nationwide.

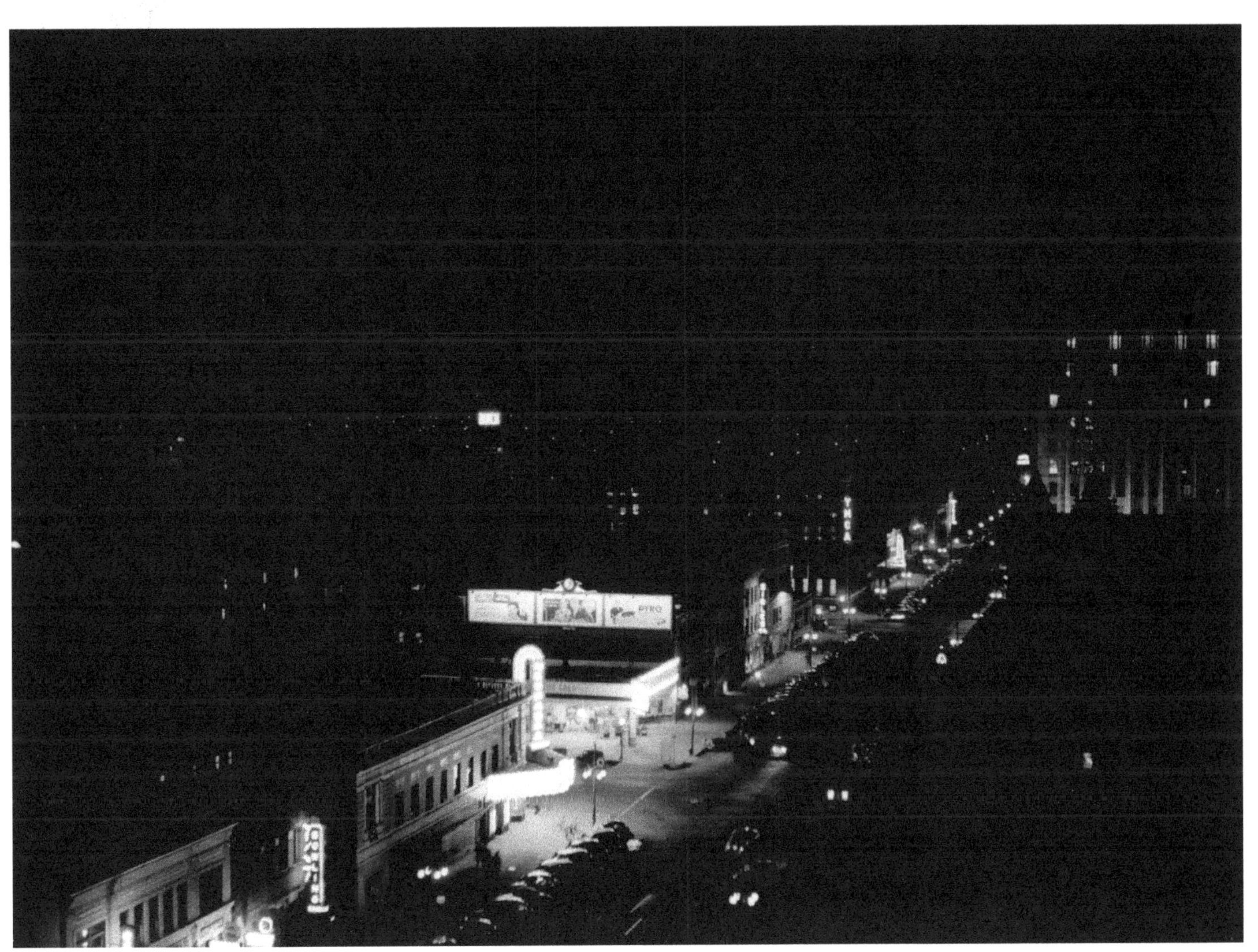

No, it's not exactly the Strip in Las Vegas, but Lincoln did have a little night life toward the end of the Great Depression, as seen here in 1940. Among the attractions are a bowling alley, the Nebraska Theater, and, in the distance, the Y.M.C.A.

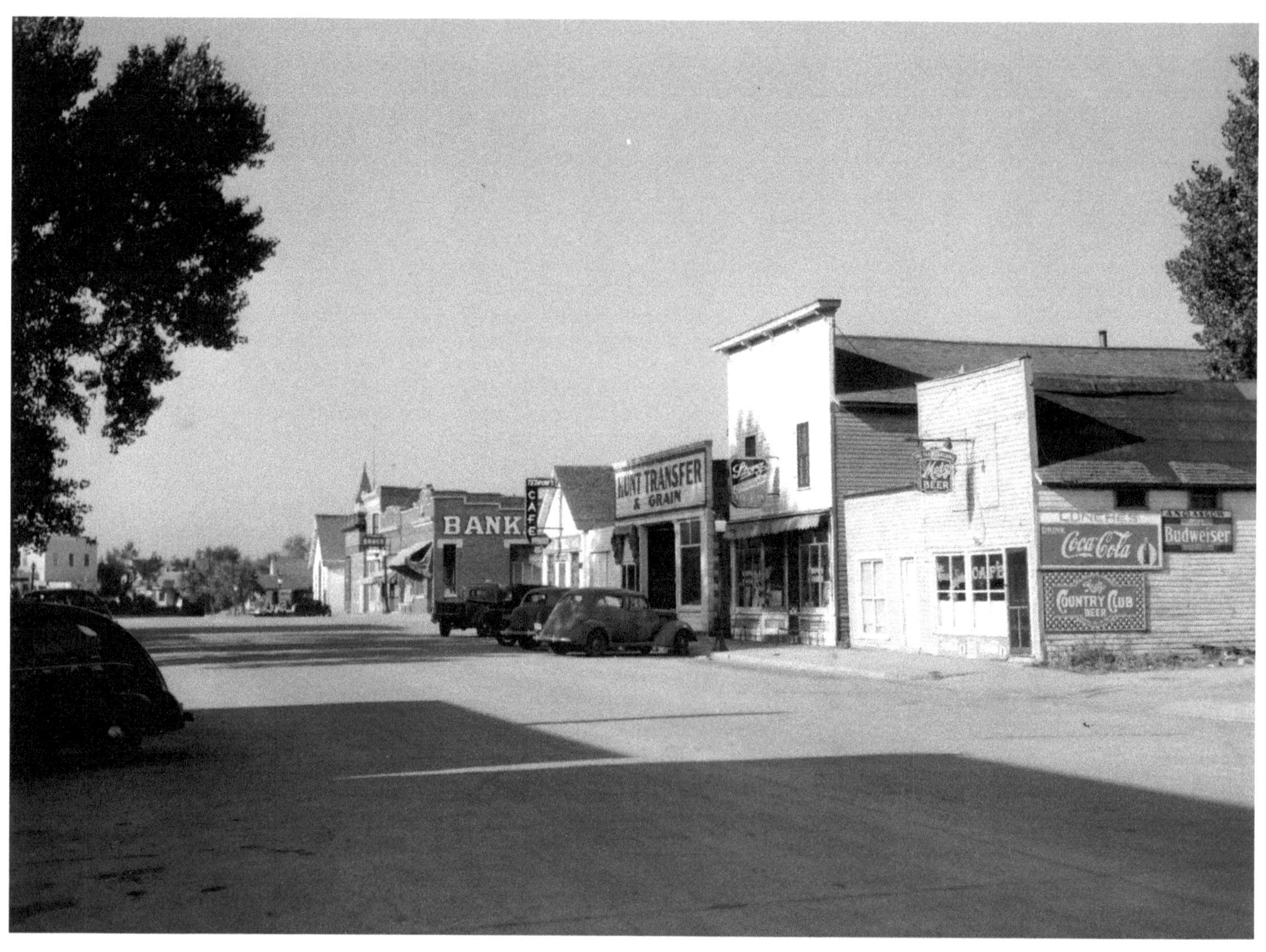

On the eve of the United States' entrance into World War II, the local football team's chances on Friday night were probably still a big topic of conversation in September 1941 along Main Street in Waterloo.

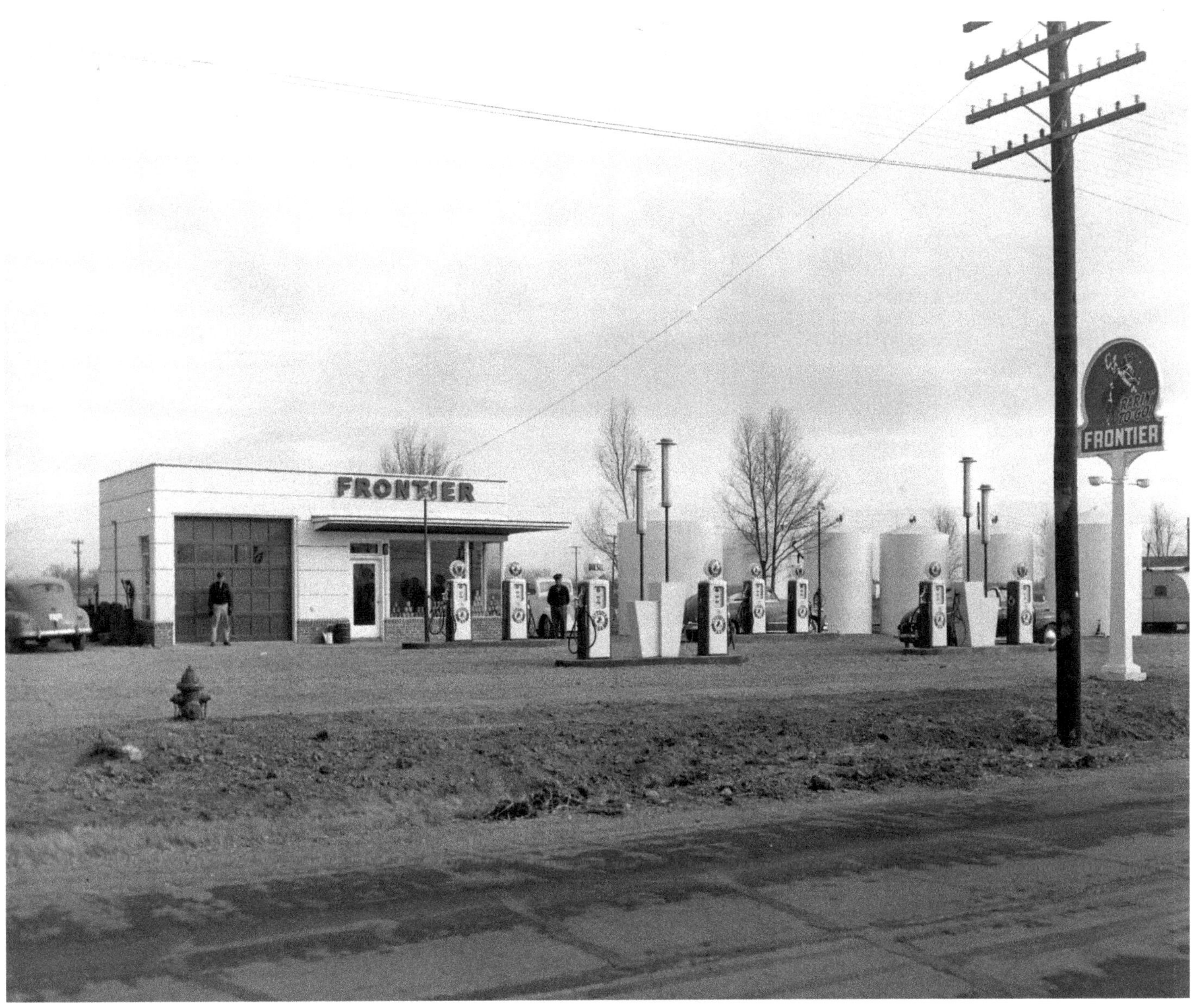

The mechanic is ready and waiting for business at this Frontier service station at the edge of Lexington along Highway 30.

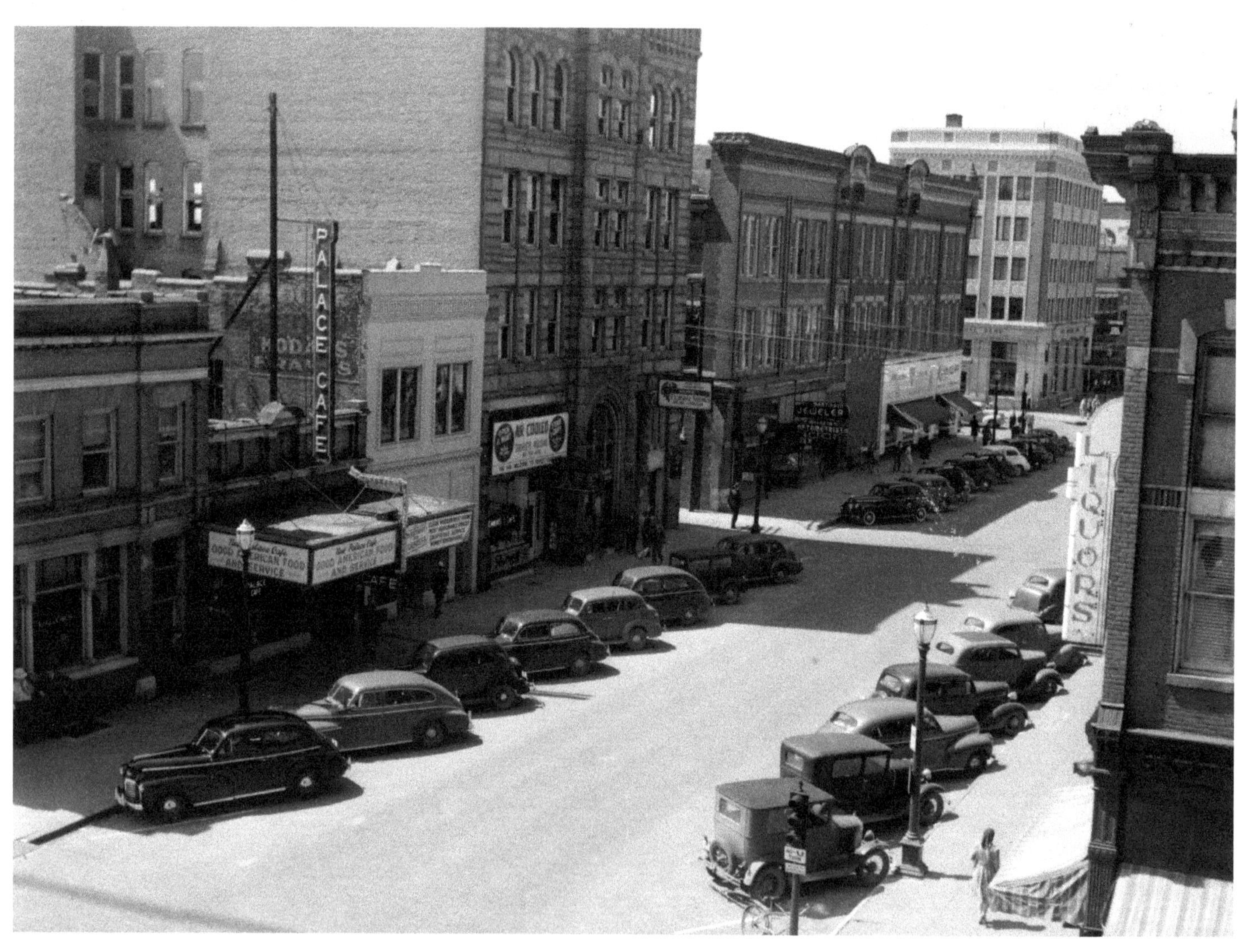

In May 1942, the United States had been at war with the Axis powers only five months. Jimmy Doolittle's raid over Japan in April had given the troops and the nation a badly needed morale boost, and the Battle of Midway in June would bring a decisive victory in the Pacific against the Imperial Japanese Navy. At the Palace Cafe in Grand Island, a sizable crowd has turned out to share news of the front and some "good American food."

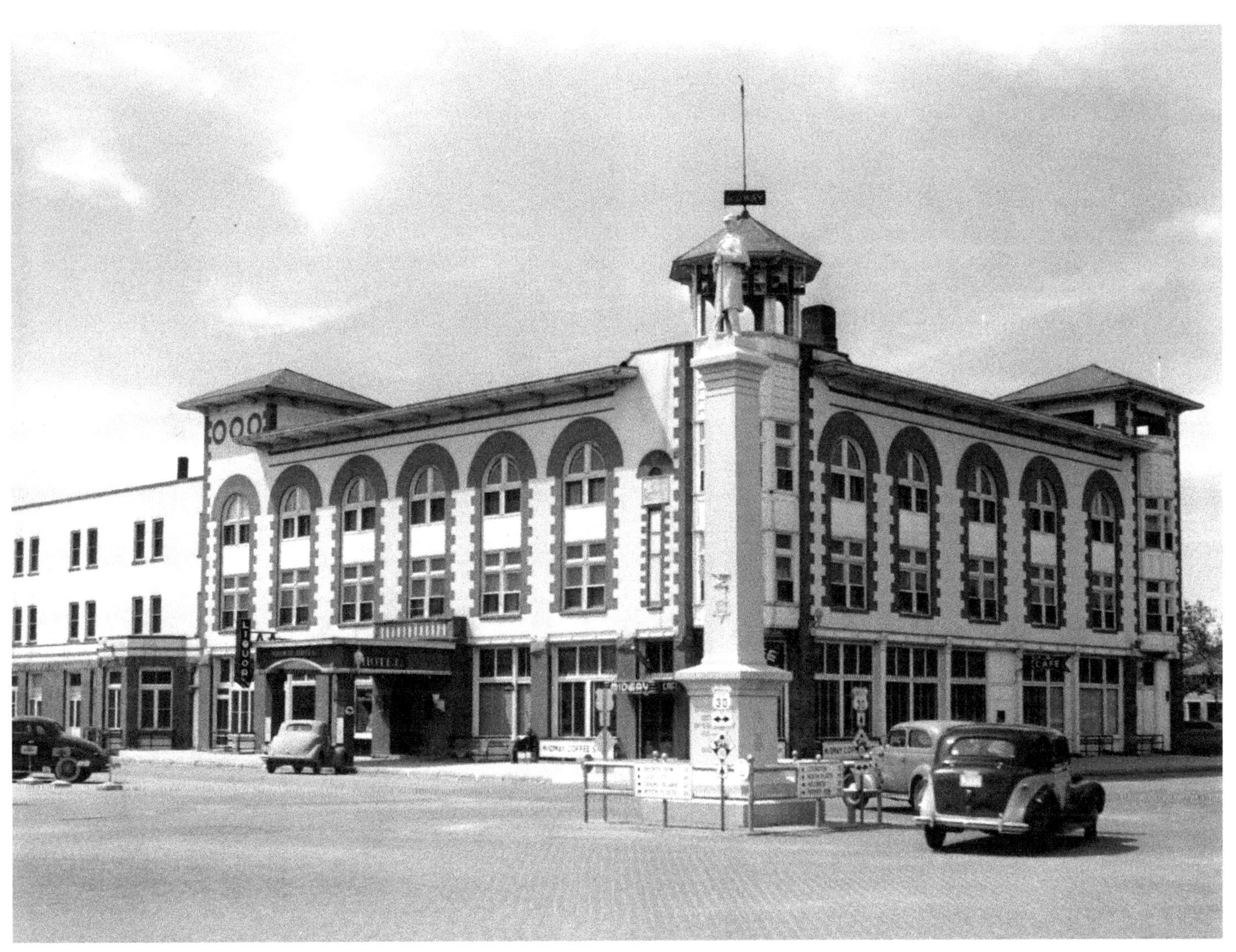

The first Midway Hotel burned to the ground, but the second was completed in 1891, at the end of Kearney's economic boom. Located at the busy intersection of 25th Street and Central Avenue, it was known as one of the finest hotels in the state. The Midway is pictured here in 1942, 25 years before it was sold and razed.

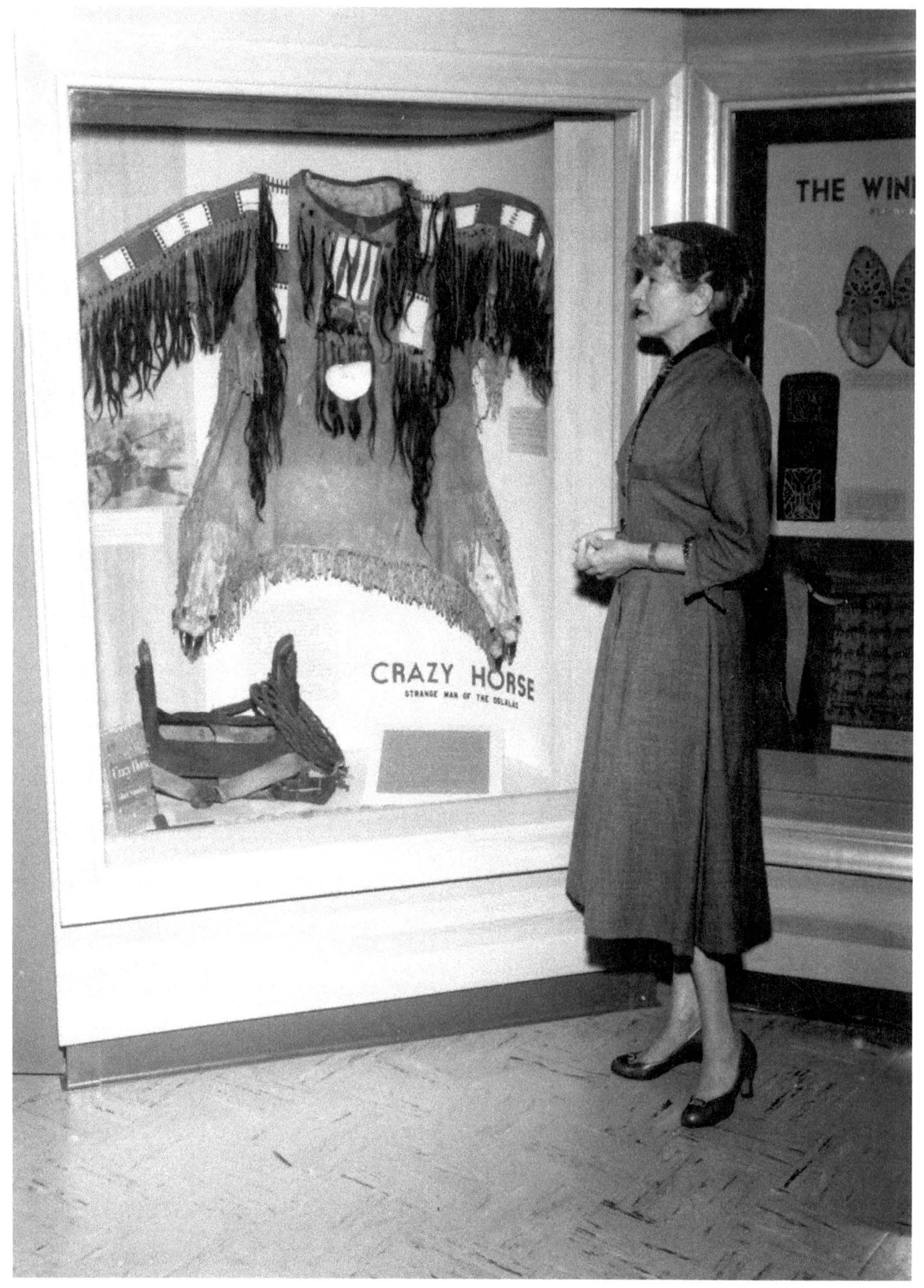

Author Mari Sandoz views an exhibit of Crazy Horse memorabilia at the Nebraska State Historical Society, where she had worked as an editor and researcher. Her 1942 biography of Crazy Horse was written from a Lakota point of view, as were several other related books. Born near Hay Springs, she grew up in hard circumstances on a Sandhills ranch and portrayed Nebraska in a gritty, realistic way to readers around the world.

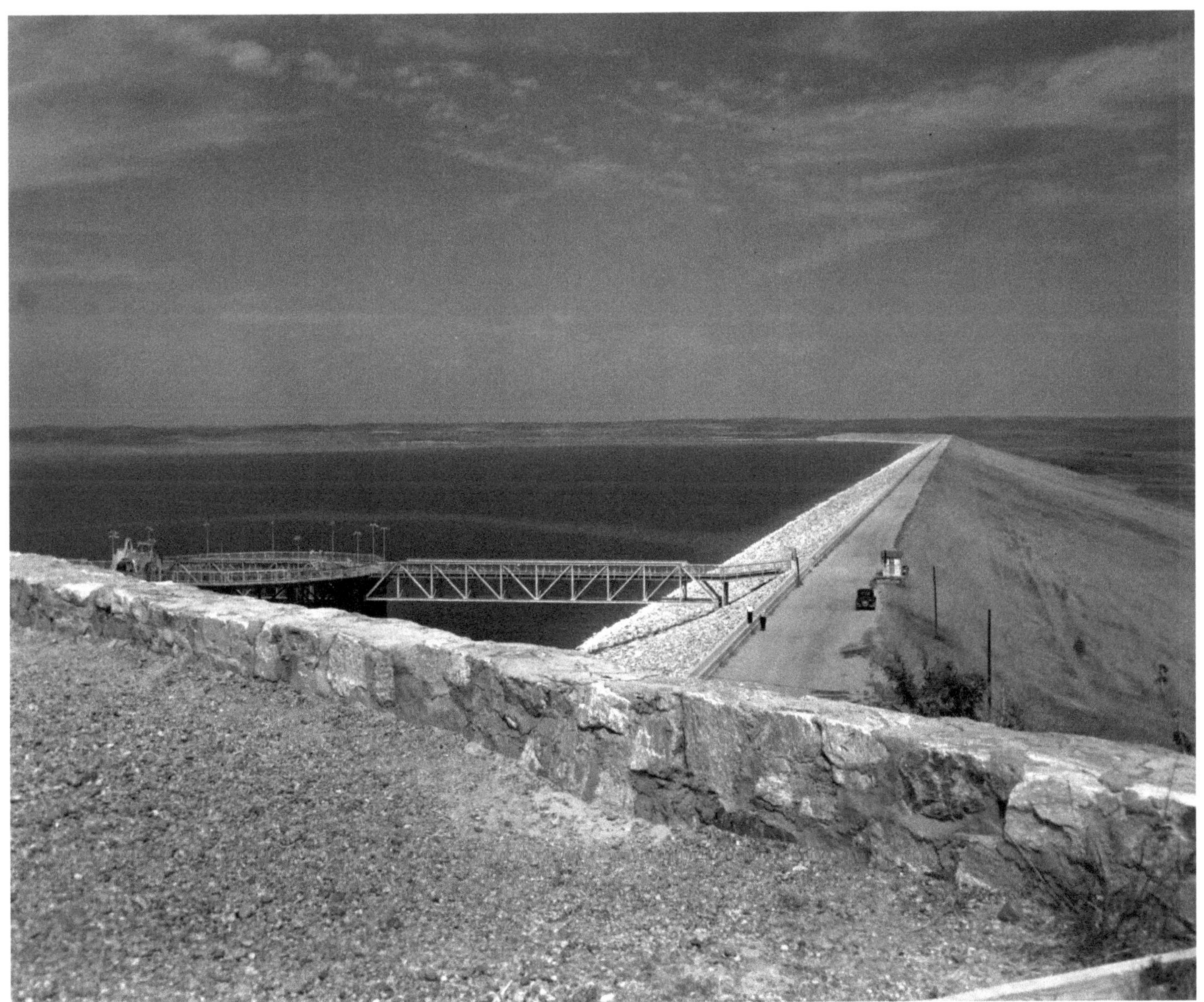

The construction of Kingsley Dam on the North Platte River north of Ogallala began in 1936 and ended five years later at a cost of $43.5 million. One of the largest public works projects in Nebraska history, the completion of the 3.5-mile-long earth dam created Lake McConaughy, a source of hydroelectric power and a popular recreational attraction.

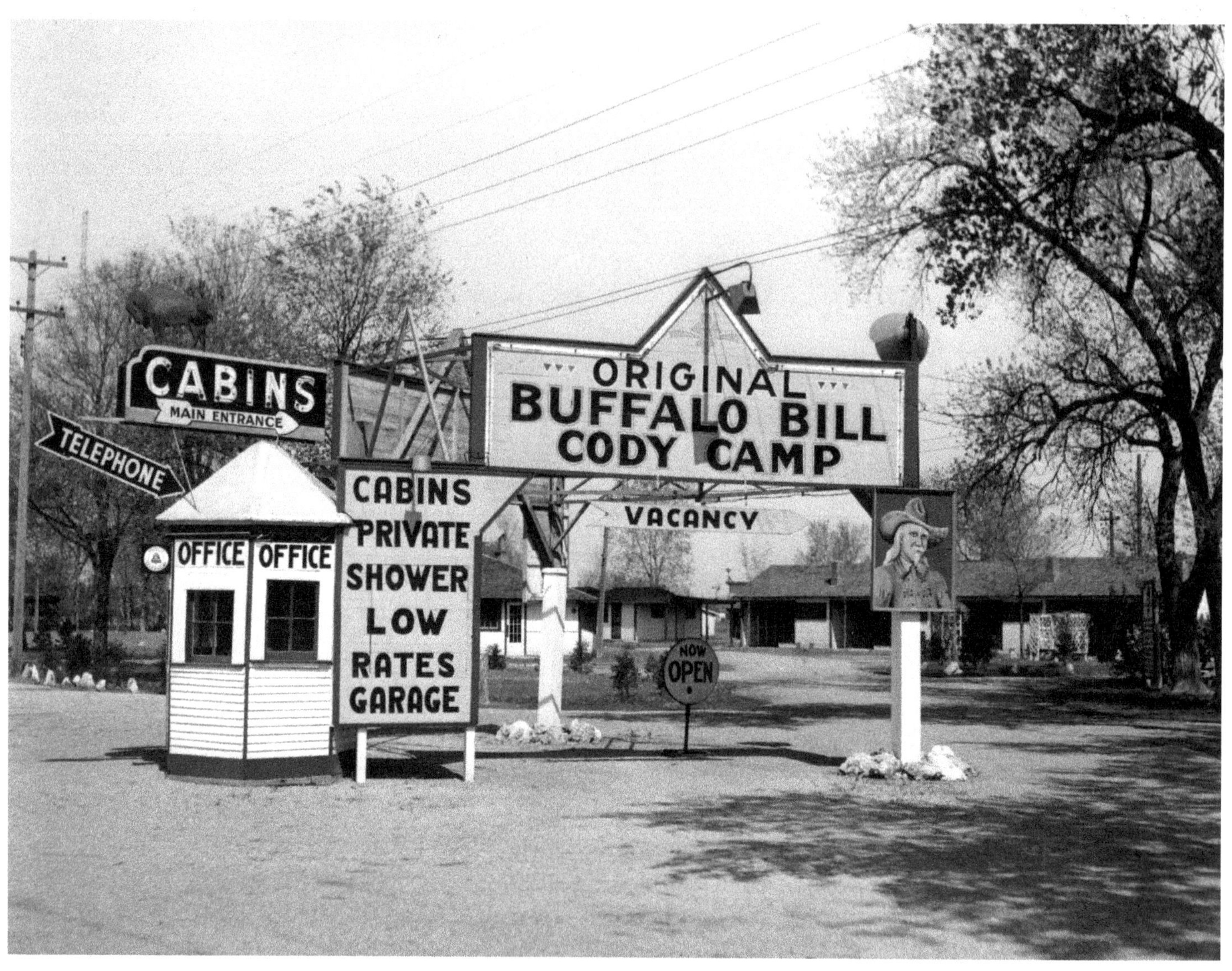

A quarter-century after his death, William F. Cody's name was still well known and used for marketing purposes in his old hometown of North Platte. Here in 1942, an establishment of rustic roadside cabins at the edge of town, typical of those around the nation that catered to cross-country motorists, takes Buffalo Bill's persona as its theme.

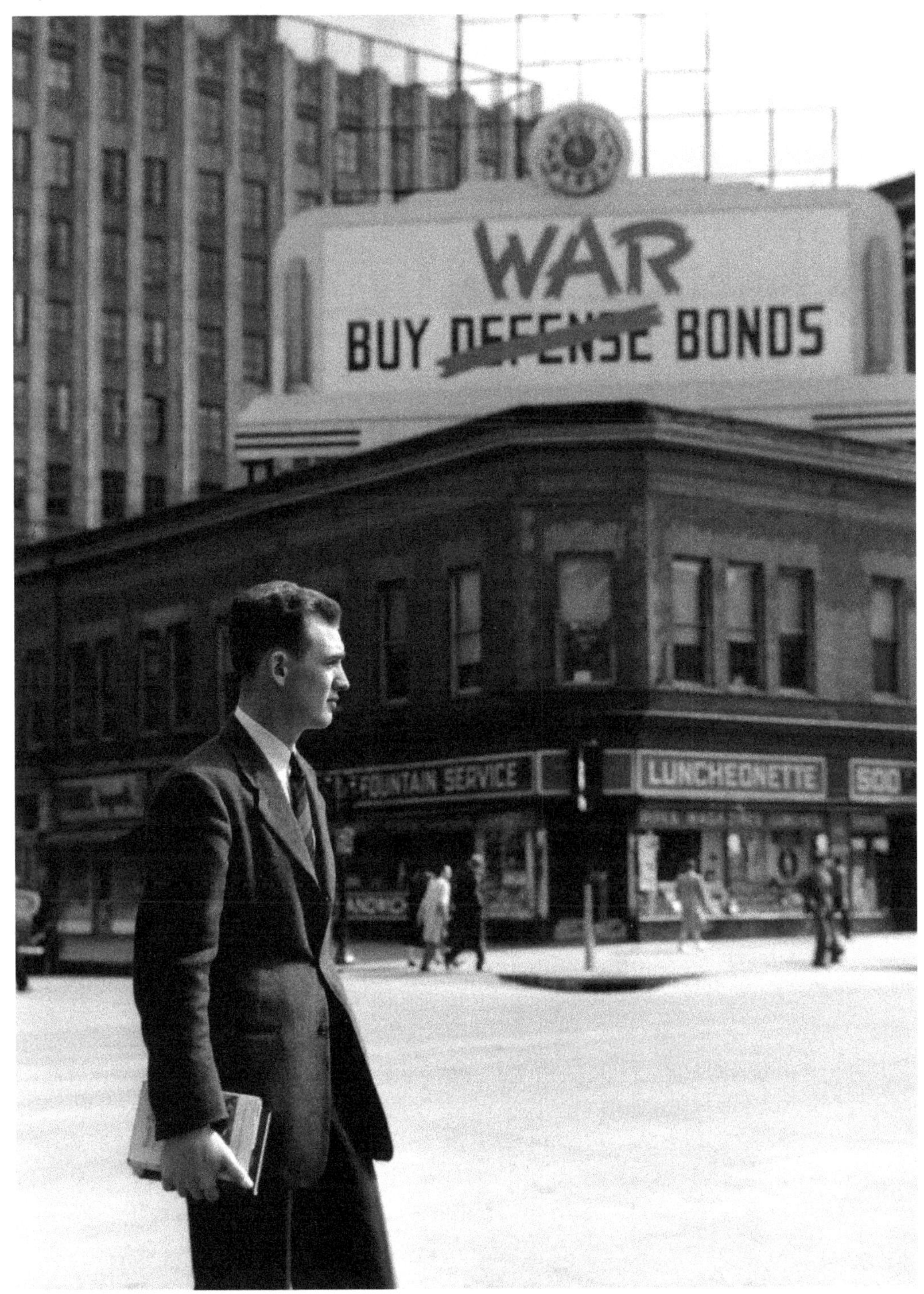

In May 1942, this large billboard in Lincoln underscores the changed circumstances in the United States after Japan bombed Pearl Harbor. When war was declared on the Axis powers, the nation threw every effort into winning the conflict, winning quickly, and bringing the troops home. In less than four years, the United States and its allies would put down the ambitions of the enemy.

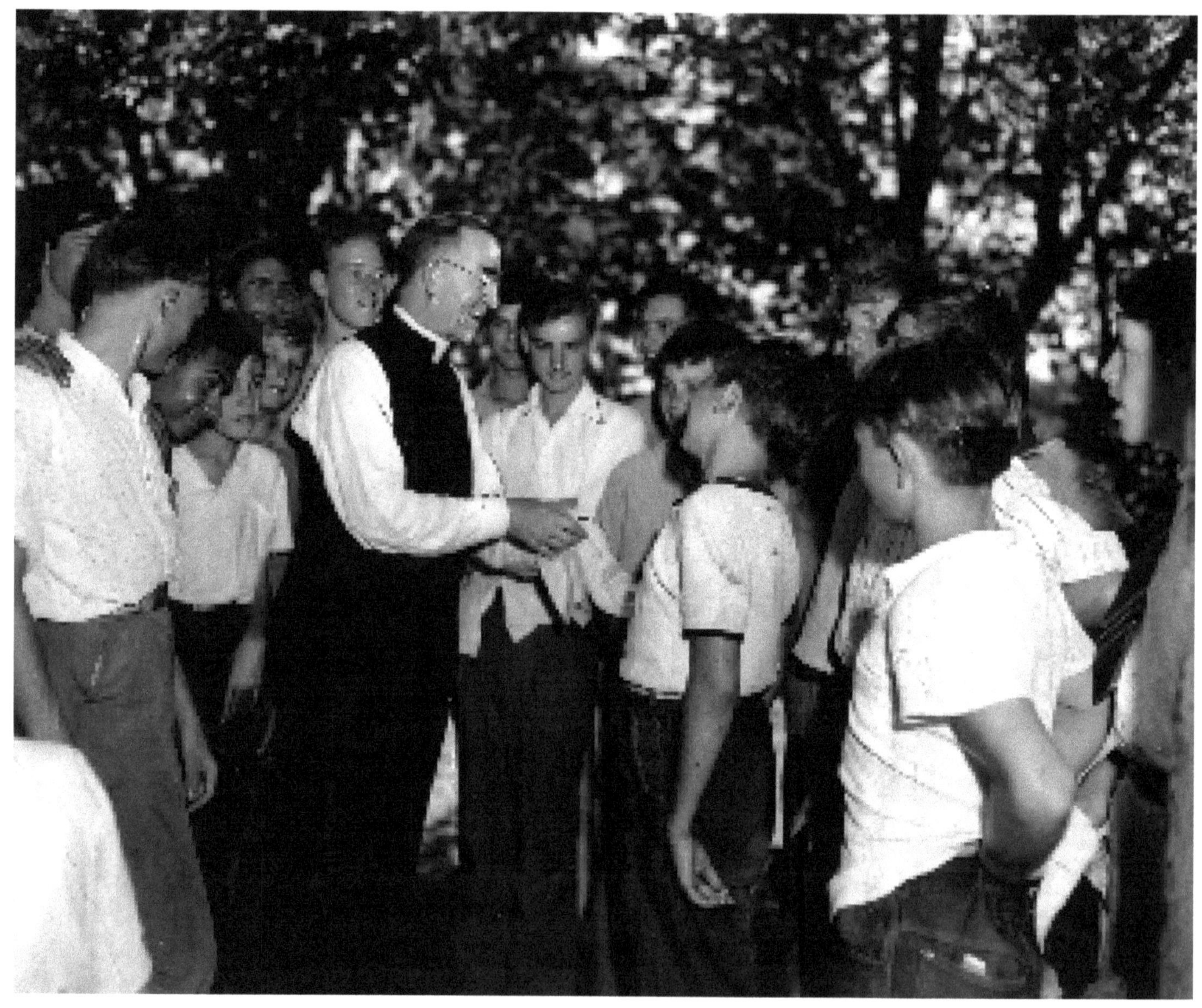

Convinced that helping neglected boys of all races and religions would be his best way to help society, Irishman Edward J. Flanagan borrowed money to start Father Flanagan's Boys Home at Omaha in 1917. With help from publicity generated by a 1938 Oscar-winning film, it grew into Boys Town, still based on his precepts of work, prayer, and education. Here, Flanagan and Boys Town residents enjoy their annual Fourth of July picnic in 1942.

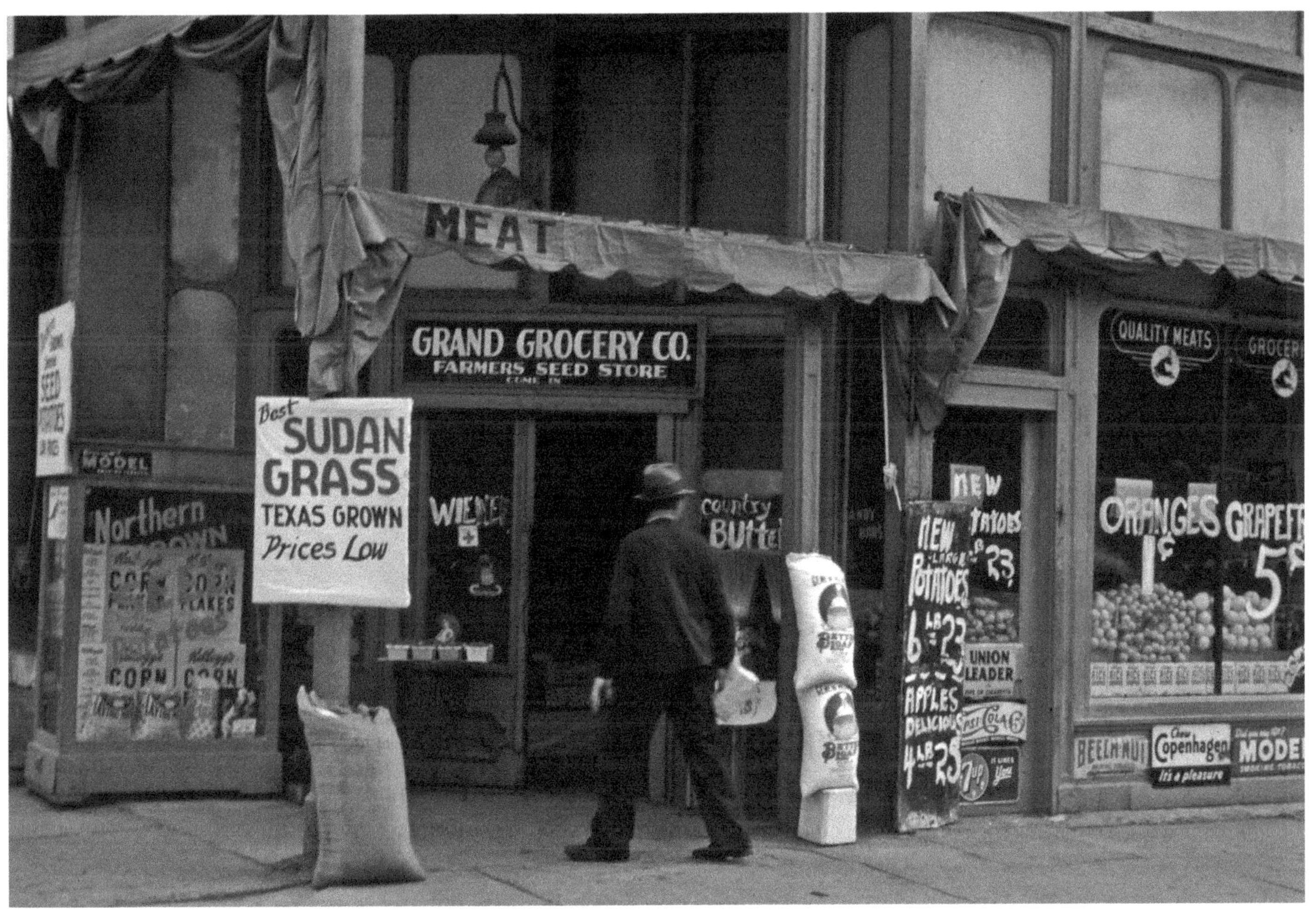

In May 1942, a variety of produce was available at Grand Grocery in Lincoln at what today seem like incredibly low prices. An orange could be purchased for a penny and a soft drink for five cents.

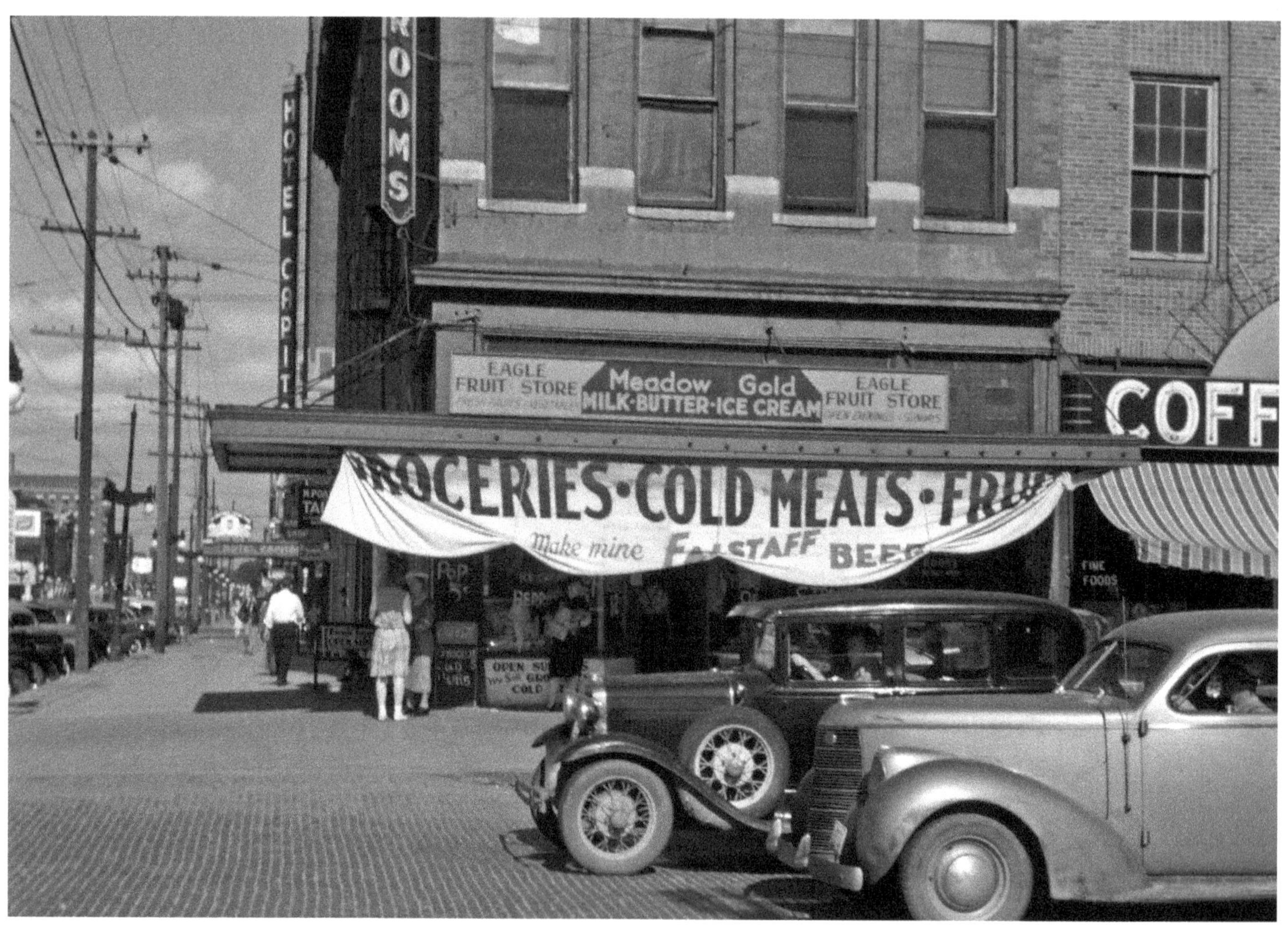

The Eagle Fruit Store at 139 N. 11th Street in Lincoln still advertised meat and butter in May 1942, but those commodities would soon grow scarce as wartime rationing came to the region.

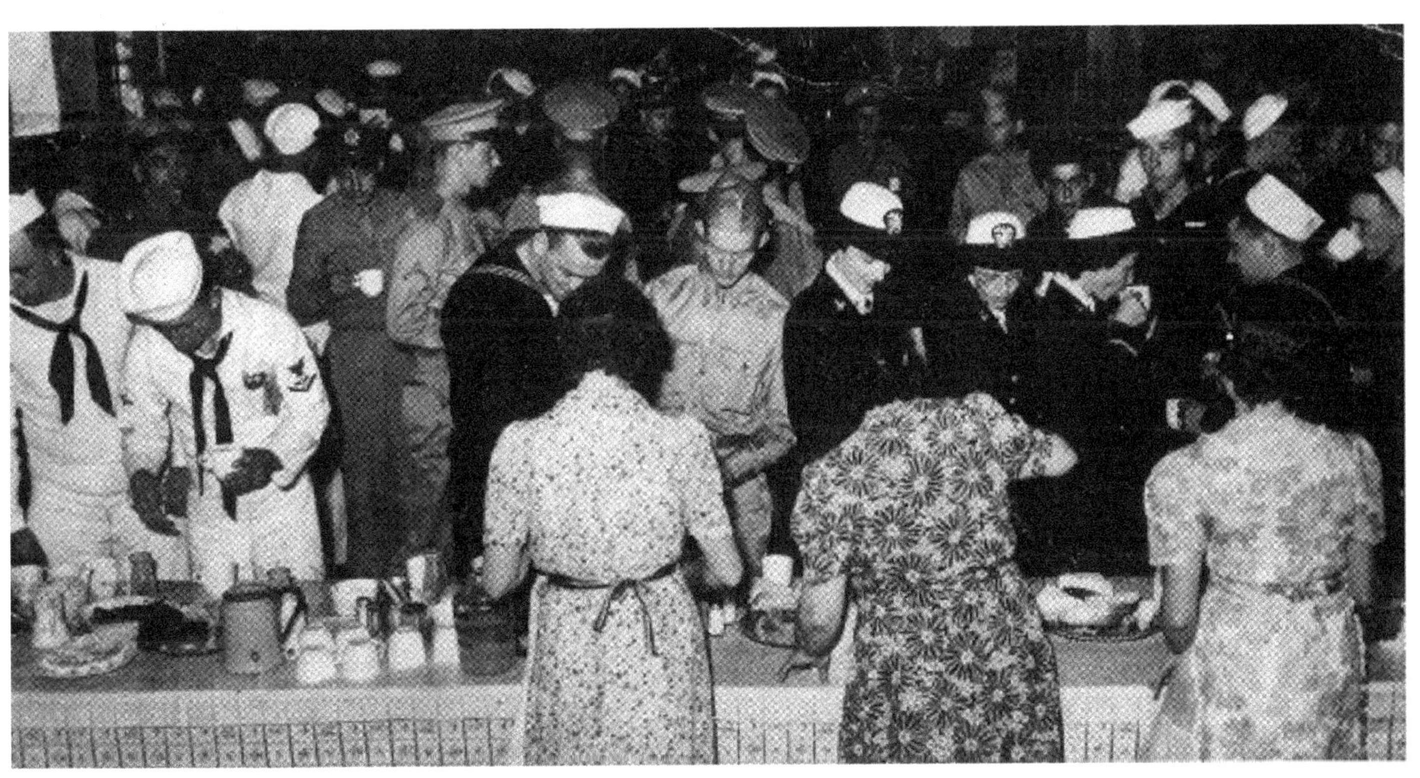

During the war, a canteen opened at the Union Pacific depot in North Platte, where local homemakers volunteered their time to serve the incoming troops. Coffee, fruit, sandwiches, and even birthday cakes were among the items on the menu, a taste of home and tangible encouragement for those bravely defending the nation. Thankful service personnel held fond memories of the canteen for many years afterward.

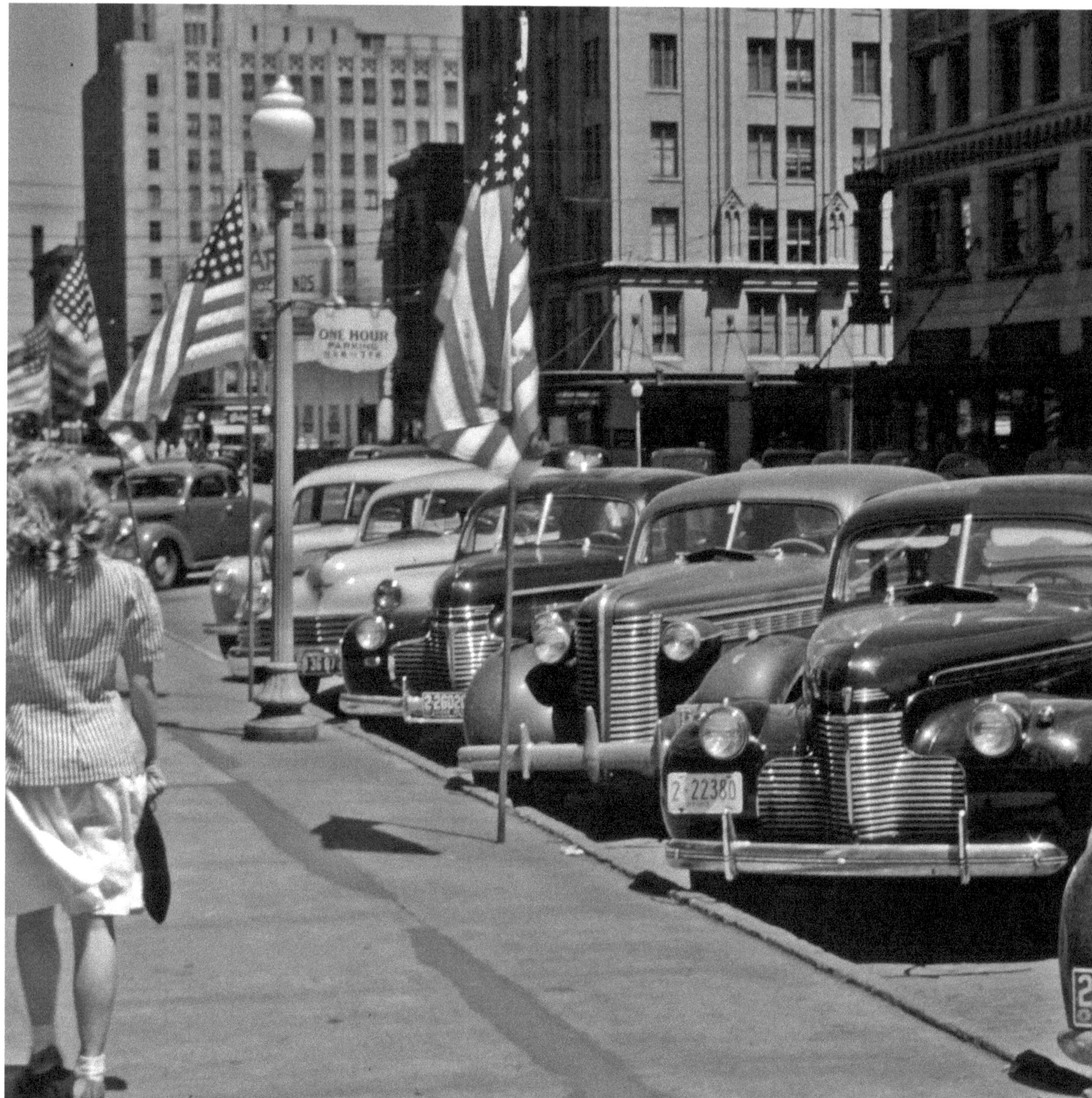
ONE HOUR
PARKING
2-22380

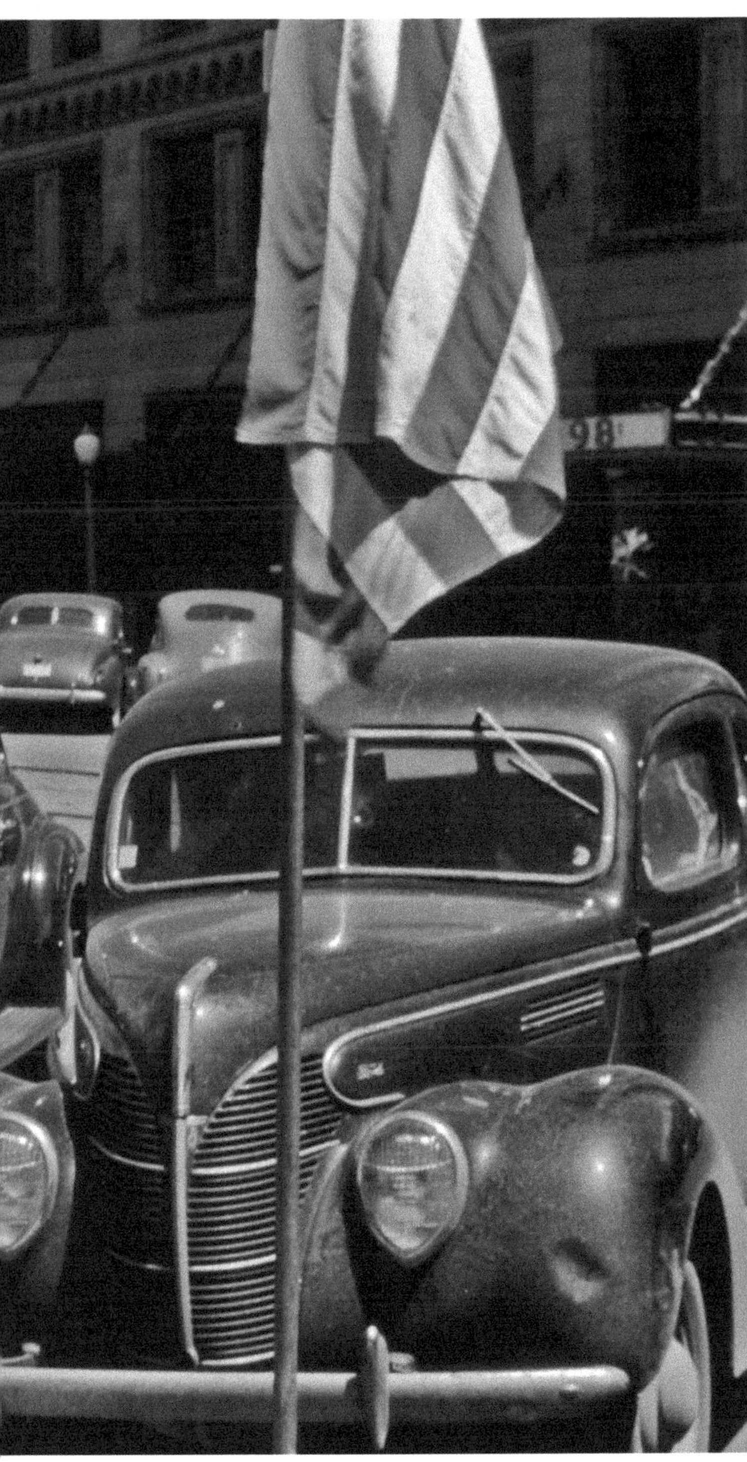

Patriotic fervor swept over the United States at the beginning of World War II, and Nebraska was no exception. In this image, the Stars and Stripes flies in downtown Lincoln in 1942.

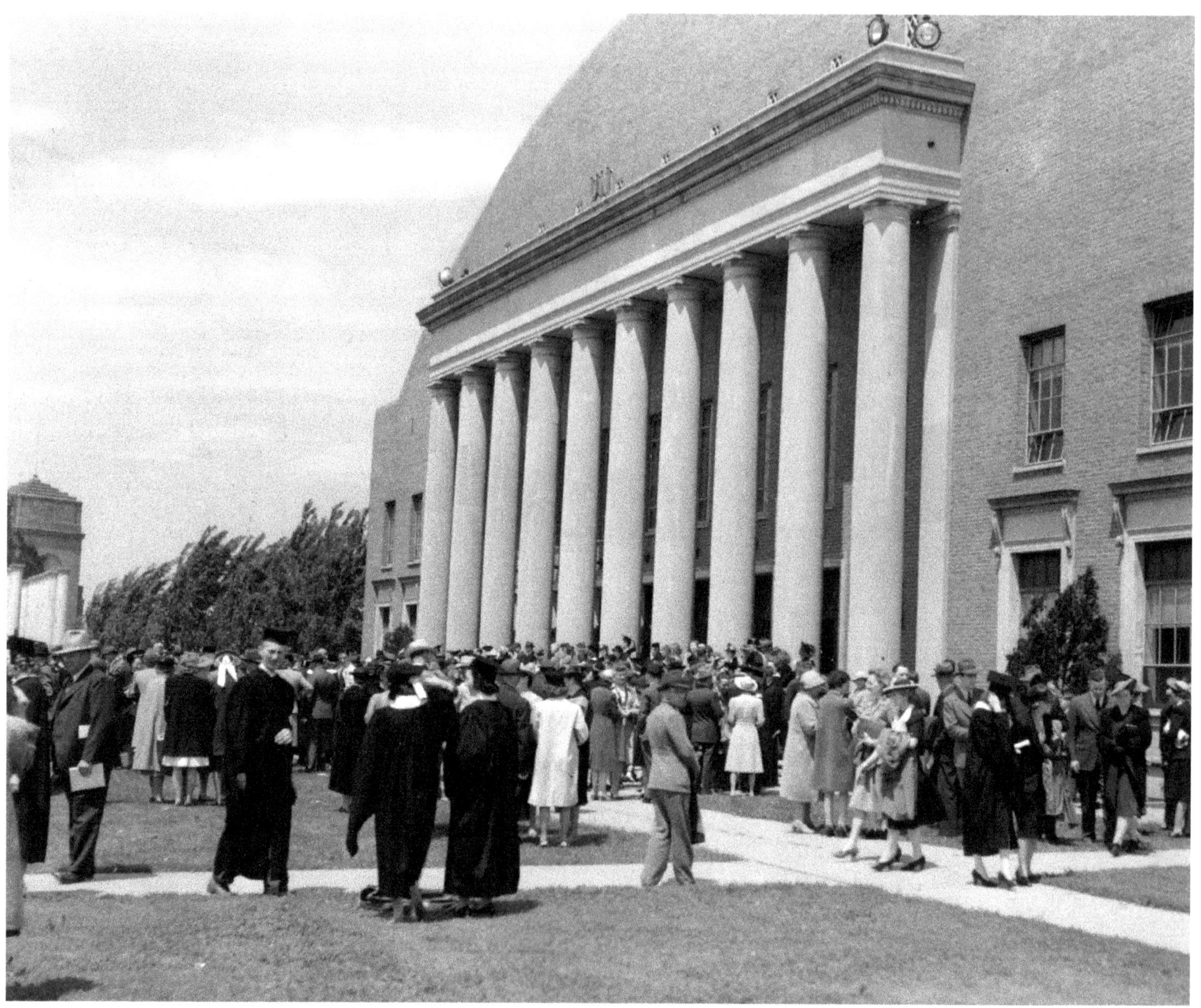

Graduates of the University of Nebraska gather with their families outside the Coliseum in May 1942. Americans of every stripe were united in opposition to the aggressions of Adolf Hitler, and many of them would soon be serving overseas, including young Nebraskans like those shown here.

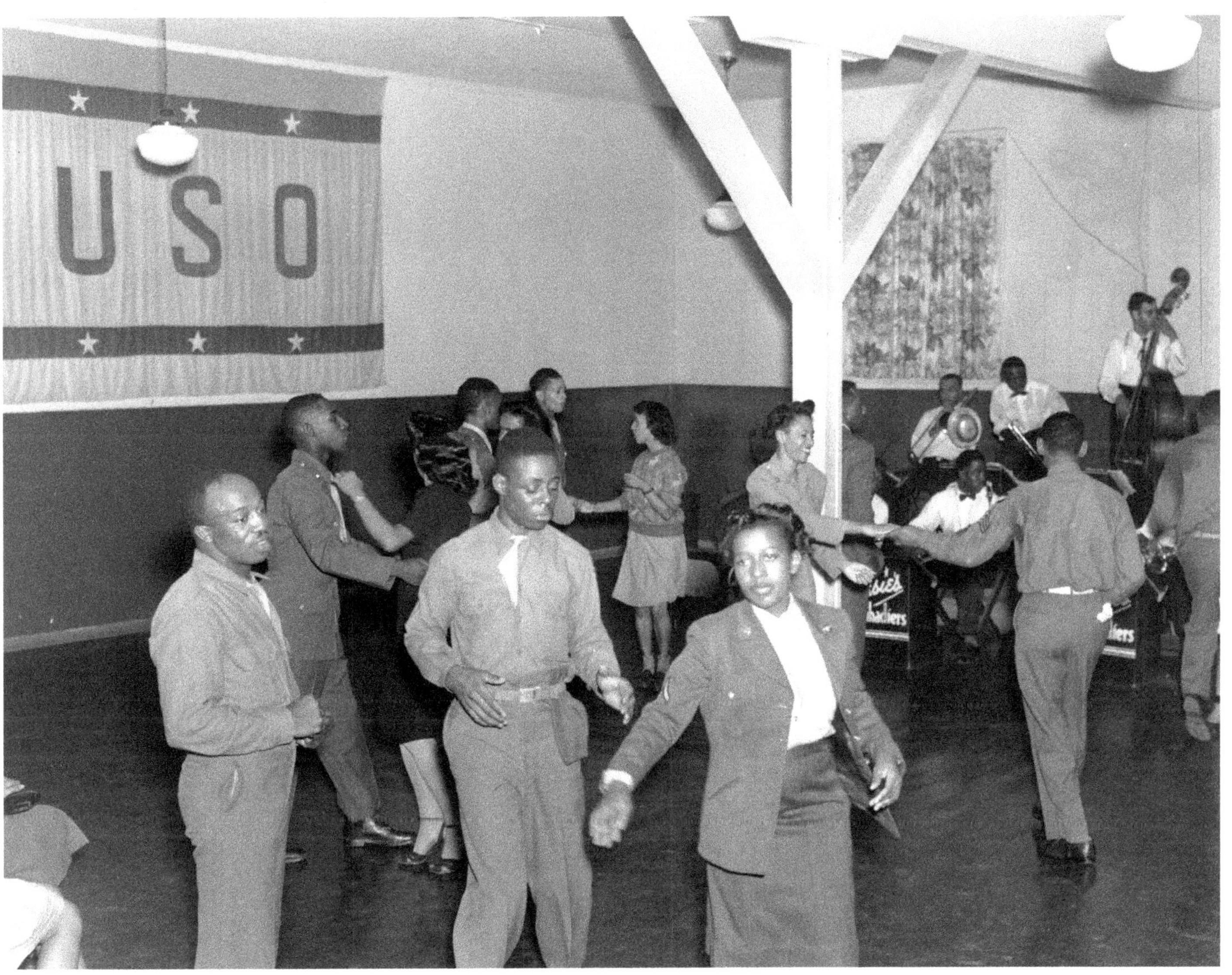

Just a few weeks after the end of World War II, veterans enjoy dancing to the music of Basie's Bombardiers at the United Services Organization Club at 212 S. 12th St. in Lincoln. The war had ended with the dropping of the atomic bomb on Japan.

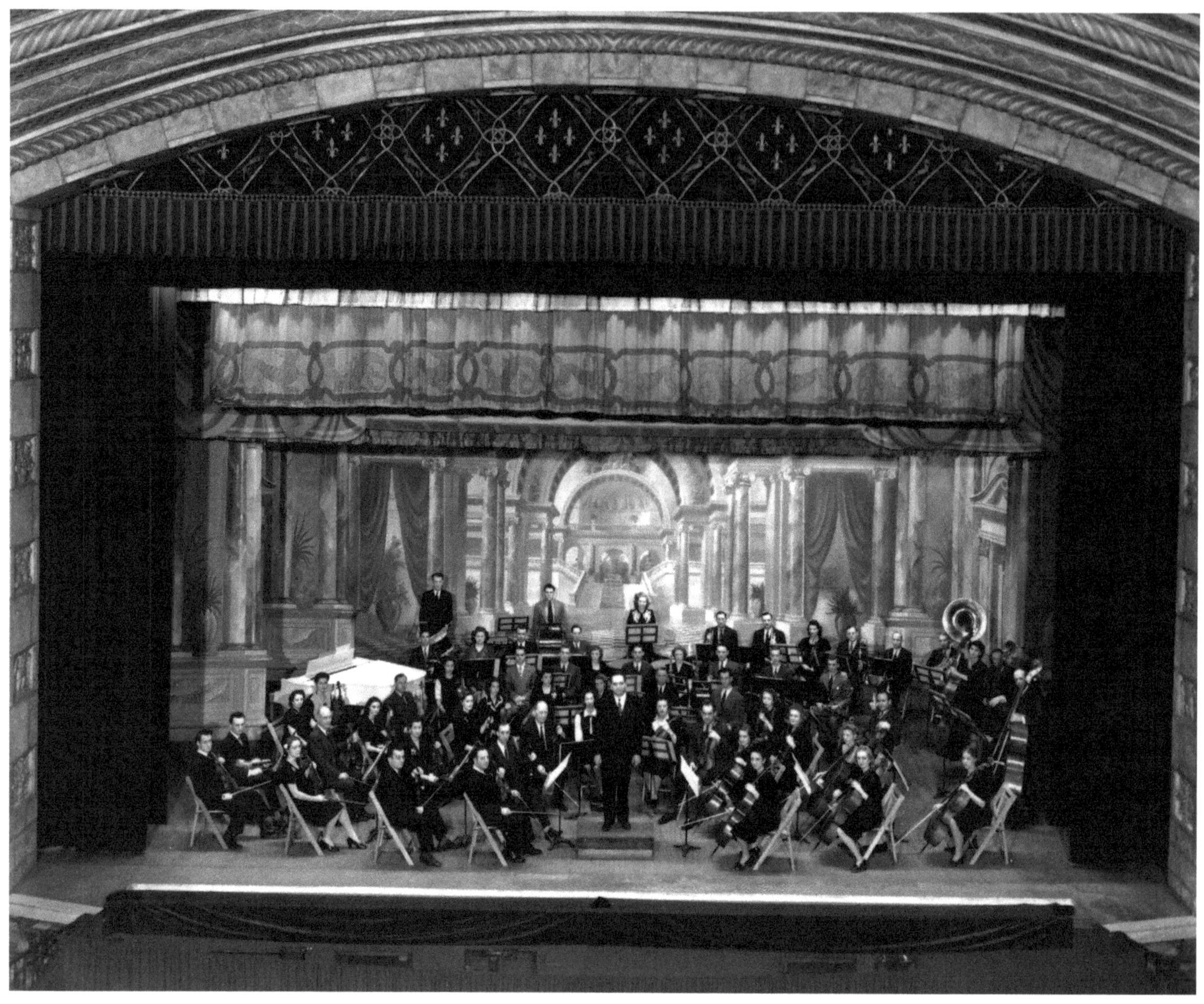

The Lincoln Symphony Orchestra, founded in 1927, was onstage in all its finery for a Christmas concert at the Stuart Theater, 140 N. 13th St., on December 13, 1945. The orchestra continues to augment Lincoln's cultural heritage into the twenty-first century.

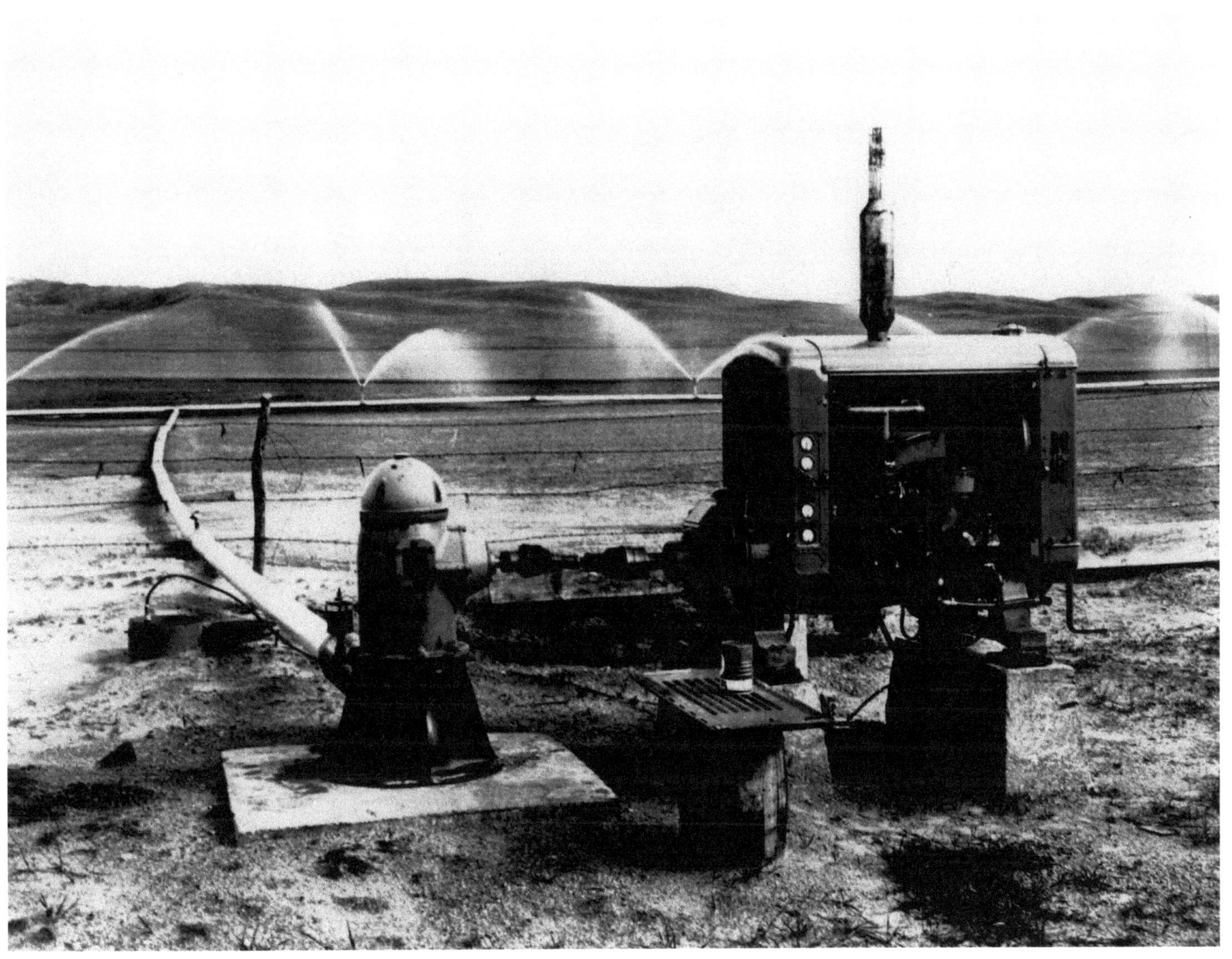

The sound of diesel motors ricocheted throughout the western half of Nebraska during the 1950s as farmers installed irrigation pumps to promote crop growth in a semi-arid environment. This photo by B. C. McLean shows a field in Grant County in 1951.

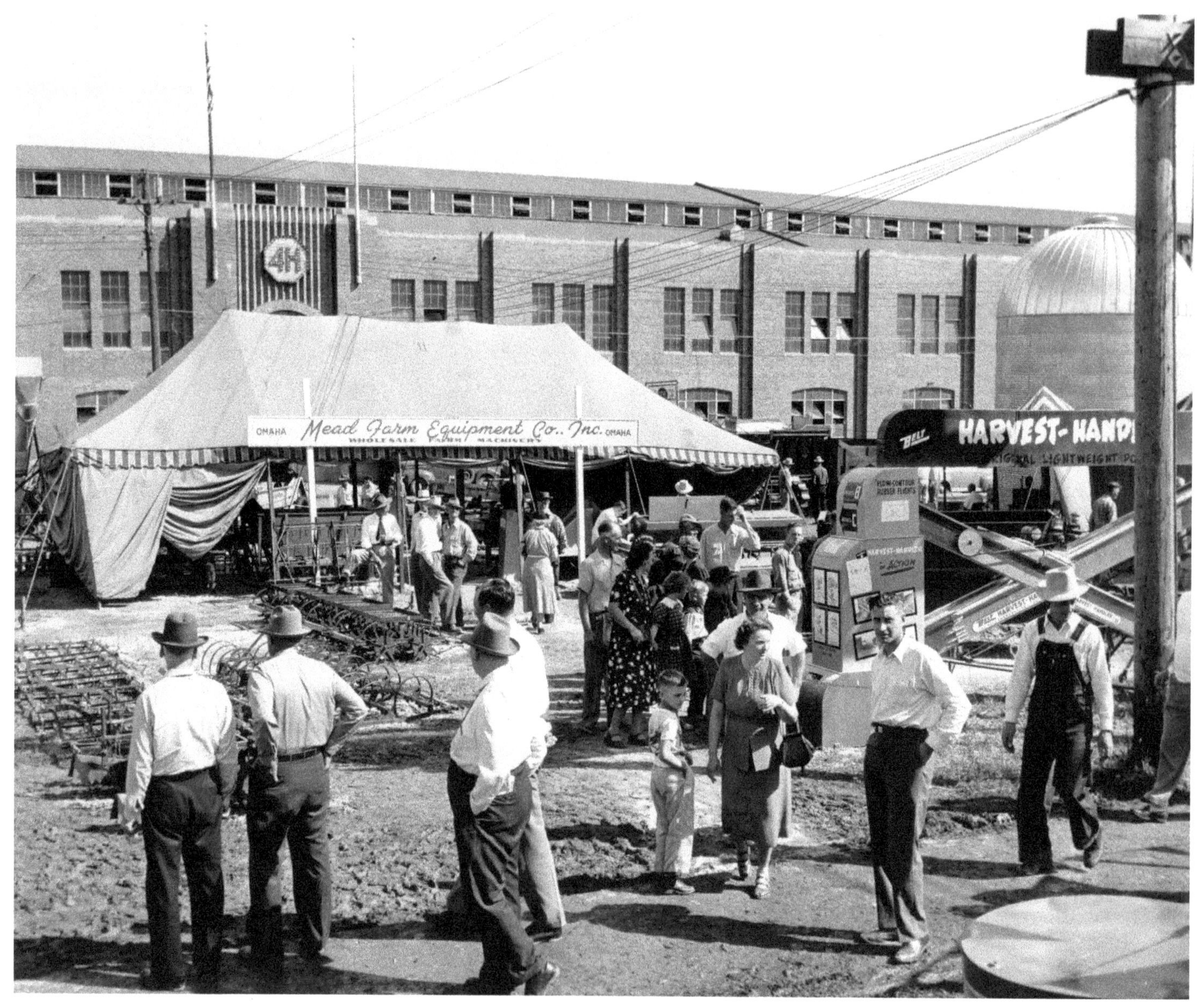

The Mead Farm Equipment booth drew a crowd during the 1951 Nebraska State Fair. The latest in farm implements has typically been part of the lure of fairs in a state always known for its agriculture.

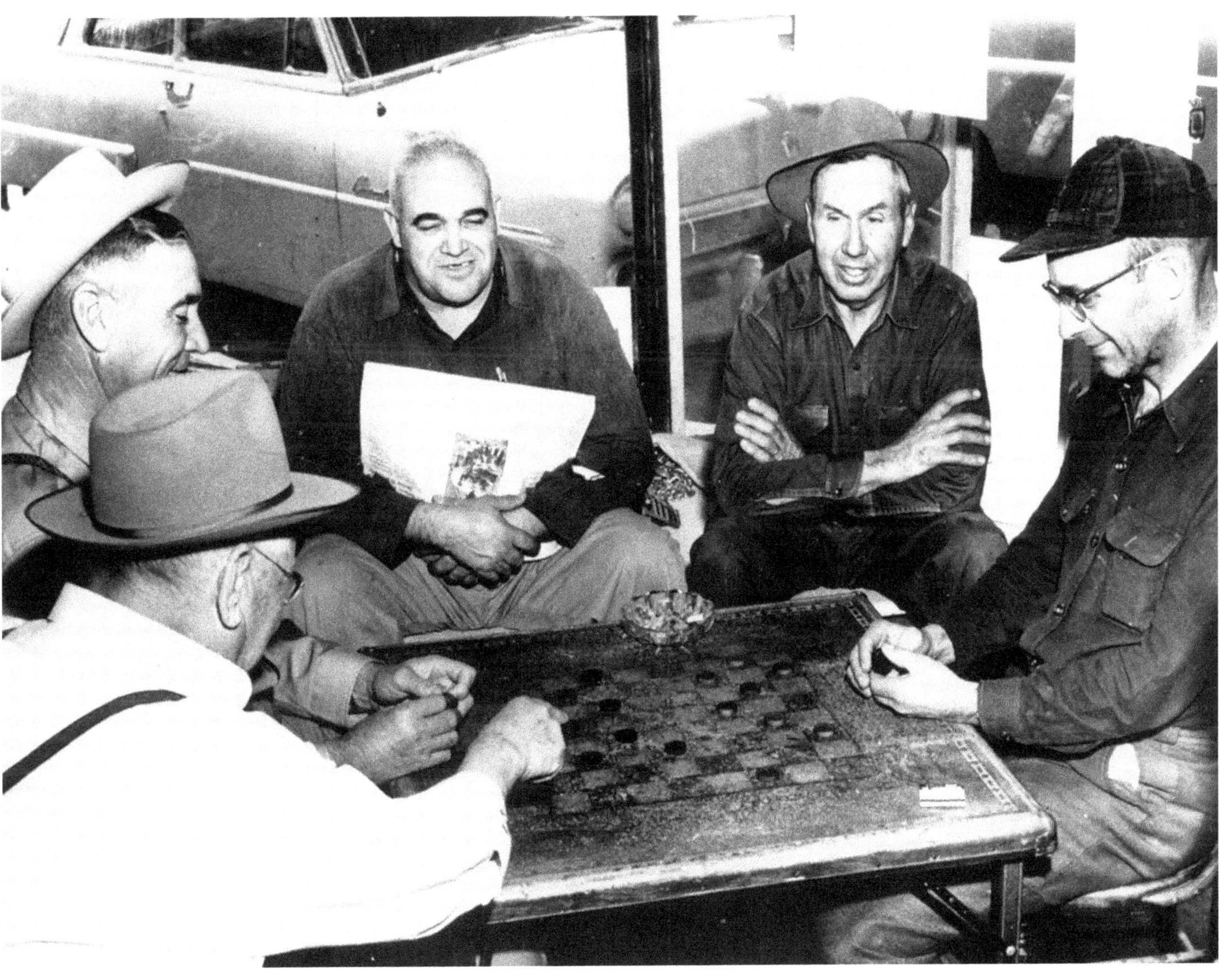

Indulging a favorite small-town diversion of the era, two weatherbeaten men play checkers near the front of a store in Mullen as three others offer unsolicited advice.

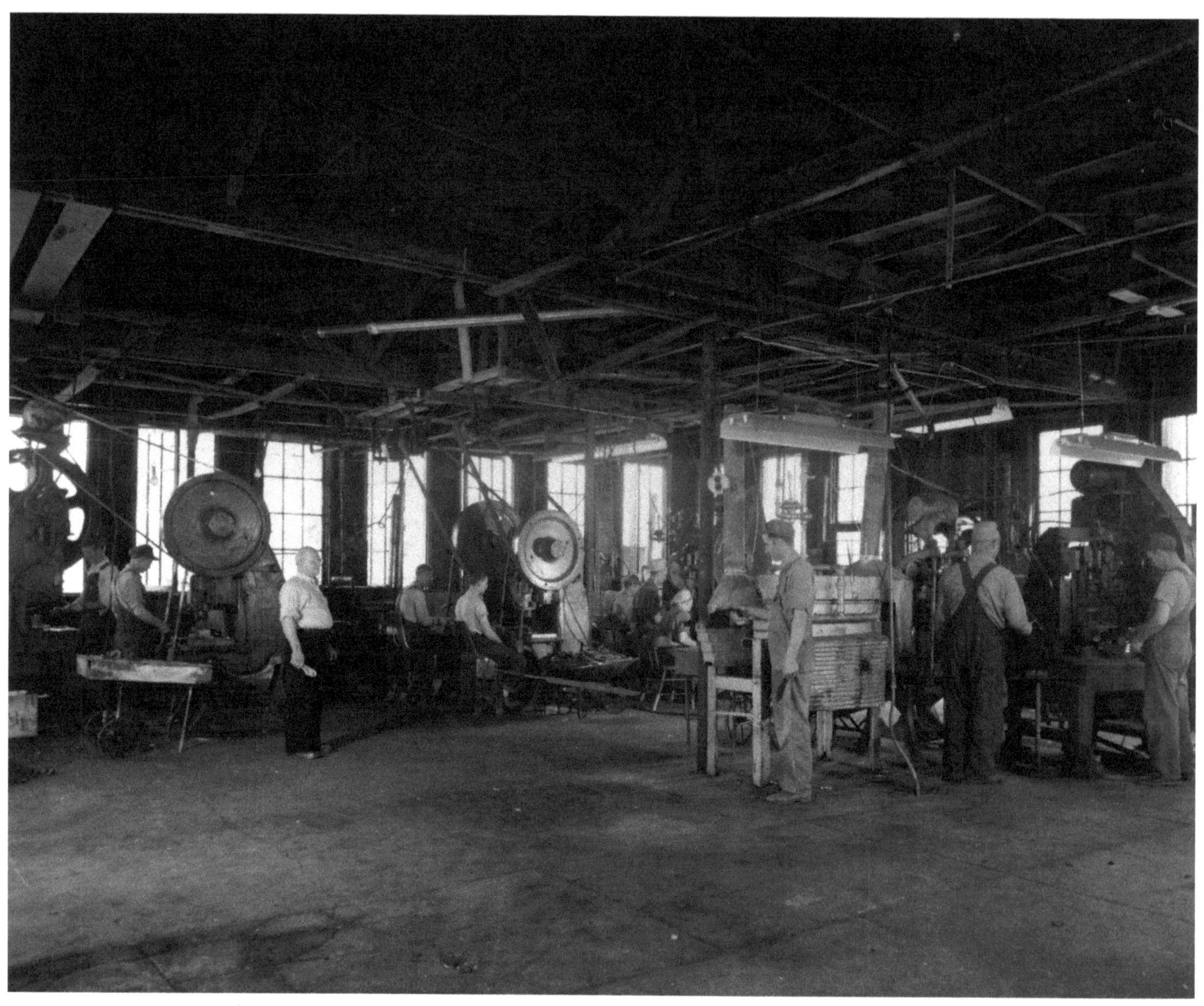

William Petersen (third from left) supervises a group of employees at the Vise-Grip factory in DeWitt. Petersen, a Danish immigrant, got his first patent in 1921 and his family business flourished for decades, employing as many as 600 people at one time, but it was eventually sold to Newell-Rubbermaid, which shut down the factory in 2008 and moved the jobs overseas.

Omaha had the state's first radio and television stations, and Johnny Carson got his start on both of them. As a 14-year-old, he was "the Great Carsoni" at the Norfolk Rotary Club before graduating from the University of Nebraska. His career took a leap forward at WOW, and he would move to Hollywood in the 1950s. Carson made NBC's *Tonight Show* one of the most-watched programs in history, hosting it 30 years before retiring in 1992.

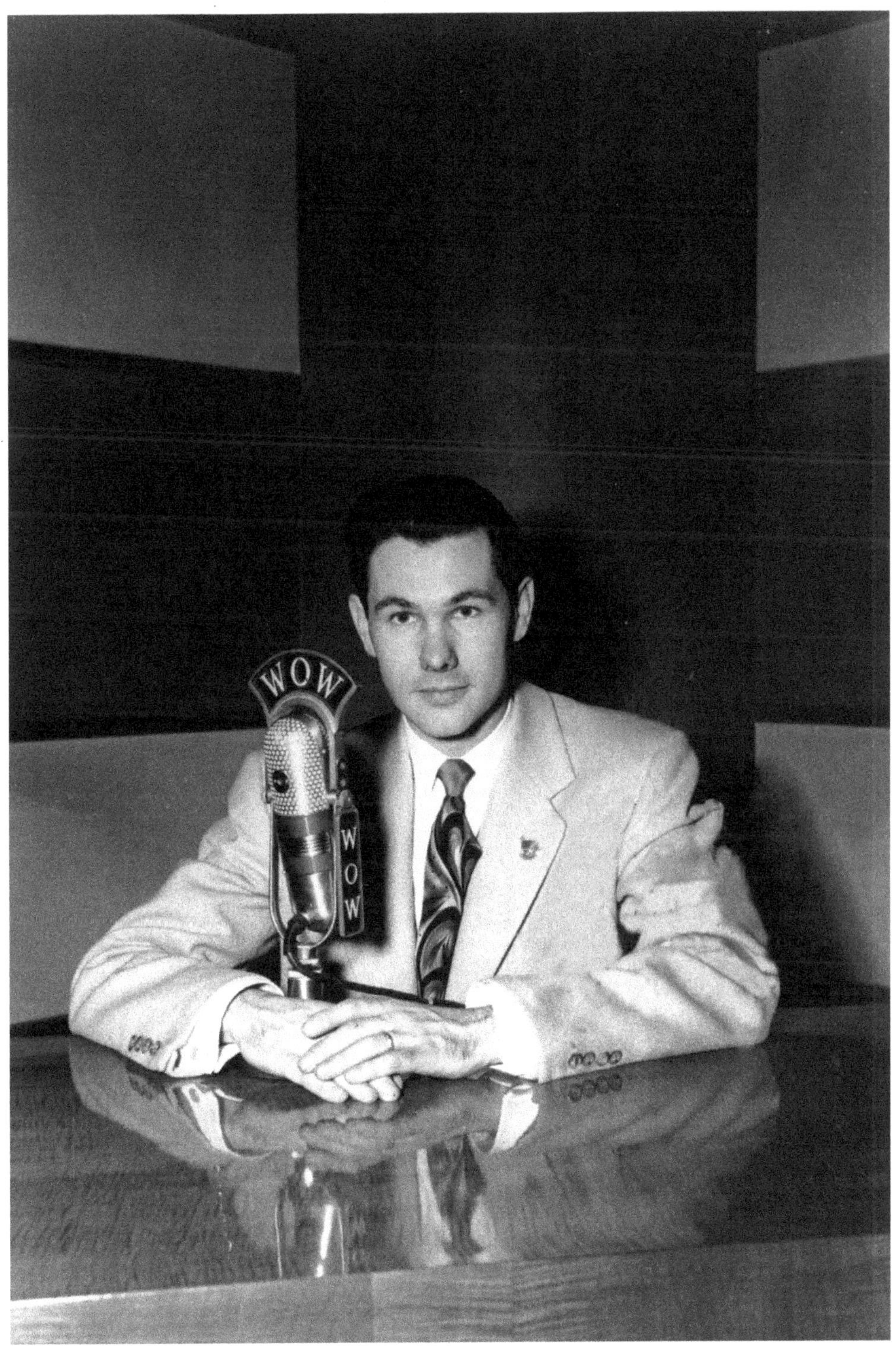

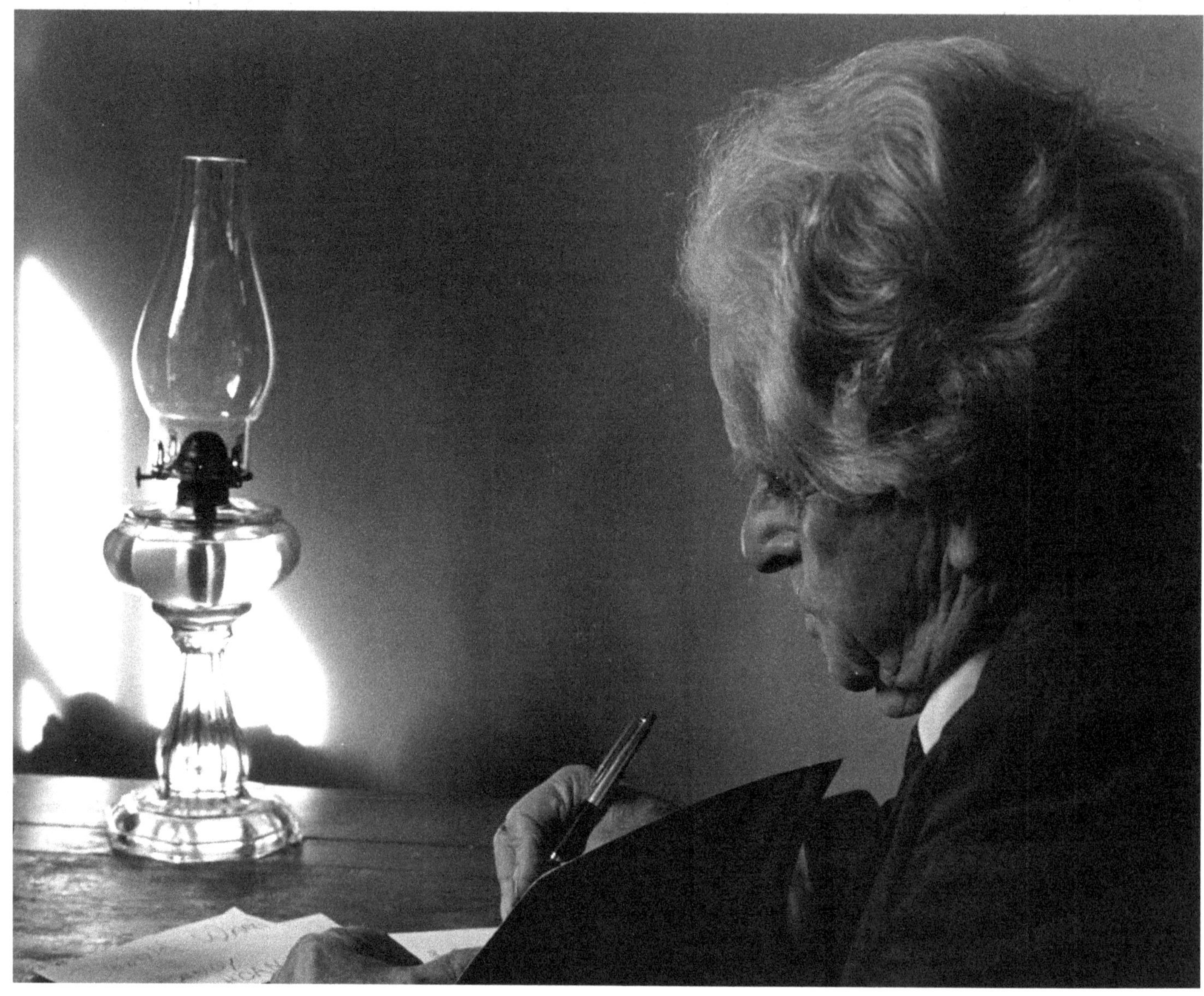

A resident of Bancroft, John G. Neihardt graduated from Nebraska Normal College at age 16 and started writing lyric poetry at 19—much of it about the American Indian. *Black Elk Speaks,* based on the life of the Lakota Sioux holy man, is possibly the most influential work ever written on American Indian culture and religion. The Nebraska Legislature named him the state's poet laureate in 1921, a title he held 52 years until his death.

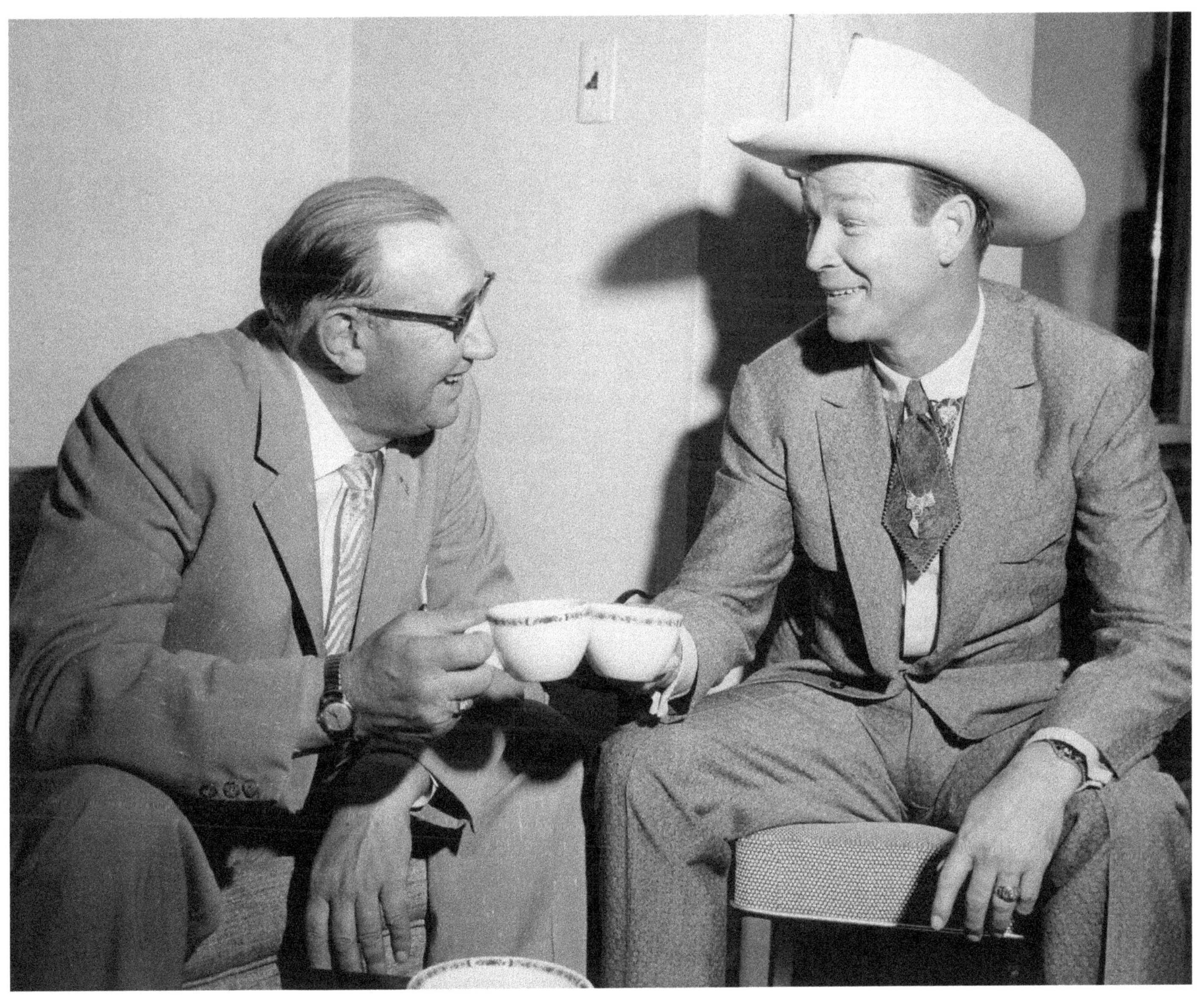

Cowboy actor Roy Rogers spread happiness and goodwill at his many public appearances, including this one at the Nebraska State Fair in 1957. He is pictured with a state fair official.

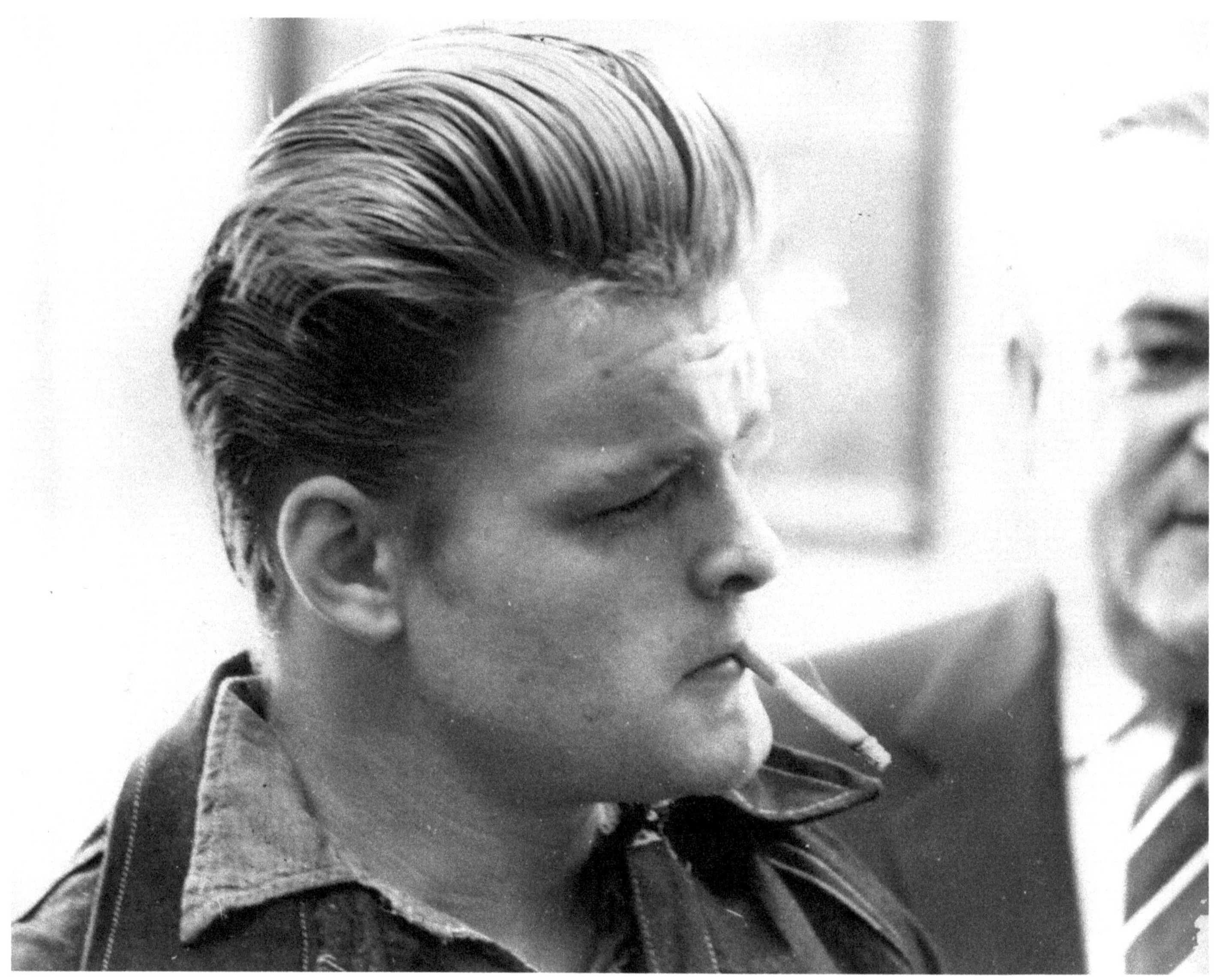

In 1958, Charles Starkweather, a 19-year-old high school dropout and James Dean aspirant, went on one of the most famous murder rampages in history, killing 11 people as he drove his young girlfriend in a variety of cars around Lincoln and then on a cross-country trip that terrorized thousands of people across Nebraska and Wyoming. He is shown talking to reporters while in custody before being executed at the Nebraska State Penitentiary in 1959.

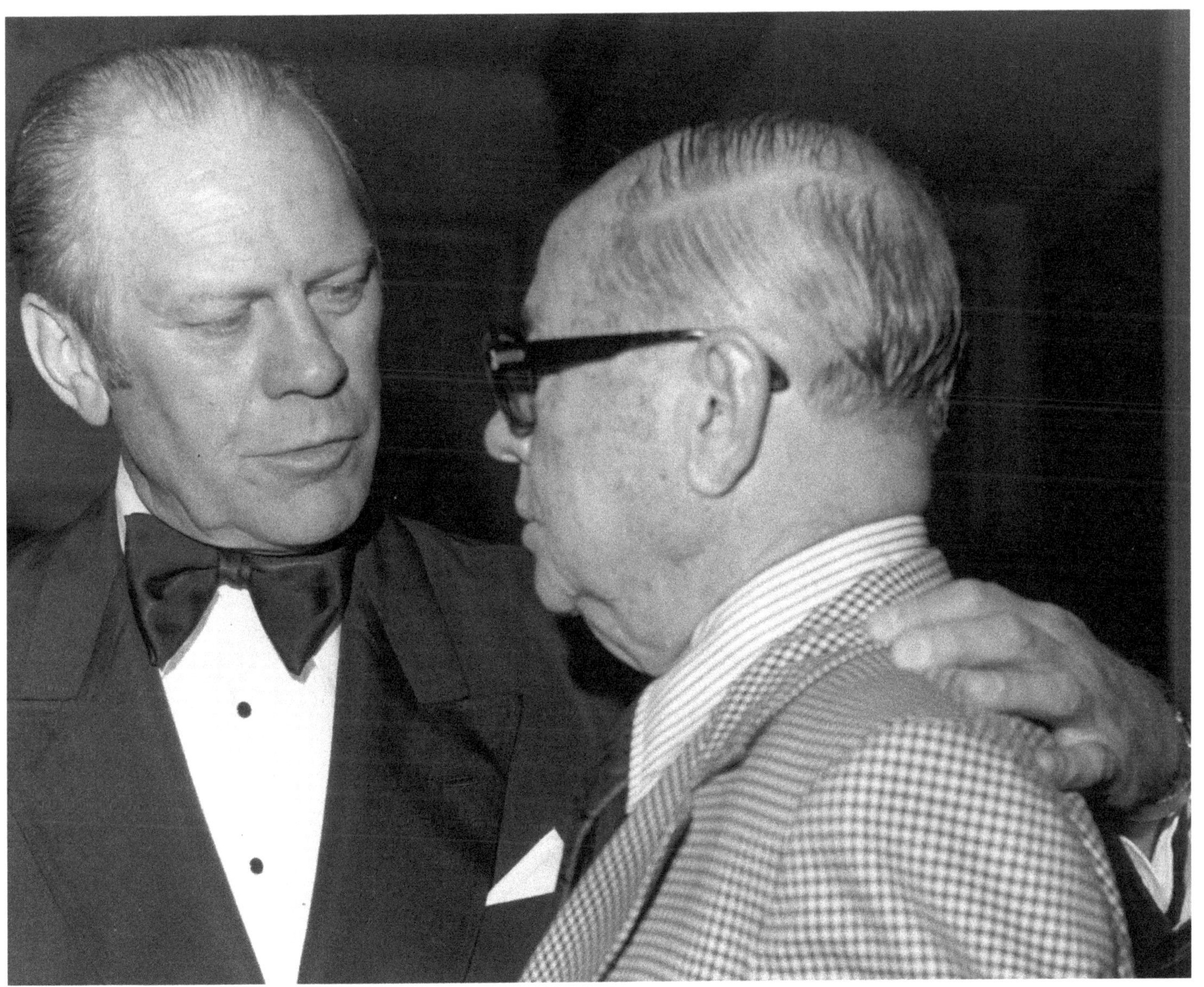

President Gerald R. Ford, who was born in Omaha before spending most of his life in Michigan, chats with Nebraska senator Carl Curtis during Curtis's last term in office in the mid-1970s. The personification of a rock-ribbed conservative Republican, the Kearney County native was a counterpoint to the populist mentality of George Norris and served 24 years before being succeeded by a moderate Democrat, the former governor J. James Exon.

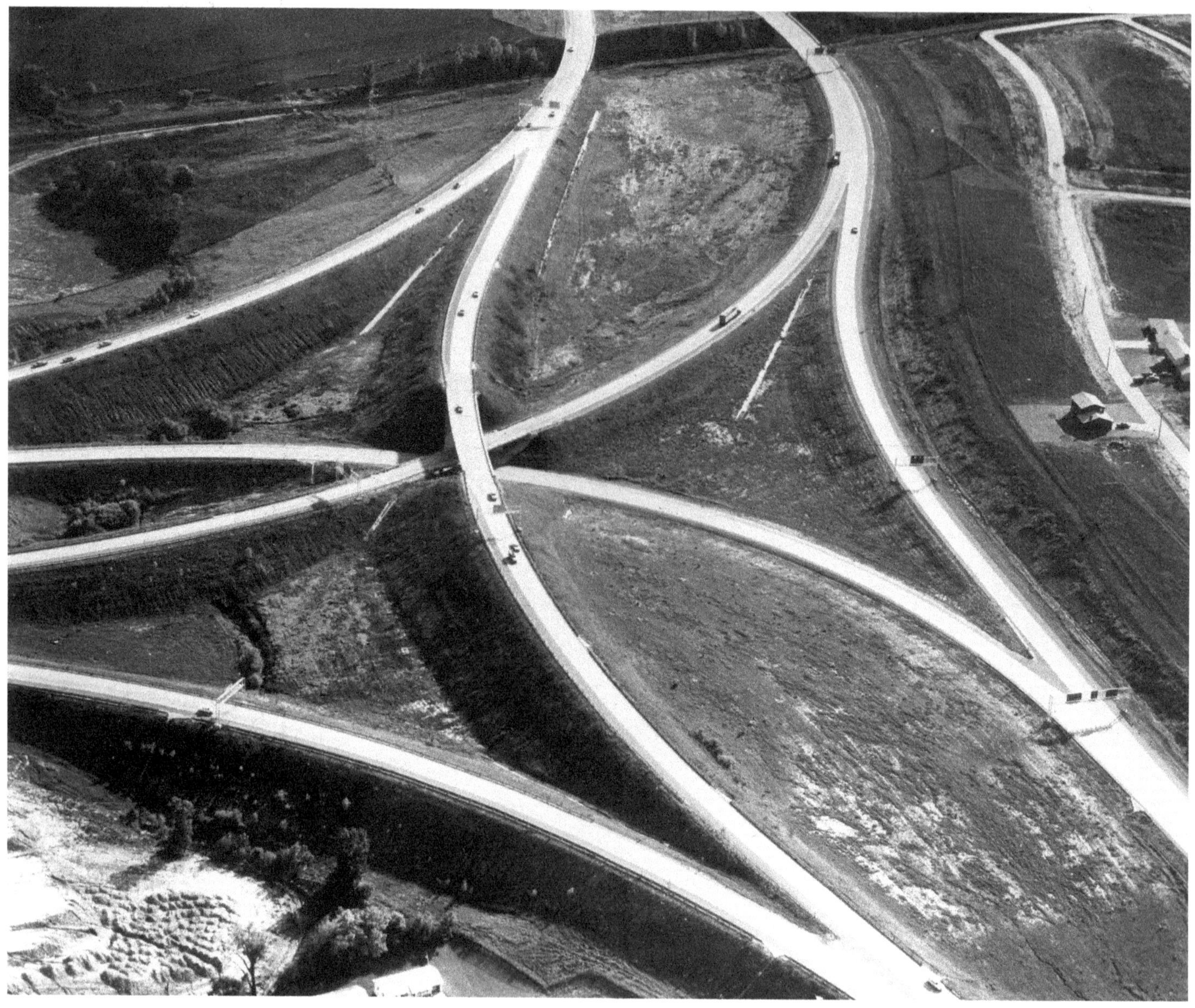

Newly constructed Interstate 80 near Omaha was not a very busy place in 1966, 10 years after President Dwight Eisenhower signed legislation that launched the nationwide Interstate highway system. In 1957, work began on I-80 south of Gretna, and it made its way west across the state during the 1960s. Nebraska's 455 miles of I-80 were completed in 1974 at a cost of just under $1 million a mile.

Notes on the Photographs

These notes, listed by page number, attempt to include all aspects known of the photographs. Each of the photographs is identified by the page number, photograph's title or description, photographer and collection, archive, and call or box number when applicable. Although every attempt was made to collect all data, in some cases complete data may have been unavailable due to the age and condition of some of the photographs and records.

ii **Omaha in 1868**
Denver Public Library
11005832

vi **Early Nebraska Farm Family**
Library of Congress
08375u

x **Trenton Real Estate Office, 1880s**
Nebraska State Historical Society
RG3839-4-12

2 **Scott's Bluff**
Library of Congress
LC-USF34-059252-D

3 **Crow Butte near Crawford**
Library of Congress
02653u

4 **Fort Kearny, 1858**
Nebraska State Historical Society
RG2102-1-2

5 **Pioneers at Fort Kearny**
Nebraska State Historical Society
RG2102-1-3

6 **First Territorial Capitol**
Nebraska State Historical Society
RG1234-2-10

7 **James Butler "Wild Bill" Hickok**
Nebraska State Historical Society
RG2603-6

8 **Sioux Tepees near North Platte**
Denver Public Library
11005822

9 **Omaha's Ware Block**
Denver Public Library
11005830

10 **Second Territorial Capitol**
Library of Congress
LC-USZ62-062484

11 **Panorama of Fort McPherson**
Nebraska State Historical Society
RG0951-3

12 **J. Sterling Morton**
Nebraska State Historical Society
RG1013-1-1

13 **Standing Bear with Family**
Nebraska State Historical Society
RG2066-5-2

14 **Grasshopper Humor on Locust Plague**
Library of Congress
09649u

15 **Chuckwagon Chow near Sutherland**
Denver Public Library
10021930

16 **C. H. Peters Store at West Union**
Library of Congress
13109v

17 **Weilers Butcher Shop in Lincoln**
Nebraska State Historical Society
RG2158-1864

18 **Sylvester Rawding Family with Cow**
Library of Congress
08372u

19 Broken Bow Hardware
Library of Congress
Photo by Solomon D. Butcher
08380u

20 The J. D. Semler Family
Library of Congress
Photo by Solomon D. Butcher
08370u

21 Solomon Butcher Self-portrait
Library of Congress
10216v

22 William Moore and His Family
Library of Congress
08371u

23 Buffalo Bill at Scouts Rest
Denver Public Library
11006260

24 Early Trenton
Nebraska State Historical Society
RG3839-5-7

25 Grain Elevators at Blue Hill
Nebraska State Historical Society
RG0802-83-5

27 Threshing Day near Wilber
Nebraska State Historical Society
RG0813-109

28 Wintry Street in Early Ewing
Nebraska State Historical Society
RG3841-3-10

29 Fort Robinson Barracks
Nebraska State Historical Society
RG1517-119-2

30 Lakota Family
Nebraska State Historical Society
RG2068-3-1

31 Holt County Teacher and Schoolchildren
Nebraska State Historical Society
RG3841-8-11

32 Lincoln's Haymarket District
Nebraska State Historical Society
RG2158-0218

33 Frank Roach Sod House, 1890
Library of Congress
13792v

34 Rooftop View of Lexington
Library of Congress
16291v

36 Platte Valley Institute, 1892
Library of Congress
LC-USZ62-088924

37 Devil's Gap near Oconto
Library of Congress
13202v

38 William Jennings Bryan
Nebraska State Historical Society
RG3198-15-12

39 Kretzschmar Grocery at Sartoria
Library of Congress
12974v

40 Advocate Office at Ansley
Library of Congress
Photo by Solomon D. Butcher
14478v

41 Willa Cather
Nebraska State Historical Society
RG2639-1-82

42 Trans-Mississippi and International Exposition
Library of Congress
3b15603u

43 President McKinley at Lincoln
Nebraska State Historical Society
RG2158-1104

44 The Women's Auxiliary at Mullen
Nebraska State Historical Society
RG3842-1-1

45 Nebraska National Guard Band
Library of Congress
13173v

46 Tremont Hotel at Springview
Photo by Solomon D. Butcher
13510v

47 Elam Bean Ranch at Amherst
Photo by Solomon D. Butcher
12184v

48 Roosevelt Train at Fairmont
Library of Congress
3c02880u

49 Roosevelt at Grand Island
Library of Congress
3c16512u

50 Hygeia Creamery Stand at County Fair in Broken Bow
Library of Congress
13275v

51 Scene at the Overton Bank
Library of Congress
13146v

52 Crowd at Cozad's City Restaurant, 1904
Library of Congress
13092v

53 Overton Drugstore Interior
Library of Congress
13354v

54 P. F. Forney Livery & Feed at Merna
Library of Congress
12968v

55 **New Era Office at Kearney**
Library of Congress
13423v

56 **Cowboy Farley on Horse, 1904**
Library of Congress
12549v

57 **National Guardsmen Camp at Kearney**
Library of Congress
Photo by Solomon D. Butcher
13174v

58 **Hay Day at the Empire Ranch**
Library of Congress
14159v

59 **Hall County Courthouse at Grand Island**
Library of Congress
LC-USZ62-073166

60 **Burlington & Missouri Station at Lincoln**
Nebraska State Historical Society
RG2158-2049

61 **Union Stockyards at Omaha**
Library of Congress
6a07580u

62 **Oglala at Fort Robinson**
Denver Public Library
10031877

63 **Second State Capitol**
Library of Congress
LC-USZ62-058279

64 **Kearney's Midway Hotel Cigar Stand**
Photo by Solomon D. Butcher
13428v

65 **Pipe Layers at Kearney**
Photo by Solomon D. Butcher
13040v

66 **Main Street in Hordville**
Nebraska State Historical Society
RG0802-37-13

67 **Lunch Bunch at the Amherst School**
Library of Congress
Photo by Solomon D. Butcher
13350v

68 **Crowd at C. F. Bodinson Store in Kearney**
Library of Congress
13029v

69 **Daniel Freeman**
Library of Congress
3c04167u

70 **Pilger General Store, 1908**
Nebraska State Historical Society
RG0802-76-7

71 **Salt Valley Floodwaters**
Nebraska State Historical Society
RG2158-3029

72 **On the Street in Nebraska City**
Library of Congress
6a07515u

73 **The Town of Blair**
Library of Congress
6a07539u

74 **Overton Storefronts**
Photo by Solomon D. Butcher
13147v

75 **Sunny Day in Alliance**
Library of Congress
6a07439u

76 **Beatrice at Sixth and Court Streets**
Library of Congress
6a07531u

77 **Downtown Falls City, 1908**
Photo by Frederick Bandholtz
6a07475u

78 **Scribner and Residents**
Library of Congress
6a07467u

79 **Sells-Floto Circus at Kearney**
Library of Congress
13274v

80 **Rushing for the Taft Train at DeWitt**
Library of Congress
3c02524u

81 **Candidate Taft in Lincoln**
Library of Congress
02224u

82 **A View of Fremont**
Photo by Frederick Bandholtz
6a07459u

83 **At Lake Doris, 1909**
Photo by Solomon D. Butcher
13222v

84 **A Growing Lexington**
Library of Congress
6a07491u

85 **On the Street in Crawford**
Photo by Frederick Bandholtz
6a07547u

86 **North Platte at Sixth and Dewey Streets, 1909**
Library of Congress
6a07507u

87 **Shelton Business District**
Library of Congress
12967v

88 **Eighth U.S. Cavalry at Fort Robinson**
Library of Congress
6a30096u

90 **The Kearney Opera House**
Library of Congress
13078v

91 **Jefferson County Courthouse at Fairbury**
Library of Congress
6a07499u

92 **Steam Power at the Ike Buck Farm**
Library of Congress
10112v

93 **Switch Engine at Wymore Coal Chute**
Library of Congress
3b44999u

94 **William Jennings Bryan at Home**
Nebraska State Historical Society
RG3198-108-38

95 **Union Pacific Depot at Kearney**
Library of Congress
14531v

96 **A View of Downtown Hastings**
Library of Congress
6a07483u

98 **Fighting a Prairie Fire, 1911**
Nebraska State Historical Society
RG3841-8-13

99 **Tornado Approaching Alliance**
Library of Congress
3b37813u

100 **Tornadoes of 1913 Scene of Devastation**
Library of Congress
3b35506u

101 **Tornadoes of 1913 Scene of Devastation no. 2**
Library of Congress
3c00397u

102 **Ceremony at Ash Hollow Cemetery**
Nebraska State Historical Society
RG3013-6-4

103 **Oregon Trail Marker at Ash Hollow**
Nebraska State Historical Society
RG3013-5-1

104 **Horse and Mule Barn at Union Stockyards**
Library of Congress
6a26971u

105 **Farmers State Bank of Talmage**
Nebraska State Historical Society
RG0802-58-36

106 **Brickyards at Humboldt**
Nebraska State Historical Society
RG0802-66-6

107 **Railroad Water Tower**
Nebraska State Historical Society
RG0802-60-1

108 **Waterloo High School Group Shot**
Nebraska State Historical Society
RG3348-9-5

109 **Downtown Omaha, 1916**
Library of Congress
6a07572u

110 **Fremont Tractor Show**
Library of Congress
6a28267u

111 **Automobile Tractor near Ogallala**
Nebraska State Historical Society
RG0716-34-6

112 **Omaha High School ROTC**
Library of Congress
6a25461u

115 **National Guard Company Group Shot, 1917**
Library of Congress
6a29969u

116 **Baseball Champions from West Point**
Nebraska State Historical Society
RG0802-17-12

117 **McCook World War I Victory Garden**
Nebraska State Historical Society
RG2442-6-67a

118 **John J. Pershing at Lincoln**
Nebraska State Historical Society
RG2183-1926-0930-1

119 **Park Barber Shop at Columbus**
Library of Congress
LC-USZ61-692

120 **Lovers' Lane at Champion, 1920**
Library of Congress
3b46640u

121 **Early Combine on the Ben hawkins Farm**
Nebraska State Historical Society
RG3358-132

123 **Dog Gone Wagon**
Nebraska State Historical Society
RG3841-5-18

124 **Aerial Panorama of Lincoln**
Nebraska State Historical Society
RG2159-2137

125 **Digging out of Trouble**
Nebraska State Historical Society
RG3021-9-2

126 **Ogallala Campground**
Nebraska State Historical Society
RG0802-46-25

127 **Pawnee Man Holding Peace Pipe at Trenton**
Library of Congress
3c18298

128 **Parade in Honor of Charles G. Dawes**
Nebraska State Historical Society
RG2158-2139

129 **Charles G. Dawes and Admirers in Lincoln**
Nebraska State Historical Society
RG2158-2141

130 DeHavilland-4 at Lee Bird Field
Denver Public Library
00020706

132 Edward E. Perkins
Nebraska State Historical Society
RG3348-927

133 Pastoral Scene near Bennington
Nebraska State Historical Society
RG3348-10-7

134 Chimney Rock near Bayard
Nebraska State Historical Society
RG3319-1-21

135 Red Breckinridge Stunt at Burwell Rodeo
Nebraska State Historical Society
RG3375-2-30

136 Lincoln High School, 1929
Nebraska State Historical Society
RG2183-1929-0429

137 Aerial View of State Penitentiary
Nebraska State Historical Society
RG2418-3-18

138 University of Nebraska Cheerleaders
Library of Congress
3c00227

139 Tornado near Gothenburg
Library of Congress
LC-USZ62-056449

140 Bird's-eye View of State Capitol Construction
Nebraska State Historical Society
RG1234-40-18

141 The Nebraska State Capitol
Nebraska State Historical Society
RG2183-1934-0418-1

142 Nebraska Farmer Operating Single-row Corn Picker
Nebraska State Historical Society
RG3358-12a

143 Blustery Day at 13th and O Streets
Nebraska State Historical Society
RG2183-1931-0410-1

144 Indian Industrial School at Genoa
Nebraska State Historical Society
RG4422-1-20

145 Red Cloud Agency Ceremony, 1932
Denver Public Library
10031565

146 North Platte River Bridge near Scottsbluff
Nebraska State Historical Society
RG0802-71-23

147 Depression-era Farm Family at Home
Nebraska State Historical Society
RG2183-1943-1021-3

148 George Norris
Nebraska State Historical Society
RG3298.PH3-3

149 George Norris at Legislative Ceremony
Nebraska State Historical Society
RG2183-1937-0105-2

150 The First Unicameral State Legislature
Nebraska State Historical Society
RG2183-1937-0105-1

152 Workers' Alliance of America Meeting
Library of Congress
3c22463

153 Unemployed Father and Son
Library of Congress
3c22480

154 4-H Baby Beef on the Scales
Library of Congress
3c18225

155 Dawson County Cattle Drive, 1938
Library of Congress
LC-USF34-00805-D

156 Seward County Farm Girl
Library of Congress
8a03619u

157 Outside Omaha's Union Station
Library of Congress
8a03545u

158 On the Beat in Lincoln, 1938
Library of Congress
Photo by John Vachon
LC-USF33-T01-01257-M4

159 North Platte Saturday Morning Matinee
Library of Congress
LC-USF33-T01-01327-M1

160 Scene in Depression-era Lincoln
Library of Congress
LC-USF33-T01-01262-M2

161 Omaha Schoolchildren on the Playground
Library of Congress
LC-USF34-008828-D

162 Sheep at Union Stockyards
Library of Congress
Photo by John Vachon
LC-USF34-008852-D

163 Scene in Depression-era Omaha
Library of Congress
LC-USF34-701-8883

164 Smokes and Brews
Library of Congress
Photo by John Vachon
LC-USF34-008829-D

165 The Henshaw Cafeteria
Library of Congress
LC-USF34-008897-D

166 Armistice Day Parade in Omaha, 1938
Library of Congress
8a03947u

167 Scene on Omaha's Lower Douglas Street
Library of Congress
8a03936u

168 Alex's Bargain Center
Library of Congress
LC-USF34-008927-D

169 Meat Delivery in Omaha
Library of Congress
LC-USF3301-1277-M4

170 North Platte Union Pacific Depot
Denver Public Library
11005618

171 Farmstead on the High Plains near Imperial
Library of Congress
LC-USF34-029562-D

172 Zimmerman Farm Auction, 1940
Library of Congress
Photo by Arthur Rothstein
LC-USF34-029609-D

173 Lincoln Night Life
Library of Congress
Photo by John Vachon
LC-USF34-061767-D

174 Main Street in Waterloo
Library of Congress
LC-USF34-059870-D

175 Service Station in Lexington
Denver Public Library
10024217

176 Grand Island During World War II
Library of Congress
LC-USF34-065757-D

177 Kearney's Second Midway Hotel
Library of Congress
LC-USF34-065719

178 Mari Sandoz
Nebraska State Historical Society
RG0014-24-1

179 Kingsley Dam and Lake McConaughy
Library of Congress
17333U

180 Roadside Motor Lodge at North Platte
Library of Congress
LC-USF34-065755-D

181 War-era Billboard in Lincoln
Library of Congress
LC-USF34-003030-D

182 Father Flanagan Boys Town Picnic
Courtesy of the Boys Town Hall of History, Boys Town, NE

183 Signage at Grand Grocery in Lincoln
Library of Congress
1a34282u

184 The Eagle Fruit Store in Lincoln
Library of Congress
1a34274u

185 At the North Platte Canteen
Nebraska State Historical Society
RG2154-6-43

187 Patriotic Fervor in Wartime Lincoln
Library of Congress
1a34271u

188 University of Nebraska Graduates
Library of Congress
LC-USF34-065763-D

189 Dance at the USO
Nebraska State Historical Society
RG2183-1945-0922-5

190 The Lincoln Symphony Orchestra
Nebraska State Historical Society
RG2183-1945-1213-1

191 Irrigation Pumps for Crop Growth
Library of Congress
LC-USZ62-066032

192 Scene at the 1951 Nebraska State Fair
Nebraska State Historical Society
RG2183-1951-0907-10

193 Game of Checkers at Mullen
Nebraska State Historical Society
RG3842-1-13

194 William Petersen and Vise-Grip Employees at DeWitt Plant
Nebraska State Historical Society
RG5623-11

195 Johnny Carson at WOW
Nebraska State Historical Society
RG2411-867

196 John G. Neihardt
Nebraska State Historical Society
RG1042-3-2

197 Roy Rogers at the Nebraska State Fair
Nebraska State Historical Society
RG3356-55-4

198 Convicted Murderer Charles Starkweather
Nebraska State Historical Society
RG0809-4-1

199 President Gerald Ford with Senator Carl Curtis
Nebraska State Historical Society
RG4340-SFN97875

200 Newly Constructed Interstate 80
Nebraska State Historical Society
RG3348-10-2

HISTORIC PHOTOS OF NEBRASKA

It has been home to the Lakota and Pawnee, to Buffalo Bill and the "Great Commoner." From its earliest days, Nebraska has held a strategic place in the history of the nation's westward expansion. The spirit of the state is visible in the faces of its pioneer settlers, its political and literary luminaries, and its epic landmarks.

Historic Photos of Nebraska will take one back to 1880s sod houses and frontier forts, to one-room schoolhouses and laborers putting in a hard day's work. It includes faces of both the famous and the obscure, cityscapes from yesteryear and the farmers who helped build the state's agricultural heritage. The struggles caused by severe weather and economic downturns are chronicled here, as are moments of triumph and achievement.

With nearly 200 black-and-white images reproduced in vivid detail and captions and introductions provided by a fifth-generation Nebraskan, this book strikes a tone that is sometimes poignant, sometimes humorous, but always faithful to the soul of Nebraska.

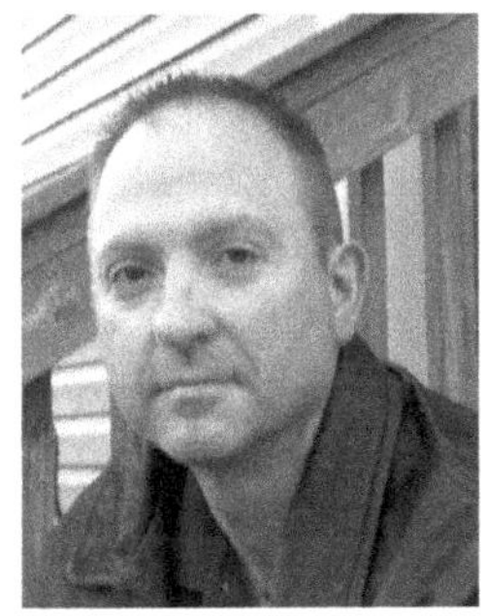

Tad Stryker is a freelance writer with a lifelong interest in Nebraska and its history. He is editor of NebraskaPedia.com, an online encyclopedia where he links historical articles about Nebraska and its various towns.

He co-wrote and edited a 2005 Turner publication, *Maranatha: The Miracle Camp on the Plains,* chronicling the history of a nonprofit organization based near North Platte.

A native Nebraskan, Stryker was raised in Custer County, where pioneer photographer Solomon D. Butcher settled and did the majority of his best-known work. Stryker graduated from the University of Nebraska–Lincoln with a degree in journalism and history. He and his wife, Jean, have three grown children.

WWW.TURNERPUBLISHING.COM

www.ingramcontent.com/pod-product-compliance
Lightning Source LLC
LaVergne TN
LVHW070459120826
845154LV00019BA/40